Real-Time Integration Methods for Mechanical System Simulation

NATO ASI Series

Advanced Science Institutes Series

A series presenting the results of activities sponsored by the NATO Science Committee, which aims at the dissemination of advanced scientific and technological knowledge, with a view to strengthening links between scientific communities.

The Series is published by an international board of publishers in conjunction with the NATO Scientific Affairs Division

A Life Sciences B Physics	Plenum Publishing Corporation London and New York
C Mathematical and Physical Sciences D Behavioural and Social Sciences E Applied Sciences	Kluwer Academic Publishers Dordrecht, Boston and London
F Computer and Systems Sciences G Ecological Sciences H Cell Biology	Springer-Verlag Berlin Heidelberg New York London Paris Tokyo Hong Kong Barcelona

Series F: Computer and Systems Sciences Vol. 69

Real-Time Integration Methods for Mechanical System Simulation

Edited by

Edward J. Haug

Center for Computer Aided Design
208 Engineering Research Facility
The University of Iowa
Iowa City, Iowa 52242, USA

Roderic C. Deyo

Evans & Sutherland Computer Co. Inc.
580 Arapeen Dr.
Salt Lake City, UT 84108, USA

Springer-Verlag Berlin Heidelberg New York
London Paris Tokyo Hong Kong Barcelona

Published in cooperation with NATO Scientific Affairs Division

Proceedings of the NATO Advanced Research Workshop on Real-Time Integration Methods for Mechanical System Simulation, held in Snowbird, Utah, USA, August 7–11, 1989.

ISBN 3-540-53280-3 Springer-Verlag Berlin Heidelberg New York
ISBN 0-387-53280-3 Springer-Verlag New York Berlin Heidelberg

Printed in Germany

Printing: Druckhaus Beltz, Hemsbach; Binding: J. Schäffer GmbH & Co. KG, Grünstadt
45/3140-543210 – Printed on acid-free-paper

PREFACE

This book contains the edited versions of lectures and selected contributed papers presented at the NATO Advanced Research Workshop on Real-Time Integration Methods For Mechanical System Simulation, held in Snowbird, Utah, August 7-11, 1989. The Institute was attended by 42 participants from 9 countries, including leading mathematicians and engineers from universities, research institutions, and industry. The majority of participants presented either invited or contributed papers during the Institute, and everyone participated in lively discussions on scientific aspects of the program. The Workshop provided a forum for investigation of promising new directions for solution of differential-algebraic equations (DAE) of mechanical system dynamics by mathematicians and engineers from numerous schools of thought.

The Workshop addressed needs and opportunities for new methods of solving of DAE of mechanical system dynamics, from the perspective of a broad range of engineering and scientific applications. Among the most exciting new applications addressed was real-time computer simulation of mechanical systems that, for the first time in human history, permits operator-in-the-loop simulation of equipment that is controlled by the human; e.g., driving a vehicle, operating a space telerobot, operating a remote manipulator, and operating construction equipment. The enormous potential value of this new application and the fact that real-time numerical integration methods for DAE of mechanical system dynamics is the pacing problem to be solved in realizing this potential served to focus much of the discussion at the Workshop.

The Workshop was originally intended to provide a forum for examining promising new directions for the real-time solution of DAE of mechanical system dynamics. The present status of affordable computation restricts the numerical integration methods used for complex systems to only a few function evaluations and severely constrains the range of current DAE methods that are applicable in real-time simulation. At the conclusion of the Workshop, a consensus among the majority of participants was that such limitations will remain a serious challenge in applying the current generation of successful numerical methods for DAEs. Thus, the "Real-Time Integration Method" part of the Workshop is only in its initial development.

The unique mix of scholars in mathematics, numerical analysis, and engineering who participated in this Advanced Research Workshop created a rich multidisciplinary environment for consideration of new DAE methods and identification of new directions for research. The vigorous technical discussion that permeated the entire meeting, during lectures, meals, and informal evening meetings provided new insights that will focus the activity of leading research specialists in DAE methods.

This book is organized into three parts, each addressing a technical aspect of the field of DAE of mechanical system dynamics:

Part 1 - DAE Applications and Basic Solution Methods

The first four papers provide an introduction to applications and formulation methods for dynamics of multibody systems. The remaining three papers in Part 1 provide an overview of the current state of the art in numerical solution of DAE, with a focus toward mechanical system dynamics.

Part 2 - New DAE and ODE Solution Methods

The six papers comprising Part 2 present promising new methods for effective solution of DAE of mechanical system dynamics, including consideration of parallel computer solution of ordinary differential equations.

Part 3 - Advanced DAE Applications

The five papers comprising Part 3 present a sampling of advanced applications that involve DAE of multibody dynamics and control.

The directors of the Workshop and editors of this text express their deep appreciation to NATO for sponsoring the Advanced Research Workshop; to the Evans & Sutherland Corporation for meeting preparation, local arrangements, and cordial support in conducting the Workshop; and to the lecturers and participants for their dedication and vigor throughout the Workshop. The pleasant surroundings of Snowbird, Utah created an invigorating environment for technical interaction and personal discussions.

While it is difficult to single out all persons who should receive formal thanks for making the Workshop and these Proceedings possible, a few must be noted. Ms. Vicky Roach of Evans & Sutherland tirelessly oversaw preparation for the Workshop and provided invaluable assistance throughout its conduct. Mr. Peter Doenges and Mr. John Briggs of Evans & Sutherland provided support throughout the Workshop. We also thank those employees of Evans & Sutherland who helped with transportation during the Workshop. Finally, Ms. Rozanne Huff and Ms. Pamela Ramser of the University of Iowa organized these Proceedings and prepared final manuscripts.

Edward J Haug
Iowa City, Iowa
May 1990

Roderic C. Deyo
Salt Lake City, Utah

CONTENTS

PART 1

DAE APPLICATIONS AND BASIC SOLUTION METHODS

An Example of Real-Time Simulation: Multi-body Vehicles

Roderic C. Deyo
Evans & Sutherland
600 Komas Drive
Salt Lake City, Utah 84108
USA

Abstract

This paper describes a high-performance driving simulator currently under development. It discusses the cueing requirements for man-in-the-loop simulation and a total simulator system overview is provided. A detailed description of the recursive dynamics algorithm and the real-time vehicle model in terms of the vehicle graph are presented. Subsystem models are briefly introduced. Real-time integration methods, along with constraint stabilization techniques used for the solution of the system DAEs are described. Finally, the Alliant FX/8 architecture is presented in the context of algorithm efficiency in a shared memory parallel computing environment, along with selected algorithm timing results run on Alliant and serial VAX machines.

NATO ASI Series, Vol. F 69
Real-Time Integration Methods for Mechanical System Simulation
Edited by E. J. Haug and R. C. Deyo

1 Introduction

The purpose of this NATO Workshop is to review real-time integration methods for potential use in man- and hardware-in-the-loop simulation of mechanical systems. It seems appropriate then to present an example of an advanced vehicle simulator currently under commercial development. Driving simulation provides a context in which the current "state-of-the-art" in system design and parallel dynamics algorithms can be explored, as well as providing a non-trivial example of constrained kinematic systems which give rise to differential-algebraic equations (DAEs), whose numerical solution is a major theme of the workshop.

Vehicle simulation requires the construction of a total synthetic real-time environment. An effective simulator must provide proper motion, visual, sound, and tactile cueing for the driver to respond in a natural manner. A simulated driving environment is an excellent example of a complex "real-time microworld", where a person must interact completely and naturally with an artificial, but compelling, computer controlled world.

Driving simulation is an interesting special case of vehicle simulation because it entails synthesizing a familiar, yet rich and dynamic environment. A driving simulator must provide

- accurate vehicle dynamics predicting real vehicle behavior,
- graphics which provide sufficient optical flow density for proper control and speed-distance judgments by the subject,
- optimal acceleration cueing,
- sound and control force feedback cueing mechanisms to enhance the sense of realism for the subject,
- update rates sufficiently high for minimal transport delay and hardware-in-the-loop capability.

The goal of allowing human interaction with the vehicle is to provide a designer with information about performance, stability, ride quality, and safety margins to suit human tolerances in control, task loading, and comfort. Simulation provides a safe and cost-effective method for early resolution of design compromises.

Because of the nature of the Workshop, this paper addresses only a few of the major design issues in real-time vehicle simulation. It briefly discusses the functional design and relation between the various subsystems, describes in some detail the real-time dynamics and integration method, and ends with a short discussion concerning several delicate issues of hardware implementation for the real-time algorithms.

2 The Driving Simulator System

2.1 Introduction

In the last fifteen or so years, man-in-the-loop simulation using computer-generated, real-time graphics has assumed a major role not only in pilot training, but also in engineering applications for land, sea, air, and space vehicles. Man-in-the-loop simulation uses a person in the control loop of a simulation to provide feedback to the system operations (hardware-in-the-loop simulation is similar, except that a control system complements or replaces the operator). The operator experiences a synthetic environment, manipulates his controls in response to the

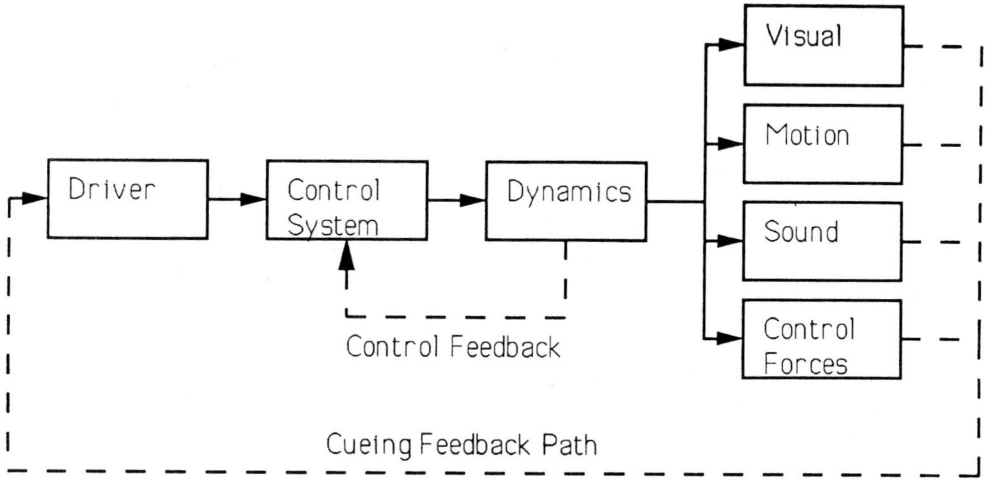

Figure 1. Simulation functional diagram.

situation, and experiences the results of his actions. In a real-time simulator, the dynamics model is continually evaluated to give feedback to the operator. On the basis of these data, the simulator provides realistic environmental cues to allow him to control the simulated vehicle in the same way that he would in the real world. The cueing feedback is shown in Figure 1, where the major simulator functional relations are indicated.

As already stated, a primary goal of simulation is to tune raw performance, stability, ride quality, safety margins, and other design or control qualities, to suit human tolerances in control, task loading, and comfort. Through the use of simulation, training or design testing can often be achieved at lower cost, experiments can be conducted under controlled, repeatable circumstances, and — important for engineering — vehicle designs can be evaluated while minimizing the number of prototypes.

An important engineering use of man-in-the-loop simulation is to determine vehicle response and to study the man-machine interface before the start of a vehicle test program. For example, a new automobile or control interface can be modeled and test driven even before it leaves the drawing board. The drivers can give valuable feedback to the designers about the car's characteristics at an early enough stage to permit changes in the design. Integration of control systems, such as anti-lock brakes (ABS) and four-wheel steering, can be achieved at an earlier time. Driver reactions can be measured, and different alternatives can be tested.

In designing a driving simulator, close attention must be paid to providing those cues needed to properly operate the vehicle. Man-in-the-loop simulators depends upon complex computer image generators to produce the dense, rapidly changing visual scenes necessary for proper cueing [13]. Ideally, new frames would be produced at a rate of 50-100 hz and would contain many thousands of smooth shaded, textured, anti-aliased polygons, lighted and displayed in proper priority. Because of the dominance of visual cueing, the requirement of good real-time computer graphics represents a large portion of the cost of man-in-the-loop simulator. Hence, as the capabilities of computer image generation have improved and the relative cost of simulation has dropped, there are better economic justifications for its use. For vehicle engineering, the cost of simulation has always been an important consideration, and, as a result, has only recently been low enough to justify simulation on a large scale.

While computer graphics is the critical element in creating a realistic operator environment, the graphics must work in concert with the rest of the system to be believable. The motion system must provide proper cueing during both translational and rotational accelerations. Since in driving simulation there are often sustained longitudinal and lateral accelerations, platform motion limitations must be considered and optimal use made of the available capacity. For audio cueing, a sound generation system must provide expected noises during vehicle maneuvers, including environmental sounds. Vehicle controls must provide the proper "feel" during their use, so control reaction forces must be determined and properly applied. The simulator system must at all times provide a complex, totally integrated synthetic driving environment.

A critical issue is the total system transport delay between the onset of a driver command and the first display of the resulting motion by the visual system (delay in the onset of motion by the platform is also important, but is easier to minimize). Ideally, the simulator should introduce no more delay then is present in the vehicle itself. Modern high-performance sports cars can achieve delays of well under 50 ms. Consequently, transport delay should be no more than 50 ms for a high-performance engineering driving simulator. This can be achieved by a carefully considered total system design.

2.2 An Advanced Driving Simulator

An advanced man-in-the-loop simulator currently under development [12] (Figure 2) is made up of a several complex subsystems that combine to create a complete synthetic driving environment for the operator:

- The host computer controls all of the real-time operations of the system, including computation of the vehicle and motion platform dynamics, which can be performed on special accelerator hardware closely coupled to the host computer. All calculations for the entire system are performed within a 10 ms time frame. An integrated data base contains visual models, geometric data on the simulated environment, data relating to the sounds encountered, and mechanical characteristics of the vehicle.

- The visual system calculates the correct image based on position information from the host computer. It removes hidden areas, computes the sun angle, smooth shades, textures, and anti-aliases the result. There is a high degree of parallelism in the foregoing operations, allowing about ten GIPS (Giga Instructions Per Second) operation in a large system.

- Multiple CRT projectors display an image on the dome. Special screen material is used for maximum brightness and contrast.

- The motion platform is a configuration of hydraulic actuators that can move the operator's cab in any direction or angle by combining motions about the x, y, z, yaw,

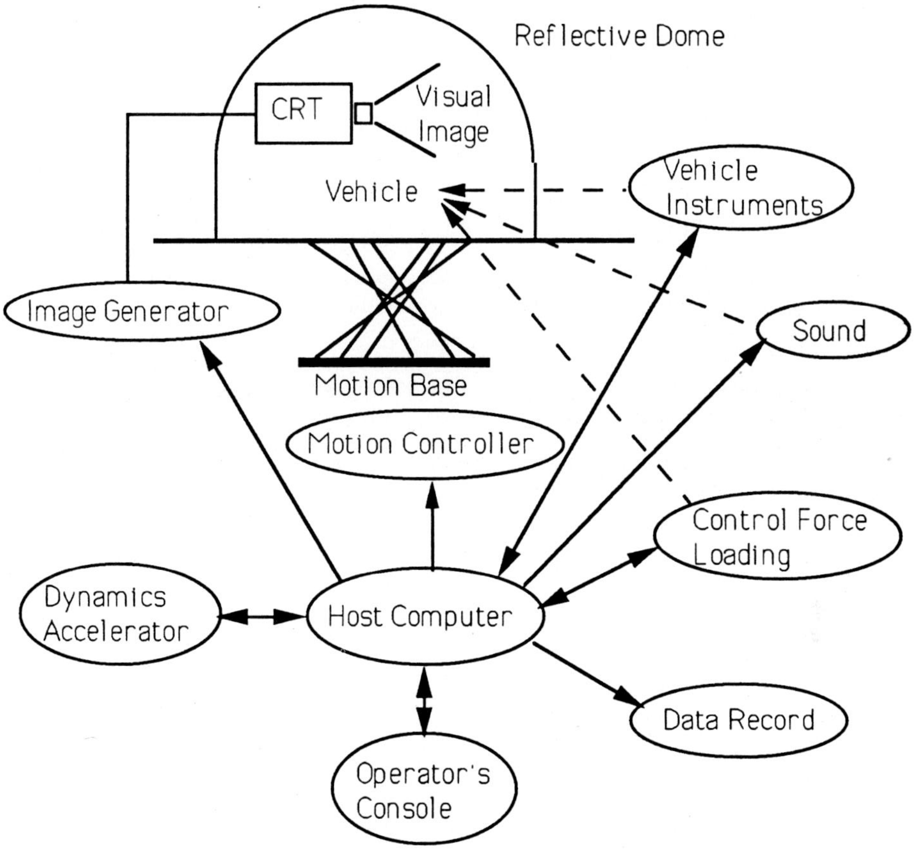

Figure 2. Modern advanced vehicle simulator system.

pitch, and roll axes. The control signals to the motion platform are filtered ("washed out") to transform the virtual real-world motion computed by the dynamics software into movements achievable by the system.

- The sound subsystem uses multiple speakers to generate appropriate sounds to simulate the engine, gear whine, wind noise, passing traffic, etc.
- Instrumentation provides data to the host computer to monitor the the entire system and ensure the driver's safety.
- Control force loaders are used to provide appropriate forces back to the operator through the steering wheel, brake pedal, and transmission lever to replicate the reaction forces found in a real car.
- The operations console allows a single person to oversee all of the simulation activities, allowing flexible control over vehicle tests.

Possibly the most challenging aspect of a modern simulator is its systems software design and integration. Special techniques must be used to avoid communications congestion, while retaining real-time control over multiple processes.

3 Real-Time Dynamics Algorithms

3.1 Previous Dynamics Modeling Techniques

Computational multi-body dynamics is currently a very active area of research [19]. Many algorithm choices for both kinematic formulation (Cartesian, joint, screw space, etc.) and dynamical principle (Newton's law, Euler-Lagrange equations, principle of virtual work, etc.) are available. Two often used dynamical laws for modeling complex vehicles are the principles of virtual work and virtual power, though sometimes Lagrangian formulations are employed. A wider diversity occurs in the choice of kinematic formulation for linked multi-body systems.

Previous work in obtaining equations of motion for a complex system can be generally divided into two methods depending on choice of system coordinates [20]: In the first, no attempt to choose a minimal set of coordinates is made, opting instead for a maximal set of Cartesian coordinates for each body and a maximal set of constraints [30]; in the second method, a minimal, or at least small, set of joint coordinates are used recursively to identify an outboard body's position relative to some chosen base-body [22] (these are the so-called $O(N)$-methods, whose computational complexity grows linearly with the number of bodies N).

The first method has the advantages of generality and relatively simple equations — and the disadvantage of rarely being optimal for a given mechanism or vehicle. Commercial codes, such as DADS [32] or ADAMS [9], generate Cartesian coordinates for each body to which a maximal set of constraint conditions must be applied. This is similar to finite element methods in structural mechanics where a very large, but sparse, equation set results. In these algorithms, most of the time is spent in solving this large set of equations.

In the second method, a small set of relative joint coordinates is used, and fewer constraints must be applied, but the equations are often extremely complex. Most of the algorithm time is spent in the assembly of the final equations. A minimal coordinate description is very effective in describing spacecraft and robots, since these systems naturally form tree graphs contractible to the base-body. But a difficulty occurs when closed loops appear in the system graph, since the relative joint coordinates are then subject to additional constraints from the closing of the loop, and so are not independent. Wittenburg [33] developed the idea of cutting the closed loop to form a tree graph, and adding Lagrange multipliers to the equations of motion to provide the now missing constraint reaction forces. Once the system graph is a tree, recursive methods developed by Hooker and Margulies [22] for spacecraft, and Armstrong [2] and Luh, *et. al.* [26], for robotics, can be used to recover body accelerations. Bae [3], using these ideas in his thesis, derived an algorithm combining cut joints with recursion. In addition, he discussed issues relating to the natural parallelization of the resulting algorithm. Essentially, we have implemented Bae's work, adding additional techniques for stable integration and pipeline delay reduction to the parallel recursive algorithm.

3.2 Derivation of Recursive Dynamics Equations for Vehicle Model

3.2.1 Rigid Body Kinematics and Euler Parameters

For convenience, we summarize some standard material from rigid body kinematics. Two excellent references are [16] and [21], with the latter describing the notation used throughout this paper. As is well known, a free rigid body in space has six independent degrees of freedom: Three translational for its center of mass (CM) and three rotational for orientation about its CM. Traditionally, Euler angles have been used to describe a body's orientation. But such a parameterization has singular configurations where its differential vanishes and the

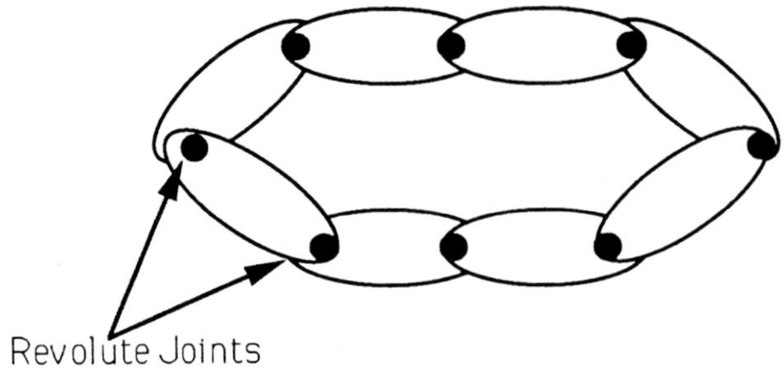

Figure 3. Linked rigid bodies forming a close loop.

inverse transformation fails to exist. To avoid this potential difficulty, we use four Euler parameters e_0, e_1, e_2, e_3, describing the angular orientation of the body fixed coordinate frame with respect to the global coordinate frame and satisfying a single normalization condition $e_0^2 + e_1^2 + e_2^2 + e_3^2 = 1$. The Euler parameters (which are unit Quaternions) are related to space rotations in the following way: If the rotation has unit axis vector $\vec{\eta}$ and angle θ about the axis, then $e_0 = \cos(\theta/2)$ and $\vec{e} = (e_1, e_2, e_3)^T = \vec{\eta}\sin(\theta/2)$. Euler parameters describe SU(2), a unit 3-sphere in Euclidean 4-space, which represents a two-fold covering of the rotation group SO(3), and so clearly they have no singular configuration. For this reason, Euler parameters are a convenient choice of parameterization when arbitrary vehicle orientations are possible. For notational convenience, we write the Euler parameters as a four component object $\vec{p} = (e_0, e_1, e_2, e_3)^T$, but we must remember that rotations themselves do not commute and so are not vectors. Simple quadratic *algebraic* formulas allow the expression of direction cosine matrices, virtual rotations, and angular velocities in terms of Euler parameters and their derivatives.

3.2.2 Kinematic Relations - The Vehicle Graph

As an example, Figure 3 shows a planar multi-body system of rigid bodies linked together by revolute joints. A revolute joint allows only rotation about the common joint axis between bodies. These bodies are not independent in their motion, but are constrained to move so that certain relations between the coordinates of each linked body are satisfied: Both the distances from the joint center to each body's CM and the angles between the joint axis and each vector from the joint location to the body's CM remain constant.

We can abstract this picture and describe the same multi-body system in terms of a *graph*, where the vertices (nodes) represent rigid bodies and the edges joints. This is shown in Figure 4. A *directed* graph is a graph where an ordering between vertices is given, so each edge has a direction from the ordering of its endpoints. It is clear that any configuration of linked rigid bodies can be described in this way, since we make no assumption that the graph have any embedding properties in the plane.

We now order the bodies by numbering outward from a chosen base-body. To derive our

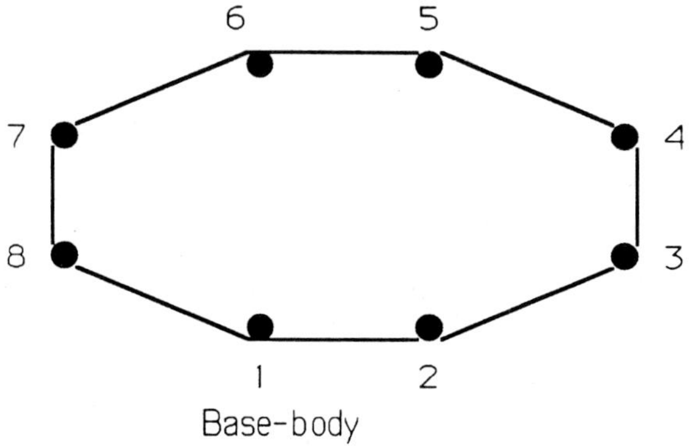

Figure 4. Graph associated to multi-body system.

kinematic relations, we need only examine pairs of linked bodies. Suppose we consider the ith and j^{th} bodies linked together as shown in Figure 5. We require several coordinate systems which are indicated in the Figure: An inertial global frame; body i's centroidal frame; body j's centroidal frame; body i's joint frame ij connecting body i and j; body j's joint frame ji describing the same joint as ij between body j and i. $\vec{d}_{i,j}$ is the joint vector between the ij and ji joint frames. The orientation matrices $A_i, A_j, A''_{i,j}, C_{i,j}, C_{j,i}$ relating the frames are also indicated. The global centroidal coordinates of body i are $\vec{r}_i$ and the joint attachment vectors in the local body frame are $\vec{s}'_{i,j}$. The A_i are used to transform local vectors, such as $\vec{s}'_{i,j}$, to global coordinates $\vec{s}_{i,j} = A_i \vec{s}'_{i,j}$.

We assume that the joint between the two bodies can be fully described by a set of relative joint coordinates $\vec{q}_{i,j}$. For example, in a revolute joint, a single angle about the joint axis vector; for a spherical joint, the three Euler angles or four Euler parameters between the ij and ji joint coordinate frames; for a translational joint, the length extension along the translational axis definition vector.

The following relations are easy to deduce:

$$A_j = A_i C_{i,j} A''_{i,j} C^T_{j,i}, \tag{1}$$

$$\vec{r}_j = \vec{r}_i + \vec{s}_{i,j} + \vec{d}_{i,j} - \vec{s}_{j,i}, \tag{2}$$

$$\vec{\omega}_j = \vec{\omega}_i + \vec{\omega}_{i,j}, \tag{3}$$

$$\dot{\vec{r}}_j = \dot{\vec{r}}_i + \dot{\vec{s}}_{i,j} + \dot{\vec{d}}_{i,j} - \dot{\vec{s}}_{j,i}, \tag{4}$$

where the $\vec{\omega}_i$ are the global angular velocities and $\vec{\omega}_{i,j}$ is the global joint angular velocity between the ij and ji joint frames. A linear relation between $\vec{\omega}_{i,j}$ and the relative joint coordinate velocities $\dot{\vec{q}}_{i,j}$ exists. We write it as

$$\vec{\omega}_{i,j} = H_{i,j} \dot{\vec{q}}_{i,j},$$

where $H_{i,j}$ must be calculated for each joint type. Then the jth-body's rotational velocity is

$$\vec{\omega}_j = \vec{\omega}_i + H_{i,j} \dot{\vec{q}}_{i,j}.$$

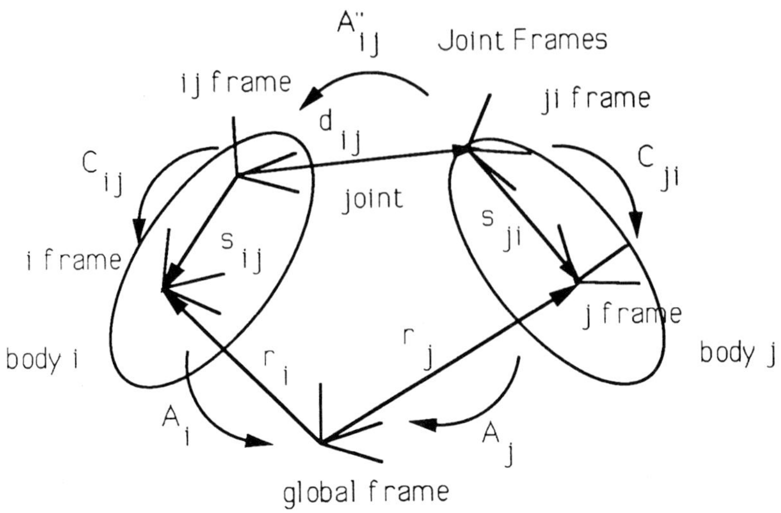

Figure 5. Adjacent linked bodies.

Since $\vec{s}_{i,j}$ is a vector fixed on body i,

$$\dot{\vec{s}}_{i,j} = \tilde{\omega}_i \vec{s}_{i,j}.$$

Similarly, for body j,

$$\dot{\vec{s}}_{j,i} = -\tilde{s}_{j,i}\vec{\omega}_j.$$

In terms of the relative joint velocities,

$$\dot{\vec{s}}_{j,i} = -\tilde{s}_{j,i}(\vec{\omega}_i + H_{i,j}\dot{\vec{q}}_{i,j}).$$

The derivative of the joint displacement vector $\vec{d}_{i,j}$ is

$$\dot{\vec{d}}_{i,j} = \tilde{\omega}_i \vec{d}_{i,j} + d_{i,j,q_{i,j}} \dot{\vec{q}}_{i,j} \tag{5}$$

where $d_{i,j,q_{i,j}}$ is the Jacobian of the joint vector $\vec{d}_{i,j}$ with respect to the relative joint coordinates $\vec{q}_{i,j}$. Putting all this together, we can write the relations between the velocities in terms of certain matrices $B_{i,j,1}$ and $B_{i,j,2}$ as

$$\begin{aligned} \begin{pmatrix} \dot{\vec{r}}_j \\ \vec{\omega}_j \end{pmatrix} &= \begin{pmatrix} I & (\tilde{r}_i - \tilde{r}_j) \\ 0 & I \end{pmatrix} \begin{pmatrix} \dot{\vec{r}}_i \\ \vec{\omega}_i \end{pmatrix} + \begin{pmatrix} d_{i,j,q_{i,j}} + \tilde{s}_{i,j} H_{i,j} \\ H_{i,j} \end{pmatrix} \dot{\vec{q}}_{i,j} \\ &= B_{i,j,1} \begin{pmatrix} \dot{\vec{r}}_i \\ \vec{\omega}_i \end{pmatrix} + B_{i,j,2} \dot{\vec{q}}_{i,j}. \end{aligned} \tag{6}$$

A similar formula holds for each body's virtual translation $\delta\vec{r}_i$ and virtual rotation $\delta\vec{\pi}_i$ (which, being infinitesimal, is a true 3-vector)

$$\begin{pmatrix} \delta\vec{r}_j \\ \delta\vec{\pi}_j \end{pmatrix} = B_{i,j,1} \begin{pmatrix} \delta\vec{r}_i \\ \delta\vec{\pi}_i \end{pmatrix} + B_{i,j,2}\delta\vec{q}_{i,j}. \tag{7}$$

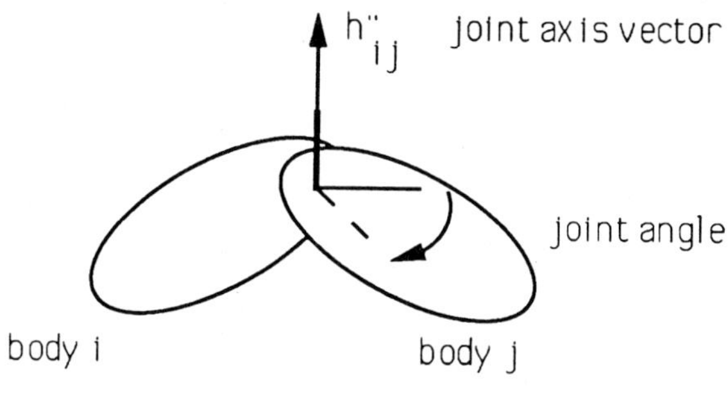

Figure 6. Two bodies linked by a revolute joint.

The acceleration relations are

$$\begin{pmatrix} \ddot{\vec{r}}_j \\ \dot{\vec{\omega}}_j \end{pmatrix} = B_{i,j,1} \begin{pmatrix} \ddot{\vec{r}}_i \\ \dot{\vec{\omega}}_i \end{pmatrix} + B_{i,j,2}\ddot{\vec{q}}_{i,j} + D_{i,j}, \tag{8}$$

where $D_{i,j}$ contains the velocity terms

$$D_{i,j} = \dot{B}_{i,j,1} \begin{pmatrix} \dot{\vec{r}}_i \\ \vec{\omega}_i \end{pmatrix} + \dot{B}_{i,j,2}\dot{\vec{q}}_{i,j}. \tag{9}$$

The matrices $B_{i,j,1}$ and

$$\dot{B}_{i,j,1} = \begin{pmatrix} 0 & (\tilde{\dot{r}}_i - \tilde{\dot{r}}_j) \\ 0 & 0 \end{pmatrix} \tag{10}$$

are independent of joint type, while $B_{i,j,2}$ and $\dot{B}_{i,j,2}$ depend upon the joint type and its relative coordinates. Reference [3] contains an extensive table of joint types and their corresponding B_2 and $\dot{B}_2$ matrices.

Example of revolute joint: Figure 6 shows two bodies linked by a revolute joint. Here $d_{i,j} = 0$. Choose the joint axis vector $\vec{h}''$ parallel to the $z''_{i,j}$-axis and let θ be the rotation angle about this axis. Then

$$\vec{\omega}_j = \vec{\omega}_i + H_{i,j}\dot{\theta}_{i,j}$$

where

$$H_{i,j} = \vec{h}_{i,j} \tag{11}$$

$$= A_i C_{i,j} \begin{pmatrix} 0 \\ 0 \\ 1 \end{pmatrix}. \tag{12}$$

The joint transformation matrix $A''_{i,j}$ is just the usual rotation matrix about the local ij joint frame by the angle θ. Also,

$$B_{i,j,2} = \begin{pmatrix} \tilde{s}_{j,i}\vec{h}_{i,j} \\ \vec{h}_{i,j} \end{pmatrix} \tag{13}$$

and

$$\dot{B}_{i,j,2} = \begin{pmatrix} \dot{\tilde{s}}_{j,i}\vec{h}_{i,j} + \tilde{s}_{j,i}\dot{\vec{h}}_{i,j} \\ \dot{\vec{h}}_{i,j} \end{pmatrix}. \tag{14}$$

Since

$$\dot{\vec{h}}_{i,j} = \tilde{\omega}_i \vec{h}_{i,j},$$

$$\dot{B}_{i,j,2} = \begin{pmatrix} \tilde{h}_{j,i}\tilde{\omega}_j s_{j,i} + \tilde{s}_{j,i}\tilde{\omega}_i \vec{h}_{i,j} \\ \tilde{\omega}_i \vec{h}_{i,j} \end{pmatrix}. \tag{15}$$

3.2.3 Virtual Work Equations

The D'Alembert's virtual work principle [17] states that for a system of N bodies, the sum of the virtual work (work of a virtual displacement $\delta\vec{q}$ against a force $\vec{Q}$) due to inertial and external forces under virtual kinematically admissible displacements (virtual displacements which satisfy the constraints), added to the the work of the internal forces, must vanish in dynamic equilibrium. For a rigid body we ignore this last term, because the internal forces can do no work. We treat springs and dampers connecting rigid bodies as external force elements.

For a rigid body, we must consider the virtual displacements from both translation and rotation. Again, we follow the notation of [21]. If the position and orientation are given in the global inertial frame by $\vec{r}_i$ and $\vec{p}_i$, we write the ith body's global velocity as the vector $\vec{Y}_i$

$$\vec{Y}_i = \begin{pmatrix} \dot{\vec{r}}_i \\ \vec{\omega}_i \end{pmatrix}, \tag{16}$$

where its rotational velocity is $\vec{\omega}_i$; the body's acceleration and virtual displacement-rotation are

$$\dot{\vec{Y}}_i = \begin{pmatrix} \ddot{\vec{r}}_i \\ \dot{\vec{\omega}}_i \end{pmatrix}, \tag{17}$$

$$\delta\vec{Z}_i = \begin{pmatrix} \delta\vec{r}_i \\ \delta\vec{\pi}_i \end{pmatrix}. \tag{18}$$

If the motion of the system of bodies must satisfy a set of constraint equations $\vec{\Phi}(\vec{r}_i, \vec{p}_i) = 0$, D'Alembert's ***principle of virtual work*** states that for every set of ***kinematically admissible*** virtual displacements $\delta\vec{Z}_i$ satisfying orthogonality with the rows of the constraint Jacobian $\vec{\Phi}_{\vec{Z}_i}$ (the matrix of partial derivatives of each component of $\vec{\Phi}$ with respect to each coordinate)

$$\sum_{i=1}^{N} \vec{\Phi}_{\vec{Z}_i}\delta\vec{Z}_i = 0, \tag{19}$$

the virtual work must vanish:

$$\sum_{i=1}^{N} \delta\vec{Z}_i^T(M_i\dot{\vec{Y}}_i - \vec{Q}_i) = 0, \tag{20}$$

where the symmetric and positive-definite generalized mass matrix M_i and force vector $\vec{Q}_i$ are written as as

$$M_i = \begin{pmatrix} m_i & 0 & 0 & 0 \\ 0 & m_i & 0 & 0 \\ 0 & 0 & m_i & 0 \\ 0 & 0 & 0 & J_i \end{pmatrix} \tag{21}$$

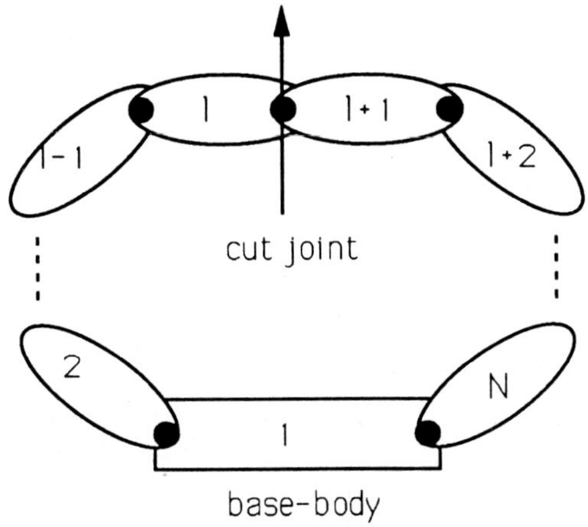

Figure 7. Closed graph for derivation of recursive elimination equations.

and

$$\vec{Q}_i = \begin{pmatrix} \vec{f}_i \\ \vec{n}_i - \tilde{\omega}_i J_i \vec{\omega} \end{pmatrix}. \tag{22}$$

These contain the body mass m_i, moment of inertia tensor J_i, and external forces $\vec{f}_i$ and torques $\vec{n}_i$. Geometrically, kinematic admissibility requires that the virtual displacement be in the tangent hyperplane to the configuration manifold.

In our case, the virtual displacements $\delta\vec{Z}_i$ are not independent when subject to the constraint conditions Equation 19, and so we cannot assume each of their coefficients must vanish. If we add the virtual work of these constraint forces, by means of Lagrange multipliers, then the virtual displacements can be assumed independent. So we replace Equation 20 by

$$0 = \sum_{i=1}^{N} \delta\vec{Z}_i^T (M_i \dot{\vec{Y}}_i - \vec{Q}_i) + \sum_{(j,k)-cutjoint} \delta\vec{Z}_i^T \vec{\Phi}_{Z_i}^{(j,k)T} \vec{\lambda}_{(j,k)}, \tag{23}$$

where the $\vec{\lambda}_{(j,k)}$ are the Lagrange multipliers from the cut joint between body j and k.

3.2.4 Recovery of Accelerations from the Recursive Equations

We demonstrate (following Bae's thesis [3], [4], [5], [6]) how the recursive equations for the accelerations are derived by considering the single closed loop graph shown in Figure 7. Body 1 is the base body, and we cut the loop between bodies l and $l+1$. Equation 23 is then

$$0 = \sum_{i=1, i\neq l, l+1}^{N} \delta\vec{Z}_i^T (M_i \dot{\vec{Y}}_i - \vec{Q}_i) + \sum_{i=l}^{l+1} \vec{Z}_i^T (M_i \dot{\vec{Y}}_i - \vec{Q}_i + \vec{\Phi}_{Z_i}^{(l,l+1)T} \vec{\lambda}_{(l,l+1)}). \tag{24}$$

If we now substitute our kinematic relations relating acceleration and virtual displacement of body l in terms of those of body $l-1$ and the relative joint coordinates $\vec{q}_{(l-1)l}$ between them, we get

$$
\begin{aligned}
0 = & \sum_{i=1}^{l-1} \delta \vec{Z}_i^T (M_i \dot{\vec{Y}}_i - \vec{Q}_i) + \\
& \delta \vec{Z}_i^T (B_1^T (M_l B_1 \dot{\vec{Y}}_{l-1} + M_l B_2 \ddot{\vec{q}}_{(l-1)l} + M_l D_{(l-1)l} - \vec{Q}_i) + \vec{\Phi}_{Z_l}^{(l,l+1)T} \vec{\lambda}_{(l,l+1)})) + \\
& \delta \vec{q}_{(l-1)l}^T (B_2^T (M_l B_1 \dot{\vec{Y}}_{l-1} + M_l B_2 \ddot{\vec{q}}_{(l-1)l} + M_l D_{(l-1)l} - \vec{Q}_i + \vec{\Phi}_{Z_l}^{(l,l+1)T} \vec{\lambda}_{(l,l+1)})) + \\
& \sum_{i=l+2}^{N} \delta \vec{Z}_i^T (M_i \dot{\vec{Y}}_i - \vec{Q}_i) + \vec{Z}_{l+1}^T (M_i \dot{\vec{Y}}_{l+1} - \vec{Q}_{l+1} + \vec{\Phi}_{Z_{l+1}}^{(l,l+1)T} \vec{\lambda}_{(l,l+1)}).
\end{aligned}
\tag{25}
$$

Since the virtual relative joint displacements $\delta \vec{q}_{(l-1)l}$ are arbitrary (after making the cut), its coefficient must vanish and we can solve for the relative joint acceleration

$$
\ddot{\vec{q}}_{(l-1)l} = -(B_2^T M_l B_2)^{-1} (B_2^T (M_l B_1 \dot{\vec{Y}}_{l-1} + M_l D_{(l-1)l} - \vec{Q}_i + \vec{\Phi}_{Z_l}^{(l,l+1)T} \vec{\lambda}_{(l,l+1)})) \tag{26}
$$

If we substitute the relative acceleration back into Equation 26, we have eliminated all body l accelerations. Continuing in this manner backwards along each branch gives an equation for the base body acceleration $\dot{\vec{Y}}_1$ and Lagrange multipliers $\vec{\lambda}$

$$
0 = \delta \vec{Z}_1^T ((M_1 + K_1^1 + K_1^2) \dot{\vec{Y}}_1 - (Q_1 + L_1^1 + L_1^2) + (\Phi M_1^{1T} + \Phi M_1^{2T}) \vec{\lambda}), \tag{27}
$$

where the superscripts 1 and 2 indicate the result of recursive elimination along each branch to the base body for the accumulated mass (K), force (L), and Jacobian (ΦM) matrices.

If the system has nc constraints, Equation 27 does not yet determine the base body acceleration since we have only 6 equations and $6 + nc$ unknown accelerations and Lagrange multipliers. To arrive at the extra equations needed, we differentiate the constraint equations twice to get

$$
\begin{aligned}
\ddot{\vec{\Phi}}_{(l-1)l} & \equiv \vec{\Phi}_{\vec{Z}_l} \dot{\vec{Y}}_l + \vec{\Phi}_{\vec{Z}_{l+1}} \dot{\vec{Y}}_{l+1} - \gamma \\
& = 0
\end{aligned}
\tag{28}
$$

where γ includes all other non-acceleration terms. We can now proceed as before to eliminate recursively the intermediate bodies down to the base body, arriving at

$$
0 = (\Phi M_1^1 + \Phi M_1^2) \dot{\vec{Y}}_1 + (\Phi L_1^1 + \Phi L_1^2) \vec{\lambda} - RHS_1^1 - RHS_1^2 - \gamma, \tag{29}
$$

where again we have accumulated Jacobian mass (ΦM), force (ΦL), and mixed term (RHS) matrices along each branch.

We can combine Equations 27 and 29 as

$$
\begin{pmatrix} K_1 & \Phi M_1^T \\ \Phi M_1^T & \Phi L_1 \end{pmatrix} \begin{pmatrix} \dot{\vec{Y}}_1 \\ \vec{\lambda} \end{pmatrix} = \begin{pmatrix} L_1 \\ RHS_1 \end{pmatrix}, \tag{30}
$$

where we have collected terms from both branches. Equation 30 is then used to find the base body acceleration $\dot{\vec{Y}}_1$. Once the base body acceleration is known, we recover each outboard body relative joint acceleration using Equation 26 and then the Cartesian acceleration using the kinematic formulas.

4 Vehicle Dynamics Model

4.1 Real-Time Dynamics for Vehicle Simulation

Evans & Sutherland has devised efficient real-time dynamics algorithms applicable to arbitrary vehicle types. Non-real-time computer simulation of complicated mechanical linkages has been performed for machines, robots, spacecraft, and ground vehicles. True real-time simulation is more difficult and hitherto done only for relatively simple mechanical systems, such as aircraft, when the governing equations can be approximated, as with linearized equations of motion, or with specialized computer hardware. Engineering simulation of modern vehicles, such as high performance sports cars, requires a multi-body non-linear model in order to provide a high fidelity of motion; software flexibility is required to deal with the general nature of vehicle engineering problems. A solution to real-time engineering simulation demands both cost-effective computational capacity and the adaptability of general purpose computers and software. Simulator system integration and introduction into the real-time software of motion-base washout and vehicle subsystem models are facilitated by the use of standard operating systems and programming languages.

Two previous approaches to real-time vehicle dynamics modeling, albeit at very different levels, are those implemented by the Swedish Road and Traffic Research Institute (VTI) [29] and Daimler-Benz [14] [18]. The VTI model considers a simple planar 3 degree-of-freedom car, but carefully considers tire and other forces. Daimler-Benz achieves real-time with a much more sophisticated, but still simplified model. They incorporate an implicit integration scheme with a quasi-Newton method [11] to achieve stability in a dual processor system. Details of how constraint stabilization is performed are not available.

We are primarily interested in the accurate prediction of vehicle dynamics, rather than kinematics or inverse dynamics [23]. The approach we use decomposes the system into a set of rigid bodies (a rigid body requires distances between points within the body to be fixed) connected by joints (which allow relative motion between the bodies), subject to various external forces, moments, and constraints. The resulting linked system can be represented, as discussed in the previous section, by a directed closed graph [33] (see Figure 8), where the bodies form vertices and joints the edges joining the vertices.

As shown in Section 3.2.2, for a tree graph, outboard body Cartesian positions and velocities can be expressed in terms of inboard body and relative joint coordinates and velocities. This chaining recursively provides the coordinates needed for determining the total system motion. In our lexicon, *recursive* is used to mean either moving inward or outward along the tree graph, using data from previous bodies along the branch, along with the joint coordinates, to determine the position and motion of the next.

General multi-body graphs, with embedded closed loops, are necessary to represent more complicated systems, such as high-performance sports cars. The existence of closed loops obstructs the graph from being a contractible tree graph, so the system must be transformed. We open the closed loops by adding "cut-joint constraints", so that a recursive relative joint coordinate kinematic description can be employed with the resulting tree graph. Next, D'Alembert's virtual work principle [17] is utilized to derive the equations of motion, augmented by reaction forces from the cut-joint constraints introduced via Lagrange multipliers. This relative joint coordinate formulation, implemented in a recursive parallel algorithm, leads to greater efficiencies for real-time simulation than Cartesian coordinate formulations. External forces are computed from the tires, drivetrain, wind resistance, brakes, springs, dampers, stabilizer bars, and suspension stops. Because our vehicle bodies are subject to kinematic constraints

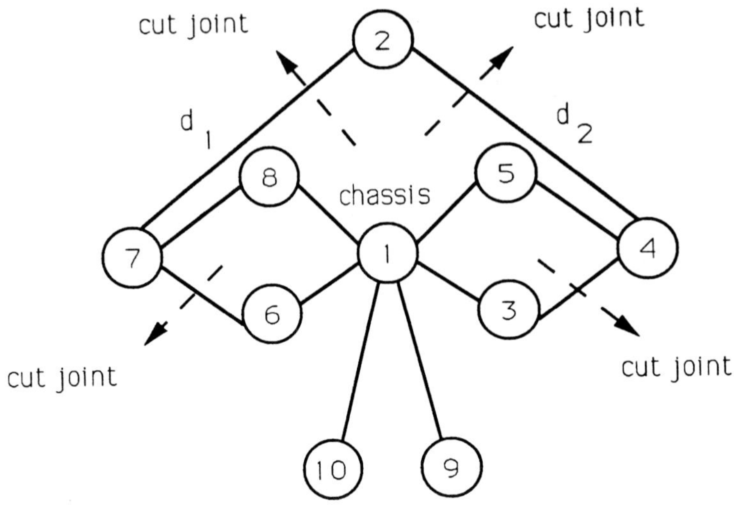

Figure 8. Vehicle graph with cut-joints indicated.

from cutting the closed loops in the graph, a set of coupled differential-algebraic equations (DAE's), in which differential equations of motion and algebraic equations of constraint must be simultaneously solved, results. At all times, the numerical solution must closely satisfy the imposed kinematic constraints, so some form of constraint stabilization is mandatory. In addition, integration and control stability must be preserved even with high frequency force inputs.

In the rest of this section, we describe in more detail our recursive vehicle kinematics and equations of motion. We discuss the numerical integration techniques used to solve our DAE's, along with the important concept of constraint stabilization. Lastly, we mention computer hardware issues and present the timing results for our algorithm on various serial and parallel machines.

4.2 Vehicle Description

A typical modern high-performance sports sedan is shown schematically in Figure 9. It consists of a chassis, the two Macpherson front suspension subsystems [8], the steering rack, and the two rear suspension arms. The Macpherson front suspension subsystem is detailed in Figure 10. This suspension allows both jounce (spindle vertical motion) and steer (the rotation of the spindle) as independent motions. Steering is done by motion of the tie-rods (which act as distance constraints) connecting the rack and spindle.

The initial step is to break the vehicle into its independent structural components, each of which can be approximated as a rigid body. These will include everything *except* compliant members, such as shock absorbers, bushings, and springs, which have important internal degrees of freedom. These compliant elements can themselves be modeled using deformation mode analysis, with the coefficient of the mode introduced as another generalized degree-of-freedom. For example, a model might contain 10 independent bodies: Chassis, rack, two Swiss arms, two struts, two spindles, and two rear trailing arms. Shock absorbers and springs are attached to the front and rear suspensions. Torsion bars are included to provide the proper vehicle roll stability.

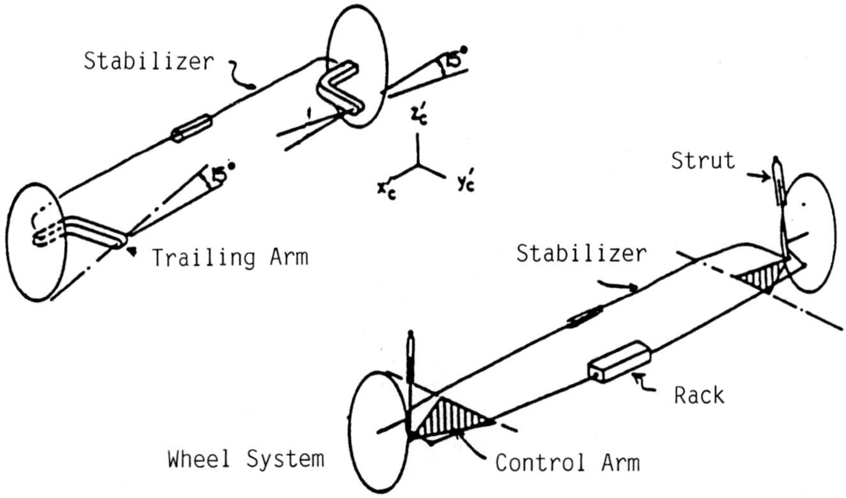

Figure 9. Schematic diagram of modern high-performance sports sedan.

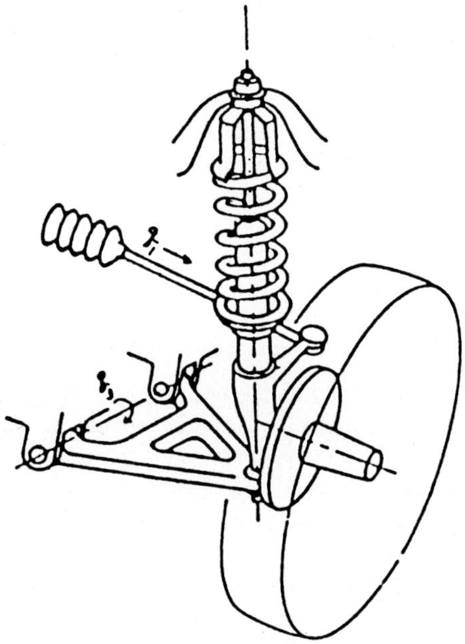

Figure 10. Macpherson front suspension.

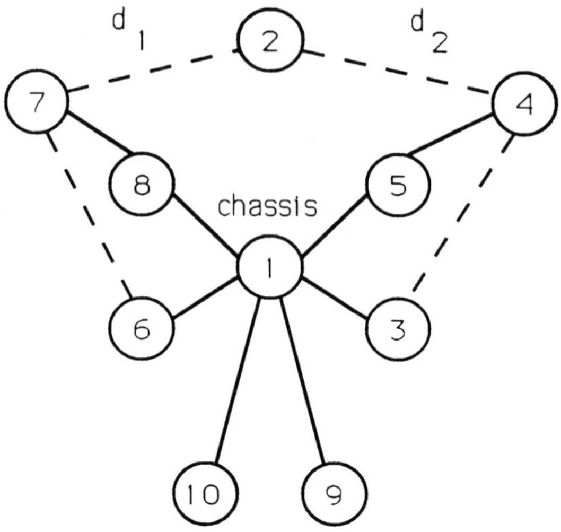

Figure 11. Vehicle tree graph with cut loops.

Even though each rigid body needs six coordinates to describe its motion, they are constrained in their collective motion because the rigid bodies are connected to one-another. For example, the Macpherson front strut assembly has only two motions: A vertical "jounce" and a rotational "steer". When we account for all the constraints from the joints, we have just ***ten*** independent degrees of freedom left. The joint constraints effectively convert the dependent individual body coordinates into a smaller set of independent relative joint coordinates. For example, the rear trailing wheel only needs the relative angle between it and the chassis to describe its position. The model takes as its basic variables the chassis Cartesian coordinates and relative joint coordinates. These, along with the associated velocities, are the coordinates that must be propagated through time by the numerical integrator while preserving the constraint relations.

4.3 Real-time Algorithm

4.3.1 Decomposition in terms of a Vehicle Graph

The vehicle is described in its assembly by a directed graph in which closed loops will exist. For example, in the front suspension, a closed loop occurs among the chassis, Swiss arm, spindle, and strut. These closed loops will cause problems for the relative coordinates, so they are removed by applying a "cut-joint" constraint in place of an actual joint. This produces a tree-structure graph, without closed loops, but adds additional constraint equations that must ultimately be satisfied by the coordinates.

The corresponding vehicle graph is shown in Figure 8. There are four closed loops from the front suspension and steering linkages. If we cut the links between rack and spindle and lower control arm and spindle on both sides, we produce the tree graph shown in Figure 11.

4.3.2 Vehicle Coordinates

In Figure 11, the chassis is the base body, whose coordinates are the three Cartesian degrees of freedom of the center-of-mass in the inertial frame $\vec{r}_1$ and four Euler parameters $\vec{p}_1$ describing

Table 1. Model coordinates.

Independent Path	Generalized Coordinate	Joint Axis
Body 1 $\xrightarrow{T_2}$ Body 2	q_1	u_1
Body 1 $\xrightarrow{R_1}$ Body 6	q_2	u_2
Body 1 $\xrightarrow{R_2}$ Body 3	q_3	u_3
Body 1 $\xrightarrow{R_3}$ Body 9	q_4	u_4
Body 1 $\xrightarrow{R_4}$ Body 10	q_5	u_5
Body 1 $\xrightarrow{S_1}$ Body 5 $\xrightarrow{T_3}$ Body 4	q_6-q_9,q_{10}	u_6-u_9
Body 1 $\xrightarrow{S_2}$ Body 8 $\xrightarrow{T_1}$ Body 7	q_{11}-q_{14},q_{15}	u_{10}-u_{13}

its orientation. The lower control arm position is determined by the chassis position and specification of the revolute joint angle (the rear suspension arms have a similar description). The strut's position is given by the chassis and spherical joint orientation (again using Euler parameters). The spindle's position can be found from the strut's position and the translational joint distance. The position of the rack relative to its translational joint with the chassis is given by the driver's steering input. Table 1 presents the system's coordinates. Notice that we have not yet "closed" any of the four loops in Figure 11 by adding constraint reaction force terms to the virtual work equations.

In our current model, the four tires are not treated as individual bodies, but are given only a single rotational degree of freedom and inertia. This ignores small gyroscopic effects. Not treating the tire as a full body is a reasonable approximation, since tire inertial forces can be separately calculated and added as additional external coupling torques to the equations of motion. Compliance in any of the rigid bodies is not considered, but can be added as a generalized degree-of-freedom.

Our model has 10 rigid bodies, 4 tires (as noted above, having only a single rotational degree-of-freedom), and 26 body and relative joint coordinates (not all independent) in the kinematic description of the vehicle tree graph. The constraints from the closed suspension and steering loops must be considered, since they restrict some of these 26 coordinates.

4.3.3 Holonomic Vehicle Constraints

The coordinates used in the vehicle description are subject to holonomic constraints [16] $\vec{\Phi}(\vec{Z}_i) = 0$ (constraints that are expressible in terms of the variables and which can be used to eliminate dependent coordinates) from the closed loops in the graph. The Macpherson front suspension requires the spindle to meet the lower control arm at a spherical joint as shown in Figure 10. Counting both the right and left sides, this gives 6 independent constraints. The rack-spindle distance give 2 more independent constraints, while the normalization of the three sets of Euler parameters provides 3 more. The driver steering commands produce 1 more constraint on rack motion. Since each of these constraints is holonomic, and they are all independent, we have $26 - (6 + 2 + 3 + 1) = 14$ independent degrees of freedom in our vehicle (exclusive of the drivetrain and other subsystems).

Non-holonomic constraints (non-integrable relations involving the coordinates) are encountered in our model only in the kinematics of tire roll-without-slip on a surface. The resulting tire constraint forces are treated as external forces on the spindle and tire.

4.3.4 Recovery of Outboard Positions, Velocities, Accelerations

We work with a set of 26 dependent coordinates describing the tree graph structure and 12 constraint equations from the cut joints. The velocity and acceleration formulas involve joint matrices B_1 and B_2 giving the linear relation between outboard body velocity and inboard body and relative joint velocity. We write the Cartesian velocity of outboard body $i+1$ as $\dot{\vec{Z}}_{i+1} = B_1\dot{\vec{Z}}_i + B_2\dot{\vec{q}}_{(i+1)i}$ where for body i, its global Cartesian coordinates are $\vec{Z}_i = [\vec{r}_i^T \vec{\pi}_i^T]^T$.

The corresponding acceleration formula is $\ddot{\vec{Z}}_{i+1} = B_1\ddot{\vec{Z}}_i + B_2\ddot{\vec{q}}_{(i+1)i} + \vec{D}_{(i+1)i}$, where the *velocity coupling* terms $\vec{D}_{(i+1)i}$ contain the coordinate velocities and derivatives of the joint matrices B_1 and B_2. The B_2 and D matrices must be individually constructed for each specific joint type.

These kinematic formulas are used to express the global Cartesian position, velocity, and acceleration of an out-board body in terms of an inboard body and relative joint position, velocity, and acceleration. All body coordinates, velocities, and accelerations are determined recursively moving outward in the graph from the initial base body.

4.3.5 Recovery of Coordinate Accelerations

We generate our dynamical equations using D'Alembert's principle of virtual work. This is done in a way that generates maximum parallelism in the algorithm. By using relative joint coordinates, rather than Cartesian coordinates, the unknown joint constraint forces are automatically eliminated from our equations. Using virtual work has the advantage that alternative variational methods require the additional step of forming either Lagrangians or Hamiltonians, and so are cumbersome for complex systems. Added difficulties with variational formulations occur when non-conservative forces (such as friction) are present. With virtual work, we can consider both conservative and non-conservative forces in a straightforward manner, while the cut joint constraints are easily incorporated using Lagrange multipliers.

The result of the equations of motion is a parallel algorithm that allows the inward recursive elimination of the relative joint accelerations, and accumulation of terms into a single matrix equation for the base body accelerations and Lagrange multipliers. The remaining coordinate accelerations are then recursively recovered by moving outward in the graph. The organization of the algorithm closely follows the system tree graph, and so exhibits the inherent parallelism of each independent branch. Accelerations are numerically integrated to determine the new positions and velocities at the next frame time. The recursive algorithm is fully non-linear in that velocity coupling terms $\vec{D}$ are not assumed negligible. The assumption of slow rates of angular change, so coupling from the Euler terms $\tilde{\omega}J\vec{\omega}$ is small, fails during high speed maneuvering of vehicles. The inclusion of these non-linear terms is critical for simulating the effects of anti-lock braking systems (ABS) [24] and four-wheel traction controls.

4.3.6 External Forces

We include various external forces such as tire forces, wind resistance, engine and brake torque, springs, dampers, stabilization bars, and internal reactions in the model. The most critical, and difficult, for accurate road vehicle simulation are the tire forces [10]. The major components of tire forces and moments are shown in Figure 12. Because of the complexity of interaction, the forces and moments are taken from measured data as a function of normal force, slip angle, and camber angle. Attention is paid to how the tire forces change during conversion from a no-slip to a slip condition in order to minimize longitudinal force discontinuities.

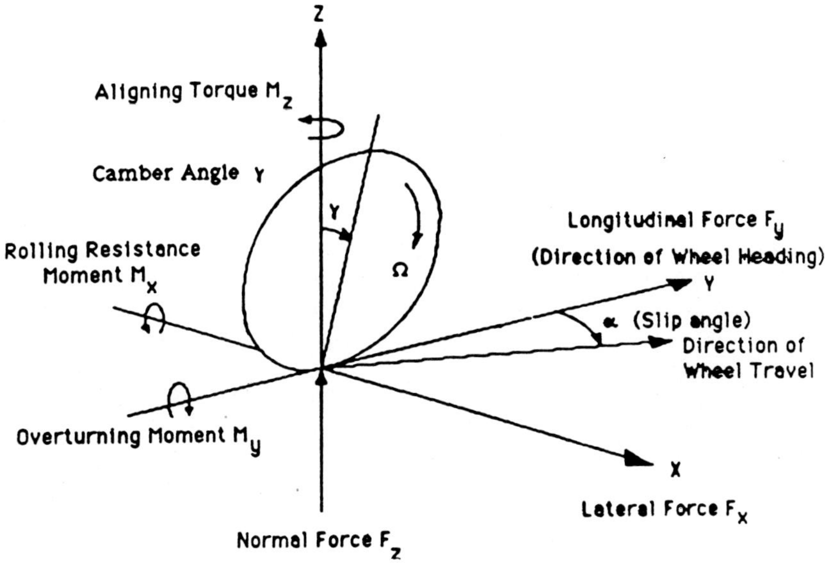

Figure 12. Tire forces and moments.

Complex drivetrain models for both manual and automatic transmissions have been developed. They are based on combining drivetrain components such as engine, clutch, transmission, torque converter, and differential together with proper feedback [27]. Each separate component is modeled using table lookups of data provided for individual designs. Our current drivetrain models have a single degree of rotational freedom which is independently integrated to find rotational velocity and applied wheel torques.

4.3.7 Integration of Accelerations

We can symbolically write the result of the recursive algorithm determining the accelerations as recovering the right-hand side $\vec{f}(t, Y)$ of the first-order vector equation

$$\dot{\vec{Y}} = \vec{f}(t, Y), \tag{31}$$

where $\vec{Y}$ is the state vector of 26 chassis and joint coordinates and their velocities. This equation includes both the dynamics equations and the differential form of the algebraic cut joint constraints. If it is solved using ODE methods, small errors can accumulate and the solution will ultimately fail to satisfy the constraints. If we add the constraint equations to Equation 31, the resulting DAE's are difficult to solve by standard ODE methods [15]. Our approach is to solve Equation 31 as an ODE, but add an additional independent step stabilizing the solution so it satisfies the constraints.

Equation 31 can be solved using linear multistep methods from numerical analysis to advance $\vec{Y}(t)$ to $\vec{Y}(t+\Delta t)$. Because of real-time limitations, methods that require only a single updated evaluation of $\vec{f}$ for each time step can currently be used. This limits us to conditionally-stable explicit methods such as Adams-Bashforth and Adams-Moulton Predictor-Corrector schemes [25] without a final update. Experiments have shown that accuracy is relatively insensitive to method order. High accuracy is not required for most vehicle simulation, since the driver's perception is the dominant factor. Stability becomes the main issue for the integration technique.

During vehicle simulation, large external force discontinuities can occur, for example, when the suspension stops close from high impact forces generated during hitting a pothole. These forces manifest themselves in sharp discontinuities in the right-hand-side of Equation 31. Since it is not possible to reduce the time step, a restarting procedure is employed, where momentum is conserved and the order of the Predictor-Corrector method is gradually increased. An option to improve the restart would be to use low-order Runge-Kutta methods. These have adequate accuracy, with enlarged stability regions, and are self-starting. When using explicit methods, great care must be taken in how the resulting equations are partitioned and solved to avoid instabilities resulting from natural high frequency force inputs. To improve total system bandwidth, after the system has been properly partitioned into slow (chassis) and fast (suspension) components, a hybrid integration scheme where the low frequency slow components are integrated with an explicit method and the high frequency fast components with an implicit method is advantageous.

Guidance in partitioning the components can be gained by the use of an eigenvalue analysis of the Jacobian matrix for the differential equation system. This linear analysis, though only approximate, will help reveal the potentially troublesome high-frequency oscillatory modes (those with large imaginary parts) and stiff, fast decaying modes (those with large negative real parts). When combined with a stability region analysis of the ODE method, an informed guess as to stable step size can be made. Since it is very difficult to calculate the system Jacobian analytically, a difference approximation about a reference state of interest is used. The zero eigenvalue, rigid body modes must be first removed from matrix before EISPACK or other standard eigenvalue software is used.

4.3.8 Constraint Stabilization

The numerical solution to Equation 31 must satisfy all cut joint constraints. These additional algebraic equations (forcing us to solve the differential equations on the curved configuration manifold, rather than in flat Euclidean space) require special techniques in correcting the solution produced by the integration method, while retaining accuracy and stability. For short times, since the differential form of the constraints are incorporated into Equation 31, the solution will approximately satisfy the cut joint constraints. For longer times, either Baumgarte's method [7] of modifying the equations to make the configuration manifold (the manifold determined by the constraints on which the system trajectories move) a stable attractor (points close to the configuration manifold move nearer in time along their trajectories), or a coordinate partitioning method [32] of updating the dependent coordinates can be used. Baumgarte's method essentially introduces a feedback loop to control error growth, while the partitioning method uses Newton-Raphson iteration to make the dependent coordinates satisfy all constraint conditions. Either of these ensures that accumulated numerical error will not cause the solution to drift too far off the configuration manifold.

4.4 Organization of Parallel Recursive Algorithm

The efficiencies required by real-time demand a careful decomposition of the algorithm data flow and attention to mapping the algorithm to a particular computer architecture. You can't expect real-time performance with algorithms and architectures that don't match.

4.4.1 Algorithm Flow

Figure 13 shows an implementation of the recursive algorithm without constraint stabilization.

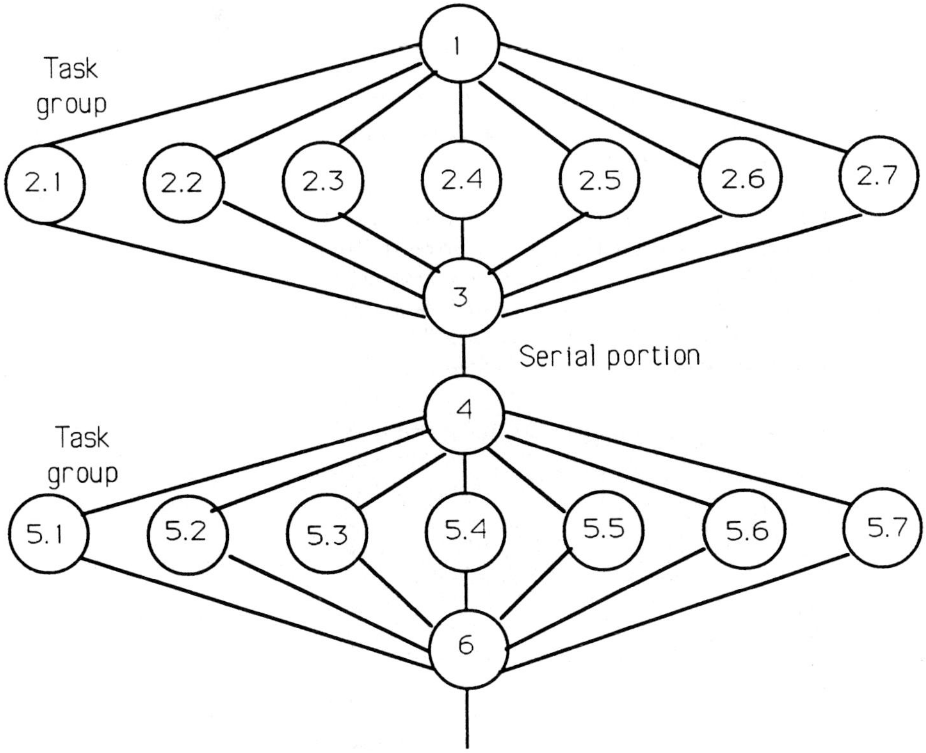

Figure 13. Organization of parallel tasking in recursive algorithm.

At the start of each time step, Cartesian positions and velocities of each body are recovered from the relative joint positions and velocities moving outward in the graph from the chassis base body. Each separate branch is computed concurrently with the others. The driver steering, brake and accelerator pedal position and other inputs are obtained from sensors and used to determine rack position and velocity, brake, and drivetrain parameters. External forces and moments are next calculated; tire, brake, spring, damper, stabilizer bar, aerodynamic, gravitational, and drivetrain are independently determined by special subsystem models. Next, the accelerations are recursively eliminated moving inward in the graph toward the base body. Again, these eliminations are performed concurrently. When the base body Equation 30 has been assembled, it is solved for the chassis Cartesian accelerations using Gaussian elimination, and recovery of the outboard body Cartesian and relative joint accelerations is made moving outward in the graph. When this is completed, the right hand side of Equation 31 has been calculated and the integration scheme advances the solution to the next time frame.

4.4.2 Computer Architectures and Software

The requirement of implementing a parallel algorithm with a small number (4-8) of concurrent tasks leads to considering a single bus or cross-bar architecture with a shared global memory. Care must be taken to avoid potential bus contention from simultaneous memory access or message passing. Modern optimizing FORTRAN and C compilers running under POSIX-type operating systems provide software flexibility. Specialized simulation computers with non-standard languages suffer from insufficient adaptability, limited transportability, and narrow growth potential. Upgrading of a simulator computer system is simplified by writing software in standard languages.

A solution to these problems is to choose a standard vector-concurrent mini-supercomputer, like the Alliant FX/8, running a UNIX operating system. Figure 14 shows the architecture of the Alliant FX/8 [1].

In the Alliant FX/8, up to 8 compute elements (CE) are connected by a 376MB/sec cross-bar to two large computational processor caches (CPC). Each CPC is a two-way interleaved 256KB cache for up to 4 CEs. Cache coherency is maintained by a write-back cache protocol[1] watching the main memory bus. The CPC are connected to a 4-way interleaved 64MB main memory by two independent 188 MB/sec 72 bit (64 bits data and 8 bits SECDED) data buses, a 28 bit address bus, and a concurrency control bus. Each individual CE contains an integer, floating point, and vector register set. The floating point units are fully segmented, and can perform simultaneous scalar multiply-adds. Special vector operations are available that will chain standard vector calculations using adds and multiplies together. All floating point operations are in 64 bit, and the vector lengths are 32 64-bit vectors (CRAY has a length of 64 64-bit vectors). The peak "macho-flops", with all 8 CEs, are 188 MFLOPS. A more realistic number would be a sustained 20-40 MFLOPS.

The operating system and all I/O operations are done with interactive processors (IP). These are essentially Motorola 68020 units with some possibility of doing floating point operations. These IPs access main memory through the IP caches (IPC), each of which share up to 3 IPs. Each IP also has a local memory to hold operating system kernel text pages. Direct memory access (DMA) is available to VME devices through special VME IPs. The design of the Alliant allows computation to occur concurrently with I/O operations. If the majority of

[1] A write-back cache is one where writes to memory are stored in cache and written to memory only when a rewritten item is removed from cache. In a write-through cache, writes to memory are written concurrently to both the cache and memory.

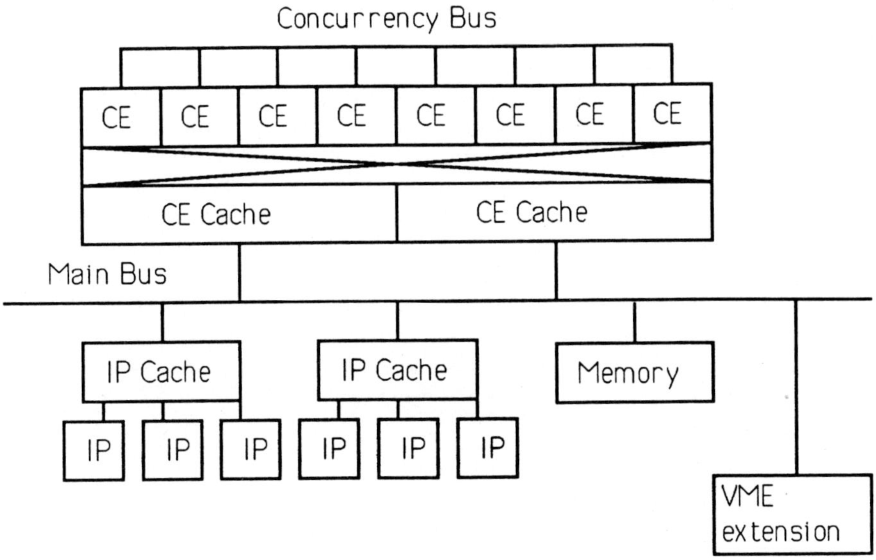

Figure 14. Organization of the Alliant FX/8.

the executing process is cache resident, I/O operations have no effect on system performance. This is important for a simulator, since a modest amount of (fewer than 100 bytes) output must be delivered without slowing the real-time computations.

Concurrency control is done through the existence of concurrency registers on each CE, and global control of the concurrency is done by concurrency instructions communicating via the concurrency bus. Synchronization of parallel execution of loops does not require access to main memory by the use of spin-locks and semaphores, but is done directly in the concurrency registers.

Very good optimizing vector-concurrent FORTRAN and C compilers are available for this class of architecture. They are limited in their detection of parallelism by the inability to fully trace all data dependencies, and so really only automatically produce COVI — concurrent outer, vector inner — loop breaking. If the algorithm does not allow for its description in terms of single or multiple loops, the programmer must provide explicit directions to enable the compiler to parallelize the code. If execution of multiple concurrent threads is required, a time consuming analysis of the algorithm data flow must be performed, resulting in a decomposition into serial groups of parallel tasks. The compiler can then proceed to automatically insert instructions for the required data coherence and task synchronization. The goal of the algorithm analysis and optimization is to provide as many task groups of up to 8 course-grained (to reduce the need for memory conflicts over shared data) concurrent tasks as possible, with the smallest possible number of single serial tasks separating the concurrent task groups. Such a design will maximize the parallel speed-up, hopefully approaching one linear in the number of processors. Practical algorithms rarely achieve linear speed-up. The recursive algorithm on the Alliant FX/8 achieves a speed-up of 3.2 with 8 CEs (cf. Table 2).

Table 2. Timing results for recursive algorithm.

Computer	Relative time to finish one algorithm step (Alliant FX/8 with 8 CEs = 1 unit) Number of CEs	Relative Time
Alliant FX/8	8	1
Alliant FX/8	4	1.25
Alliant FX/8	2	2.0
Alliant FX/8	1	3.2
Alliant FX/80	8	0.7
VAX 8800	serial code	4.5
VAX 780	serial code	21.5

4.4.3 Algorithm Timing

The recursive algorithm for the vehicle model described in section 4.3 has been run on the Alliant FX/8, FX/80 (an improved FX/8, with faster CE clock), and a serial VAX-8800 and VAX-780.

Table 2 shows the results of timings taken on these computers, both serial and parallel, using optimized FORTRAN codes for each machine.

Several final remarks are in order about the algorithm and timing results:

- The choice of relative joint coordinate can effect algorithm speed. An optimal choice can eliminate additional matrix multiplications in the backward and forward recursions.

- The algorithm as presently partitioned is flat in its timing, in that any given module is a small percent of the total time. The dominant computation within this partitioning is the Gaussian elimination to find the base-body accelerations and Lagrange multipliers.

- The algorithm, being organized around a tree structure without closed loops, clearly lends itself to various levels of parallel implementation. The left-right symmetry produces the greatest improvement in speed, with additional marginal improvements among each set of branches on each side. Algorithm speed-up is almost directly proportional to the number of independent suspension elements. This is reflected in independent branches of the opened tree graph.

5 Concluding Remarks

The necessity of taking only a single function evaluation severely limits the range of applicable methods for solving the system DAEs. An fully implicit integration method, combined with Baumgarte's method, would hold promise if low-rank Jacobian update methods can be used to solve the resulting non-linear equations. A hybrid method based upon partitioning into "fast" and "slow" components is also attractive. Experiments have indicated this to be useful.

If control systems are added, then the total system eigenvalues, including both subject and control hardware, should be considered. Physiologists have characterized to some extent the transfer functions of human perception mechanisms. By adding these differential equations to those from the dynamics, a combined total simulation system description would result. The numerical solution of the total system equations might require a different approach from the dynamics equations alone. A optimal DAE solver could take this total man-in-the-loop system into account in its choice of method, step size, and order.

I want to thank the members of the Driving Simulation Project at Evans & Sutherland, and in particular David Ingebretsen, Steve Winters, and Steve Gough, for their efforts towards real-time vehicle simulation. I also want to thank E. Haug, J. Kuhl, D-S. Bae, R-S. Hwang, D. Andersen, and W-S. Lee.

References

[1] Alliant Computer Systems Corp. *Alliant FX/Series Product Summary*, June 1987.

[2] Armstrong, W. Recursive Solution to the Equations of Motion of An N-Link Manipulator. In *Proc. 5th World Congress on Theory of Machines and Mechanism*, Vol. 2, (Montreal, 1979), 1343-1346.

[3] Bae, D. and Haug, E. A Recursive Formulation for Constrainted Mechanical System Dynamics. *Technical Report* 86-14, Center for Computer Aided Design, College of Engineering, University of Iowa, 1986.

[4] Bae, D. and Haug, E. A Recursive Formulation for Constrained Mechanical System, Part I - Open Loop. *Mechanics of Structures and Machines*, 15 (1987), 359-382.

[5] Bae, D. and Haug, E. A Recursive Formulation for Constrained Mechanical System, Part II - Closed Loop. *Mechanics of Structures and Machines*, 15 (1987).

[6] Bae, D., Haug, E., and Kuhl, J. A Recursive Formulation for Constrained Mechanical System, Part III - Parallel Processor Implementation. *Mechanics of Structures and Machines*, 16 (1988).

[7] Baumgarte, J. Stabilization of Constraints and Integrals of Motion in Dynamic Systems. *Computer Methods in Applied Mechanics in Engineering*, 1 (1972), 1-16.

[8] Campbell, C. *New Directions in Suspension Design*. Robert Bentley, Cambridge, Mass. 1981.

[9] Chace, M. Methods and Experience in Computer Aided Design of Large-Displacement Mechanical Systems. In *Computer Aided Analysis and Optimization of Mechanical System Dynamics*, E. Haug. (ed.). Springer-Verlag, Heidelberg, 1984.

[10] Clark, S. (ed.) *Mechanics of Pneumatic Tires*. U. S. Dept of Transportation, Washington, D. C., 1975.

[11] Dennis, J. and More, J. Quasi-Newton Methods, Motivation and Theory. *SIAM Review* 19, 1 (1977), 46-89.

[12] Deyo, R., Briggs, J., and Doenges, P. Getting Graphics in Gear. *Computer Graphics* 22, 4 (1988), 317-326.

[13] Doenges, Peter K. *Overview of Computer Image Generation in Visual Simulation*, Presented at ACM Siggraph Technical Courses, July, 1985.

[14] Drosdol, J. and Panik, F. The Daimler-Benz Driving Simulator: a Tool for Vehicle Development. *SAE Technical Paper* Series, 850334, (Feb. 1985).

[15] Gear, W. Differential-Algebraic Equations. In *Computer Aided Analysis and Optimization of Mechanical System Dynamics*, E. Haug (ed.) Springer-Verlag, Heidelberg, 1984.

[16] Goldstein, H. *Classical Mechanics*. Addison-Wesley, Reading, Mass., 1980.

[17] Greenwood, D. *Classical Dynamics*. Prentice-Halll, Englewood Cliffs, N.J., 1977.

[18] Hahn, S., and Kalb, E. The Daimler-Benz Driving Simulator Set-Up and Results of First Experiments. In *Summer Computer Simulation Conference Proceedings* Simulation Councils, Inc., San Diego, 1987, pp. 993 - 998.

[19] Haug, E. *Computer Aided Analysis and Optimization of Mechanical System Dynamics.* Springer-Verlag, Heidelberg, 1984.

[20] Haug, E. Elements and Methods of Computational Dynamics. In *Computer Aided Analysis and Optimization of Melchanical System Dynamics*, E. Haug (ed.).

[21] Haug, E. *Intermediate Dynamics.* Manuscript (to be published), 1986.

[22] Hooker, W. and Margulies, G. The Dynamical Attitude Equations for an n - Body Satellite. *J. Astronaut. Sci.* 12 (1965), 123-128.

[23] Issacs, P. and Cohen, M. Controlling Dynamic Simulation with Kinematic Constraints, Behavior Functions and Inverse Dynamics. *Computer Graphics* 21, 4 (July 1987), 215-224.

[24] Kempf, D., Bonderson, L., and Slater, L. Real Time Simulation for Application to ABS Development. *SAE Technical Paper* 870336, 1987.

[25] Lambert, J. *Computational Methods in Ordinary Differential Equations.* John Wiley, New York, 1973.

[26] Luh, J., Walker, M., and Paul, R. On-line Computational Scheme for Mechanical Manipulator. *J. Dyn. Syst. Measurement Control* 102 (1980), 69-76.

[27] Mitsche, M. *Dynamik der Kraftfahrzeuge.* Springer-Verlag, Berlin, 1982.

[28] Nikravesh, P. and Chung, I. Applications of Euler Parameters to the Dynamic Analysis of Three-Dimensional Constrainted Mechanical Systems. *J. Mechanical Design* 104 (1982), 785-791.

[29] Nordmark, S. VTI Driving Simulator - Mathematical Model of a Four-wheeled Vehicle for Simulation in real Time. *VTI Rapport* Nr 267A 1984. Statens vag-och trafikinstitut, Linloping, Sweden, 1984.

[30] Orlandea, N., Chace, M., and Calahan, D. A Sparsity-Oriented Approach to the Dynamic Analysis and Design of Mechanical Systems- Parts 1 and 2. *J. of Engineering for Industry* (1977), 773-784.

[31] Roberson, R. and Schwertassek, R. *Dynamics of Multibody Systems.* Springer-Verlag, New York, 1988.

[32] Wehage, R. and Haug, E. Generalized Coordinate Partitioning for Dimension Reduction in Analysis of Constrained Mechanical Systems. *J. of Mechanical Design*, 104 (1982), 247-255.

[33] Wittenburg, J. *Dynamics of Systems of Rigid Bodies.* B. G. Teubner, Stuttgart, 1977.

INDUSTRIAL PRACTICES AND EXAMPLES
SPACE STRUCTURES AND ROBOTS

Harold P. Frisch
NASA/Goddard Space Flight Center
Greenbelt Maryland

ABSTRACT

Engineers responsible for the design and analysis of spacecraft attitude control and stabilization systems have been actively contributing to multibody system simulation software development efforts for more than 2 decades. In like manner engineers responsible for ground based mechanical system design and analysis have also been contributing for the same duration. During this period both groups have watched numerical integration methods and associated software develop. The mechanical system group has drawn from this work, while the aerospace group has relied almost exclusively on methods defined by Adams, Bashford, Runge, and Kutta, at the turn of the century. The intent of this contribution is to provide a rational for "why?". This is done by first defining generic response characteristics of typical aerospace control of flexible structure problems and then listing common modeling and simulation needs. The needs list is restricted to those which have placed extraordinary demands on the numerical integration procedure. It is hoped that this aerospace user's view of underlying requirements for numerical integration procedures will motivate the developers of emerging Order N multibody system simulation software to provide a sufficiently general set of numerical integration options.

NATO ASI Series, Vol. F 69
Real-Time Integration Methods for Mechanical System Simulation
Edited by E. J. Haug and R. C. Deyo

PROBLEM CLASSIFICATION

There is general agreement on the fact that stiff problems require special numerical solution techniques. However, there is no generally accepted practical method for defining the demarcation between stiff and non stiff problems. Within the community concerned with design and manufacturing of non-aerospace mechanical systems, stiff problems occur often enough to make them a cause for concern. These problems are characterized by the presence of both very short and long time constant effects within the simulation time span of interest. The prediction of automotive vehicle response to road surface hazards (ditch, rock, etc.) is a classic example. Conversely, within the spacecraft attitude control community, stiff problems are the rare exception. For example, if one has a classic control of flexible space structure problem, and if an attempt is made to select a "best" integration method, stiff integrator methods are usually found to be the least efficient.

OSCILLATORY RESPONSE

System flexibility at joints and/or within the structure itself is one of the prime factors considered during the design of an attitude control system for a spacecraft and its independently controlled instruments and antennae. Characteristically, observable motion is oscillatory with minimal structural damping; that is, the viscous damping ratio is within an order of magnitude or so of .005. From a modelling and simulation point of view all motion that can be observed by the control system's sensors can be passed on to the controller and must be included in the simulation model. The control algorithm then defines actuator control signals. These may be oscillatory, bang-bang, or shaped pulse commands. Control algorithms are designed to keep the spacecraft and its various instruments pointing or scanning in a manner defined by mission objectives. The controller attempts to insulate line of sight motion from attitude sensor noise and all other unplanned external disturbances, such as system flexibility. Control may also be used to enhance naturally occurring structural damping. From the perspective of numerical integration requirements, the integrator cannot be allowed to step coarsely over system response oscillations within the band width of the attitude sensors and control actuators. If coarse stepping is allowed, phase information from the sensors and to the actuators is significantly degraded. Knowledge of both phase and amplitude is essential, since control is frequently via many small precisely phased actuator pulses. Accurate phase information is essential if the sensors and actuators are noncollocated, and, indeed mission critical, from the standpoint of predicting system stability.

EXTREME ACCURACY

Pointing requirements for some astronomy experiments and strategic defense initiative tasks require line of sight pointing to an accuracy of less than an arc second. Performance simulations must take into account both the dynamics of the control system, the flexibility of the structure to which the instrument is attached, and all other on board disturbance factors. The resultant steady state response is normally oscillatory, within an envelop that may either decay or beat within bounds. The boundaries of the steady state response envelop provide a measure of expected system performance. From the standpoint of numerical integration, the user needs to be assured that predictions are real and not just numerical integration noise. In application, the integrator's error tolerance factors are normally used to exercise some control on allowable step size. These tolerance factors often provide an error measure which is too conservative for high precision work. A more reliable measure of computation error is obtained by monitoring a set of dynamic invariants for the system at hand; for example, momentum, energy, quaternion magnitude, etc.

WEAK NEGATIVE AND POSITIVE DAMPING

Many spacecraft have been successfully spin stabilized. On a few isolated occasions, unanticipated effects have caused spinning spacecraft to very slowly despin or to experience a very weak nutational instability. In these cases, spin periods were measured in seconds or tens of seconds, while the associated despin and nutation buildup time constants were measured in days. The underlying cause was traced to a complex dynamic interaction between thermal bending and spacecraft spin. After extensive study, the phenomena was understood and mathematically characterized for simulation and parameter variation analysis. The nutational instability phenomena can be loosely viewed as negative damping, while the despin phenomena can be loosely viewed as positive damping. During the mathematical modelling studies, great difficulty was experienced in showing that the phenomena was real and not numerical noise from the integration process. In a broader context, users must be assured that integrator performance is not enhanced by the unintentional addition of artificial damping. If this is done important physical phenomena can be masked.

JUMP DISCONTINUITIES

The existence of jump discontinuities can be almost assured in space system application. On-off (bang-bang) control laws are frequently used to define the control signal that is sent to the spacecraft actuator system. Sensors used to monitor system state frequently have threshold limits. Signals within certain bounds are ignored, while signals above the bounds trigger responses that are passed to the control system. Other types of sensors monitor system state continuously, but only sample magnitude at regularly spaced intervals. The output of these sensors is a signal that changes magnitude only at a designated sampling period. Control laws are frequently implemented within an on board digital computer. Within the control law, gains and limiters are used to amplify and then limit command signals. In summary, frequently occurring jump discontinuities are a fact of life. Numerical integration methods must accommodate these without excessively cutting step size every time one is encountered. Discontinuity occurence, with the exception of controller sampling, is a function of system state. It cannot be predicted a-priori.

PARALLEL PROCESSING

Parallel processing computational methods are becoming more readily accessible to the project support engineer. Their ability to enhance numerical integration solution speed is discussed elsewhere in these proceedings. There is also a possibility to use parallel processing methods to overcome the jump discontinuity problem for an important practical class of problems. The controls engineer frequently encounters a system that must be actively controlled to prevent it from drifting away from a planned trajectory. Pulse control is initiated when a certain function of system state variables exceed a preset threshold. Otherwise, control actuators are dormant. This translates into the need to simulate short duration position state pulses into the controller, a short computational delay for the signal to be processed, and a short duration control actuator pulse that may be either shaped or bang-bang. Fixed step methods are costly from the standpoint that step size must be small enough to insure that pulses are found and that their shape is adequately modelled. Variable step methods may unintentionally step over the pulse or spend too much time cutting step size every time a pulse is encountered. An interesting alternative possibility is to use a parallel processor to compute a leading low order solution estimate. This could be used to locate the next jump discontinuity. This information can then be used by the high order, variable step integrator to make a one step adjustment to step size. At the discontinuity, the more accurate solution data can be used to reinitialize the discontinuity locator's state vector. If logic can be developed to insure that the next step precedes the discontinuity, by an epsilon tolerance factor the costly step size cutting process can be avoided.

MIXED DIFFERENTIAL AND FINITE DIFFERENCE EQUATIONS

Digital controllers are becoming the norm for spacecraft and robot control systems. These require the simultaneous solution of the finite difference equations (FDE) that characterize the response dynamics of digital filters, estimators, regulators, and compensators within the digital controller, and ordinary differential (ODE) or differential-algebraic equations (DAE) that characterize multibody system dynamics. The mixing of fixed step FDE solution methods with variable step DAE or ODE methods provide for a difficult implementation problem. In typical modeling and simulation problems associated with the design of digital controllers for flexible structures, step size is simply fixed at an integer fraction of the control system's sample period.

DIGITAL DELAYS

Digital delays must frequently be incorporated into a spacecraft or robot system response simulation. For example, they are encountered in digital control systems which derive rate from current and past state information, they are used to simulate delays associated with computational processing within complex controllers, the time delay between actuator signal arrival and load initiation, and when fixed delays are intentionally built into the control algorithm. The need to continually track past system state can be done with variable step methods. However this requires the special coding of an interpolator. This added degree of complexity is usually not implemented. Users simply use a fixed step integration method.

FEEDFORWARD AND ACCELERATION FEEDBACK

In order to improve system performance, control system designers often use lead or feedforward logic within the system's control algorithms. In addition to feedfoward logic, they may also use the output of accelerometers and also compute and use the first derivative of acceleration (jerk) in the control algorithm. These control design techniques cause major simulation problems. The control command that defines the load that the actuator will apply to the system is always placed on the right side of the equations of motion. But, it is a function of acceleration and jerk that the integration algorithm expects to see on the left side of the motion equations. Special coding logic is normally needed to circumvent this problem. The standard approximation is to use a fixed step method with a step size small enough to insure that acceleration and jerk computed at the previous time step provides an adequate approximation.

REAL-TIME MAN IN LOOP CONTROL AND ANIMATION

Real-time man in the loop control requires high speed integration techniques. The output is used to drive graphics animation for visual cues and to provide force reflection feedback to the operator for tactile cues. Screen refreshing is most easily accomplished if it can be synchronized with a fixed step integration method. Both visual and tactile feedback to hand controllers must be fast enough to provide cueing that has the illusion of realism. This can only happen if data transport delays between the various computing, hand control, and visualization systems can be minimized. From a numerical integration point of view, it appears that fixed step methods within a parallel processing computer environment provide the most straight forward solution to this problem.

DRIFTING FROM THE SOLUTION MANIFOLD

Differential-algebraic equations have the characteristic that their solutions can drift from the solution manifold. Various methods have been developed to continuously force the solution back onto the manifold. Baumgarte's method which is discussed by other authors in these proceedings, is the most popular method used by multibody dynamics specialists. Another approach to this problem has been successfully used within the DISCOS program. At every integration step, the DISCOS program performs a check to determine if all kinematic constraints are satisfied. As the numerical solution drifts away from the solution manifold, these conditions will not be exactly satisfied. To bring the solution back to the manifold, DISCOS computes the impulsive load that could have caused the constraint violation. It's negative is then applied to the system, implemented via a direct renormalization of the state vector. By renormalizing the state vector at every integration step, motion is kept on the manifold. This technique has worked well in applications if the integration step size is sufficiently small. The fundamental problem with the method is that it requires a renormalization of the state vector at every integration step. This is forbidden by nearly all general purpose integration methods.

TIME VARYING SYSTEM ORDER

Most spacecraft are launched in a packaged configuration. Once inserted into a correct orbit, deployment is initiated. This usually provides a wealth of complex dynamics problems for preflight study. Multisegment antenna unfold in a manner that mathematically requires the integrator to accommodate a varying number of differential equations. Degrees of freedom increase as joints are uncaged and decrease as they are sequentially locked into their fully deployed configuration. Scanning antennas that rest against stops at their travel extremes, robot systems that make and break contact as they attempt to grasp a payload, and dual arm payload handoff are problems of practical interest that involve time varying kinematic constraints, hence a system with time varying order.

The standard approach for simulating each of the above problems is to define a nonlinear viscoelastic contact spring. Stiffness and damping constants are zero before contact and large during contact. With this method system order stays constant. However, it introduces the needed to define large arbitrary numbers which must satisfy the conflicting goals of realism and computational efficiency.

If the time varying system order approach is attempted, a momentum pulse will occur in the simulation whenever the integration step is not synchronized to the exact instant of degree of freedom locking (caging). The momentum impulse method defined above was actually developed to solve this problem. Rather than attempt to cut step size to search for the exact time of locking, it was found to be more efficient to simply accept this time estimation error and to use a knowledge of the kinematic constraints to put the system back on the solution manifold by renormalization of the state vector. Renormalization of the state vector every integration step is not recommended for the new multibody solution algorithms. However, the concept may still be the best solution to the time varying system order problem.

CONSTRAINING MOTION ON THE SOLUTION MANIFOLD

Projection methods that are based on a knowledge of kinematic constraint invariants have proven to be a convenient means for bringing a drifting numerical solution back to the solution manifold. Dynamic invariants such as conservation laws for momentum and energy may be used in like manner to add an additional degree of error control to the trajectory that is traced on the solution manifold. The concept is that once motion is kept on the solution manifold by a Baumgarte like approach, additional Lagrange multipliers can be defined that will force the trajectory to continuously satisfy dynamic motion invariants. These may also provide the potential for stepping over and averaging out insignificant high frequency weakly damped effects that cannot be readily removed at the modeling step. Of course, this latter capability must be used with extreme caution.

SUBROUTINE PLANT DYNAMICS vs CONTROL DYNAMICS

Multibody dynamics specialists will normally include a provision to call a subroutine to define all nongyroscopic loads that act on the system. They imagine that "subroutine control dynamics" can be easily written. Conversely, the control system designer normally includes provision to call a subroutine to obtain all gyroscopic loads that act on the system. With appropriate small angle and other simplifying assumptions, they imagine that "subroutine plant dynamics" can be easily written.

As a new generation of multibody system simulation software evolves, the needs of both groups must be accommodated without bias. It is difficult for the multibody dynamics specialist to imagine all multibody theory encapsulated into a callable subroutine. Conversely, the controls designer cannot imagine encapsulating all intertwining control logic loops into a callable subroutine. For multibody dynamics software technology to reach deeper into the controls design community, the needs of the controls analysis must be accommodated. The challenge will be to devise methods that will allow the numerical integrator to be a utility that is provided by the controls program. Techniques must be developed that will accommodate the algebraic constraint component of the differential-algebraic equations within "subroutine plant dynamics" and the solution of the ordinary differential equation component by the integrator that is provided by the controls design and analysis program. It is unreasonable to expect that the controls analysis program will have a differential-algebraic equation solver in its library of optional integration methods.

SUMMARY

There is no question that solution methods for differential-algebraic equations comprise a rich area of research. From the point of view of one who needs to apply these methods to non stiff problems, a bias toward the stiff problem appears to be occurring in DAE and some multibody specialist communities. To date multibody methods have quite successfully serviced a range of problems far greater than ever imagined when the field of study began to evolve 20 years ago. The need for using differential- algebraic equation solution methods is now clear. The problem is that the solution methods appear to be evolving with a bias. This should be corrected. In order for multibody simulation software technology to support a full range of current and future applications, users must have access to a library of alternative integration methods. As a practical matter, the need for fixed step integration options is essential. Users should be provided with the option to readily disable step size control computation. Furthermore, multibody dynamics software developers should not intertwine the integrator with equation development methodology. No one integration method will ever satisfy all of the needs of the ever growing application community.

REAL-TIME MOTION BASE SIMULATION

Ronald R. Beck
U.S. Army Tank-Automotive Command
Warren, MI 48397-5000

ABSTRACT

The use of military vehicle performance simulation methods is playing an increasing role in the design and development of combat and tactical vehicle systems. Analytical and physical simulation tools are being used to reduce the time and high cost associated with conventional prototype-based "build-test-break-fix" military vehicle design and development programs. Their use also ensures, prior to fabricating prototypes, that new system designs meet specified performance levels. The emphasis of this paper is on the application of real-time physical simulation tools to structural integrity investigations in support of reliability forecasting.

INTRODUCTION

The U.S. Army Tank-Automotive Command (TACOM) has lead the way in sponsoring the development and application of large-displacement dynamic analysis and reliability forecasting software which permits engineering performance simulation of a broad class of combat and tactical vehicle systems. Interdisciplinary effects including electro-hydraulic and electro-mechanical servo control systems are easily handled. Analysts use these tools to explore, experiment, and study the synergistic effects on system performance by changing design parameters and operating conditions at will. One of the main uses of dynamic simulation is for the analysis of the dynamics of military vehicles and trailers. The reader may be surprised to learn that (from the viewpoint of dynamics) tactical vehicles and trailers pose a more complex and harder to analyze problem than combat vehicles. Combat vehicles have a turret, a hull and a relatively simple suspension system. Hence, the total number of bodies comprising the vehicle system is small. Stability is rarely a problem for combat vehicles. Modeling the track is not too difficult, but it adds to the computational requirements imposed on the computer.

Dynamic simulation is also used to design tests, by focusing testing in areas of concern, reducing testing in areas of confidence, and investigating system behavior well beyond the range of safe operation without endangering lives or damaging equipment.

NATO ASI Series, Vol. F 69
Real-Time Integration Methods for Mechanical System Simulation
Edited by E. J. Haug and R. C. Deyo

In addition to analytically examining vehicle behavior, motion time history data are generated via dynamic simulations to create the control signals for the electro-hydraulic actuators in TACOM's ride and motion base (physical) simulator facility. Physical simulators are being used to examine the structural integrity of complete vehicle systems or components, chassis/turret interaction dynamics, gun/turret drive weapon stabilization and control performance, and man/machine interface devices, displays and control issues. During a test, the motion simulator is used to closely emulate the same shock and vibration environment that the test specimen would encounter in the field. There are many advantages to combining analytical simulation with laboratory physical simulation. The primary ones are: absolute control over the test conditions and environment, repeatable tests, the ability to chose from a wide sample of terrain profiles, and the elimination of the influence and effects of the driver and weather and during testing.

The following section describes concrete examples of how analytical and physical simulation tools have been and are being used in all aspects of vehicle design, development, testing, and acquisition at TACOM. In particular, the simulation and analysis of:

- Military vehicle ride and shock dynamics
- Weapon system platform stability
- System structural integrity

Physical simulation tests are very appropriate for the validation of analytical models, for testing the dynamic performance of complete vehicle systems or subsystems and for the quick and objective determination of weak spots which would fail in the field. Physical simulation tests in the laboratory can provide a definite answer as to the ability of a component or a system to withstand vibrations and dynamic loads in the field. However, when a delicate mechanism is to be examined, the effect of rain, dust, mud, extreme cold, or heat cannot be discounted. Initial testing of such systems, in the Physical Simulation Laboratory, is still beneficial because it provides a quick and relatively inexpensive means to "catch" weaknesses which would certainly show in the field later on. Laboratory tests, therefore, ensure a quicker and less expensive way for "shaking down" the design. Since test conditions can be replicated exactly, a revised and improved design can be re-tested and, if it passes, one can be sure that the problem has been solved. However, the final proof is testing in the field where the system is exposed to the elements (and to the soldier).

In the past, shock and vibration input data for physical simulator systems were gathered by instrumenting vehicles and recording data as they traversed test courses. The disadvantages of this approach include the difficulty of having to instrument and test an existing vehicle, the need for extensive signal processing, the unavailability of heavily used test sites, and the risk of attempting dangerous maneuvers. TACOM has developed a new approach using Computer Automated Measurement and Control (CAMAC) systems, whereby output data generated via dynamic simulation is used to provide input control signals for physical simulators (Fig. 1). First, a high resolution dynamics model is created to mathematically represent the vehicle or the subsystem to be tested. This model is then used to

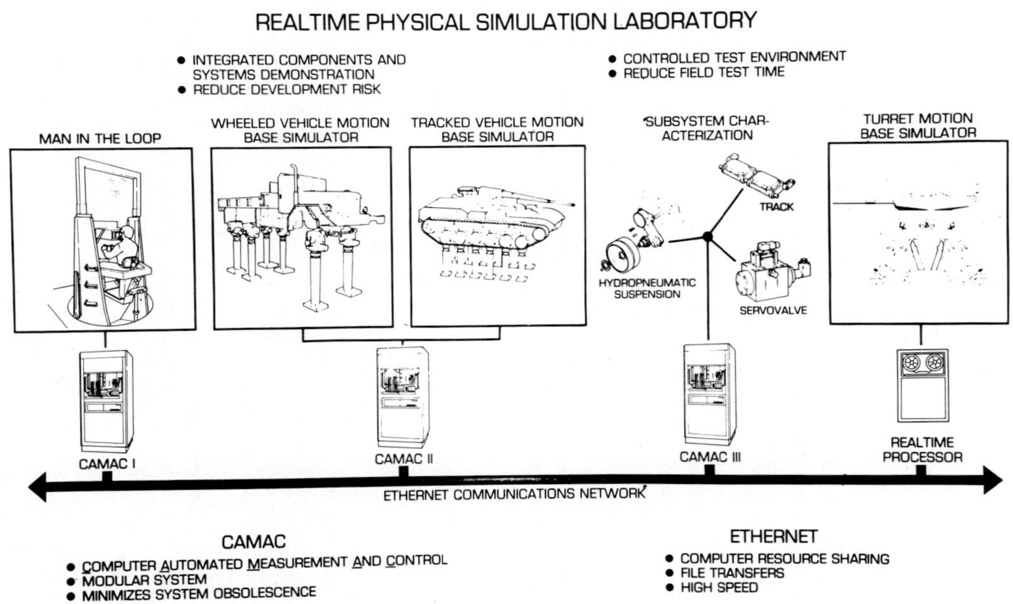

Figure 1 Realtime Physical Simulation Laboratory

analytically generate duty cycle data for any desired speed and a variety of available terrain profiles which represent various test sites and mission profiles. These duty cycle load and position data are filtered and detrended for input into the simulator system. The CAMAC system will then "drive" the actuators accordingly.

Figure 2 is a photo of the Mobile Protected Gun System (MPGS) suspension test rig mounted on hydraulic actuators in TACOM's motion base simulation laboratory. It is equipped with micro processor controlled shock absorbers to vary suspension system damping. The purpose of the test was to quantify the improved ride quality of the vehicle by controlling the damping at roadwheel stations one and five on each side of the vehicle. The computer controlled laboratory environment permitted direct comparison of the performance of the variable damping suspension system with the baseline system, because identical test conditions were maintained. For this limited test, it was shown that ride quality was improved. However, the reliability of the active shock absorbers was extremely poor. The tests proved that they could not survive the shock and vibration environment a combat vehicle is exposed to during typical cross-country operation.

Figure 2 Suspension Test Rig

A new machine gun mount designed for the 2-1/2 and 5 Ton Trucks was tested in the Laboratory. The new design has a heavier structure than the old design which caused structural integrity problems in the field. Structural vibrations resulted in cracks in the cab wall where the machine gun mount was attached. It was not expected that the heavier design would produce these failures.

The truck was mounted on six hydraulic actuators (Fig. 3) which created the necessary dynamic motion. The actuators were attached to the wheel spindles and, to account for the effect of the tires and wheels and their interaction with terrain, a mathematical model was used to generate the motion time histories which controlled the actuators.

Figure 3   2.5 Ton Truck Cab "Weapons Mount" Structural Integrity Test

Various structural failures were found. Each failure was remedied by modifying the truck cab and machine gun mount. These modifications consisted of "beefing up" appropriate elements of the structure which supported the machine gun mount. Once the modification was completed, testing was resumed and the modified structure was subjected to the same dynamic loads which caused the initial failure.

After 2400 miles of simulated off-road operation, the final design was considered to be adequately strong. Subsequently, this design passed the safety certification testing at Aberdeen Proving Ground. It is clear that the Physical Simulation Laboratory provided a controlled, quantifiable and repeatable test environment which lead to the desired solution quicker and cheaper than field testing could have.

Figure 4 is a photograph of the High Survivability Test Vehicle-Light (HSTV-L) mounted on hydraulic actuators in the laboratory. It was used to determine the stabilization and control system requirements associated with the main gun of a combat vehicle when it is in or out of mass balance. Several different stabilization and control algorithms were explored under very controlled repeatable conditions. Information gained from those tests was used to help structure further research in weapon system stabilization.

Figure 4 HSTV-L Stabilization and Control

Subsequently, an experimental automatic gun loading mechanism (Fig. 5) was tested in the Laboratory. This device was mounted on a ring supported by three hydraulic actuators. A mathematical model of the dynamics of the M1 Abrams Combat Vehicle was created and simulations were conducted to predict the vehicle's motion as it was driven over various rough cross country terrain profiles. The displacement time-histories of the three points where actuators were attached to the turret ring were generated from the simulations. These served as the basic input data for the development of the actuator control signals. This permitted the autoloader to be "shaken" in the laboratory as if it were mounted in a vehicle negotiating rough cross country terrain. The autoloader had performed well prior to these tests under static conditions. The dynamic tests were to answer the question of whether it could function under typical off-road conditions. The controlled laboratory tests revealed some minor problems which were remedied easily in the laboratory and thus eliminated costly time delays during the field test portion of the program.

Figure 5 Experimental Autoloader

Another example (Fig. 6) for testing a new design in the laboratory before releasing it for field use is the hatch of the M9 ACE Armored Combat Earthmover. A prototype driver's hatch was mounted on three actuators, just as the Autoloader was and it was subjected to the same dynamic forces the mechanism would encounter as the M9 ACE vehicle traversed various characteristic terrain-profiles. A total of 88 hours of simulation testing was executed. Several hatch hinge failures occurred throughout the 88 hours of testing. Generally, the hatch assembly required realignment and excessive play and wear were noted. These problems would not have surfaced until initial production testing scheduled for two years after the laboratory study. These tests eliminated problems prior to production of the vehicle. Currently, a redesigned hatch is being tested in the laboratory before fielding the vehicle to the troops.

Figure 6 M9 ACE Driver´s Hatach

TACOM´s Physical Simulation Laboratory cannot accommodate a heavy combat vehicle. Therefore, it was decided that a six degree-of-freedom simulator (Fig. 7) would be designed and constructed which would impart dynamic motions on a heavy combat vehicle turret. This, so called, Crew Station/Turret Motion Base Simulator (CS/TMBS) will be able to generate a maximum of 6 G acceleration on a 25 ton turret at 10 Hz frequency. (Current flight simulators are capable of low frequency motion and can accommodate light pay loads only). Additionally, this simulator will be the first of its kind because it will be able to accommodate an active payload, i.e., the turret will turn and the gun elevation will be varied during the testing.

This facility will provide the means to compare and evaluate different crew station configurations, weapon station control systems, and it will be well suited to test any other system in the turret which is influenced by shock and vibration (optics, for example). Clearly, the facility will be well suited for human engineering research, especially when equipped with a computer generated imaging system.

To achieve the design goals, a sophisticated instrumentation and control system employing a time-varying gain adaptive control system based on a model reference feed-forward architecture was chosen. An intense safety interlock hardware system with redundant software design is incorporated, which will trigger an abort sequence if anomalous conditions occur. Operation of the CS/TMBS is accomplished via a supervisor computer which receives and transmits data to an AD100 computer and, in turn, controls the independent processors for each actuator. The AD100 is a state-of-the-art computer capable of performing real-time simulation, permitting man-in-the-loop operation of the CS/TMBS.

Figure 7 Crew Station/Turret Motion Base Simulator (CS/TMBS) 6 D.O.F. System

CONCLUDING REMARKS

The U.S. Army Tank-Automotive Command's experience over the past 8-10 years has clearly demonstrated that analytical and physical simulation are viable tools for drastically improving the military vehicle design, acquisition, and field support process. The examples described in this paper provide irrefutable evidence that simulation can provide a better answer faster and at a fraction of the cost of the conventional "build-test-break-fix" approach. The Commanding General of TACOM recognized this and issued Commanding General Policy No. 22-88, which states that analytical tools will be used to the maximum extent feasible in the acquisition process for generating quantitative performance requirements and for the evaluation of competing proposals, and that the necessary input data will be a required part of the bids.

The Army and TACOM, in particular, has backed this policy by providing TACOM and other Army engineers with the most modern high technology tools available. In particular, in the form of a CRAY-2 Supercomputer, a host of Intergraph and other high quality graphics work stations and unique physical simulation facilities. Considering the magnitude of the vehicle procurement budget, the entire investment could pay for itself after only a few successful applications.

Industry is also interested in using TACOM's facilities. FMC, for example, would like to test their Advanced Mobility Test Bed and certain turret designs in the physical simulation laboratory in support of their IR&D programs. The legal aspects of the proposed cooperative activity are being ironed out by government and company lawyers. This precedent will pave the way for others to use these unique facilities in support of combat and tactical vehicle research and development.

The U.S. Army Tank-Automotive Command is a founder member of an NSF Industry/University Cooperative Research Center (I/UCRC) for simulation and design optimization which supports tool development, integration, and technology transfer. Twenty-six companies, universities and government laboratories participate and pool their resources for the development of common simulation tools. TACOM's application of these tools will greatly enhance the development and acquisition of a superior next-generation fleet of combat and tactical vehicles.

Aspects of Efficient and Reliable Multibody System Simulation

R. Schwertassek and W. Rulka[1]

Institut für Dynamik der Flugsysteme
DLR, Oberpfaffenhofen
W. Germany

Abstract

Multibody system equations can be generated in various forms. All of these may be interpreted as results of two basic approaches, the augmentation- and the elimination-method. The former method yields the descriptor form of the system motion, a set of differential-algebraic equations (DAE), and the latter the state space representation, a minimal set of ordinary differential equations (ODE). Both of these methods are surveyed. Particular emphasis is on the discussion of recursive computational schemes, generating the equations of motion with a number of operations, which is proportional to the number N of system bodies ($O(N)$-formulations).

For simulation purposes one would like to create that set of system equations, which can be generated most efficiently and for which the most efficient and reliable solution techniques are available. Numerical solution techniques for ODE have been studied in great detail and they are well-developed. By contrast, DAE have not been investigated for such a long time. In view of new developments in the latter field the generation of all the equations required for an efficient and reliable solution of DAE describing multibody system motion is discussed. These methods, i.e. an $O(N)$-formulation and new techniques for solving DAE, are implemented in the SIMPACK code. Its capabilities are illustrated by simulation of multibody mechanisms and robots.

1. Problems in Multibody System Simulation

The status of development of *multibody dynamics* is documented by the proceedings of five symposia and workshops on the topic [27], [17], [25], [5], [28]. A survey on the rise of the subject has been given in [33] and in [36]. *Multibody systems* are mechanical models for computer aided analysis and synthesis of complex technological systems such as spacecraft, mechanisms, robots or vehicles. Multibody models of man have been used for the development of safety devices such as seat belts or for the design of prosthetic limbs.

Elements of the systems considered here are (see Fig. 1):

- *rigid* or *gyrostatic bodies* (representing geometric and material properties of the system) together with known applied external forces and torques (e. g. gravity) acting upon the system bodies;

[1] MAN Technologie, München, West-Germany

NATO ASI Series, Vol. F 69
Real-Time Integration Methods for Mechanical System Simulation
Edited by E. J. Haug and R. C. Deyo

- a *global reference frame* (not necessarily corresponding to a material body), which characterizes any gross system motion;
- *interconnections* representing mobility and forces within the system;
- *control systems* interacting with actuators between and sensors on the system bodies.

The interconnections can be subdivided into *joints* and into *force elements*. The former constrain the relative motion across the interconnections and result in unknown constraint forces and torques, whereas the latter represent the known applied interactions. *Feedback control* of the motions of the multibody system is provided by controling its internal and external interactions represented by the applied forces and torques upon the system bodies.

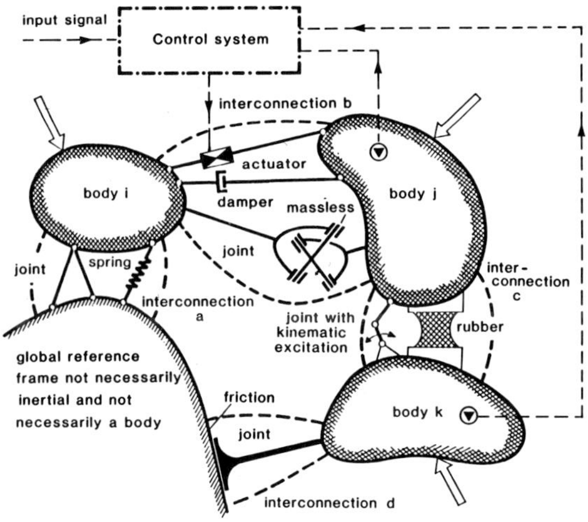

ELEMENTS OF MULTIBODY SYSTEMS:

bodies	dimensions, inertia, applied external forces (⇨)
reference frame	global system motion
interconnections	interaction between bodies
force elements	result in applied forces
supports, joints	result in constraint forces
control system	control of relative motion (sensors)

Figure 1. Typical Multibody System and its Elements

Multibody simulation programs generate the system equations from a description of the system elements and the system topology, numerically solve these equations and provide assistance for evaluating the results. The core of such programs are symbolical or numerical implementations of *multibody formalisms*, i.e. of computer oriented procedures for generating the system equations.

Some of the system elements cannot be described by parameters only - the specification of external forces and torques upon the system bodies, of the global frame's motion, of applied interaction forces and torques and of constraints resulting from the joints requires the formulation of functions depending on the system's state and on time. To make multibody programs a useful tool for system analysis and design, those functions, as required for a specific field of application, must be available in *libraries of system elements*.

Multibody system equations may be generated in various forms. A basic problem of multibody system simulation is the *selection of the "best" form* - one would like to create that set of equations, which can be generated most efficiently and for which the most efficient and reliable solution techniques are available. Solving this problem requires combined efforts in multibody dynamics and numerical mathematics.

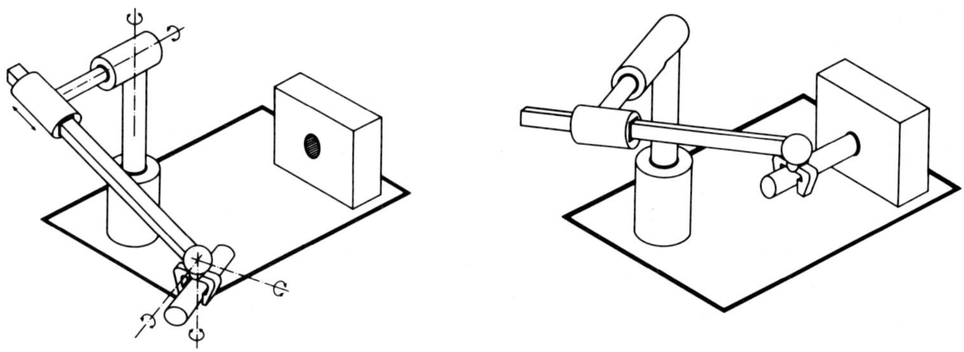

Figure 2. A Robot Operating in a Tree Configuration and in a Closed Loop Configuration

A second major class of problems concerns the *modeling options in multibody simulation codes*. Fig. 1. visualizes some of the necessities of multibody system modeling, e. g. the demand to simulate kinematic excitation, joints with massless intermediate bodies or interactions resulting from dry friction. Such capabilities are available in many of the simulation programs, being used at present. The following examples demonstrate specific needs, which cannot be handled easily with existing general purpose codes often. Fig. 2 shows a robot inserting a cylinder into a hole, i.e. a multibody system whose topological structure may change during the motion from a tree configuration into one with kinematically closed loops. Similar problems appear when analysing rendezvous- and docking-maneuvers of spacecraft, Fig. 3.

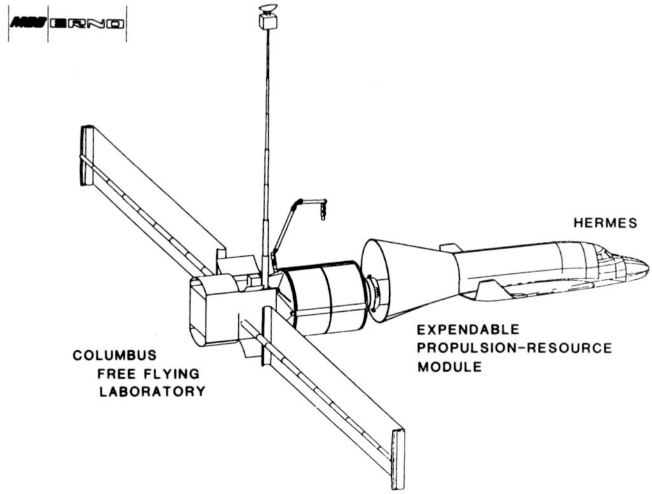

Figure 3. Spacecraft Performing a Docking Maneuver

A simulation of such systems becomes even more complicated, when impacts between the system bodies must be modeled carefully. A similar type of systems with variable structure is machinery with components having small finite clearances as examplified by the gear box shown in Fig. 4.

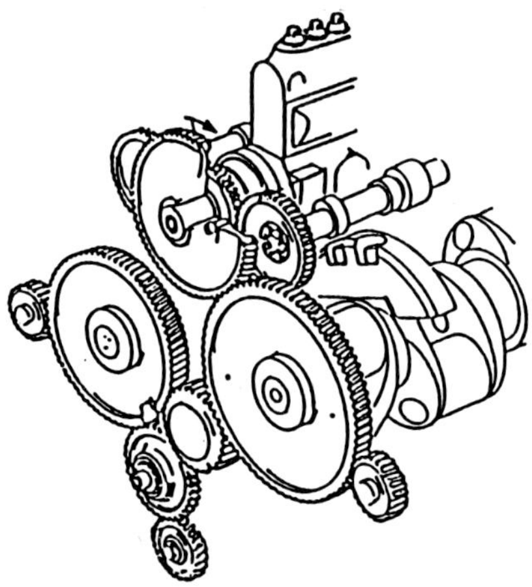

Figure 4. Machinery Yielding Multibody Models with Interconnections Having Small Finite Clearances

Impact generated vibration may cause undesirable noise or significant dynamic loads calling for a detailed analysis [31]. The modeling of the actions upon and the interactions between the system bodies in the various technological contexts often is much more complicated than the derivation of the system equations. Examples are the interactions across a wheel rail interface [51], Fig. 5, or between the rubber tire of a car and the road, Fig. 6.

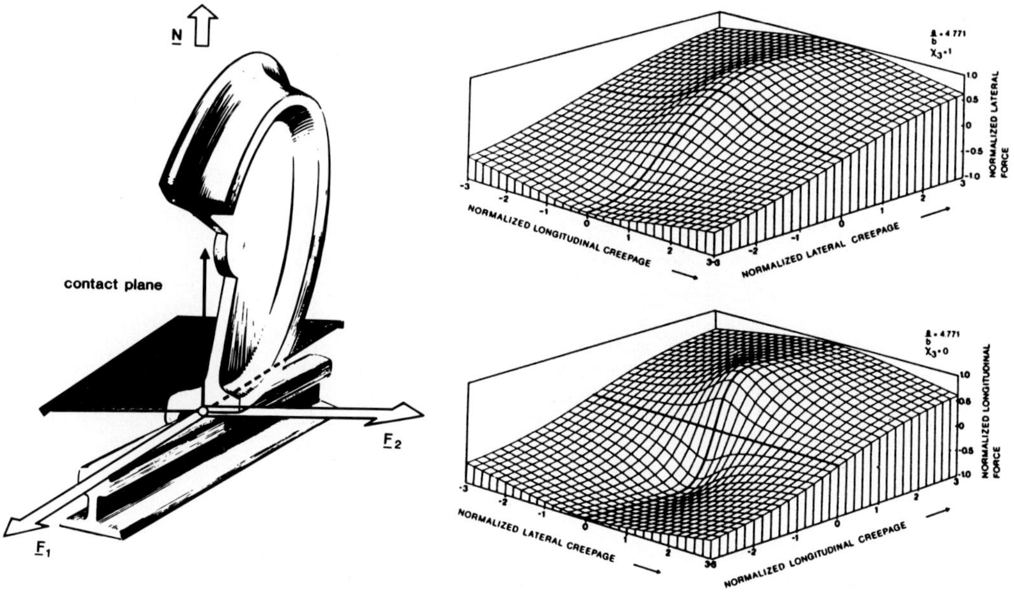

Figure 5. Interactions Across a Wheel-Rail Interface

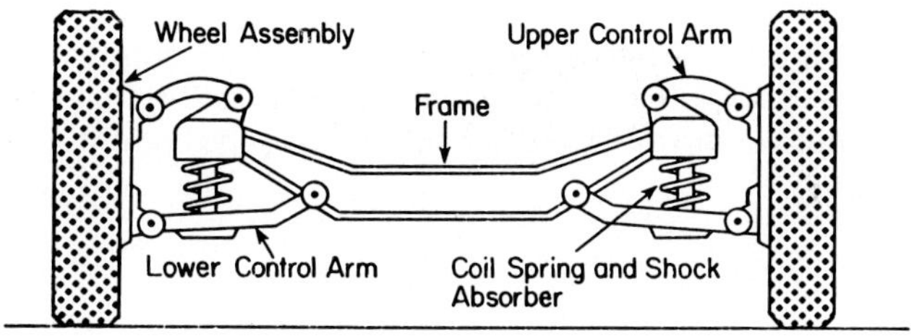

Figure 6. Multibody Suspension System of a Car

The derivation of such complicated force laws and their implementation into a multibody code may become a limiting factor for efficient simulation. Multibody systems including feedback control, e. g. the magnetically levitated vehicle shown in Fig. 7, call for a capability to describe control systems in multibody simulation packages conveniently, e. g. by using data available from control system design software. This requires capabilities for comfortable interaction between such software and multibody simulation codes.

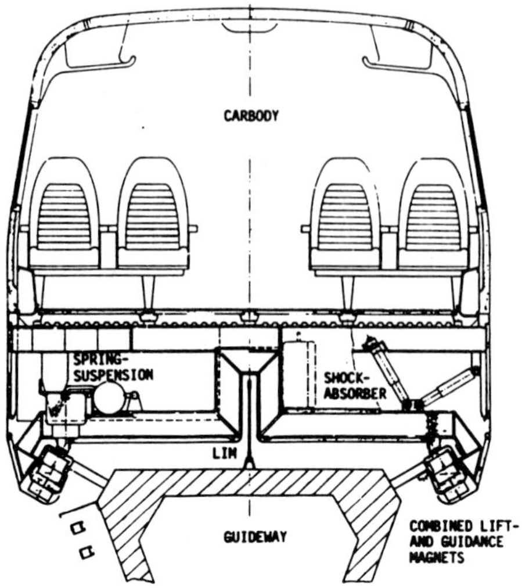

Figure 7. A Multibody MAGLEV Vehicle with Combined Lift and Guidance Requiring Feedback Control of the Interaction with the Guideway

Multibody simulation software is just one of the tools required in a design process of a technological system. Other examples are the control system design software packages just mentioned or identification- or optimization-software and CAD-packages. Multibody simulation software should not be considered as a stand alone tool - it must be able to *interact with other software* easily [8].

A requirement to multibody simulation software, which is getting more and more important, is *real time capability* in such applications as man in the loop simulation, Fig. 8, or feedback control based on nonlinear plant compensation [2].

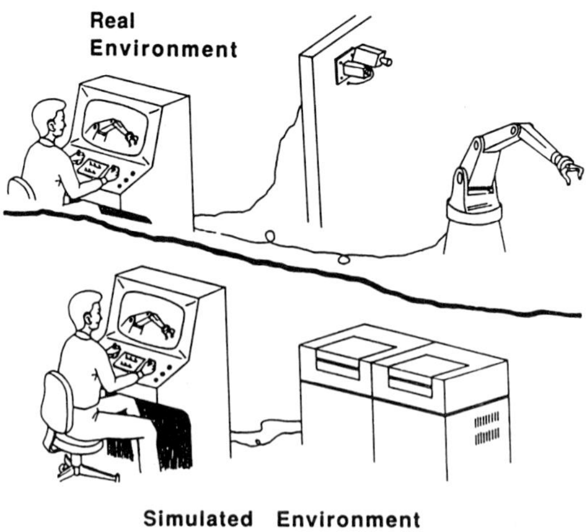

Figure 8. Man in the Loop Simulation

In [22] high computational speed is considered to be among the most important demands, when multibody simulation software is used in a control system design environment.

Particularly in space applications the *elasticity of the system bodies* is the most important topic in multibody analysis. It adds a completely new dimension to the problem of simulating the system of rigid bodies visualized in Fig. 1. The contributions collected in [28] together with other recent publications [24] demonstrate that the simulation of deformable bodies undergoing large rotational motion is still a research problem area.

This paper deals with the first one of the problems mentioned here, the appropriate interaction of methods for generating and solving the system equations. In particular, the methods for recursive generation of multibody system equations will be surveyed here. Corresponding methods for solving the system equations are discussed in a companion paper [15]. Both of these have been implemented in the SIMPACK code. Some of its capabilities will be illustrated by simulation of mechanisms and robots.

2. Basic Concepts for Generation of System Equations

Various approaches for generating multibody system equations have been described in [36] and [14] and in the survey papers cited there. The starting point of all of these methods is a set of "primitive" equations of motion. Its manipulation yields the descriptor form of the mechanical system, a set of differential algebraic equations (DAE), or its state space representation, a minimal set of ordinary differential equations (ODE). The general form of both types of equations will be discussed here, together with concepts required to generate the corresponding system matrices.

2.1 Primitive Equations of Motion

The N bodies of a multibody system are labeled $i = 1, 2, \dots N$ and the global reference frame is given the label $i = 0$. The bodies interact with each other and with points in the reference frame across N_I interconnections labeled $s = 1, 2, \dots N_I$. Position and velocity of a body i can be represented by any set of six position variables x_I^i and by any six velocity variables x_{II}^i, i.e.

$$x_I^i = [x_{Ij}^i] , \quad x_{II}^i = [x_{IIj}^i] , \quad j = 1, 2, \dots 6 . \tag{2.1}$$

Variables x_I^i and x_{II}^i may be *absolut* (describing the motion of the system bodies with respect to inertial space) or *relative* (representing the motion of interacting bodies). Collecting all of the $2{\times}N$ sets of variables required to describe the system motion in the two partitioned $6N{\times}1$-matrices

$$x_I = [x_I^i] , \quad x_{II} = [x_{II}^i] , \quad i = 1, 2, \dots N , \tag{2.2}$$

the *"primitive forms"* of the kinematical and dynamical equations of motion of the whole system can be written as [36]

$$\dot{x}_I = \hat{X}_I\,(x_I)\,x_{II} \tag{2.3.a}$$

$$J\dot{x}_{II} = Q + \Lambda. \tag{2.3.b}$$

The dimension of matrices $\hat{X}_I$ and J is $6N{\times}6N$ and matrices Q and Λ have dimensions $6N{\times}1$. The elements of matrix $\hat{X}_I$ in the kinematical equations depend on the choice of variables x_I and x_{II}. Matrix J in the dynamical equations contains generalized inertia terms corresponding to the generalized velocities x_{II} and matrix $Q + \Lambda$ summarizes the actions (forces and torques) upon the system bodies. In particular, matrix Q contains all the inertial forces and torques (such as centrifugal and Coriolis terms) together with the known external actions (such as gravity) upon the system bodies. Matrix Λ contains the contributions from the interactions across the interconnections.

Because of *constraints* on the system motion the $2{\times}6N$ variables x_I and x_{II} are redundant. For simplicity we consider holonomic constraints only. Then both, x_I and x_{II}, must satisfy a set of N_C constraint equations, which may be written as

$$f\,(x_I,t) = 0, \qquad f = [f_j], \qquad j = 1, 2, \dots N_C \tag{2.4}$$

and

$$w^T x_{II} = \zeta \tag{2.5.a}$$

where

$$w^T = \frac{\partial f}{\partial x_I^T}\,\hat{X}_I\,, \qquad \zeta = -\frac{\partial f}{\partial t}\,, \tag{2.5.b}$$

concluded by differentiating*) Eq. 2.4 and using the kinematical equations, Eq. 2.3.a, to replace $\dot{x}_I$ by x_{II}. Differentiating once more one finds the constraints on the accelerations

$$w^T \dot{x}_{II} = \xi\,, \qquad \xi = \frac{\partial^2 \zeta}{\partial t^2} - \dot{w}^T x_{II}\,. \tag{2.6}$$

Because of the constraints the $6N$ generalized interaction forces Λ are separated into $6N$ known, applied forces Λ_e and into $6N$ constraint forces Λ_z, which are unknown:

$$\Lambda = \Lambda_e + \Lambda_z, \quad \Lambda = [\Lambda_j]\,, \quad \Lambda_e = [\Lambda_{ej}], \quad \Lambda_z = [\Lambda_{zj}], \quad j = 1, 2, \dots 6N. \tag{2.7}$$

Starting from these basic equations two routes have been followed for developing computer oriented multibody formalisms. One of them, called the *augmentation method,* keeps the unknown constraint forces in the equations of motion. These are augmented by the constraint equations. The complete set of DAE, i.e. the equations of motion and the constraint equations, is called the *descriptor form* of the (mechanical) system [26]. By the second approach, the *elimination method*, the system motion is represented by a minimum set of variables, called state variables, and the unknown constraint forces are eliminated. The resulting set of ODE

*) The notation $\partial f/\partial x_I^T$ used to denote the $N_C{\times}6N$-matrix of partial derivatives (of the N_C functions in f with respect to the $6N$ variables collected in x_I) is discussed in [40].

is the system's *state space representation*. The constraint forces or any subset may be computed from a second set of equations. In the sequel both of these methods will be discussed together with mixed forms of *partially reduced system equations*.

2.2 Augmentation Method

Applying the principles of dynamics as formulated by d'Alembert, Lagrange or Jourdain and using Lagrange's method of undetermined multipliers, one concludes from Eq. 2.5.a that the $6N$ constraint forces Λ_z can be represented by just N_C unknown Lagrange multipliers

$$\mu = [\mu_j], \quad j = 1, 2, \ldots N_C \tag{2.8}$$

as

$$\Lambda_z = -\, w\mu \,. \tag{2.9}$$

Introducing this representation of Λ_z into Eq. 2.7 and the result into the unreduced dynamical equations, Eq. 2.3.b, one can rewrite the whole set of Eqs. 2.3 as

$$\dot{x}_I \quad = \hat{X}_I\,(x_I)\,x_{II} \tag{2.10.a}$$

$$J\dot{x}_{II} + w\mu = Q + \Lambda_e \tag{2.10.b}$$

These are $12N$ equations for the $12N + N_C$ unknowns x_I, x_{II} and μ. Augmenting Eqs. 2.10 by the constraint equations, Eqs. 2.4, 2.5 or 2.6, one obtains a set of DAE or an implicit system of ODE with enough relations to determine all of the unknowns. These equations, called Lagrange's equations of type one, are an often used basis for multibody formalisms, e.g. [16], [29], [30]. Usually absolute variables, i.e. variables x_I^i and x_{II}^i describing position and velocity of body i with respect to inertial space, are selected in this approach. For this choice the generation of the matrices $\hat{X}_I$, J and Q, appearing in the equations of motion, is particularly simple. Matrix Λ_e and matrices f, w, ζ and ξ in the constraint equations can be generated easily as well from data in a library of interconnections, as described in [14] and in the literature cited there.

2.3 Elimination Method

In this method relative variables are selected to represent the system motion. Relative position and velocity of two bodies interacting across any interconnection $s = 1, 2, \ldots N_I$ is described by variables

$$P^s = [P_j^s]\,, \quad G^s = [G_j^s]\,, \quad j = 1, 2, \ldots 6. \tag{2.11}$$

The definition of a set of $2 \times 6N$ relative variables, representing the whole system motion, requires the definition of a spanning tree, thus separating the N_I interconnections s into N primary ones, labeled $a = 1, 2, \ldots N$, and $N_I - N$ secondary ones, having the labels $c = N + 1, N + 2, \ldots N_I$. The variables x_I and x_{II} in Eqs. 2.3 now are chosen to be

$$x_I = P_A = [P^a], \quad x_{II} = G_A = [G^a], \quad a = 1, 2, \ldots N. \tag{2.12}$$

The remaining relative variables, collected in the partitioned matrices

$$P_C = [P^c], \quad G_C = [G^c], \quad c = N+1, N+2, \ldots N_I, \tag{2.13}$$

represent the motion across the secondary interconnections. They may be computed from P_A and G_A using the kinematic consistency conditions, which describe that bodies forming closed loops must remain hooked together during the motion. On the position level these equations are nonlinear and have the general form

$$P_C = P_C(P_A). \tag{2.14}$$

On the velocity level they are linear in the velocities, i.e.

$$G_C = W^T G_A \tag{2.15}$$

with matrix W^T depending on the position variables P_A [36].

The generalized interactions across an interconnection s, corresponding to the velocity variables G^s, are denoted by

$$\Lambda^s = [\Lambda_j^s], \quad j = 1, 2, \ldots 6. \tag{2.16}$$

In these terms the unreduced system equations have the general form given by Eq. 2.3, where matrix Λ is found to be

$$\Lambda = \Lambda_A + W \Lambda_C. \tag{2.17}$$

Here, matrix W is already known from the consistency condition for the velocities, Eq. 2.15, and the partitioned matrices

$$\left.\begin{aligned} \Lambda_A &= [\Lambda^a] \quad a = 1, 2, \ldots N \\ \Lambda_C &= [\Lambda^c] \quad c = N+1, N+2, \ldots N_I \end{aligned}\right\} \tag{2.18}$$

summarize the generalized interactions across the primary ($s = a$) and secondary ($s = c$) interconnections. The unreduced system equations in terms of relative variables are much more complex than the corresponding equations in terms of absolute variables, but the dynamical equations can be reduced conveniently to state space form.

In a first *reduction step* the constraints across the primary joints only are considered. Because of n_c^s holonomic constraints across joint s the corresponding relative motion can be described by minimal sets of $n_f^s = 6 - n_c^s$ position- and velocity-variables $p^s = [p_j^s]$ and $g^s = [g_j^s]$, $j = 1, 2, \ldots n_f^s$. The variables P_A and G_A defined by Eq. 2.12 thus can be replaced by a set of *partially reduced system variables*

$$p_A = [p^a], \quad g_A = [g^a], \quad a = 1, 2, \ldots N. \tag{2.19}$$

In these terms one finds the *partially reduced kinematical equations* having the general form

$$\dot{p}_A = Y_{IA}\, g_A \tag{2.20}$$

in case of the holonomic constraints considered here. Eqs. 2.20 are accompanied by the constraint equations

$$f_C(p_A, t) = 0, \quad f_C = \left[f^c\right], \quad c = N+1,\ N+2, \dots N_I\,, \tag{2.21.a}$$

resulting from kinematic consistency conditions, Eq. 2.15, and from the constraints across the secondary joints. In Eq. 2.21.a matrix f^c is a set of functions f_j^c, whose number corresponds to the number n_c^c of constraints across the secondary joint c

$$f^c = \left[f_j^c\right], \quad j = 1, 2, \dots n_c^c. \tag{2.21.b}$$

The generation of matrices Y_{IA} and f_C from data in a joint kinematics library [42] has been described in [36] and [43].

For the reduction of the dynamical equations one needs the statements about the nature of the constraint forces described by the principles of mechanics. In [36] they have been incorporated into definitions of modes of motion across the interconnections and of corresponding generalized applied and constraint forces. Applying these concepts the reduction to state space form and the derivation of the equations for computing the constraint forces can be described as an appropriate projection of the unreduced system equations on the corresponding modes. We have introduced n_f^s velocity variables g^s describing the unknown motion in the n_f^s free or dynamic modes. In addition there are n_c^s constrained or kinematic modes (subdivided into locked and kinematically excited modes) for which the corresponding velocities $\bar{g}^s = \left[\bar{g}_j^s\right]$, $j = 1, 2, \dots n_c^s$ are known. They are zero or given functions of time. The generalized forces across an interconnection s corresponding to the velocities g^s and $\bar{g}^s$ are the n_f^s known generalized applied forces $\lambda^s = \left[\lambda_j^s\right]$, $j = 1, 2, \dots n_f^s$ and the n_c^s generalized constraint forces $\bar{\lambda}^s = \left[\bar{\lambda}_j^s\right]$, $j = 1, 2, \dots n_c^s$, which are unknown. Now introduce in addition to matrix g_A defined by Eq. 2.19 the matrix

$$g_C = \left[g^c\right], \quad c = N+1, N+2, \dots N_I \tag{2.23}$$

of unknown velocities across the secondary interconnections $s = c$ and matrices

$$\bar{g}_A = \left[\bar{g}^a\right], \quad a = 1, 2, \dots N, \qquad \bar{g}_C = \left[\bar{g}^c\right], \quad c = N+1,\ N+2, \dots N_I \tag{2.24}$$

with the known velocities across the primary ($s = a$) and secondary ($s = c$) interconnections. The generalized forces are collected correspondingly in the partitioned matrices

$$\left.\begin{aligned} \lambda_A &= [\lambda^a], & \bar{\lambda}_A &= \left[\bar{\lambda}^a\right], & a &= 1, 2, \dots N \\ \lambda_C &= [\lambda^c], & \bar{\lambda}_C &= \left[\bar{\lambda}^c\right], & c &= N+1, N+2, \dots N_I\,. \end{aligned}\right\} \tag{2.25}$$

The unreduced dynamical equations, Eqs. 2.3.b in terms of variables $x_{II} = G_A$ and with Λ given by Eq. 2.17 are now reformulated, introducing the mode velocities g_A and $\bar{g}_A$ and the corresponding forces λ_A to $\bar{\lambda}_C$. Projecting those reformulated equations on the free modes across the primary joints, one gets the *partially reduced dynamical equations*

$$J_I\,\dot{g}_A - W_{II}\,\bar{\lambda}_C = \chi + \lambda_A + W_I\,\lambda_C\,. \tag{2.26}$$

These are accompanied by the constraint equations for the velocity variables g_A

$$W_{II}^T\,g_A = \bar{g}_C - \bar{W}_{II}^T\,\bar{g}_A\,, \tag{2.27}$$

derived by projecting the consistency conditions, Eq. 2.15, on the dual constrained modes. Matrices J_I, χ and W_I to $\overline{W}_{II}$ in Eqs. 2.26 and 2.27 can be computed from the system data as described in [36].

To evaluate laws for the applied forces λ_C across the secondary interconnections one still needs equations giving position variables $p_C = [p^c]$ and velocity variables g_C (which describe the motion across those interconnections) in terms of the dependent variables p_A and g_A used in Eqs. 2.20 and 2.26. On the position level these are nonlinear functions

$$p_C = p_C(p_A, t) , \tag{2.28}$$

which can be developed from the consistency conditions, Eq. 2.15, as described in [36]. The relations for computing the velocities g_C are linear and found by projecting the consistency conditions, Eq. 2.15, on the dual free modes. The result is

$$g_C = W_I^T g_A + \overline{W}_I^T \overline{g}_A . \tag{2.29}$$

The constraint forces $\overline{\lambda}_A$ across the primary joints have been eliminated from Eq. 2.26. Once these equations together with Eqs. 2.27, 2.20 and 2.21 have been solved to get $p_A(t)$, $g_A(t)$ and $\overline{\lambda}_C(t)$, the constraint forces $\overline{\lambda}_A$ can be generated from

$$\overline{\lambda}_A = \overline{J}_I \, \dot{g}_A - \overline{\chi} - \overline{W}_I \, \lambda_C - \overline{W}_{II} \, \overline{\lambda}_C , \tag{2.30}$$

a relation derived by projecting the unreduced dynamical equations on the constrained modes across the primary joints.

In case of systems with tree configuration the set of secondary joints is empty, the constraint equations, Eqs. 2.21 and 2.27, disappear and Eqs. 2.20 and 2.26 go into the state space representation

$$\dot{p}_A = Y_{IA} \, g_A \tag{2.31.a}$$

$$J_I \, \dot{g}_A = \chi + \lambda_A . \tag{2.31.b}$$

The relation for computing the constraint forces $\overline{\lambda}_A$, Eq. 2.30, becomes

$$\overline{\lambda}_A = \overline{J}_I \, \dot{g}_A - \overline{\chi} . \tag{2.32}$$

In case of systems with closed loops a *second reduction step* is needed to develop the state space form from the partially reduced system equations, Eqs. 2.20 and 2.26 by incorporating the constraint equations, Eqs. 2.21 and 2.27. An analytical procedure for reducing the kinematical equations, Eq. 2.20, is not known, because the constraint equations, Eqs. 2.21, are nonlinear, in general. By contrast, the constraint equations on the velocity variables, Eq. 2.27, are linear in the velocities g_A. Using basic linear algebra the reduction can be described analytically [36]. But it is important to know that matrix W_{II} in Eq. 2.27 and thus the Jacobian Φ satisfying $\Phi^T W_{II} = 0$ (which is needed in the reduction process) depends on the position variables and must be generated numerically therefore during each integration step. Thus, the reduction to state space form of both, the kinematical and the dynamical equations, can be done numerically only, in general. An exception are multibody mechanisms with specific types of joints, for which an analytical derivation of the state space representation has been described in [19], [49], [20] and [50], applying a "method of the characteristic pair of joints". There are mechanisms for which the method fails to yield the state space representation, but even in such cases it results in a description of the system motion with less constraints of the type of Eqs. 2.21 and 2.27 than the general approach outlined here.

3. Recursive Computational Schemes

In some applications, e.g. spacecraft dynamics, the relative motion of the system bodies is given in terms of absolute variables by small differencies of large numbers. In such cases it is advisable to use relative variables. The computational burden of generating the system matrices in Eqs. 2.26 to 2.32 can be reduced significantly when applying recursive computation. Corresponding computational schemes will be described now.

3.1 Basic Concepts

3.1.1 Recursions Implied by System Topology

To create a computer oriented multibody formalism, one must devise a means for telling the computer how the system bodies are interconnected, i.e. a set of parameters describing the system topology. For an analytical development of the system equations it is most appropriate to define a system graph and to introduce matrices representing its topological properties. When programming the formalism one should use pointer arrays or adjacency lists containing all the information about the sparse graph matrices. Products involving graph matrices, which appear in the analytical developments, can be computed efficiently using specific index lists derived from the graph matrices, as will be demonstrated now.

A graph, representing the topological aspects of the multibody system visualized in Fig. 1, is defined as follows: It has

- N vertices, representing the N system bodies, labeled $i = 1,2,...N$,
- a reference vertex, corresponding to the global reference frame, labeled $i = 0$,
- N_l oriented branches, interconnecting the vertices and characterizing the interconnections between the system bodies. Both, interconnections and branches are labeled $s = 1,2,...N_l$.

A "spanning tree" of the graph is a tree - i.e. a graph falling into two parts, if any one of its branches is removed - which includes all the vertices (bodies and global reference frame) of the original graph . The N branches in the spanning tree, representing the primary interconnections, are called arcs and the remaining $N_l - N$ branches closing circuits are called chords. They represent the secondary interconnections. The set of vertex indices excluding the reference vertex (i.e. the set of body indices) is **N** and the set of all vertices (including $i=0$) is **O**. The sets of branches, arcs and chords are respectively **B, A** and **C**.

Properties of the graph are described by incidence matrix $\bar{S} = [\bar{S}^{is}]$, $i \in \mathbf{O}$, $s \in \mathbf{B}$, path matrix $T = [T^{ai}]$, $a \in \mathbf{A}$, $i \in \mathbf{N}$ and mesh matrix $U = [U^{\bar{a}c}]$, $a \in \mathbf{A}$, $c \in \mathbf{C}$. Deleting the row $i=0$ from $\bar{S}$ one obtains the reduced incidence matrix $S = [S^{is}]$, $i \in \mathbf{N}$, $s \in \mathbf{B}$. The reduced incidence matrix S may be partitioned as

$S = [S_A,\ S_C]$ where $S_A = [S^{ia}]$, $i \in \mathbf{N}$, $a \in \mathbf{A}$ and $S_C = [S^{ic}]$, $i \in \mathbf{N}$, $c \in \mathbf{C}$. These matrices satisfy the relations [36].

$$TS = T[S_A,\ S_C] = [E,\ U] \tag{3.1.a}$$

with $N \times N$ unit matrix E , i.e.

$$TS_A = S_A T = E\ , \qquad TS_C = U\ . \tag{3.1.b}$$

The dimensions of matrices S, T and U are $N \times N_I$, $N \times N$ and $N \times (N_I - N)$, respectively. The elements of the matrices are zero or $+1$ or -1. The interpretation of the rows and columns of the various matrices is as follows:

Nonzero elements in

$S = [S^{is}]$

- column s show, which vertices (bodies) i are adjacent to (or contiguous to or connected by) branch (interconnection) s;
- row i show, which branches (interconnections) s are attached to (or incident on) vertex (body) i;

$T = [T^{ai}]$

- column i show, which arcs (primary interconnections) a are inboard of vertex (body) i, i.e. on the way from vertex (body) i to the root of the spanning tree (the global reference frame) $i = 0$;
- row a show, which vertices (bodies) i are outboard of arc (primary interconnection) a, i.e. on those chains, which connect arc a to terminal vertices of the spanning tree but do not pass through $i = 0$;

$U = [U^{ac}]$

- column c show, which arcs (primary interconnections) a are in the circuit defined by chord (secondary interconnection) c - there are N_C different circuits;
- row a show, which chords (secondary interconnections) c form a cutset of the system graph together with arc (primary interconnection) a. Removing the (primary and secondary) interconnections of a cutset causes the multibody system to fall into two parts - there are N different cutsets.

In all of the cases the signs of the nonzero elements of the matrices specify the branch orientation, i.e. an orientation assigned to the interconnections, which is required to define relative motion of the interacting bodies.

The relations given by Eqs. 3.1 have been used in analytical developments of multibody system equations in terms of relative variables [32], [48], [36]. and [47]. Terms appearing in the equations of motion are given by products of graph matrices and other matrices, representing geometrical, kinematical and inertia properties of the system elements or forces acting upon or within the system. An efficient evaluation of such products is suggested by the interpretations of the nonzero elements of the graph matrices given previously: These products imply summations over the various index sets, describing those topological aspects of the multibody system, which are characterized by the columns and rows of the graph matrices. In particular, products involving the T-matrix appear in the following forms:

$$X = T^T x, \quad X = [X^i], \quad i \in \mathbf{N}, \quad x = [x^a], \quad a \in \mathbf{A} \tag{3.2.a}$$

and

$$Y = T y, \quad Y = [Y^a], \quad a \in \mathbf{A}, \quad y = [y^i], \quad i \in \mathbf{N}. \tag{3.3.a}$$

The computation of matrices X and Y requires the evaluation of the expressions

$$X^i = \sum_{a \in \mathbf{A}} T^{ai} x^a, \qquad i \in \mathbf{N} \tag{3.2.b}$$

and

$$Y^a = \sum_{i \in \mathbf{N}} T^{ai} y^i, \qquad a \in \mathbf{A}. \tag{3.3.b}$$

The interpretation of the rows and columns of the path matrix T suggests recursive computational schemes for evaluating these sums. To formulate the recursions it is convenient but not necessary to introduce a special canonical labeling scheme proposed in [34]. After defining a spanning tree all chords of the system graph are given higher labels than the arcs, i.e. $a = 1, 2, \ldots N$ and $c = N+1, N+2, \ldots N_l$ as suggested previously. Moreover, each node is assigned a number smaller than the node immediately outboard of it and the (unique) inboard arc a on node i is given the same number as this node, i.e. $a = i$. Denoting the node immediately inboard of node i by $\kappa(i)$, the set of nodes connected to the reference node $i = 0$ by $\mathbf{N}_o$ and the set of the other nodes by $\overline{\mathbf{N}}_o$, the X^i are generated by the *"forward recursion"*:

$$\left.\begin{aligned} X^i &= T^{ai} x^a, & a &= i, & i &\in \mathbf{N}_0 \\ X^i &= X^{\kappa(i)} + T^{ai} x^a, & a &= i, & i &\in \overline{\mathbf{N}}_0 . \end{aligned}\right\} \tag{3.4}$$

Correspondingly denote the arc immediately inboard of arc a by $\alpha(a)$ with $\alpha(a) = 0$ for arcs attached to node $i = 0$. Introducing $\mathbf{A}_t$ to denote the set of arcs attached to terminal nodes and $\overline{\mathbf{A}}_t$ for the set of remaining arcs, parameters Y^a are generated by the *"backward recursion"*

$$\left.\begin{aligned} Y^a &= T^{ai} y^i, & i &= a, & a &\in \mathbf{A}_t \\ Y^{\alpha(a)} &= \sum_{a:\, \alpha=\alpha(a)} Y^a + T^{\alpha(a)i} y^i, & i &= \alpha(a), & a &\in \overline{\mathbf{A}}_t . \end{aligned}\right\} \tag{3.5}$$

The summation in Eq. 3.5 runs over all arcs a, for which α is immediately inboard of a, i.e. over the outboard arcs on node $i = a$. Thus the sum has more than one element only at nodes where the graph forks.

In the forward recursion, Eq. 3.4, the "outboard" X^i are computed from known "inboard" values $X^{\kappa(i)}$, whereas the backward recursion, Eq. 3.5, gives the "inboard" values $Y^{\alpha(a)}$ in terms of the "outboard" Y^a. Thus one must start at the root of the tree and follow the arcs to the terminal nodes when evaluating Eq. 3.4. In case of Eq. 3.5 one proceeds in the opposite direction begining with the arcs attached to the terminal nodes. When using canonical labeling both of the recursions are evaluated correctly, when following respectively the sequences $i = 1, 2, \ldots N$ and $a = N, N-1, \ldots$ until $\alpha(a) = 1$. The recursions, described by Eqs. 3.4 and 3.5, have been applied in [41]. An ALGOL-procedure based on Eq. 3.5 has been published in [35].

3.1.2 Kinematics of Absolute, Relative and Constrained Motion

The basic laws of dynamics are stated in their most simple form when refering to an inertial frame. To reformulate them in terms of constrained relative motion between the bodies of a multibody system, one needs the transformations between absolute and relative variables. Moreover, concepts for introducing the minimum sets of joint variables are required. All of these will be summarized now.

Applying notation described in [36], an inertial frame is $\{O^I, \underline{e}^I\}$, the reference frame is $\{O^0, \underline{e}^0\}$ and a body fixed frame is $\{CM^i, \underline{e}^i\}$, $i \in \mathbf{N}$. *Absolute motion* of the reference frame and of the system bodies is measured as described in Fig. 9.

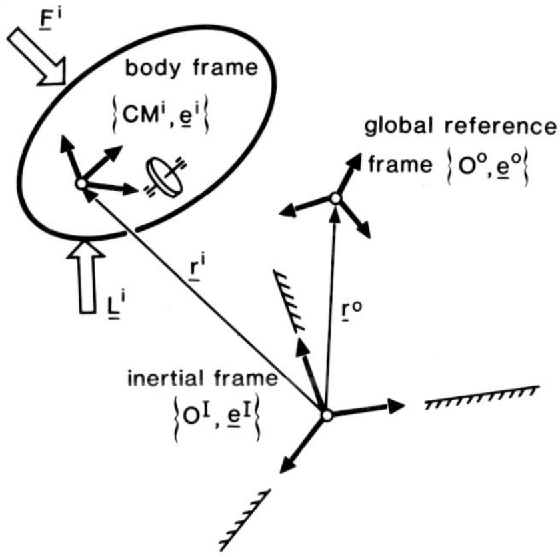

Figure 9. Notation Describing Position and Velocity of a Typical Body and of the Global Reference Frame with Respect to Inertial Space

Absolute location of the reference frame origin O^0 and of the center of mass CM^i are given by vectors $\underline{r}^i$, $i \in \mathbf{O}$ and the absolute orientation of the (dextral and orthonormal) vector basis $\underline{e}^i = [\underline{e}^i_\alpha]$ is described by the direction cosine matrix A^i according to

$$\underline{e}^i = A^i \underline{e}^I, \quad A^i = [A^i_{\alpha\beta}], \qquad i \in \mathbf{O}. \tag{3.6}$$

Greek subscripts α, β as used here always have the range 1,2,3. Velocities of CM^i and $\underline{e}^i$ with respect to the inertial frame $\{O^I, \underline{e}^I\}$ are $\underline{v}^i = \dot{\underline{r}}^i$ and $\underline{\omega}^i$, respectively. The absolute accelerations are $\dot{\underline{v}}^i$ and $\dot{\underline{\omega}}^i$, $i \in \mathbf{O}$, with dots indicating absolute derivatives, i.e. time derivatives with respect to inertial space.

The concepts for describing *relative motion* (Fig. 10) of a body $t = t(s)$ with respect to a body $f = f(s)$ across any interconnection $s \in \mathbf{B}$ have been detailed in [36].

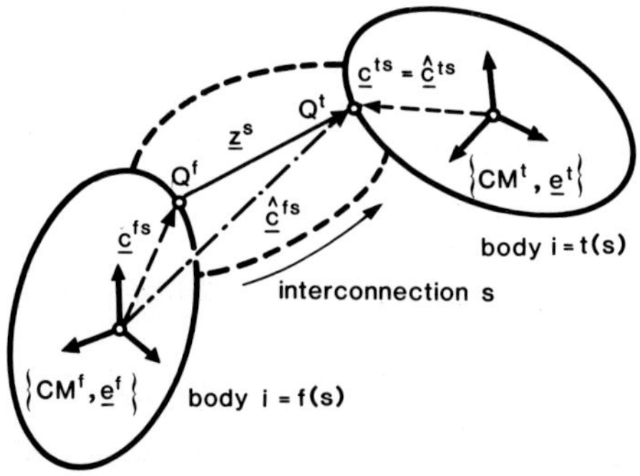

Figure 10. Notation Describing Relative Position and Velocity of Bodies Interacting Across a Typical Interconnection

Relative displacement is measured by vectors $\underline{z}^s$, defined after specifying attachment vectors $\underline{c}^{is}$, $i=f$ or $i=t$, which locate the attachment points Q^f and Q^t of interconnection s on bodies $i \in \mathbf{N}$ and in the reference frame $i=0$ (Fig. 10). Modified attachment vectors $\hat{\underline{c}}^{is}$ locating point Q^t are obtained from $\underline{c}^{is}$ when adding the $\underline{z}^s$-vector, which emanates from body i - see Fig. 10. Relative orientation across the interconnection is described by direction cosine matrix B^s as

$$\underline{e}^t = B^s\,\underline{e}^f, \quad B^s = \left[B^s_{\alpha\beta}\right], \qquad s \in \mathbf{B}\,. \tag{3.7}$$

The relative velocity of the attachment points is measured by

$$\frac{{}^f d\,\underline{z}^s}{dt} = \overset{\circ}{\underline{z}}{}^s = \underline{V}^s, \qquad s \in \mathbf{B} \tag{3.8}$$

and the relative angular velocity is

$$\underline{\Omega}^s = \underline{\omega}^t - \underline{\omega}^f\,, \qquad s \in \mathbf{B}\,. \tag{3.9}$$

Relative accelerations are

$$\overset{\circ}{\underline{\Omega}}{}^s = \frac{{}^f d\,\underline{\Omega}^s}{dt}\,, \quad \overset{\circ}{\underline{V}}{}^s = \frac{{}^f d\,\underline{V}^s}{dt} \qquad s \in \mathbf{B}\,. \tag{3.10}$$

Symbol ${}^f d/dt$ (or the open circle) represents the relative derivative of the vectors with respect to basis $\underline{e}^f$.

The relations representing *absolute motion in terms of relative motion* across the primary interconnections $s=a$ can be formulated conveniently applying graph theoretic concepts. The motion of $\underline{e}^i$ is found to be [36]:

$$A^i = A^{io}\,A^o, \quad A^{io} = \prod_{a \,\in\, \mathbf{A}} (B^a)^\sigma\,, \quad \sigma = -T^{ai}, \qquad i \in \mathbf{N} \tag{3.11}$$

$$\underline{\omega}^i = \underline{\omega}^o - \sum_{a \in \mathbf{A}} T^{ai}\, \underline{\Omega}^a, \qquad i \in \mathbf{N} \tag{3.12}$$

$$\dot{\underline{\omega}}^i = \dot{\underline{\omega}}^o - \sum_{a \in \mathbf{A}} T^{ai}\, (\overset{\circ}{\underline{\Omega}}{}^a + \underline{\omega}^{f(a)} \times \underline{\Omega}^a), \qquad i \in \mathbf{N}\,. \tag{3.13}$$

Matrix A^{io} is a direction cosine matrix describing the relative orientation of $\underline{e}^i$ and $\underline{e}^o$ as $\underline{e}^i = A^{io}\, \underline{e}^o$.

When representing the absolute motion of CM^i in terms of relative motion, path vectors $\underline{d}^{ji}$ and modified path vectors $\hat{\underline{d}}^{ji}$ appear naturally [36] - see Figs. 12 and 13.

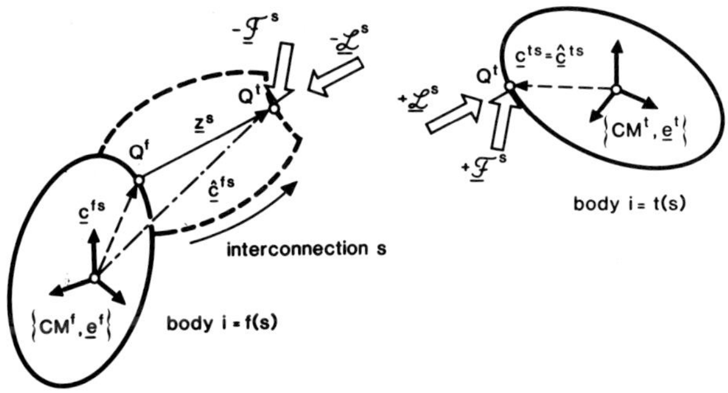

Figure 11. Interaction Across a Typical Interconnection

Denoting by $\underline{c}^{ja(o)}$ and by $\underline{c}^{ja(i)}$ the attachment vectors on body j locating the unique inboard attachment point (the one on the way to the reference frame $i = 0$) and an outboard attachment point (the one on the way to any body i) respectively, one finds

$$\underline{d}^{ji} = \begin{cases} \underline{c}^{ja(o)} & \text{if } \; j = i \\ \underline{c}^{ja(o)} - \underline{c}^{ja(i)} & \text{if } \; 0 < j < i \\ -\,\underline{c}^{oa(i)} & \text{if } \; 0 = j < i \\ 0 & \text{otherwise.} \end{cases} \tag{3.14}$$

The notation $j < i$ used here means that body j is inboard of body i, i.e. closer to the reference frame $i = 0$. For $j \neq i$ the nonzero path vectors $\underline{d}^{ji}$ connect that outboard attachment point on body j, which is on the way to body i, with the inboard attachment point O^j, which is on the way to the global frame $i = 0$. For $j = i$ the outboard attachment point is replaced by the center of mass CM^j, i.e. vector $\underline{d}^{jj}$ connects CM^j and O^j. Modified path vectors $\hat{\underline{d}}^{ji}$ are now defined by adding the

$\underline{z}^a$-vectors, i.e. by replacing $\underline{c}^{ia}$ by $\hat{\underline{c}}^{ia}$ in Eq. 3.14. In these terms the motion of CM^i can be represented as

$$\underline{r}^i = \underline{r}^o - \sum_{j \in \mathbf{O}} \hat{\underline{d}}^{ji}, \qquad i \in \mathbf{N} \quad (3.15)$$

$$\underline{v}^i = \underline{v}^o - \sum_{j \in \mathbf{O}} \underline{\omega}^j \times \hat{\underline{d}}^{ji} - \sum_{a \in \mathbf{A}} T^{ai}\, \underline{V}^a, \qquad i \in \mathbf{N} \quad (3.16)$$

$$\dot{\underline{v}}^i = \dot{\underline{v}}^o - \sum_{j \in \mathbf{O}} (\dot{\underline{\omega}}^j \times \hat{\underline{d}}^{ji} + \underline{\underline{w}}^j \cdot \hat{\underline{d}}^{ji}) - \sum_{a \in \mathbf{A}} T^{ai}\, (\mathring{\underline{V}}^a + 2\,\underline{\omega}^f \times \underline{V}^a), \qquad i \in \mathbf{N} \quad (3.17)$$

where $f = f(a)$ in Eq. 3.17.

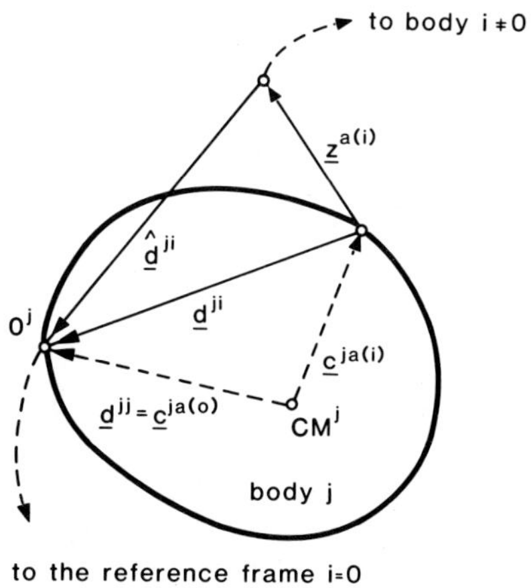

Figure 12. Path-Vectors and Attachment-Vectors for Body j

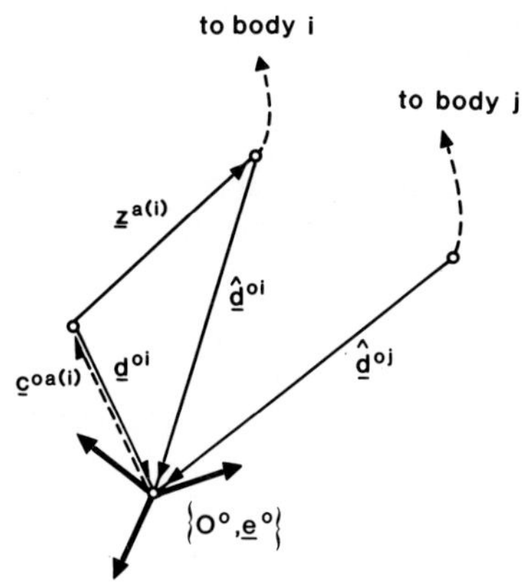

Figure 13. Path- and Attachment-Vectors for the Reference Frame j = 0

Dyadic $\underline{\underline{w}}^j$, appearing in the same equation is defined as

$$\underline{\underline{w}}^j = (\underline{\omega}^j \underline{\omega}^j - \underline{\omega}^j \cdot \underline{\omega}^j \underline{\underline{E}}), \qquad j \in \mathbf{O}. \tag{3.18}$$

It is a convenient device for representing the centrifugal terms $\underline{\omega}^j \times (\underline{\omega}^j \times \hat{\underline{d}}^{ji}) = \underline{\underline{w}}^j \cdot \hat{\underline{d}}^{ji}$. Symbol $\underline{\underline{E}}$ denotes the unit tensor (whose coordinates are given by unit matrix E) and two vectors standing together as $\underline{\omega}^j \underline{\omega}^j$ represent a dyadic with the coordinates $\omega^j \omega^{j^T}$. Matrix $\omega^j = [\omega^j_\alpha]$ contains the coordinates of vector $\underline{\omega}^j$ in basis $\underline{e}^j$. Matrix B^s and vector $\underline{z}^s$ as well as vectors $\underline{\Omega}^s$ and $\underline{V}^s$ can be represented by six position- and six velocity-variables P^s and G^s, Eq. 2.11. Here we select any set of three variables*) parameterizing B^s and the coordinates $z^s = [z^s_\alpha]$ of vector $\underline{z}^s$ in basis $\underline{e}^{f(s)}$ as position variables P^s. The velocity variables are defined to be

$$G^s = \begin{bmatrix} \Omega^s \\ V^s \end{bmatrix}, \quad s \in \mathbf{B} \tag{3.19}$$

with matrices $\Omega^s = [\Omega^s_\alpha]$ and $V^s = [V^s_\alpha]$ containing the coordinates of vectors $\underline{\Omega}^s$ and $\underline{V}^s$ in basis $\underline{e}^{f(s)}$.

Usually the motion across an interconnection is *constrained* because of joints between the bodies and less than six joint position state variables $p^s = [p^s_j]$ and joint velocity state variables $g^s = [g^s_j]$ are sufficient to describe the relative motion of the interacting bodies. In case of holonomic constraints the numbers of position and velocity state variables are identical and the variables satisfy kinematical equations of motion having the general form

$$\dot{p}^s = Y^s_l(p^s, t)\, g^s . \tag{3.20}$$

Matrices B^s and z^s required for evaluating Eq. 3.11 and the matrix forms of Eqs. 3.12 to 3.17 may be obtained from the explicit forms of the joint constraint equations

$$B^s = B^s(p^s, t), \qquad z^s = z^s(p^s, t). \tag{3.21}$$

The relative velocities G^s defined by Eq. 3.19 are obtained from the explicit forms of the velocity constraint equations, i.e. from the joint variables g^s and from any known motion $\overline{g}^s(t)$ across the interconnection as

$$G^s = \varphi^s g^s + \overline{\varphi}^s \overline{g}^s . \tag{3.22}$$

Here the columns of matrices φ^s and $\overline{\varphi}^s$ are the mode vectors characterizing the free and the constrained modes of motion across the joint. Introducing the dual vectors ψ^s, $\overline{\psi}^s$ satisfying

$$\varphi^{s^T} \psi^s = E, \qquad \overline{\varphi}^{s^T} \psi^s = 0, \qquad \varphi^{s^T} \overline{\psi}^s = 0, \qquad \overline{\varphi}^{s^T} \overline{\psi}^s = E, \tag{3.23}$$

one observes that the mode velocities g^s and $\overline{g}^s$ are the projections of G^s on the dual modes, i.e.

$$g^s = \psi^{s^T} G^s, \qquad \overline{g}^s = \overline{\psi}^{s^T} G^s . \tag{3.24}$$

---

*) To avoid the singularities of any three parameter representation of a direction cosine matrix one may decide to use the four Euler parameters or other representations [36].

The information required to evaluate Eqs. 3.20 to 3.24, i.e. the definitions of the variables p^s and g^s and the functions Y_i^s, B^s, z^s, φ^s, $\overline{\varphi}^s$, ψ^s and $\overline{\psi}^s$ are available in the joint kinematics library described in [42].

3.1.3 Recursive Evaluation of Kinematical Equations

As mentioned in Sect. 2.3 the system motion can be represented by the partially reduced set of variables p^a and g^a - see Eq. 2.19. From Eqs. 2.20 and 3.20 one concludes that the system matrices in the corresponding kinematical equations of motion are

$$Y_{IA} = [Y_i^a] \tag{3.25}$$

with matrices Y_i^a available in a joint kinematics library.

Given the variables p^a and g^a the kinematical relations, Eqs. 3.11 to 3.13 and 3.15 to 3.17, can be evaluated recursively. First recall the resolutions of vectors $\underline{z}^a$, $\underline{\Omega}^a$ and $\underline{V}^a$ introduced when discussing Eq. 3.19 and use Eqs. 3.21 and 3.22 to represent B^a, $\underline{z}^a$, $\underline{\Omega}^a$ and $\underline{V}^a$ in terms of p^a and g^a. Then observe that the sums involving T^{ai} can be evaluated recursively as discussed in Sect. 3.1.1. Sums involving the path vectors $\hat{\underline{d}}^{ji}$ - see Eqs. 3.15, 3.16 and 3.17 - can be computed recursively as well, because these vectors are defined in terms of T^{ai} - see [44] Giving all arcs the same orientation, e.g. towards the terminal nodes, the computations become particularly simple and one arrives at the following forward recursions to compute the absolute motion of

body bases $\underline{e}^i$ in terms of relative motion:

$$A^i = A^{i\kappa(i)}\, A^{\kappa(i)} = B^a\, A^{\kappa(i)}, \qquad a = i \tag{3.26}$$

$$\underline{\omega}^i = \underline{\omega}^{\kappa(i)} + \underline{\Omega}^a, \qquad a = i \tag{3.27}$$

$$\dot{\underline{\omega}}^i = \dot{\underline{\omega}}^{\kappa(i)} + \underline{\omega}^{\kappa(i)} \times \underline{\Omega}^a + \overset{\circ}{\underline{\Omega}}{}^a, \qquad a = i \tag{3.28}$$

center of mass CM^i in terms of relative motion:

$$\underline{r}^i = \underline{\rho}^i - \underline{d}^{ii} \tag{3.29.a}$$

where

$$\left.\begin{aligned} \underline{\rho}^0 &= \underline{r}^0 \\ \underline{\rho}^i &= \underline{\rho}^{\kappa(i)} - \hat{\underline{d}}^{\kappa(i)i} \end{aligned}\right\} \tag{3.29.b}$$

$$\underline{v}^i = \underline{u}^i - \underline{\omega}^i \times \underline{d}^{ii} \tag{3.30.a}$$

where

$$\left.\begin{aligned} \underline{u}^0 &= \underline{v}^0 \\ \underline{u}^i &= \underline{u}^{\kappa(i)} - \underline{\omega}^{\kappa(i)} \times \hat{\underline{d}}^{\kappa(i)i} + \underline{V}^a, \qquad a = i \end{aligned}\right\} \tag{3.30.b}$$

$$\dot{\underline{v}}^i = \underline{a}^i - (\dot{\underline{\omega}}^i \times \underline{d}^{ii} + \underline{\underline{w}}^i \cdot \underline{d}^{ii}) \tag{3.31.a}$$

where

$$\left.\begin{array}{l} \underline{a}^{o} = \underline{\dot{v}}^{o} \\ \underline{a}^{i} = \underline{a}^{\kappa(i)} - (\underline{\dot{\omega}}^{\kappa(i)} \times \underline{\hat{d}}^{\kappa(i)i} + \underline{\underline{w}}^{\kappa(i)} \cdot \underline{\hat{d}}^{\kappa(i)i}) + 2\,\underline{\omega}^{\kappa(i)} \times \underline{V}^{a} + \overset{\circ}{\underline{V}}{}^{a}, \quad a = i \end{array}\right\} \qquad (3.31.b)$$

Vectors $\underline{\rho}^{i}$, $\underline{u}^{i}$ and $\underline{a}^{i}$, $i \in \mathbf{N}$, appearing naturally these equations, represent respectively the absolute location, velocity and acceleration of the inboard attachment point O^{i} on body i, $i \in \mathbf{N}$. For $i = 0$ the vectors represent those quantities for the origin O^{0} of the reference frame $\{O^{0}, \underline{e}^{0}\}$.

To implement the above relations on a computer one needs their matrix forms. It is gotten when representing each body associated quantity, characterized by body labels i or $\kappa(i)$ into the corresponding body frame and each interconnection related vector, characterized by arc index a, into vector basis $\underline{e}^{f(a)} = \underline{e}^{\kappa(i)}$ for the choice of arc orientations mentioned previously. Then matrices $A^{i\kappa(i)} = B^{a}$ are used to combine all the resolutions of vectors and dyads in one basis. Here we develop the matrix form of the expression for the accelerations only. It will be required later when manipulating the dynamical equations. Introduce the partitioned matrices

$$b^{i} = \begin{bmatrix} \dot{\omega}^{i} \\ a^{i} \end{bmatrix}, \quad i \in \mathbf{O}\ , \qquad (3.32)$$

where $\dot{\omega}^{i}$, a^{i}, $i \in \mathbf{O}$ are the resolutions of vectors $\underline{\dot{\omega}}^{i}$, $\underline{a}^{i}$ in basis $\underline{e}^{i}$. The matrix forms of Eqs. 3.28 and 3.31 are found to be

$$b^{i} = C^{i}(D^{\kappa(i)^{T}}\, b^{\kappa(i)} + \alpha^{\kappa(i)} + \dot{G}^{a}), \qquad a = i, \quad i \in \mathbf{N} \qquad (3.33)$$

with the partitioned matrices

$$C^{i} = \begin{bmatrix} A^{i\kappa(i)} & 0 \\ 0 & A^{i\kappa(i)} \end{bmatrix} \qquad (3.34)$$

$$D^{\kappa(i)} = \begin{bmatrix} E & -\widetilde{\left(\hat{d}^{\kappa(i)i}\right)} \\ 0 & E \end{bmatrix} \qquad (3.35)$$

$$\alpha^{\kappa(i)} = \begin{bmatrix} \tilde{\omega}^{\kappa(i)} & 0 \\ 0 & 2\tilde{\omega}^{\kappa(i)} \end{bmatrix} G^{a} - \begin{bmatrix} 0 \\ w^{\kappa(i)}\, \hat{d}^{\kappa(i)i} \end{bmatrix}, \qquad a = i \qquad (3.36)$$

and with the relative accelerations

$$\dot{G}^{a} = \varphi^{a}\, \dot{g}^{a} + \dot{\varphi}^{a}\, g^{a} + \frac{d}{dt}\, (\overline{\varphi}^{a}\, \overline{g}^{a}) \qquad (3.37)$$

obtained by differentiating Eq. 3.22. Notations $\omega^{\kappa(i)}$, $w^{\kappa(i)}$ and $\hat{d}^{\kappa(i)i}$ represent the resolutions of $\underline{\omega}^{\kappa(i)}$, $\underline{\underline{w}}^{\kappa(i)}$ and $\underline{\hat{d}}^{\kappa(i)i}$ in basis $\underline{e}^{\kappa(i)}$.

3.2 Implicit Dynamical Equations

3.2.1 Basic Equations

Denoting angular and linear momentum of body $i \in \mathbf{N}$ (see Fig. 9) of a multibody system by $\underline{H}^i$ and $\underline{P}^i$, applied external torque and force by $\underline{L}^i$ and $\underline{F}^i$ and the totality of interaction torques and forces across interconnection s by $\underline{L}^s$ and $\underline{F}^s$ - see Fig. 11 - the dynamical equations of motion are

$$\left.\begin{aligned} \dot{\underline{H}}^i &= \underline{L}^i - \sum_{s \in \mathbf{B}} S^{is} (\underline{L}^s + \hat{\underline{c}}^{is} \times \underline{F}^s) \\ \dot{\underline{P}}^i &= \underline{F}^i - \sum_{s \in \mathbf{B}} S^{is} \underline{F}^s \end{aligned}\right\} \quad i \in \mathbf{N}. \tag{3.38}$$

Interactions $+\underline{L}^s$ and $+\underline{F}^s$ act on body $t(s)$, $s \in \mathbf{B}$, which implies that the reactions $-\underline{L}^s$ and $-\underline{F}^s$ act upon body $f(s)$. The forces $\underline{F}^s$ are applied at points Q^t located by vectors $\hat{\underline{c}}^{is}$ on the bodies $i \in \mathbf{N}$.

Eqs. 3.38 can be reformulated in terms of velocity variables G^a, defined by Eq. 3.19 for $s = a$, to obtain the general form of the dynamical equations, Eqs. 2.3.b with the generalized interactions given by Eq. 2.17. For the following discussion it is helpful to rewrite those $6N$ equations as N sets of six equations corresponding to the interconnection a, i.e.

$$\sum_{b \in \mathbf{A}} J^{ab} \dot{G}^b = Q^a + \Lambda^a + \sum_{c \in \mathbf{C}} W^{ac} \Lambda^c, \qquad a \in \mathbf{A}. \tag{3.39}$$

Here J^{ab} are 6×6 generalized inertia matrices corresponding to velocity variables G^a. The $6{\times}1$-matrices Q^a summarize external and inertial effects and the partitioned matrices

$$\Lambda^s = \begin{bmatrix} L^s \\ F^s \end{bmatrix}, \quad s = a \text{ or } s = c, \tag{3.40}$$

contain the coordinates L^s, F^s of the interactions $\underline{L}^s$, $\underline{F}^s$ in vector bases $\underline{e}^{f(s)}$. As the totality of interactions, Eq. 2.7, the interactions Λ^s across an interconnection s can be subdivided into the known applied interactions Λ^s_e resulting from force elements and into the constraint interactions Λ^s_z, which are unknown and result from the joints, i.e. $\Lambda^s = \Lambda^s_e + \Lambda^s_z$. The $6{\times}6$-submatrices W^{ac} of W are the transposes of the coefficient matrices appearing in the kinematic consistency conditions for the velocities, Eq. 2.15. By analogy with Eq. 3.39 these conditions can be rewritten as

$$G^c = \sum_{a \in \mathbf{A}} W^{ac^T} G^a, \qquad c \in \mathbf{C}. \tag{3.41}$$

To generate the partially reduced dynamical equations, Eq. 2.26, the unreduced system equations, Eqs. 3.39, are reformulated, using the description of joint kinematics, Eq. 3.22 for $s = a$ and representing the interactions Λ^s in terms of dual modes ψ^s and $\overline{\psi}^s$

$$\Lambda^s = \psi^s \lambda^s + \overline{\psi}^s \overline{\lambda}^s. \tag{3.42}$$

An interpretation of the coordinates λ^s and $\bar{\lambda}^s$ of Λ^s is obtained, recalling the definition of dual bases. Using Eqs. 3.23 in Eq. 3.41 one concludes

$$\lambda^s = \varphi^{s^T} \Lambda^s = \varphi^{s^T} \Lambda^s_e , \qquad \bar{\lambda}^s = \bar{\varphi}^{s^T} \Lambda^s , \tag{3.43}$$

which are the n_f^s known generalized applied forces corresponding to the unknown mode velocities g^s and the n_c^s unknown constraint forces corresponding to the known mode velocities $\bar{g}^s$.

Introducing the velocities G^a and the interactions Λ^a and Λ^c, as given by Eqs. 3.22 and 3.42, into Eq. 3.39 and projecting the result on the mode vectors φ^a and $\bar{\varphi}^a$ one obtains the partially reduced dynamical equations, Eq. 2.26, and the relations for computing the constraint forces $\bar{\lambda}^a$, Eq. 2.30, i.e.

$$\sum_{b \in \mathbf{A}} J_I^{ab} \dot{g}^b - \sum_{c \in \mathbf{C}} W_{II}^{ac} \bar{\lambda}^c = \chi^a + \lambda^a + \sum_{c \in \mathbf{C}} W_I^{ac} \lambda^c \tag{3.44.a}$$

and

$$\bar{\lambda}^a = \sum_{b \in \mathbf{A}} \bar{J}_I^{ab} \dot{g}^b - \bar{\chi}^a - \sum_{c \in \mathbf{C}} (\bar{W}_I^{ac} \lambda^c + \bar{W}_{II}^{ac} \bar{\lambda}^c). \tag{3.45}$$

Here

$$\left.\begin{aligned} J_I^{ab} &= \varphi^{a^T} J^{ab} \varphi^b & \bar{J}_I^{ab} &= \bar{\varphi}^{a^T} J^{ab} \varphi^b \\ W_I^{ac} &= \varphi^{a^T} W^{ac} \psi^c & \bar{W}_I^{ac} &= \bar{\varphi}^{a^T} W^{ac} \psi^c \\ W_{II}^{ac} &= \varphi^{a^T} W^{ac} \bar{\psi}^c & \bar{W}_{II}^{ac} &= \bar{\varphi}^{a^T} W^{ac} \bar{\psi}^c \\ \chi^a &= \varphi^{a^T} X^a & \bar{\chi}^a &= \bar{\varphi}^{a^T} X^a \end{aligned}\right\} \tag{3.46.a}$$

where

$$X^a = Q^a - \sum_{b \in \mathbf{A}} J^{ab} \left(\dot{\varphi}^b g^b + \frac{d}{dt} (\bar{\varphi}^b \bar{g}^b) \right) . \tag{3.46.b}$$

Introducing G^s, $s = a$ and $s = c$ as given by Eq. 3.22 into the kinematic consistency conditions, Eq. 3.41 and projecting the result on the dual modes ψ^c and $\bar{\psi}^c$, one gets in view of Eqs. 3.23

$$g^c = \sum_{c \in \mathbf{C}} W_I^{ac^T} g^a + \bar{W}_I^{ac^T} \bar{g}^a, \tag{3.47}$$

which is a relation for computing the unknown velocities g^c from the system variables g^a and

$$\sum_{a \in \mathbf{A}} W_{II}^{ac^T} g^a = \bar{g}^c - \sum_{a \in \mathbf{A}} \bar{W}_{II}^{ac^T} \bar{g}^a, \tag{3.44.b}$$

i.e. the constraint equations to be satisfied by the velocities g^a when solving Eq. 3.44.a. Because these constraints, resulting from the kinematic consistency conditions and the constraints across the secondary joints c, have not been incorporated into the system equations, Eqs. 3.44.a still contain the unknown constraint forces $\bar{\lambda}^c$.

3.2.2 Recursive Generation of System Matrices

A detailed discussion of Eqs. 3.44 to 3.47 may be found in [36]. Here it is sufficient to know that the elements of matrices $J = [J^{ab}]$ and $Q = [Q^a]$ have the general forms

$$J^{ab} = \sum_{i,k} T^{ai} T^{bk} M^{ik}, \quad Q^a = \sum_i T^{ai} Z^i, \qquad a \in \mathbf{A}, \; b \in \mathbf{A}, \tag{3.48}$$

where M^{ik} and Z^i are functions of the absolute motion of the system bodies, which have been developed in [36].

For a system with tree configuration the W-matrices disappear and the equations of motion reduce to the forms given as Eqs. 2.31 and 2.32. The discussions of Sect. 3.1.3 demonstrate that J^{ab} and Q^a (and thus the system matrices J_l^{ab}, $\bar{J}_l^{ab}$, χ^a and $\bar{\chi}^a$) can be developed efficiently by backward recursion - see Eqs. 3.3.b, 3.5 and 3.46, 3.48. In case of systems with closed loops, terms involving the W-matrices must be developed as well. Without giving the details it is mentioned that they can be derived from the absolute motion of the system bodies computed previously.

Summarizing the results of Sects. 3.2.1 and 3.1.3 one observes that, given the motion across the primary interconnections in terms of p^a and g^a together with the constraint forces $\bar{\lambda}^c$ across the secondary interconnections, one can generate the

1. kinematical equations, Eq. 2.20, and the relative motion in terms of B^a, z^a and G^a from data in a joint kinematics library - see Eqs. 3.25, 3.21 and 3.22;
2. absolute motion (position and velocity) of the system bodies by forward recursion, Eqs. 3.26, 3.27 and 3.29, 3.30;
3. relative position and velocity across the secondary interconnections, Eqs. 2.28 and 2.29 or 3.47, together with the loop constraint equations on variables p^a and g^a, Eqs. 2.21 and 2.27 or 3.44.b;
4. system matrices in the dynamical equations by a backward recursion, Eqs. 3.48, 3.44.a or 2.26.

Two recursions, a forward and a backward one, are required to generate the system equations. These computations can be done efficiently, but considerable computational effort must be spent for the inversion of matrix $J_l = [J_l^{ab}]$ when integrating the system equations. Formalisms generating the resolved form

$$\dot{g}^a = \dot{g}^a(p^a, g^a, \bar{\lambda}^c, t), \qquad a \in \mathbf{A} \tag{3.49}$$

yield an important improvement. Such formulations have been developed as early as 1974 and will be described in the next section. The constraint forces

$$\bar{\lambda}^a = \bar{\lambda}^a (p^a, g^a, \bar{\lambda}^c, t), \qquad a \in \mathbf{A} \tag{3.50}$$

have been eliminated from the system equations, but they may be required, e. g. for system evaluation. They can be computed recursively as well, when generating Eq. 3.49.

3.3 Explicit Dynamical Equations

3.3.1 Origins

Recursive computation as implied by the T-matrix of graph theory has been used when generating the *implicit* forms of multibody system equations [41], but the subject was not discussed in the literature on general purpose multibody system simulation. Most efforts in the seventies were oriented towards increasing the *generality* of the multibody models to be handled by a computer oriented formalism. This was in contrast to developments for applications in robotics. Much effort has gone into producing efficient computer implementations of multibody formalisms to realize the possibility of real-time dynamic control based on multibody robot models [2], [9]. It appears quite natural that the robotics community also concentrated on increasing the efficiency of the simulation of robots and that a major step to improve the *efficiency* of simulation, the development of recursive $O(N)$-formulations, has its roots in this field of application. The basic advantage of the $O(N)$-formulations is not their recursive nature but the fact that they generate the *explicit* form of the dynamical equations, Eq. 3.49, (i.e. the form required for the numerical solution of ODE) with a number of operations, which increases linearly with the number N of the system bodies. By contrast, the generation of the explicit system equations, Eq. 3.49, from their implicit form, Eq. 2.26, requires the inversion of matrix J_l, i.e. a number of operations, which is proportional to the third power of the dimension of J_l. For tree configured systems having joints with one degree of freedom only, the dimension of J_l equals the number N of bodies. If N is sufficiently large, simulations based on $O(N)$-formulations are certain to be more efficient than those calling for a solution of the implicit equations. At present, the magic number N seems to lie somewhere between 5 and 7, when the system allows rotational motion only.

The first one to propose an $O(N)$ computational scheme for the simulation of multibody system motion was A. F. Vereshchagin as early as 1974 [45]. He mentions that writing special simulation programs for each special robot manipulator is unsatisfactory, because it calls for an "extremely cumbersome" derivation of the system equations. Moreover, within such programs one must evaluate complicated nonlinear functions to generate the accelerations for a given time and a given set of position- and velocity-variables. By contrast, in Gauss's principle the determination of the explicit equations of motion, Eq. 3.49, reduces to the algebraic problem of minimizing a quadratic form in terms of redundant accelerations, considering the (linear) velocity constraint equations. Interpreting this procedure as a dynamic programming problem for determining the accelerations, Vereshchagin demonstrates how to write the resolved form of the equations of motion in an algorithmic way, i.e. in a way, which can be implemented easily on a computer. Specializing to single open chain systems having prismatic and revolute joints only, he observes that the relations between the absolute velocities of the system bodies and the joint velocity state variables, i.e. the form of the constraint equations required in his approach, can be generated recursively and that these recursions can be combined with recursive relations to generate the accelerations.

The equations of motion are obtained in terms of second derivatives of a minimal set of joint coordinates. It is stated explicitely that a computer code based on this method has been developed and used successfully and that the computational work increases linearly with the number of bodies in the system. The scheme is shown to be superior to an alternative, based on the Gibbs-Appel equations, which applies to more general systems. This early paper on the subject is written remarkably clear and it is amazing to observe that such an important contribution to multibody system simulation got known in the community working on the development of general purpose codes only after the method had been reinvented by other authors.

The next contribution, also motivated by simulation of manipulators, has been given by W. W. Armstrong, five years later [1]. As Vereshchagin's approach, Armstrong's method applies to single open chain systems and again it is pointed out explicitely that the resolved form of the equations of motion is obtained by computation, which grows linearly with the number of bodies. It is stated that the method has been generalized to deal with flexible links and that it has been applied to simulate the Shuttle Remote Manipulator Arm.

Armstrong hypothesizes and proofs the existence of linear, recursive relations representing both, the absolute angular acceleration of body i and the force between body i and the interior body $i-1$ across the inboard joint in terms of the linear acceleration at the inboard joint of body i. He gives the expressions for the coefficient matrices in these linear relations and demonstrates that the matrices can be computed recursively begining at the terminal body. Having determined all these linear relations, he solves for the linear and angular accelerations of the system bodies, begining with the most interior body and proceeding outward to the terminal body. As a result one obtains the explicit forms of the equations of motion. The constraint forces across the joints may be computed as well during the recursions. In this form the method applies to systems with spherical joints only. Modifications required to deal with revolute joints increase the computational burden significantly [9]. They are described in an appendix of the paper. Aspects of improving computational speed by updating not all the terms when integrating the system equations are discussed there as well. To summarize, the method is of order N, but the coefficient of N seems to be rather large [9]. as compared to Vereshchagin's approach.

Being aware of Armstrong's approach, Featherstone reinvented Vereshchagin's more efficient method in 1983 [9]. He has found the same recursive relations, but his derivation is not based on Gauss's principle. Rather he introduces the concepts of "articulated-body inertias" and of "bias-forces" and applies these concepts to develop his algorithm. If both, articulated-body inertia and bias-force, are known for any body of the multibody system, then the acceleration of that body may be calculated directly from the external forces applied to the body. It is shown, that articulated-body inertias and bias-forces can be computed by a backward recursion and that the absolute acceleration of the system bodies and the relative accelerations across the joints then may be found by a forward recursion. Before performing both of these recursions a forward recursion is required to compute absolute position and velocity of the system bodies from the relative motion across the joints (together with some other matrices).

Apart from discussing Vereshchagin's paper, the publications of Featherstone [9], [10] and [11] give an excellent survey on the development of computational schemes for solving both, the forward and the inverse problem of robot dynamics. Detailed figures about the computational requirements of the various algorithms may be found in his publications. To be sure, these contributions are hard to read for those who are not familiar with the concept of ″spatial motion″, which is popular in some kinematics literature and which is used heavily by Featherstone. His concepts of ″articulated-body inertia″ and ″bias-force″ give a nice physical interpretation of terms appearing naturally in *O(N)*-formulations, as we will see later.

After Featherstone's first paper had been published, the possibility of constructing the explicit form of the multibody system equations was discussed also in the community working on the development of general purpose codes. Independently, and in part without any knowledge about the contributions mentioned up to now, the method has been developed and published at various places [3], [4], [6], [7], [37], [47]. The basic idea to generate the explicit form and the resulting algorithms of the various procedures are those of Vereshchagin and Featherstone, but the different ″schools″ have used their own terminology to describe the derivation of the algorithms. Bae and Haug have used the ″variational form″ of the system equations, Brandl, Johanni and Otter use the Newton/Euler equations as a starting point and incorporate the joint constraints by applying the concept of modes of motion and in Rosenthals derivation appears the flavor of ″Kane's equations″ [23]. A forthcoming paper of R. Wehage [47] describes the recursive algorithm very clearly using graph theoretic concepts. As Haug [18] he discusses the benefits of using parallel computer architecture. In some of the latter publications, the algorithm has been generalized to deal with arbitrary joints and system topology. In particular, closed loop systems are incorporated by defining a spanning tree of the system graph, formulating the loop closure conditions and introducing the constraint forces across the secondary joints into the system equations. As a result one finds a set of partically reduced system equations in the explicit form, Eq. 3.49, accompanied by the corresponding constraint equations, Eqs. 2.21. Most of the procedures mentioned previously have been used for developing efficient codes and some data on their performance have been published. A careful comparison of the relative performance of the various codes is not available at present, and I doubt, whether it is worth clarifying this point for general purpose codes. Of course, such details become important in specific applications with stringent requirements on real time capabilities for simulation of specific multibody models.

3.3.2 Recursive Generation of Resolved Dynamical Equations

A description of the *O(N)* recursive computational scheme, yielding the algorithm first published by Vereshchagin, is given now applying the terminology used heretofore. The starting point are the basic laws of Newton and Euler and the concepts of modes of motion and corresponding generalized forces, Eqs. 3.22 to 3.24 and 3.42, 3.43. The latter are used to incorporate the joint constraint equations. First the special case of systems with tree configuration will be considered and the resulting equations are generalized afterwards for systems with closed loops.

We rewrite the basic dynamical equations, Eqs. 3.38, in matrix form. They apply for the general case of closed loop systems. After selecting a spanning tree one can distinguish inboard and outboard bodies, joints, attachment points etc.. From the general theory given in [36] it is concluded that it is the inboard attachment point O^i (Fig. 12) rather than CM^i, which is used most conveniently as a reference point for the formulation of the dynamical equations. Denoting the mass of body i by m^i, its inertia tensor with respect to CM^i by $\underline{\underline{I}}^i$ (Fig. 9), the inertia tensor with respect to O^i is ${}_o\underline{\underline{I}}^i = \underline{\underline{I}}^i + m^i\,(\underline{d}^{ii} \cdot \underline{d}^{ii}\,\underline{\underline{E}} - \underline{d}^{ii}\,\underline{d}^{ii})$. Collecting the coordinates of ${}_o\underline{\underline{I}}^i$ with respect to vector basis $\underline{e}^i$ in inertia matrix ${}_oI^i$, the resolutions of external actions $\underline{L}^i$, $\underline{F}^i$ with respect to $\underline{e}^i$ in matrices L^i, F^i and introducing matrices

$$J^i = \begin{bmatrix} {}_oI^i & -m^i\,\tilde{d}^{ii} \\ m^i\,\tilde{d}^{ii} & m^i\,E \end{bmatrix}, \qquad Q^i = \begin{bmatrix} L^i - \tilde{d}^{ii}\,F^i - \tilde{\omega}^i\,{}_oI^i\,\omega^i \\ F^i + m^i\,w^i\,d^{ii} \end{bmatrix}, \qquad i \in \mathbf{N} \tag{3.51}$$

the dynamical equations, Eq. 3.38, can be rewritten in the matrix form

$$J^i\,b^i = Q^i + C^i\,\Lambda^i - \sum_{b\,:\,b\,\neq\,i} S^{ib}\,D^{\kappa(b)}\,\Lambda^b, \qquad i \in \mathbf{N}. \tag{3.52}$$

Matrices b^i, C^i, $D^{\kappa(b)}$ and Λ^b appearing here have been defined previously, Eqs. 3.32, 3.34, 3.35 and 3.40. Body and joint labels used in Eq. 3.52 are visualized in Fig. 14.

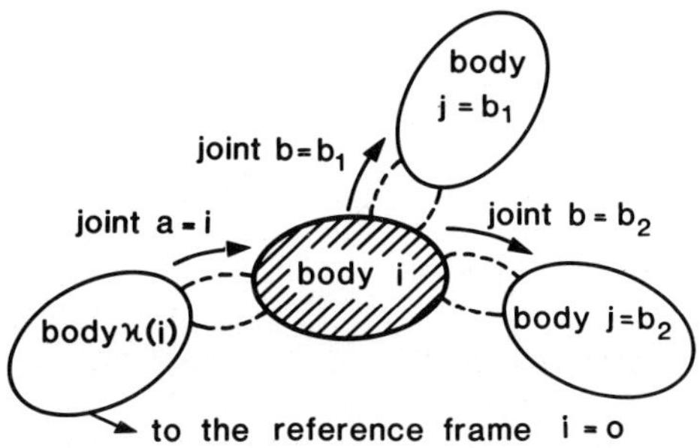

Figure 14. Labels of Bodies and Joints Contiguous to Body i in Case of Canonical Labeling

In case of canonical labeling, as used here, the inboard joint on body i is $a = i$. Thus the interaction across the inboard joint on body i is Λ^a, $a = i$, i.e. Λ^i (a notation, which avoids adding $a = i$ to Eq. 3.52 and to all relations to be developed in the sequel, and which makes the recursions in those equations more apparent). The interaction across the inboard joint has been written separately and excluded from the summation. It appears with a positive sign, because $S^{ii} = -1$, when orienting all arcs towards the terminal bodies as proposed in Sect. 3.1.3. The contributions from the interactions across the outboard joints appear under the summation sign. An outboard joint b connects body i with an outboard body $j = b$. Thus $\kappa(b)$, appearing as an index in Eq. 3.52, is the body inboard of both joint b and body $j = b$, i.e. body i whenever $S^{ib} \neq 0$ and $b \neq i$.

We now consider the special case of tree configured systems, which implies that $\bar{\lambda}^c$ is absent from the resolved form of the dynamical equations, Eq. 3.49, we want to derive. These equations can be generated observing that Eqs. 3.52 can be transformed (in case of tree configured systems) for any $i \in \mathbf{N}$ into the specific forms

$$\hat{J}^i\,b^i = \hat{Q}^i + C^i\,\Lambda^i, \qquad i \in \mathbf{N}\,, \tag{3.53}$$

i.e. into forms, in which the acceleration b^i of body i depends on the interaction Λ^i across the inboard interconnection on that body only. For terminal bodies the corresponding matrices $\hat{J}^i$ and $\hat{Q}^i$ are found to be

$$\hat{J}^i = J^i, \quad \hat{Q}^i = Q^i \quad \text{for } i \in \mathbf{N}_t, \tag{3.54}$$

because $S^{ib} = 0$ for $b \neq i$ and $i \in \mathbf{N}_t$, i.e. because there are no outboard interconnections attached to the terminal bodies in case of a system with a tree configuration. For interior system bodies it will be demonstrated later that matrices $\hat{J}^i$ and $\hat{Q}^i$ can be computed by a backward recursion. Once these matrices are available the unreduced equations, Eqs. 3.53, must be reduced to an explicit state space representation, Eq. 3.49. Thus two problems must be solved, the transformation of the equations of motion, Eq. 3.52, into the special form given by Eq. 3.53 and the derivation of Eqs. 3.49 and 3.50 from this equation.

We consider the latter problem first. Representing b^i as given by Eqs. 3.33 and 3.37 and recalling that $C^{i^T} C^i = E$ one concludes from Eq. 3.53

$$K^i \varphi^i \dot{g}^i = X^i - K^i (D^{\kappa(i)^T} b^{\kappa(i)} + \alpha^{\kappa(i)}) + \Lambda^i . \tag{3.55}$$

Here

$$K^i = C^{i^T} \hat{J}^i C^i, \quad X^i = C^{i^T} \left(\hat{Q}^i - K^i \left(\dot{\varphi}^i g^i + \frac{d}{dt} (\overline{\varphi}^i g^i) \right) \right) \tag{3.56}$$

are the inertia and inertial terms $\hat{J}^i$ and $\hat{Q}^i$ (the latter including contributions from variable modes and from kinematic excitations) resolved in basis $\underline{e}^{\kappa(i)}$ instead of $\underline{e}^i$. Now use Eq. 3.42 to rewrite Eq. 3.55 in the form

$$K^i \varphi^i \dot{g}^i = X^i - K^i (D^{\kappa(i)^T} b^{\kappa(i)} + \alpha^{\kappa(i)}) + \psi^i \lambda^i + \overline{\psi}^i \overline{\lambda}^i . \tag{3.57}$$

Introducing the reduced inertia matrix

$$K_I^i = \varphi^{i^T} K^i \varphi^i \tag{3.58}$$

having a dimension corresponding to the number of free modes (or degrees of freedom) across the inboard joint $a = i$ on body i and applying Eq. 3.23 one can solve for the unknowns $\dot{g}^i$ and $\overline{\lambda}^i$

$$\dot{g}^i = (K_I^i)^{-1} \left(\varphi^{i^T} \left(X^i - K^i (\alpha^{\kappa(i)} + D^{\kappa(i)^T} b^{\kappa(i)}) \right) + \lambda^i \right) \tag{3.59}$$

$$\overline{\lambda}^i = \overline{\varphi}^{i^T} \left(K^i (\varphi^i \dot{g}^i + \alpha^{\kappa(i)} + D^{\kappa(i)^T} b^{\kappa(i)}) - X^i \right) . \tag{3.60}$$

Eqs. 3.59 and 3.60 represent the accelerations $\dot{g}^i$ and the constraint forces $\overline{\lambda}^i$ across the inboard joints $a = i$ in terms of the accelerations $b^{\kappa(i)}$ for the inboard body $\kappa(i)$. The acceleration b° of the reference frame $i = 0$ is known. Thus $\dot{g}^i$ and $\overline{\lambda}^i$ can be computed by Eqs. 3.59 and 3.60 for the layer of bodies attached to the reference frame. Using Eq. 3.33, the acceleration b^i can be computed for those bodies and now one can use Eqs. 3.59 and 3.60 again to obtain $\dot{g}^i$ and $\overline{\lambda}^i$ for the next layer of outboard bodies. In other words: Using Eqs. 3.33, 3.59 and 3.60 one can generate $\dot{g}^i$ and $\overline{\lambda}^i$ by a forward recursion.

To evaluate these equations we still need matrices $\hat{J}^i$ and $\hat{Q}^i$ appearing in Eqs. 3.53 for interior bodies - for terminal bodies they are given by Eq. 3.54. To develop those expressions, consider a body $\kappa(i)$ inboard of a terminal body i, $i \in \mathbf{N}_t$. Its dynamical equation is Eq. 3.52 for $i = \kappa$, i.e.

$$J^{\kappa(i)}\, b^{\kappa(i)} = Q^{\kappa(i)} + C^{\kappa(i)}\, \Lambda^{\kappa(i)} - \sum_{b\,:\,b\, \neq\, \kappa(i)} S^{\kappa(i)b}\, D^{\kappa(b)}\, \Lambda^{b}\,. \tag{3.61.a}$$

The only nonzero terms in the sum on the right side correspond to outboard joints $b = i$ on body $\kappa(i)$, which implies $\kappa(b) = \kappa(i)$. Thus it is no longer necessary to keep the argument of $\kappa = \kappa(i) = \kappa(b)$ explicit and Eq. 3.61.a can be rewritten as

$$J^{\kappa}\, b^{\kappa} = Q^{\kappa} + C^{\kappa}\, \Lambda^{\kappa} - \sum_{b\,:\,b\, \neq\, \kappa} S^{\kappa b}\, D^{\kappa}\, \Lambda^{b}, \qquad \kappa = \kappa(i)\,. \tag{3.61.b}$$

To transform Eq. 3.61.b into the form given by Eq. 3.53, the actions Λ^b across the outboard joints b of body κ must be represented in terms of the acceleration b^κ. Such a relation is gotten, when replacing index i by index b in Eq. 3.55 after introducing $\dot{g}^i = \dot{g}^b$ as given by Eq. 3.59 and solving for Λ^b. The result is

$$\left.\begin{aligned} \Lambda^b &= K^b\, \varphi^b\, (K_I^b)^{-1} \left(\varphi^{b^T} (X^b - K^b\, \alpha^\kappa) + \lambda^b\right) - \left(X^b - K^b\, \alpha^\kappa\right) \\ &\quad + \left(K^b - (K^b\, \varphi^b)\, (K_I^b)^{-1}\, (K^b\, \varphi^b)^T\right) D^{\kappa^T}\, b^\kappa \end{aligned}\right\} \tag{3.62}$$

Introducing this expression for Λ^b into Eq. 3.61.b and rearranging the terms one gets Eq. 3.53 with $i = \kappa$. Matrices $\hat{J}^\kappa$ and $\hat{Q}^\kappa$ are found to be

$$\hat{J}^\kappa = J^\kappa + \sum_{b\,:\,b\, \neq\, \kappa} S^{\kappa b}\, D^\kappa \left(K^b - (K^b\, \varphi^b)\, (K_I^b)^{-1}\, (K^b\, \varphi^b)^T\right) D^{\kappa^T} \tag{3.63}$$

$$\left.\begin{aligned} \hat{Q}^\kappa = Q^\kappa &- \sum_{b\,:\,b\, \neq\, \kappa} S^{\kappa b}\, D^\kappa \left((K^b\, \varphi^b)\, (K_I^b)^{-1}\, \varphi^{b^T} - E\right) X^b \\ &- \sum_{b\,:\,b\, \neq\, \kappa} S^{\kappa b}\, D^\kappa \left(K^b - (K^b\, \varphi^b)\, (K_I^b)^{-1}\, (K^b\, \varphi^b)^T\right) \alpha^\kappa \\ &- \sum_{b\,:\,b\, \neq\, \kappa} S^{\kappa b}\, D^\kappa\, (K^b\, \varphi^b)\, (K_I^b)^{-1}\, \lambda^b \end{aligned}\right\} \tag{3.64}$$

Recalling Eqs. 3.56 one observes that these relations give $\hat{J}^{\kappa(i)}$ and $\hat{Q}^{\kappa(i)}$ in terms of matrices $\hat{J}^i$ and $\hat{Q}^i$ corresponding to bodies i outboard of body κ. Manipulating the dynamical equation, Eq. 3.52 for the body inboard of body κ in the very same way, one arrives again at the relations just developed. Thus matrices $\hat{J}^i$ and $\hat{Q}^i$ can be computed by a backward recursion, using Eqs. 3.63, 3.64 and 3.56, 3.57. The recursion is initialized, considering Eq. 3.54, which applies for the terminal bodies.

3.3.3 O(N) Computational Scheme

The results of Sects. 3.3.2 and 3.1.3 can be summarized as follows: Given the system parameters together with the state variables p^i, g^i and time t, the resolved forms of the kinematical and dynamical equations of a tree configured system and the corresponding constraint forces can be generated recursively by the following computational scheme:

1. *Forward Recursion:*

For $i = 1,2,...N$ generate:

- direction cosine matrices B^a, displacements z^a and velocities G^a, $a = i$, by Eqs. 3.21 and 3.22;
- direction cosine matrices A^i by Eq. 3.26 and absolute motion of CM^i, described in terms of r^i and v^i, by the matrix forms of Eqs. 3.29 and 3.30, if required, e. g. for evaluating laws of external actions L^i, F^i;
- angular velocities ω^i by the matrix form of Eq. 3.27 with Ω^a available in matrix G^a - see Eq. 3.19;
- matrices C^i, $D^{\kappa(i)}$, $\alpha^{\kappa(i)}$, J^i and Q^i by Eqs. 3.34 to 3.36 and 3.51;
- right side of the kinematical equations of motion, Eq. 3.25, available in a joint kinematics library together with all the other information needed about the constraints on the relative motion across the interconnections.

2. *Backward Recursion:*

Initialize $\hat{J}^i$, $\hat{Q}^i$, K^i, X^i and K^i_i for $i \in \mathbf{N}_t$ as given by Eqs. 3.54, 3.56 and 3.58 and generate for $i = N, N\text{-}1,...$ until $\kappa(i) \in \mathbf{N}_o$:

- $\hat{J}^\kappa$, K^κ and K^κ_i by Eqs. 3.63, 3.56 and 3.58;
- $\hat{Q}^\kappa$ and X^κ by Eqs. 3.64 and 3.56 with λ^b available from a force element library.

3. *Forward Recursion:*

For $i = 1,2,...N$ generate:

- right side $\dot{g}^i$ of dynamical equations by Eq. 3.59;
- constraint forces $\bar{\lambda}^i$ by Eq. 3.60, if needed;
- acceleration b^i by Eqs. 3.33 and 3.37.

A backward and two forward recursions are required to solve the problem. The inversion of the large matrix $J_l = \left[J_l^{ab}\right]$ in Eq. 2.31 is replaced by the inversion of N small matrices K^i_i having a maximum dimension of 6×6 , i.e. the maximal number of free modes across a joint. In many applications the order of matrices K^i_i will be just one, two or three, making trivial the computation of the inverse. The reason for this basic advantage of the $O(N)$ formulation is as follows: When generating the system equations, Eqs. 2.31 and 2.32, the unreduced equations of motion for *the whole system* are formulated first. This set of equations is separated into two subsets yielding the equations of motion, Eq. 2.31.a, and the equations for the constraint forces, Eq. 2.32. The computations of the accelerations $\dot{g}_A$ and of the constraint forces $\bar{\lambda}_A$ are separated strictly. By contrast, these computations are intermingled in the $O(N)$ computational scheme. Comparing the right sides of Eqs. 3.59 and 3.60 one observes that practically all the information for calculating $\bar{\lambda}^i$ is available, once $\dot{g}^i$ has been computed. The equations for the $O(N)$ computational scheme are derived by considering *each system body separately* and representing the interactions across its outboard joints (including the constraint forces) in terms of the body's acceleration (see Eq. 3.62) which is known, once all the computations to generate $\dot{g}^i$ have been completed - see Eqs. 3.59, 3.33 and 3.37.

Some comparisions with other derivations of the computational scheme may be helpful at this place. Comparing with Featherstone's paper [9] one concludes that his "articulated-body inertias" and "bias-forces" correspond to the terms K_I^i and X^i given by Eqs. 3.54, 3.63, 3.56, 3.58 and 3.54, 3.64, 3.56, respectively. These relations are more complicated than those given in [9], because general tree configured systems with arbitrary joints are included here. The relations have been given in [3] as well; just the arguments used for their derivation are different. Here we have applied the concepts of modes of motion and corresponding generalized forces to obtain Eqs. 3.59 and 3.60, which represent the joint accelerations and the constraint forces in terms of the acceleration of the inboard body and which yield the expressions for the "articulated-body inertias" and the "bias-forces". By contrast, these equations are found in [3] when writing the variational total system equations as sums, whose terms are premultiplied by independent and redundant virtual displacements. Eqs. 3.59 are found, considering that the coefficients of the independent virtual displacements must be zero.

Up to now we have considered systems with tree configuration only. It has been shown how to generate the kinematical equations, Eq. 2.31a, the resolved form of the dynamical equations, i.e.

$$\dot{g}_A = J_I^{-1}\,(\chi + \lambda_A) \tag{3.65}$$

and the equations for computing the constraint forces $\bar{\lambda}_A$, Eq. 2.32. The algorithm can be generalized easily to provide the partically reduced system equations for closed loop systems, i.e. the kinematical equations, Eq. 2.20, accompained by the constraint equations on the position level, Eq. 2.21, and the resolved form of the dynamical equations

$$\dot{g}_A = J_I^{-1}\,W_{II}\,\bar{\lambda}_C + J_I^{-1}\,(\chi + \lambda_A + W_I\,\lambda_C) \tag{3.66}$$

accompained by the velocity constraint equations, Eq. 2.27. We also discuss how to obtain the constraint forces $\bar{\lambda}_A$, Eq. 2.30, and the constraint equations on the acceleration level

$$W_{II}^T\,\dot{g}_A + \dot{W}_{II}^T\,g_A - \frac{d}{dt}\left(\bar{g}_C - \overline{W}_{II}^T\,\bar{g}_A\right) = 0\,. \tag{3.67}$$

The latter relation may be needed in numerical solution procedures [15].

Starting with a discussion of the equations of motion one observes that the kinematical equations remain unchanged. In the dynamical equations the additional terms $J^{-1}\,W_I\,\lambda_C$ and $J_I^{-1}\,W_{II}\,\bar{\lambda}_C$ must be computed within the algorithm. This is accomplished, considering that the additional actions

$$\Lambda^c = \psi^c\,\lambda^c + \overline{\psi}^c\,\lambda^c \tag{3.68}$$

are applied with opposite sign at those terminal bodies of the system represented by the spanning tree, which are connected by secondary joints c. These additional actions must be treated in the formalism in the same way as the external actions L^i, F^i upon the terminal bodies in question. The external actions appear in matrices Q^i only, see Eq. 3.51. Thus, in case of closed loops systems, one simply modifies Q^i for the terminal bodies, i.e. one changes Eq. 3.54 into

$$\hat{Q}^i = Q^i - S^{ic}\,(\psi^c \lambda^c + \overline{\psi}^c \overline{\lambda}^c)\,, \qquad i \in \mathbf{N}_t\,. \tag{3.69}$$

Here, the elements S^{ic} of the incidence matrix ensure that the actions Λ^c are added with the correct sign just to those bodies i, which interact across secondary interconnections c. Separating the actions Λ^c, as proposed in Eq. 3.69, into contributions from applied forces λ^c and constraint forces $\overline{\lambda}^c$ is required, because the λ^c must be computed from the motion across the secondary interconnections, whereas the $\overline{\lambda}^c$ are among the system variables.

To evaluate the constraint equations observe that absolute position, velocity and acceleration of any terminal bodies are available, once the second forward recursion of the algorithm has been completed. The functions $P^c = P^c\,(p_A,\ t)$, $G^c = G^c\,(p_A,\ g_A,\ t)$ and $\dot{G}^c = \dot{G}^c\,(p_A,\ g_A,\ t)$, describing the relative motion across the secondary interconnections, are computed easily from the known absolute motions. They are required to generate the generalized applied forces λ^c, given by Eq. 3.43, and to evaluate the constraints. To get the constraint equation on the position level, Eq. 2.21.a, introduce values $P^c\,(p_A,\ t)$ into the implicit constraint equations $f^c\,(P^c,\ t) = 0$ across the secondary joints c. On the velocity level compute matrix

$$\left[\overline{\psi}^{c^T} G^c - \overline{g}^c\,(t)\right], \qquad c \in \mathbf{C}\,. \tag{3.70}$$

Recalling Eqs. 3.24, one concludes that this expression is identical with the value by which the velocity constraint equation, Eq. 2.27, i.e. the relation

$$W_{II}^T g_A + \overline{W}_{II}^T \overline{g}_A - \overline{g}_C = 0\,, \tag{3.71}$$

is violated. This is all of the information about the velocity constraint equations required in a DAE-solver; the values of the individual terms in Eq. 3.71 are not needed. To evaluate the acceleration constraint equations one proceeds by analogy, projecting $\dot{G}^c$. Adding these computations to the algorithm, the generation of the system equations for closed loop systems is complete. The modification described by Eq. 3.69 guarantees that the constraint forces $\overline{\lambda}_A$ are computed as given by Eq. 2.30 given the time t and the system variables p_A, g_A, $\overline{\lambda}_C$.

4. Computer Simulation

Recursive $O(N)$ computational schemes have been implemented in various multibody simulation programs. Some of them are described in [28]. Here we summarize the main features of the SIMPACK code.

4.1 Properties of the SIMPACK-Code

The structure of the code is visualized in Fig. 15 - see also [38] and [39]. It is based on an $O(N)$ formulation as described here. The explicit form of the partially reduced equations of motion is generated for closed loop systems together with the equations to compute the constraint forces across the primary joints and the constraint equations on the position-, velocity- and acceleration-level as required for the numerical solution techniques described in [15]. The formalism has been implemented numerically and the code has been structured into modules, which may be evaluated in parallel, taking precautions to use parallel computer architecture. Present implementations are on serial machines.

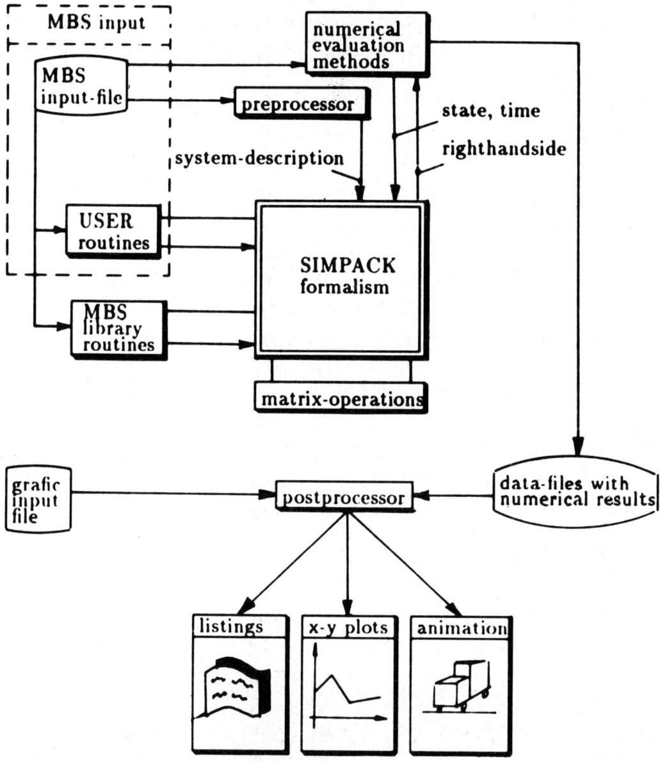

Figure 15. Schematic Structure of the SIMPACK Program Package

A library of constraints resulting from the joints in the interconnections is available as well as libraries of force elements to compute the external and the applied interaction forces. In particular, interaction forces depending not only on the relative motion of the interconnected bodies but also on additional state variables have been included. This allows to model interaction with substructures or control systems. Some basic control laws are available in a library as well. The interface between the library functions and other modules of the package (see Fig. 15) has been defined in a general way to allow a user to add his specific routines as required for his field of application.

Besides the routines for numerical solution of the differential-algebraic equations the block of numerical evaluation methods shown in Fig. 15 contains routines for numerical linearization of the system equations and for linear sytem analysis (in particular routines for the computation of eigenvalues and eigenvectors as functions of the system parameters).

An important aspect during the development of the code, which has not been discussed here, is the elasticity of the system bodies. A general interface has been defined to allow modeling of elastic bodies and the code has been structured accordingly. At present, the specific equations for including flexible beams are being implemented. These equations have been developed considering all the terms required for a complete representation of small elastic deformations superimposed on large rigid body motions - see [24] and [38] and literature cited there.

4.2 Examples

The SIMPACK code has been used for the simulation of a variety of multibody systems with feedback control including trucks and mechanisms as documented in [38] and [39]. Here its usage is described to analyze a problem, which appeared during the design of the gripper mechanism for a printing machine, Fig. 16. The gripper accelerates the paper resting in the paper storage to the speed of the printing roller. The desired gripper motion is enforced by a closed loop linkage together with a cam/follower mechanism. The closed loop linkage consists of four bodies, the follower, the pull rod, the gripper and a cylinder, rotating at an angular velocity $\Omega = const.$ and enforcing a circular motion of the endpoint of the lever attached to the gripper. The printing roller and the rotating cylinder are connected by a chain drive (not shown in the figure) which enforces a common angular velocity Ω of the two bodies. A spring is attached to the gripper to guarantee permanent contact between cam and follower.

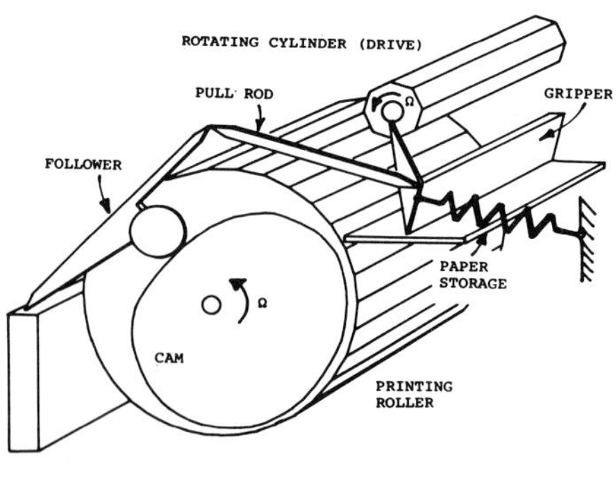

Figure 16. Gripper Mechanism of a Printing Machine

The problem to be analyzed is as follows: When increasing the speed of printing, i.e. the angular velocity of the printing roller, the quality of print is reduced, even when enforcing permanent contact between cam and follower by higher preloads of the spring. The problem was studied with the four body model shown in Fig. 17.

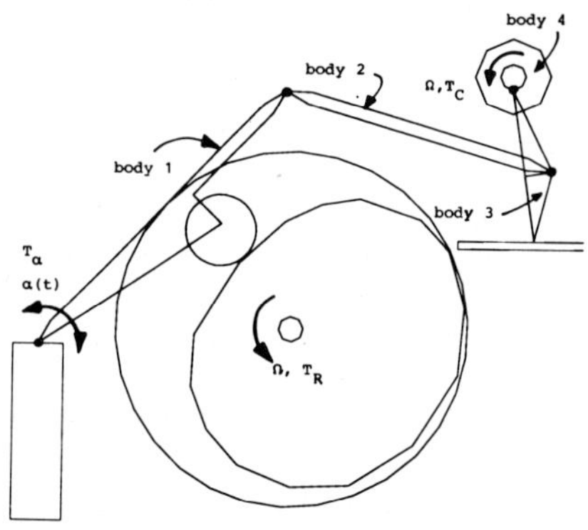

Figure 17. Multibody Model of Gripper Mechanism

Two kinematic excitations have been considered in the system, the constant angular velocity Ω of the cylinder and the angular motion $\alpha(t)$ of the follower resulting from the rotation of the cam with $\Omega = const.$. Thus we have a four body model with a closed loop and with zero (dynamic) degrees of freedom. A simulation with SIMPACK yields the driving torques T_α and T_C - see Fig. 17. The total driving torque $T = T_C + T_R$ is concluded from T_α, considering $T_R \Omega = T_\alpha \dot{\alpha}$ The results $T = T(t)$ are shown in Fig. 18 for the two angular velocities $\Omega = 2\pi$/sec. and $\Omega = 20\pi$/sec.. The spring force has been considered to be zero in this simulation.

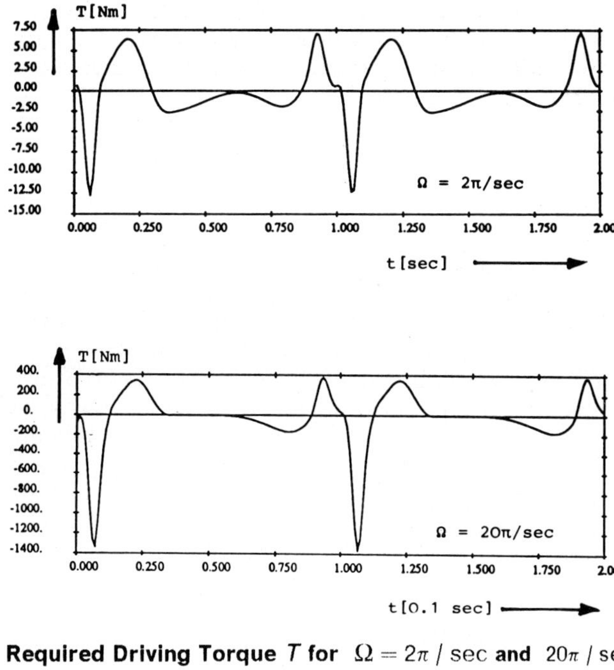

Figure 18. Required Driving Torque T for $\Omega = 2\pi$ / sec and 20π / sec

Looking at the corresponding torques $T_\alpha(t)$ - Fig. 19 - one concludes two facts:

1. When Ω is increased by an order of magnitude the required driving torque grows by two orders of magnitude thus signaling the influence of centrifugal forces, which are proportional to Ω^2.

2. The motion cannot be realized by the mechanism, when the spring force is zero. This is concluded from Fig. 19 - whenever $T_\alpha < 0$, cam and follower loose contact.

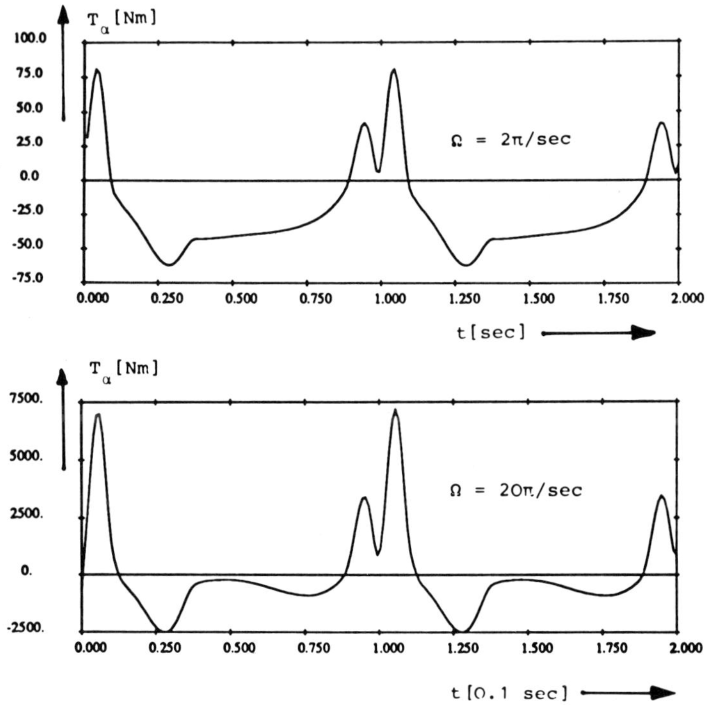

Figure 19. Torque T_α Acting Upon Follower to Press it Against Cam

In a second simulation the influence of the spring was studied. Its preload was determined in such a way that $T_\alpha > 0$ during the whole cycle of the mechanism motion - see Fig. 20. The resulting driving torque T is shown in the same figure. One observes that it is increased again considerably, now because of the influence of the spring load. The conclusion is that the problem cannot be solved by adjusting the spring force without increasing the required driving power in an unacceptable way. Rather a redesign of the mechanism is needed including provisions to balance the rotating masses for eliminating the influence of the centrifugal forces.

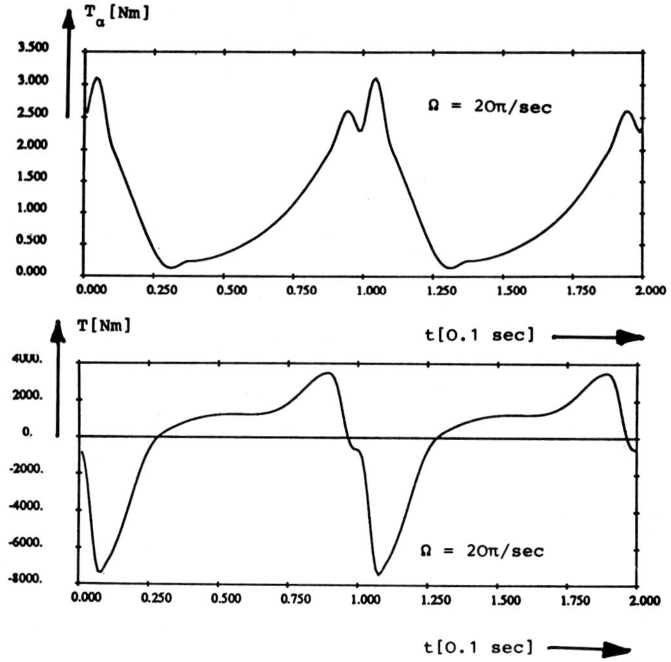

Figure 20. Torque T_α and Driving Torque T after Adjusting Preload of Spring

To summarize, a closed loop mechanism with zero (dynamic) degrees of freedom has been simulated by solving a set of DAE of the form of Eqs. 2.20, 3.66, 2.21a, 2.27 and 3.67. The simulation yields the constraint forces required to evaluate the design of the mechanism.

5. Bibliography

1. Armstrong, W. W.: Recursive Solution to the Equations of Motion of an N Link Manipulator, Proc. 5th World Congr. Theory of Machines and Mechanisms, Vol. 2, 1979, pp. 1343-1346.
2. Asada, H., Kanade, T., Takeyama, I.: Control of a Direct Drive Arm, J. Dyn. Syst. Meas. Ctrl., vol. 105 (1983) pp. 136-142.
3. Bae, D. S., Haug, E. J.: A Recursive Formulation for Constrained Mechanical System Dynamics: Part I, Open Loop Systems, Mechanics of Structures and Machines, 15 (1987) pp. 359-382.
4. Bae, D. S., Haug, E. J.: A Recursive Formulation for Constrained Mechanical System Dynamics: Part II, Closed Loop Systems, Mechanics of Structures and Machines, 15 (1987) pp. 481-506.
5. Bianchi, B., Schiehlen, W., (eds.): Dynamics of Multibody Systems, Proc. IUTAM/IFToMM-Symposium, Udine, 1985, Springer-Verlag, Berlin, 1986.

6. Brandl, H., Johanni, R., Otter, M.: A very Efficient Algorithm for the Simulation of Robots and Similar Multibody Systems Without Inversion of the Mass Matrix, IFAC/IFIP/IMACS Int. Symposium on Theory of Robots, Wien, 1986.
7. Brandl, H., Johanni, R., Otter, M.: An Algorithm for the Simulation of Multibody Systems with Kinematic Loops, Proc. 7th World Congress The Theory of Machines and Mechanisms, Sevilla, Spain, 1987, Vol. 1, pp. 407-411.
8. Ebert, K., Graul, S., Schwertassek, R.: Simulation von Mehrkörpersystemen; Methode, Stand der Technik und Anforderungen für orbitale Systemdynamik, DGLR-Jahrbuch 1988 I, pp. 226-235.
9. Featherstone, R.: The Calculation of Robot Dynamics Using Articulated-Body Inertias, Robotics Research, vol. 2, no. 1, 1983, pp. 13-30.
10. Featherstone, R.: Robot Dynamics Algorithms, Ph. D. Dissertation, Univ. of Edinburgh, 1984.
11. Featherstone, R., Robot Dynamics Algorithms, Kluwer Academic Publ., Boston, 1987.
12. Führer, C.: On the Description of Constrained Mechanical Systems by Differential/Algebraic Equations, in: Neunzert, H. (ed.). The Road-Vehicle-System and Related Mathematics, Teubner, Stuttgart, 1985.
13. Führer, C.: Differential-algebraische Gleichungssysteme in mechanischen Mehrkörpersystemen - Theorie, numerische Ansätze und Anwendungen, Dissertation, Mathematisches Institut der Technischen Universität München, 1988.
14. Führer, C., Schwertassek, R.: Generation and Solution of Multibody System Equations, to appear in Intl. Journal of Nonl. Mechanics (1989).
15. Führer, C., Leimkuhler, B.: Stabilized Differential - Algebraic Formulation of the Equations of Motion of Constrained Mechanical Systems, NATO Advanced Research Workshop Real-Time Integration Methods for Mechanical System Simulation, Snowbird, Utah, Aug. 1989.
16. Haug, E. J., Nikravesh, P. E., Sohoni, V. N., Wehage, R. A.: Computer Aided Analysis of Large Scale, Constrained, Mechanical Systems, 4th International Symposium on Large Engineering Systems, Calgary Alberta, Canada, June 1982.
17. Haug, E. J. (ed.): Nato Advanced Study Institute on Computer Aided Analysis and Optimization of Mechanical System Dynamics, Iowa City, 1983, Springer-Verlag, Berlin, 1984.
18. Haug, E. J.: Parallel Processing Real Time Dynamic Simulation, Proc. Workshop Multibody Simulation, G. Man, R. Laskin, eds., JPL D-5190, Pasadena, Cal., 1988, pp. 1019-1070.
19. Hiller, M., Kecskemethy, A., Woernle, C.: A Loop-Based Kinematical Analysis of Spatial Mechanisms, ASME Paper 86-DET-184, New York, 1986.
20. Hiller, M., Woernle, C.: The "Characteristic Pair of Joints" - an Effective Approach for the Inverse Kinematics Problem of Robots, Proc. IEEE Conf. Robotics and Automation, vol. 2, pp. 846-851, Philadelphia, April 1988.
21. Jones, R. E., Morse, T. W., Russell, W. C.: High Speed Simulation of Multi-Flexible-Body Systems with Large Rotations, Paper No. AIAA-87-0930, Dynamics Specialists Conference, Monterey, Cal., April 9-10, 1987.
22. Jones, R. E.: Multiflex Body Dynamics for Control Design, SDIO/NASA Workshop on Multibody Simulation, G. Man, R. Laskin, eds., JPL D-5190, April 1988, pp. 354-382.
23. Kane, T. R., Levinson, D. A.: Dynamics: Theory and Applications, McGraw-Hill, NY, 1985.

24. Kane, T. R., Ryan, R. R., Banerjee, A. K.: Dynamics of a Cantilever Beam Attached to a Moving Base, J. Guidance, Control, and Dynamics, vol. 10, no. 2, 1987, pp. 139-151.
25. Kortüm, W., (ed.): Software for Dynamic Analysis and Design of Mechanical Systems, Course V1.08, Carl-Cranz-Gesellschaft, Oberpfaffenhofen, 1984.
26. Luenberger, D. G.: Dynamic Equations in Descriptor Form, IEEE Trans. Automatic Control 22 (1977) pp. 312-321.
27. Magnus, K., (ed.): Dynamics of Multibody Systems, Proc. IUTAM-Symposium München, 1977, Springer-Verlag, Berlin, 1978.
28. Man, G., Laskin, R., (eds.): Proceedings of the Workshop on Multibody Simulation, JPL D-5190, vols. I, II, III, Pasadena, Cal., April 1988.
29. Orlandea, N.: Node-Analogous, Sparsity-Oriented Methods for Simulation of Mechanical Systems, Ph.D. Dissertation, Univ. Michigan, 1973.
30. Orlandea, N., Chace, M. A., Calahan, C. A.: A Sparsity-Oriented Approach to the Dynamic Analysis and Design of Mechanical Systems, J. Engrg. Ind. 99, 1977, pp. 773 - 784.
31. Pfeiffer, F.: Über unstetige, insbesondere stosserregte Schwingungen, Zeitschr. Flugwiss. Weltraumforsch. 12 (1988) pp. 358-367.
32. Roberson, R. E., Wittenburg, J.: A Dynamical Formalism for an Arbitrary Number of Interconnected Rigid Bodies, with Reference to the Problem of Satellite Attitude Control, Proc. 3rd Congr. Int. Fed. Autom. Control, London, 1966, Butterworth, Vol. 1, Book 3, Paper 46D, 1967.
33. Roberson, R. E.: Computer-Oriented Dynamic Modeling of Spacecraft: Historical Evolution of Eulerian Formalisms since 1750, 28th International Astronautical Congress (Prague, 25 Sep-1 Oct 1977), IAF Paper 77-A 11.
34. Roberson, R. E.: A Multibody Eulerian Dynamic Simulation as a Design Tool for Attitude Dynamics and Control, Proc. AOCS Conf., ESA Rept. SP-128, Noordwyk, 1977, pp. 209-220.
35. Roberson, R. E.: The Path Matrix of a Graph, its Construction and its Use in Evaluating Certain Products, Computer Meths. Appl. Mech. Engrg. 42, 1984, pp. 42-56.
36. Roberson, R. E., Schwertassek, R.: Dynamics of Multibody Systems, Springer-Verlag, Berlin, 1988.
37. Rosenthal, R.: Order N Formulation for Equations of Motion of Multibody Systems, SDIO/NASA Workshop on Multibody Simulation, JPL, Arcadia, Cal., Sept. 1-3, 1987, pp. 1122-1150.
38. Rulka, W.: SIMPACK, Ein Rechenprogramm zur Simulation von Mehrkoerpersystemen mit grossen Bewegungen, Computergestuetztes Berechnen und Konstruieren, 10. Reutlinger Arbeitstagung, April 1989.
39. Rulka, W.: SIMPACK, a Computer Program for Simulations of Large-Motion Multibody Systems, to appear in Handbook of Multibody Programs, W. Schiehlen (ed.), Springer-Verlag, Berlin.
40. Schiehlen, W.: Technische Dynamik, B. G. Teubner, Stuttgart, 1986.
41. Schwertassek, R.: Der Roberson/Wittenburg Formalismus und das Programmsystem MULTIBODY zur Rechnersimulation von Mehrkörpersystemen, DFVLR-FB-78-08, DFVLR, Wissenschaftliches Berichtswesen, Köln, 1978.
42. Schwertassek, R., Senger, K.-H.: Representation of Joints in Multibody Systems, ZAMM 68 (1988), pp. 111 - 119.
43. Schwertassek, R.: Multibody Kinematical Equations in Terms of Relative Variables, ZAMM 68 (1988), pp. 207 - 211.

44. Schwertassek, R., Eichberger, A.: Recursive Generation of Multibody System Equations in Terms of Graph Theoretic Concepts, to appear in Mechanics of Structures and Machines, Vol. 17, No.2, 1989.
45. Vereshchagin, A. F.: Computer Simulation of the Dynamics of Complicated Mechanisms of Robot-Manipulators, Engineering Cybernetics, no. 6, 1974, pp. 65-70.
46. Wehage, R. A., Haug, E. J.: Generalized Coordinate Partitioning for Dimension Reduction in Analysis of Constrained Dynamic Systems, J. Mech. Design, Vol. 134, 1982, pp. 247-255.
47. Wehage, R. A.: Solution of Multibody Dynamics Using Natural Factors and Iterative Refinement, Part I: Open Kinematic Loops, Part II: Closed Kinematic Loops, to appear.
48. Wittenburg, J.: Dynamics of Systems of Rigid Bodies, B.G. Teubner, Stuttgart, 1977.
49. Woernle, C.: Ein systematisches Verfahren für die Rückwärtstransformation bei Industrierobotern, Robotersysteme 3 (1987), pp. 219-228.
50. Woernle, C.: Ein systematisches Verfahren zur Aufstellung der geometrischen Schliessbedingungen in kinematischen Schleifen mit Anwendung bei der Rückwärtstransformation für Industrieroboter, Fortschritt-Berichte VDI, Reihe 18, Nr. 59, VDI-Verlag, Düsseldorf, 1988.
51. Jaschinski, A.: Anwendung der Kalkerschen Rollreibungstheorie zur dynamischen Simulation von Schienenfahrzeugen, DFVLR-Forschungsbericht, DFVLR-FB-87-07, DFVLR, Wiss. Berichtswesen, Köln 1987.

Generalized Coordinate Partitioning Methods for Numerical Integration of Differential-Algebraic Equations of Dynamics

Edward J. Haug

Jeng Yen

Center for Computer Aided Design
College of Engineering
208 Engineering Research Facility
The University of Iowa
Iowa City, Iowa 52242

Abstract

Explicit and implicit, stiffly stable numerical integration algorithms based on generalized coordinate partitioning are developed and demonstrated for automated simulation of multibody dynamic systems. The concept of generalized coordinate partitioning is used to parameterize the constraint set with independent generalized coordinates. A stiffly stable, backward differentiation formulas are applied to determine independent generalized coordinates and velocities. Dependent generalized coordinates, velocities, and accelerations, as well as Lagrange multipliers that account for constraints, are explicitly retained in the formulation to satisfy all of the governing kinematic and dynamic equations. The algorithm is shown to be valid and accurate, both theoretically and through solution of a numerical example.

Introduction

The field of multibody dynamics has seen a major resurgence during the past decade, owing primarily to opportunities offered by high speed workstations and compute servers to automate the process of equation formulation and solution. Recent contributions to the literature permit automated formulation of the governing equations of rigid and flexible multibody systems, using a variety of computationally oriented algorithms. Cartesian coordinate formulations that yield a maximal set of highly sparse equations form the basis for highly automated dynamic simulation computer codes [1,2] that are broadly used in industry, on a variety of engineering workstations and mainframe computers.

NATO ASI Series, Vol. F 69
Real-Time Integration Methods for Mechanical System Simulation
Edited by E. J. Haug and R. C. Deyo

Graph theoretic methods, with cut-joint concepts that lead to spanning trees and a minimal set of generalized coordinates and constraint equations, have been introduced by Roberson and Wittenburg [3,4] and form the foundation for a wide variety of new computational formulations that hold the potential for high speed dynamic simulation. Symbolic computing methods have been used effectively with these formulations [5]. Recursive formulations that build upon the topological relative coordinate foundation have recently been used to create high speed dynamic simulation methods that are well-suited for parallel computing [6,7].

These and related developments in multibody dynamics have created a variety of powerful new algorithms for efficient automation of the process of constructing the highly nonlinear equations of motion of constrained mechanical systems. Inherent in this class of engineering applications is the need to account for algebraic kinematic constraints that are due to mechanical couplings that restrict relative and absolute motion of components in a multibody system. The foundation for treating such constraints is the time-honored Lagrange multiplier method that has been known for approximately two centuries. Virtually all of the formulations noted above use this approach in constructing the equations of motion for broad classes of mechanical systems. In spite of the fact that such formulations have existed in the engineering literature for two centuries, it was only recognized by the numerical analysis community during the past decade that the equations of constrained mechanical system dynamics are not differential equations. Rather, they are differential-algebraic equations, abbreviated DAE [8].

While some progress has been made in developing and implementing numerical methods for computer solution of DAE [8-15], the lack of broadly applicable and robust integrators for DAE remains the fundamental limitation in automated application and effective use of multibody dynamic simulation methods in a computer-aided engineering environment.

Three basically different approaches have been proposed in the literature for integration of DAE. The first involves direct application of backward difference formulas to all generalized coordinates, using various combinations of configuration, velocity, and acceleration constraint equations [16]. The second approach is based on generalized coordinate partitioning algorithms that implicitly identify independent generalized coordinates that are integrated by predictor-corrector numerical integration methods [10-12]. Finally, constraint stabilization methods have been proposed that attempt to replace algebraic constraints with some form of constraint compensation that permits direct numerical integration of all generalized coordinates [17].

The direct backward differentiation formulas have been studied extensively by Petzold et al. [14,18], but have yet to yield an effective and broadly applicable integration algorithm for the DAE that arise in mechanical system dynamics [15]. The generalized coordinate partitioning approach is theoretically valid and yields accurate results for broad classes of mechanical system dynamics applications [10,13]. It suffers, however, from difficulties with stiff systems and has heretofore defied implementation with an implicit algorithm. The constraint stabilization method [17], while simple in concept, lacks a firm theoretical foundation that permits positive error control and, in fact, occasionally diverges, even for systems that have valid solutions.

The purpose of this paper is to review a broadly applicable, generalized coordinate partitioning integration methods for DAE that arise in mechanic system dynamics. The methods are presented for holonomically constrained mechanical systems.

Differential-Algebraic Equations of Constrained Multibody Dynamics

Let $\mathbf{q} = [q_1, ..., q_n]^T$ be an n-vector of generalized coordinates that describe the configuration of all bodies that make up a mechanical system. These generalized coordinates may include Cartesian coordinates of individual bodies [19] or relative coordinates between bodies that are connected by kinematic joints [4]. In either case, kinematic constraints that act on the mechanical system are represented in the form of algebraic (holonomic) constraint equations of the form

$$\mathbf{\Phi}(\mathbf{q},t) = \mathbf{0} \qquad (1)$$

where $\mathbf{\Phi}(\mathbf{q},t) = [\Phi_1(\mathbf{q},t), ..., \Phi_m(\mathbf{q},t)]^T$ is an m-vector of constraint functions that have two derivatives. For the purposes of the development presented in this paper, it is presumed that the constraints of Eq. 1 are consistent and independent; i.e., the mechanical system can be assembled and the Jacobian of the constraint functions

$$\mathbf{\Phi}_{\mathbf{q}} \equiv \left[\frac{\partial \Phi_i}{\partial q_j} \right]$$

which is an mxn matrix, has full row rank [19,20]. Under these conditions, there exists a unique Lagrange multiplier vector $\boldsymbol{\lambda} = [\lambda_1, ..., \lambda_m]^T$ for which the constrained equations of motion are [4,19]

$$\mathbf{M}(\mathbf{q}, t)\, \ddot{\mathbf{q}} + \mathbf{\Phi}_{\mathbf{q}}(\mathbf{q}, t)^T \boldsymbol{\lambda} = \mathbf{Q}^A(\mathbf{q}, \dot{\mathbf{q}}, t) \qquad (2)$$

where the mass matrix $\mathbf{M}(\mathbf{q}, t)$ is, in general, dependent on generalized coordinates and time and $\mathbf{Q}^A(\mathbf{q}, \dot{\mathbf{q}}, t)$ is an n-vector of generalized applied forces, not including workless constraint reaction forces that are due to workless kinematic constraints of Eq.1.

Equations 1 and 2, together with appropriate initial conditions, comprise a system of DAE for determining the motion of the mechanical system, under the action of applied forces. If $\mathbf{\Phi_q}$ has full row rank and if $\mathbf{a}^T\mathbf{M}\mathbf{a} > 0$ for all $\mathbf{a} \neq \mathbf{0}$ such that $\mathbf{\Phi_q a} = \mathbf{0}$, then with appropriate initial conditions these equations have a unique solution, at least locally [19]. As noted in the foregoing, equations of this form have been known for essentially two centuries, but analytical and numerical methods for their solution remain underdeveloped.

In order to progress with solution methods, constraint velocity and acceleration equations associated with Eq. 1 are needed. Differentiating Eq. 1 with respect to time yields the velocity equation

$$\mathbf{\Phi_q \dot{q}} = \mathbf{v} \equiv -\mathbf{\Phi}_t \tag{3}$$

Differentiating this equation with respect to time yields the acceleration equation

$$\mathbf{\Phi_q \ddot{q}} = \boldsymbol{\gamma} \equiv -(\mathbf{\Phi_q \dot{q}})_\mathbf{q}\, \mathbf{\dot{q}} - 2\mathbf{\Phi}_{\mathbf{q}t}\mathbf{\dot{q}} - \mathbf{\Phi}_{tt} \tag{4}$$

While Eqs. 3 and 4 are derived from the algebraic constraint equations of Eq. 1, they must nevertheless be satisfied in any valid numerical method of solution of the equations of motions.

Due to the algebraic constraints of Eq. 1, components of the generalized coordinate vector $\mathbf{q}$ are dependent. In order to identify a set of independent generalized coordinates, the Jacobian of the constraint equations is formed at an assembled configuration of the mechanical system and Gauss-Jordan reduction of the Jacobian $\mathbf{\Phi_q}$, with full row and column pivoting, is carried out to identify a nonsingular mxm submatrix. The generalized coordinates associated with columns of this nonsingular submatrix may be taken as dependent coordinates [10,19]. The implicit function theorem assures that these dependent variables may be uniquely determined, at least locally, as a function of the remaining generalized coordinates, which are declared to be independent generalized coordinates. Having carried out this computation, the generalized coordinate vector $\mathbf{q}$ is partitioned as

$$\mathbf{q} = \begin{bmatrix} \mathbf{u} \\ \mathbf{v} \end{bmatrix} \tag{5}$$

where $\mathbf{u}$ are dependent generalized coordinates, $\mathbf{v}$ are independent generalized coordinates, and $\mathbf{q}$ has been reordered to permit the simple partitioning shown in Eq. 5. Recall that the process of selecting dependent generalized coordinates $\mathbf{u}$ assures that the associated sub-Jacobian $\mathbf{\Phi_u}$ is nonsingular; i.e.,

$$|\mathbf{\Phi_u}| \neq 0 \tag{6}$$

The implicit function theorem assures that there exists a twice differentiable function **h** of **v** and **t** such that

$$\mathbf{u} = \mathbf{h}(\mathbf{v}, t) \tag{7}$$

is the solution of Eq. 1 for **u** as a function of **v**; i.e.,

$$\mathbf{\Phi}(\mathbf{h}(\mathbf{v}, t), \mathbf{v}, t) = \mathbf{0} \tag{8}$$

for arbitrary values of **v** and t.

To analyze the equations of motion of Eq. 2, they may be reordered and partitioned, according to the decomposition of **q** into **u** and **v**, as

$$\begin{aligned} \mathbf{M}^{uu}\ddot{\mathbf{u}} + \mathbf{M}^{uv}\ddot{\mathbf{v}} + \mathbf{\Phi}_u^T\boldsymbol{\lambda} &= \mathbf{Q}^{Au} \\ \mathbf{M}^{vu}\ddot{\mathbf{u}} + \mathbf{M}^{vv}\ddot{\mathbf{v}} + \mathbf{\Phi}_v^T\boldsymbol{\lambda} &= \mathbf{Q}^{Av} \\ \mathbf{\Phi}_u\ddot{\mathbf{u}} + \mathbf{\Phi}_v\ddot{\mathbf{v}} &= \boldsymbol{\gamma} \end{aligned} \tag{9}$$

where the mass matrices in the first two equations are submatrices of **M** and the vector functions on the right are a partitioning of the generalized applied force vector $\mathbf{Q}^A$. Similarly, the velocity equation of Eq. 3 may be written in the form

$$\mathbf{\Phi}_u\dot{\mathbf{u}} + \mathbf{\Phi}_v\dot{\mathbf{v}} = \boldsymbol{\nu} \tag{10}$$

For purposes of theoretical analysis, Eq. 7 may be used to write all expressions that involve the dependent generalized coordinates **u** as functions of the independent generalized coordinates **v** and time. Therefore, all terms in Eqs. 9 and 10 that depend on **u** may be written as functions of **v**. Since the coefficient matrix of $\dot{\mathbf{u}}$ in Eq. 10 is nonsingular, $\dot{\mathbf{u}}$ may be written as

$$\dot{\mathbf{u}} = \mathbf{\Phi}_u^{-1}[\boldsymbol{\nu} - \mathbf{\Phi}_v\dot{\mathbf{v}}] \tag{11}$$

which is a function of only **v** and $\dot{\mathbf{v}}$. Similarly, the third of Eqs. 9 may be solved for $\ddot{\mathbf{u}}$, to obtain

$$\ddot{\mathbf{u}} = \mathbf{\Phi}_u^{-1}[\boldsymbol{\gamma} - \mathbf{\Phi}_v\ddot{\mathbf{v}}] \tag{12}$$

which, after using Eqs. 7 and 11, is a function of only **v**, $\dot{\mathbf{v}}$, and $\ddot{\mathbf{v}}$.

Since the coefficient matrix of $\boldsymbol{\lambda}$ in the first of Eqs. 9 is nonsingular, this equation may be solved for $\boldsymbol{\lambda}$ to obtain

$$\boldsymbol{\lambda} = (\boldsymbol{\Phi}_u^{-1})^T [Q^{Au}(v, \dot{v}, t) - M^{uv}\ddot{v} - M^{uu}\ddot{u}] \tag{13}$$

Substituting this result and Eq. 12 into the second of Eqs. 9 yields

$$\hat{M}(v, t)\ddot{v} = \hat{Q}(v, \dot{v}, t) \tag{14}$$

where

$$\begin{aligned} \hat{M} &= M^{vv} - M^{vu}\boldsymbol{\Phi}_u^{-1}\boldsymbol{\Phi}_v - \boldsymbol{\Phi}_v^T(\boldsymbol{\Phi}_u^{-1})^T[M^{uv} - M^{uu}\boldsymbol{\Phi}_u^{-1}\boldsymbol{\Phi}_v] \\ \hat{Q} &= Q^{Av} - M^{vu}\boldsymbol{\Phi}_u^{-1}\boldsymbol{\gamma} - \boldsymbol{\Phi}_v^T(\boldsymbol{\Phi}_u^{-1})^T[Q^{Au} - M^{uu}\boldsymbol{\Phi}_u^{-1}\boldsymbol{\gamma}] \end{aligned} \tag{15}$$

Although the coefficient matrix $\hat{M}$ and the vector $\hat{Q}$ are extraordinarily complicated functions of their arguments, Eq. 14 is a differential equation of motion for the system in terms of the independent generalized coordinates $\mathbf{v}$. This differential equation can be integrated numerically by any valid method, to compute the time history of the independent generalized coordinates. Dependent generalized coordinates and their velocities and accelerations are then recovered from Eqs. 1, 3, and 4. This process can be reliably continued as long as the sub-Jacobian $\boldsymbol{\Phi}_{\mathbf{u}}$ is well-conditioned, which implies that Eq. 6 holds. This result yields a theoretical algorithm that is valid and, more important, forms the foundation for creating practical and implementable numerical integration algorithms.

In order to integrate the second order differential equations of Eq. 14 for $\mathbf{v}(t)$, it is conventional to introduce velocity variables that permit reduction of the second order system to a system of first order equations. More specifically, let

$$\mathbf{s} \equiv \dot{\mathbf{v}} \tag{16}$$

then, $\ddot{\mathbf{v}} = \dot{\mathbf{s}}$, which may be substituted into Eq. 14 to obtain

$$\hat{M}(v, t)\dot{s} = \hat{Q}(v, s, t) \tag{17}$$

This equation and the definition of Eq. 16, written in the form of a differential equation,

$$\dot{v} = s \tag{18}$$

forms a system of first-order differential equations of motion in the variables $\mathbf{v}$ and $\mathbf{s}$.

An Explicit DAE Solver

Any explicit ordinary differential equation solver can be used to integrate Eqs. 17 and 18 for **v**(t) and **s**(t), provided initial conditions are specified on **v** and **s** at the initial time t_0. This requires that at each time step $\dot{\mathbf{s}}$ is determined from Eq. 17. This would appear to require that the matrices $\hat{\mathbf{M}}$ and $\hat{\mathbf{Q}}$ be evaluated, which would require a great deal of computation. To avoid this complexity Eq. 2 can be solved for $\ddot{\mathbf{q}} = [\ddot{\mathbf{u}}^T, \ddot{\mathbf{v}}^T]^T = [\ddot{\mathbf{u}}^T, \dot{\mathbf{s}}^T]^T$. In this way $\dot{\mathbf{s}}$ is obtained and $\ddot{\mathbf{u}}$ may be deleted or used to obtain an estimate of $\dot{\mathbf{u}}$ at the next time step.

After $\dot{\mathbf{v}}$ and $\dot{\mathbf{s}}$ are integrated to obtain **v** and **s** at the next time step, **u** & $\dot{\mathbf{u}}$ can be obtained by solving Eqs. 1 and 3. A Newton-Raphson algorithm may be used to solve Eq. 1 for **u**, with **v** fixed. This process can be continued to the final time, or until $\mathbf{\Phi_u}$ becomes ill-conditioned. In the latter case, the generalized coordinates **q** are repartitioned and the process is continued. This algorithm has all the theoretical properties of the explicit ODE solver that is used to integrate $\dot{\mathbf{v}}$ and $\dot{\mathbf{s}}$ [19]. It has been used extensively in the DADS computer code [2] with good results. In case Eqs. 16 and 17 become stiff, which usually occurs only when a pathological model of the mechanical system is used, an implicit stiffly stable algorithm is needed.

A Theoretical Implicit DAE Solver

In order to numerically integrate the system of Eqs. 17 and 18, an implicit, stiffly stable numerical integration algorithm [21] that is based on backward differentiation formulas is introduced, as follows:

$$\dot{\mathbf{v}}_j = \frac{1}{h}\sum_{i=0}^{k} \alpha_i \mathbf{v}_{j-i} \tag{19}$$

$$\dot{\mathbf{s}}_j = \frac{1}{h}\sum_{i=0}^{k} \alpha_i \mathbf{s}_{j-i} \tag{20}$$

where t_j is the jth time step in the numerical integration process, a subscript on a variable denotes that variable evaluated at the associate time step, h is the numerical integration time step, k is the order of the integration algorithm, and α_i are coefficients in the backward differentiation formula.

Substituting the backward differentiation formulas from Eqs. 19 and 20 into Eqs. 17 and 18 yields the implicit numerical integration formulas

$$\frac{1}{h}\hat{M}(v_j, t_j)\sum_{i=0}^{k}\alpha_i \mathbf{s}_{j-i} - \hat{Q}(v_j, \mathbf{s}_j, t_j) = \mathbf{0} \tag{21}$$

$$\frac{1}{h}\sum_{i=0}^{k}\alpha_i v_{j-i} - \mathbf{s}_j = \mathbf{0} \tag{22}$$

which must be solved for the unknowns $\mathbf{v}_j$ and $\mathbf{s}_j$ at time t_j. Note that past state information $\mathbf{v}_{j-i}$ and $\mathbf{s}_{j-i}$, i=1, ..., k, is required to evaluate Eqs. 21 and 22. Since well-known self-starting numerical integration algorithms that generate this information are available [21], this topic will not be addressed here.

Note that Eqs. 21 and 22 comprise $2(n-m)$ equations in $2(n-m)$ variables. These are highly nonlinear equations, so they must be solved by some form of iterative numerical algorithm. Given the complexity of the matrix $\hat{M}$ and vector $\hat{Q}$ of Eq. 15, as functions of $\mathbf{v}$ and $\mathbf{s}$, direct implementation of an iterative algorithm such as Newton's method to solve Eqs. 21 and 22 would be extraordinarily complicated and probably impractical. Thus, Eqs. 21 and 22 should be regarded as a valid, but theoretical, numerical integration algorithm for the DAE of mechanical system dynamics.

A Numerical Implicit DAE Solver

In addition to introducing $\mathbf{s}$ as the time derivative of the independent generalized coordinate $\mathbf{v}$, the dependent velocity $\dot{\mathbf{u}}$ is defined as a new variable

$$w \equiv \dot{u} \tag{23}$$

Noting that $\ddot{u} = \dot{w}$, Eqs. 16 and 23 may be used in Eqs. 9, 1, and 10 to obtain the first order DAE

$$M^{uu}\dot{w} + M^{uv}\dot{\mathbf{s}} + \mathbf{\Phi}_u^T\boldsymbol{\lambda} = Q^{Au} \tag{24}$$

$$M^{vu}\dot{w} + M^{vv}\dot{\mathbf{s}} + \mathbf{\Phi}_v^T\boldsymbol{\lambda} = Q^{Av} \tag{25}$$

$$\mathbf{\Phi}(\mathbf{u}, v, t) = \mathbf{0} \tag{26}$$

$$\mathbf{\Phi}_u w + \mathbf{\Phi}_v \mathbf{s} = \nu \tag{27}$$

$$\mathbf{\Phi}_u \dot{w} + \mathbf{\Phi}_v \dot{\mathbf{s}} = \boldsymbol{\gamma} \tag{28}$$

The basis for the algorithm presented here is use of the backward differentiation formulas of Eqs. 19 and 20 that were employed in the theoretical algorithm and to retain all other variables, specifically $\mathbf{u}_j$, $\mathbf{w}_j$, $\dot{\mathbf{w}}_j$ and $\boldsymbol{\lambda}_j$, as explicit variables in the formulation. This approach is suggested by the theoretical algorithm of the preceding subsection, in which $\mathbf{v}_j$ and $\mathbf{s}_j$ were determined by Eqs. 21 and 22 and the remaining variables were determined by Eqs. 1, 10, and the first and third of Eqs. 9. Substituting the backward differentiation formulas of Eqs. 19 and 20 into Eqs. 24 through 28 and Eq. 16 yields the following implicit DAE integration algorithm:

$$\mathbf{M}^{uu}(\mathbf{u}_j,\mathbf{v}_j,t_j)\,\dot{\mathbf{w}}_j + \frac{1}{h}\,\mathbf{M}^{uv}(\mathbf{u}_j,\mathbf{v}_j,t_j)\sum_{i=0}^{k}\alpha_i\mathbf{s}_{j-i} + \boldsymbol{\Phi}_u^T(\mathbf{u}_j,\mathbf{v}_j,t_j)\boldsymbol{\lambda}_j - \mathbf{Q}^{Au}(\mathbf{u}_j,\mathbf{v}_j,\mathbf{w}_j,\mathbf{s}_j,t_j) = \mathbf{0} \qquad (29)$$

$$\mathbf{M}^{vu}(\mathbf{u}_j,\mathbf{v}_j,t_j)\dot{\mathbf{w}}_j + \frac{1}{h}\,\mathbf{M}^{vv}(\mathbf{u}_j,\mathbf{v}_j,t_j)\sum_{i=0}^{k}\alpha_i\,\mathbf{s}_{j-i} + \boldsymbol{\Phi}_v^T(\mathbf{u}_j,\mathbf{v}_j,t_j)\boldsymbol{\lambda}_j - \mathbf{Q}^{Au}(\mathbf{u}_j,\mathbf{v}_j,\mathbf{w}_j,\mathbf{s}_j,t_j) = \mathbf{0} \qquad (30)$$

$$\boldsymbol{\Phi}(\mathbf{u}_j,\mathbf{v}_j,t_j) = \mathbf{0} \qquad (31)$$

$$\boldsymbol{\Phi}_u(\mathbf{u}_j,\mathbf{v}_j,t_j)\,\mathbf{w}_j + \boldsymbol{\Phi}_v(\mathbf{u}_j,\mathbf{v}_j,t_j)\,\mathbf{s}_j - \boldsymbol{\nu}(\mathbf{u}_j,\mathbf{v}_j,t_j) = \mathbf{0} \qquad (32)$$

$$\boldsymbol{\Phi}_u(\mathbf{u}_j,\mathbf{v}_j,t_j)\,\dot{\mathbf{w}}_j + \frac{1}{h}\,\boldsymbol{\Phi}_v(\mathbf{u}_j,\mathbf{v}_j,t_j)\sum_{i=0}^{k}\alpha_i\,\mathbf{s}_{j-i} - \boldsymbol{\gamma}(\mathbf{u}_j,\mathbf{v}_j,\mathbf{w}_j,\mathbf{s}_j,t_j) = \mathbf{0} \qquad (33)$$

$$\frac{1}{h}\sum_{i=0}^{k}\alpha_i\mathbf{v}_{j-i} - \mathbf{s}_j = \mathbf{0} \qquad (34)$$

This system of 2n + 2m equations, in the same number of variables, is nonlinear and must be solved using iterative computational methods. It should be noted that this algorithm explicitly satisfies all kinematic relations and the equations of motion of the constrained mechanical system.

To see that this algorithm is in fact valid, it is to be shown that it yields the same solution as the theoretical algorithm of Eqs. 21 and 22. To show this, note first that Eqs. 34 and 22 are identical. Next, note that Eqs. 31 and 32 imply that $\mathbf{u}_j = \mathbf{h}(\mathbf{v}_j, t_j)$ and

$$\mathbf{w}_j = \boldsymbol{\Phi}_u^{-1}(\boldsymbol{\nu}_j - \boldsymbol{\Phi}_v\mathbf{s}_j) \qquad (35)$$

Similarly, Eq. 33 implies that

$$\dot{w}_j = \Phi_u^{-1}\left(\gamma_j - \frac{1}{h}\Phi_v \sum_{i=0}^{k} \alpha_i s_{j-i}\right) \tag{36}$$

and Eq. 29 yields

$$\lambda_j = (\Phi_u^{-1})^T \left\{ Q^{Au} - M^{uu}\dot{w}_j - \frac{1}{h} M^{uv} \sum_{i=0}^{k} \alpha_i s_{j-i} \right\} \tag{37}$$

Substituting Eqs. 36 and 37 into Eq. 30 yields

$$\frac{1}{h}\left\{ M^{vv} - M^{vu}\Phi_u^{-1}\Phi_v + (\Phi_u^{-1}\Phi_v)^T M^{uu}\Phi_u^{-1}\Phi_v - (\Phi_u^{-1}\Phi_v)^T M^{uv} \right\} \sum_{i=0}^{k} \alpha_i s_{n-1}$$

$$= Q^{Av} - (\Phi_u^{-1}\Phi_v)^T Q^{Au} + (\Phi_u^{-1}\Phi_v)^T M^{uu}\Phi_u^{-1}\gamma_n - M^{vu}\Phi_u^{-1}\gamma_n \tag{38}$$

Noting the definitions of Eq. 15, this is just Eq. 14. Thus, the solution obtained with this algorithm is identical to the solution of the theoretical algorithm, which was shown to be valid in the preceding section. This verifies the validity of the computational algorithm.

In addition to being theoretically valid, the implicit numerical algorithm defined by Eqs. 29 through 34 is also computationally practical. While it represents a rather large system of equations, application of the Newton-Raphson method for its solution will yield a highly sparse system of equations, whose coefficient matrix and right side are computable from known kinematic and kinetic information. The algorithm is, therefore, well-suited to computer automation.

Direct Application of Backward Differentiation Formulas To DAE

In order to compare a more conventional application of backward differentiation formulas to DAE [16], the full set of generalized velocities may be defined as a new variable,

$$\mathbf{a} = \dot{\mathbf{q}} \tag{39}$$

Equations 1 and 2, in first-order form, are then

$$M\dot{\mathbf{a}} + \Phi_q{}^T \lambda = Q^A \tag{40}$$

$$\dot{\mathbf{q}} = \mathbf{a} \tag{41}$$

$$\mathbf{\Phi}(\mathbf{q}, t) = \mathbf{0} \tag{42}$$

Applying backward differentiation formulas to both $\dot{\mathbf{q}}$ and $\dot{\mathbf{a}}$ at time t_j yields

$$\dot{\mathbf{q}}_j = \frac{1}{h}\sum_{i=0}^{k} \alpha_i \mathbf{q}_{j-1} \tag{43}$$

$$\dot{\mathbf{a}}_j = \frac{1}{h}\sum_{i=0}^{k} \alpha_i \mathbf{a}_{j-1} \tag{44}$$

Substituting these relations in Eqs. 40 through 42, evaluated at t_j, yields

$$\frac{1}{h}\mathbf{M}(\mathbf{q}_j)\sum_{i=0}^{k} \alpha_i \mathbf{a}_{j-1} + \mathbf{\Phi}_{\mathbf{q}}^{T}(\mathbf{q}_j, t_j)\boldsymbol{\lambda}_j - \mathbf{Q}^{A}(\mathbf{q}_j, \mathbf{a}_j, t_j) = \mathbf{0} \tag{45}$$

$$\frac{1}{h}\sum_{i=0}^{k} \alpha_i \mathbf{q}_{j-1} - \mathbf{a}_j = \mathbf{0} \tag{46}$$

$$\mathbf{\Phi}(\mathbf{q}_j, t_j) = \mathbf{0} \tag{47}$$

This alternate approach to direct integration of DAE has been shown by Petzold and coworkers [18] to have potential difficulties regarding stability and convergence. This direct formulation is included here for purposes of numerical comparison with the generalized coordinate partitioning implicit DAE solver proposed in this paper.

An Elementary Slider-Crank Example

In order to study numerical properties of the preceding algorithms, consider the elementary model of a slider-crank mechanism shown in Fig. 1, where the units of length are meters. The crank (body 1) rotates without friction about an axis perpendicular to the x-y plane. The connecting rod (body 2) is constrained so that its center point slides without friction along the x axis. The polar moments of inertia of bodies 1 and 2 are 1.0 and 2.0 kg·m^2, respectively, and the mass of body 2 is 2.0 kg. A constant torque T = 2n·m is applied to body 1. The initial condition is $\phi_1 = \pi/4$, $\phi_2 = -.36136$, $x_2 = 2.5779$, and zero velocity.

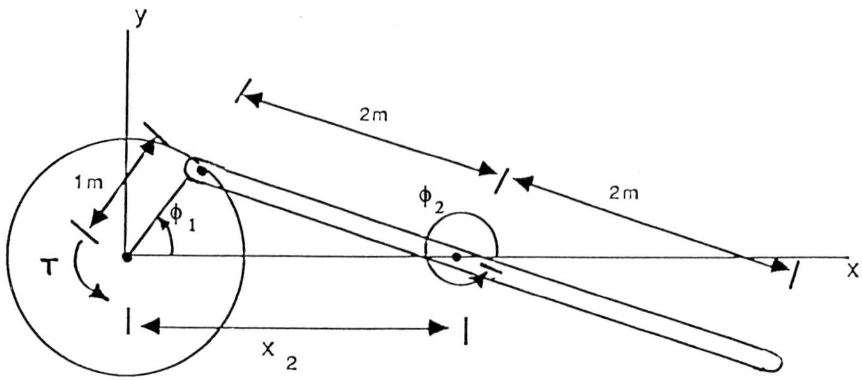

Figure 1. Elementary Slider-Crank

In this elementary example, three generalized coordinates shown in Fig. 1 may be defined as

$$\mathbf{q} = [\phi_1, x_2, \phi_2]^T \tag{48}$$

The kinematic constraint equations that define the revolute joint between the crank and connecting rod, whose center must slide along the x-axis, are

$$\boldsymbol{\Phi}(\mathbf{q},t) = \begin{bmatrix} \cos\phi_1 + 2\cos\phi_2 - x_2 \\ \sin\phi_1 + 2\sin\phi_2 \end{bmatrix} = \mathbf{0} \tag{49}$$

The Jacobian of this constraint with respect to the full set of generalized coordinates is

$$\boldsymbol{\Phi}_{\mathbf{q}} = \begin{bmatrix} -\sin\phi_1 & -1 & -2\sin\phi_2 \\ \cos\phi_1 & 0 & 2\cos\phi_2 \end{bmatrix} \tag{50}$$

Since $\cos\phi_2$ can never be zero, the 2×2 sub-Jacobian that consists of the last two columns of the matrix of Eq. 50 is always nonsingular. Thus, the variables x_2 and ϕ_2 may be chosen as dependent, leaving ϕ_1 as independent; i.e., the following partitioning may be employed:

$$\mathbf{u} = [x_2, \phi_2]^T$$
$$v = \phi_1 \quad (51)$$

For use in the implicit numerical integration algorithm, the sub-Jacobians with respect to dependent and independent variables are thus

$$\mathbf{\Phi}_u = \begin{bmatrix} -1 & -2\sin\phi_2 \\ 0 & 2\cos\phi_2 \end{bmatrix} \quad (52)$$

$$\mathbf{\Phi}_v = \begin{bmatrix} -\sin\phi_1 \\ \cos\phi_1 \end{bmatrix} \quad (53)$$

For this elementary example, the mass matrix and applied generalized force vector are

$$M = \begin{bmatrix} J_1 & 0 & 0 \\ 0 & M_2 & 0 \\ 0 & 0 & J_2 \end{bmatrix} \quad (54)$$

$$\mathbf{Q}^A = [T, 0, 0]^T \quad (55)$$

The right sides of the velocity and acceleration equations of Eqs. 3 and 4 are

$$\mathbf{v} = 0$$
$$\boldsymbol{\gamma} = \begin{bmatrix} \cos\phi_1\dot{\phi}_1^2 + 2\cos\phi_2\dot{\phi}_2^2 \\ \sin\phi_1\dot{\phi}_1^2 + 2\sin\phi_2\dot{\phi}_2^2 \end{bmatrix} \quad (56)$$

For application of the first-order implicit DAE solver, new variables are defined as

$$s = \dot{\phi}_1$$
$$w = [\dot{x}_2, \dot{\phi}_2]^T \quad (57)$$

In terms of these variables and the preceding matrices, Eqs. 29 through 34 are

$$\begin{bmatrix} m_2 & 0 \\ 0 & J_2 \end{bmatrix} \dot{w}_j + \begin{bmatrix} -1 & 0 \\ -2\sin\phi_{2_j} & -2\cos\phi_{2_j} \end{bmatrix} \lambda_j = \mathbf{0}$$

$$\frac{1}{h} J_1 \sum_{i=0}^{k} \alpha_i s_{j-i} + \begin{bmatrix} -\sin\phi_j & \cos\phi_j \end{bmatrix} \lambda_j - T = 0$$

$$\begin{bmatrix} \cos\phi_j + 2\cos\phi_{2_j} - x_{2_j} \\ \sin_{1_j} + 2\sin\phi_{2_j} \end{bmatrix} = \mathbf{0}$$

$$\begin{bmatrix} -1 & -2\sin\phi_{2_j} \\ 0 & 2\cos\phi_{2_j} \end{bmatrix} w_j + \begin{bmatrix} -\sin\phi_{1_j} \\ \cos\phi_{1_j} \end{bmatrix} s_j = \mathbf{0} \tag{58}$$

$$\begin{bmatrix} -1 & -2\sin\phi_{2_j} \\ 0 & 2\cos\phi_{2_j} \end{bmatrix} \dot{w}_j + \frac{1}{h} \begin{bmatrix} -\sin\phi_{1_j} \\ \cos\phi_{1_j} \end{bmatrix} \sum_{i=0}^{k} \alpha_i s_{j-i} - \begin{bmatrix} \cos\phi_{1_j} s_j^2 + 2\cos\phi_{2_j} w_{2_j}^2 \\ \sin\phi_{1_j} s_j^2 + 2\sin\phi_{2_j} w_{2_j}^2 \end{bmatrix} = \mathbf{0}$$

$$\frac{1}{h} \sum_{i=0}^{k} \alpha_i \phi_{1_{j-1}} - s_j = 0$$

A simple code that implements the implicit algorithm, using second order backward differentiation formulas with a constant stepsize, is used to compute the numerical solution of Eq. 58. As the starting point for Newton iteration, the code utilizes a first order polynomial extrapolation. Newton iteration is terminated when the Euclidean norm of the residual of the nonlinear system is less than $5h^2$. To estimate the accuracy of the numerical solutions, accurate numerical results for the same model were obtained with DADS [2] and are denoted as $\mathbf{q}^*$. The Euclidean norm of the global error and the average number of the Newton iterations are given at times t = 1.0, 3.0, and 5.0 in Table 1. Results are given for four values of h. The rate of convergence can be estimated by computing the ratio t of the error in the solution obtained with stepsize h and the error in the solution obtained with stepsize $\frac{h}{2}$. Here, the rate of convergence is of the order of two, since $t \geq 1.5$. Note that a very small number of Newton iterations are required.

In order to compare results obtained with the implicit algorithm and the more conventional direct application of backward differentiation formulas to DAE, Eqs. 45 through 47, for the elementary slider-crank example, are

Table 1. Error in Solution from Implicit Algorithm

Stepsize		$h = 10^{-2}$	$h = 5\times10^{-3}$	$h = 2.5 \times 10^{-3}$	$h = 10^{-3}$
	$t = 1.5$	2.28×10^{-5}	6.91×10^{-6}	4.5×10^{-6}	4.4×10^{-6}
$\lVert \mathbf{q} - \mathbf{q}^* \rVert_2$	$t = 3.5$	3.76×10^{-4}	9.53×10^{-5}	2.33×10^{-5}	3.31×10^{-6}
	$t = 5.0$	5.45×10^{-4}	1.44×10^{-4}	4.17×10^{-5}	1.55×10^{-5}
	$t = 1.5$	6.76×10^{-5}	1.74×10^{-5}	4.70×10^{-6}	1.12×10^{-6}
$\lVert \dot{\mathbf{q}} - \dot{\mathbf{q}}^* \rVert_2$	$t = 3.5$	1.30×10^{-3}	3.32×10^{-4}	8.45×10^{-5}	1.50×10^{-5}
	$t = 5.0$	2.01×10^{-3}	5.06×10^{-4}	1.23×10^{-4}	1.55×10^{-5}
Average No.	$t \le 1.5$	1	1	1	1
of Newton	$t \le 3.5$	1.5	1.5	1.5	1.5
Iterations	$t \le 5.0$	1.75	1.75	1.75	1.75

$$
\begin{aligned}
&\frac{1}{h}\begin{bmatrix} J_1 & 0 & 0 \\ 0 & m_2 & 0 \\ 0 & 0 & J_2 \end{bmatrix}\sum_{i=0}^{k} \alpha_1 \mathbf{a}_{j-1} + \begin{bmatrix} -\sin\phi_{1_j} & \cos\phi_{1_j} \\ -1 & 0 \\ -2\sin\phi_{2_j} & 2\cos\phi_{2_j} \end{bmatrix}\boldsymbol{\lambda}_j - \begin{bmatrix} T \\ 0 \\ 0 \end{bmatrix} = \mathbf{0} \\
&\frac{1}{h}\sum_{i=1}^{k} \alpha_i \mathbf{q}_{j-1} - \mathbf{a}_j = \mathbf{0} \qquad (59) \\
&\begin{bmatrix} \cos\phi_{1_j} + 2\cos\phi_{2_j} - x_{2_j} \\ \sin\phi_{1_j} + 2\sin\phi_{2_j} \end{bmatrix} = \mathbf{0}
\end{aligned}
$$

The same second order backward differentiation formula with constant stepsize was implemented to compute the numerical solution of the nonlinear system of Eq. 59. The same Newton iteration process was used to solve this system. Numerical results given in Table 2 indicate the same order of the rate of convergence as the previous method. However, the Newton iteration process diverges near time $t = 3.55$, when the peak acceleration occurs, for all four stepsizes. Note also that the number of Newton iterations is much larger than for the implicit algorithm.

Table 2. Error in Solution for Direct BDF Method

Stepsize		$h = 10^{-2}$	$h = 5\times10^{-3}$	$h = 2.5\times10^{-3}$	$h = 10^{-3}$
	$t = 1.5$	2.8×10^{-5}	4.89×10^{-6}	4.51×10^{-6}	4.43×10^{-6}
$\lVert \mathbf{q} - \mathbf{q}^* \rVert_2$	$t = 3.0$	9.65×10^{-4}	2.55×10^{-4}	6.11×10^{-5}	8.94×10^{-6}
	$t = 3.5$	1.36×10^{-3}	3.56×10^{-4}	8.88×10^{-5}	2.08×10^{-5}
	$t = 1.5$	2.08×10^{-4}	1.26×10^{-5}	2.59×10^{-6}	7.54×10^{-7}
$\lVert \dot{\mathbf{q}} - \dot{\mathbf{q}}^* \rVert_2$	$t = 3.0$	1.75×10^{-3}	4.33×10^{-4}	1.09×10^{-4}	1.50×10^{-5}
	$t = 3.5$	4.77×10^{-3}	8.29×10^{-4}	1.96×10^{-4}	3.37×10^{-5}
Average No.	$t \le 1.5$	4.3	5	5	7
of Newton	$t \le 3.0$	3.7	4.8	4.4	6
Iterations	$t \le 3.5$	4.5	5.2	5	10

Figures 2 and 3 show the error in the numerical solutions with the same stepsize $h = 2.5 \times 10^{-3}$ sec. It is easy to see the instability of the direct backward differentiation formula method.

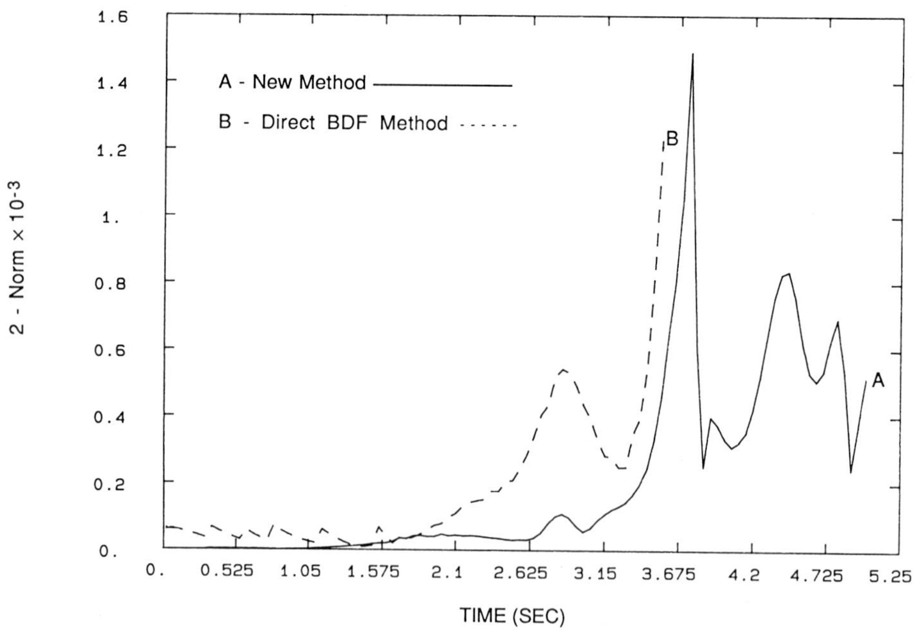

Figure 2. Velocity Error, $h = 2.5 \times 10^{-3}$ Sec.

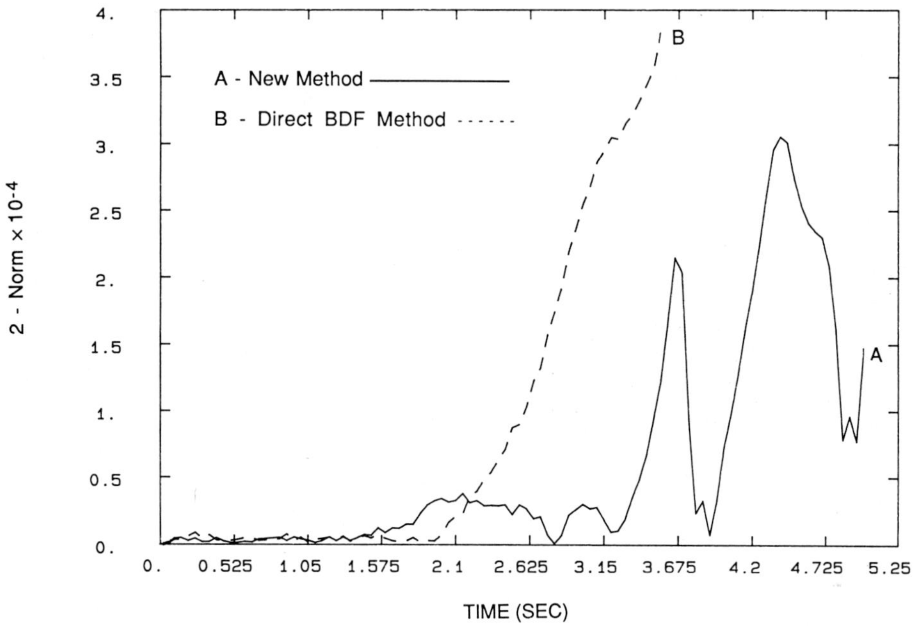

Figure 3. Position Error, $h = 2.5 \times 10^{-3}$ Sec.

Conclusions

As shown theoretically in this paper, the implicit generalized coordinate partitioning numerical integration algorithm is equivalent to solving the reduced differential equation of Eq. 14 by a stiffly stable solver. Numerical results presented verify this theory and show that Newton iteration with the new implicit method converges very rapidly. The direct backward differentiation method, in contrast, requires many Newton iterations to converge. In fact, as suggested by the theory of DAE [15,18], it diverges for even the elementary slider-crank example studied in this paper.

References

1. ADAMS users' guide: Mechanical Dynamics, Inc., 555 South Forest, Ann Arbor, Mich: USA 1981.
2. DADS users' manual: Rev. 4.0, Computer Aided Design Software, Inc., Oakdale, Iowa: USA 1987.
3. Roberson, R.E.: The path matrix of a graph, its construction and its use in evaluating certain products: Computer Methods in Applied Mechanics and Engineering, Vol. 24: pp. 47-56 1984.
4. Wittenburg, J.: Dynamics of systems of rigid bodies B.G. Teubner: Stuttgart, 1977.
5. Wittenburg, J., and Wolz, U.: Mesa Verde: A symbolic program for nonlinear articulated rigid body dynamics: ASME: Paper No. 85-DET-141 1985.
6. Bae, D.S., Hwang, R.S., and Haug, E.J.: A recursive formulation for real-time dynamic simulation: Advances in Design Automation ASME: New York, NY, USA pp. 499-508 1988.
7. Hwang, R.S., Bae, D.S., Haug, E.J., and Kuhl, J.G.: Parallel processing for real-time dynamic system simulation: Advances in Design Automation ASME: New York, NY, USA pp. 509-518 1988.
8. Petzold, L.: Differential/algebraic equations are not ODEs: SIAM J. Sci. Stat. Comput. Vol. 3: No. 3: pp. 367-384 1982.
9. Gear, C.W., and Petzold, L.R.: ODE methods for the solution of differential/algebraic systems: SIAM J. Num. Anal. Vol. 21: No. 4: pp. 716-728 1984.
10. Wehage, R.A., and Haug, E.J.: Generalized coordinates partitioning for dimension reduction in analysis of constrained dynamic system: J. of Mechanical Design Vol. 104: pp. 247-255 1982.
11. Mani, N.K., and Haug, E.J.: Singular value decomposition for dynamic system design sensitivity analysis: Engineering with Computers Vol. 1: pp. 103-109 1985.
12. Liang, C.G., and Lance, G.M.: A differentiable null space method for constrained dynamic analysis J. of Mechanisms, Transmissions, and Automation in Design, Vol. 109: pp. 405-411 1987.
13. Park, T.: A hybrid constraint stabilization-generalized coordinate partitioning method for machine dynamics: J. of Mechanisms, Transmissions, and Automation in Design Vol. 108: No. 2: pp. 211-216 1986.
14. Brenan, K.E., Campbell, S.L., and Petzold, L.R.: Numerical solution of initial-value problems in differential-algebraic equations North-Holland: New York, NY, USA 1989.
15. Fuhrer, C.: On the description of constrained mechanical systems by differential/algebraic equations German Aerospace Research Establishment (DFVLR): Institute for Flight System Dynamics: 1987.
16. Chace, M.A.: Methods and experience in computer aided design of large-displacement mechanical systems: (E.J. Haug, ed.). NATO ASI: Vol. F9: Computer Aided Analysis and Optimization of Mechanical System Dynamics, Berlin-Heidelberg: Springer-Verlag 1984.
17. Baumgarte, J.: "Stabilization of constraints and integrals of motion in dynamical systems: Computer Methods in Applied Mechanics and Engineering, Vol. 1: pp. 1-16 1972
18. Petzold, L., and Lötstedt, P.: Numerical solution of nonlinear differential equations with algebraic constraints. II: Practical Implementations SIAM J. Sci. Stat. Comput.: Vol. 7: pp. 720-733 1986.
19. Haug, E.J.: Computer aided kinematics and dynamics of mechanical systems, Vol I: basic methods: Allyn and Bacon: Boston, MA USA 1989.
20. Strang, G.: Linear algebra and its applications, 2nd ed.: Academic Press: New York, NY USA 1980.
21. Gear, G.W.: Numerical initial value problems in ordinary differential equations: Prentice-Hall: New York, NY USA 1969.

An Introduction to Numerical Methods for ODEs and DAEs

C. W. Gear*
Department of Computer Science
University of Illinois at Urbana-Champaign

Abstract

Many standard implicit methods such as multistep and Runge-Kutta can be applied to both Ordinary Differential Equations (ODEs) and Differential Algebraic Equations (DAEs). This talk first compares and contrasts their ability to handle the two types of problems. Depending on the nature of the problem, methods that are effective for ODEs may break down for DAEs. Not all DAEs are *solvable* (that is, have a smooth solution). Even those that are solvable may have pathological behavior.

A measure of the "complexity " of a DAE is its *index*. In fact, three types of index are defined in the literature. One, called the *local index*, does not seem to have any bearing on the nature of the problem unless either it is small (zero or one) or the problem has a special structure, in which case it is the same as the second index, called the *global index* or usually just the *index*. This second one probably should be called the *differential index*. It determines the important properties of the structure of the DAE. Essentially it is the number of times that the DAE must be differentiated to determine an ODE satisfied by all components of any solution of the system. (This is called the *underlying ODE*.) The third index, which should probably be called the *perturbation index*, determines the effect of perturbations to the DAE on its solution.

In our current understanding, the differential index (or just "index" below) seems to determine the difficulty of numerical integration. We cannot directly solve general problems whose index exceeds one. (By directly we mean without resort to symbolic differentiation or other specialized manipulation techniques that recognize a particular structure of the system.) However, for problems with special structure (see Petzold and Fuhrer in this conference) we can handle problems of higher index. Problems with a structure which arises very commonly in simulation and control, and is now called the *Hessenberg form*, were first treated by Petzold and Lotstedt[18] and by Brenan[1] who showed that fixed step size BDF methods solved problems through index three. That has been extended, and recently Keiper and Gear[9] have shown that variable step size generalized BDF methods of order $m-1$ solve index m problems for $m \leq 4$, and conjecture that the result is also true for larger m. (Numerical evidence suggests it is also true for $m = 5$.) However, the direct solution of high

*Work supported in part by US DOE under grant DOE DEFG02-87ER25026 and by NSF under grant DMS 87-03226

NATO ASI Series, Vol. F 69
Real-Time Integration Methods for Mechanical System Simulation
Edited by E. J. Haug and R. C. Deyo

index problems is probably not practical because of the impact of numerical perturbations. Roundoff or iteration errors of size ϵ in the computation cause errors in the solution of size ϵh^{-p}, where h is the step size used and p is the perturbation index. Since h must be small to control the truncation error in the integrator, a large p will cause serious problems unless very high precision is used. It has been shown that the perturbation index is either d or $d-1$ where d is the differential index, hence a large d will also cause numerical difficulties.

1 Introduction

An initial value problem in ODEs takes the form

$$y' = f(y), \qquad y(0) = y_0, \tag{1}$$

whereas a DAE takes the form

$$F(y', y) = 0, \qquad B(y'(0), y(0)) = 0. \tag{2}$$

Clearly, (1) is a special case of (2). If $F_{y'}$ is everywhere non singular (or non singular in a region near the solution), (2) is called an implicit ODE, and, in principal, it can be inverted into form (1). In practice, unless this inversion is simple, it is easier to deal with (2) directly.

The theories of ODEs and ODE methods are well understood. Methods such as Runge-Kutta and multistep converge under relatively weak assumptions–assumptions that are not much stronger than those needed for existence and uniqueness of solutions to the ODE itself (e.g., Lipschitz continuity). Most codes for ODEs obtain their knowledge of the ODE via a module (or subroutine) that computes the value of f in (1) for any given value of y. These codes can also be used directly for DAEs if this module can compute y' given y in (2). Clearly that requires $F_{y'}$ to be non singular. This is the essence of a proof that DAEs which are implicit ODEs can be solved by any method. However, if $F_{y'}$ is singular, the problem is no longer an implicit ODE and becomes more challenging.

ODE methods are characterized as *explicit* or *implicit*. An explicit method takes the form

$$y_n = \sum [\alpha_m y_m + h\beta_m y'_m], \tag{3}$$

where the sum is taken over previously computed values, whereas an implicit method usually takes the form

$$y_n = \Sigma_n + h\beta_n f(y_n), \tag{4}$$

where Σ_n is a sum similar to the right-hand side of (3). Here, the y_n are computed values of y at mesh or non-mesh points, depending on the type of code and method. (Implicit Runge-Kutta methods and their extensions may require y_n to be defined as a vector of values and β_n to be a matrix to use this notation.) The code may use an iterative method for the solution of (4), but it does this by evaluations of f for various values of y. Either explicit or implicit methods can be used for implicit ODEs as described above since (2) provides a recipe for computing the values of f needed by the code when $F_{y'}$ is non singular.

When $F_{y'}$ is singular, we can no longer compute y' from (2) given y so the above approach cannot be used. However, an alternate statement of the implicit method if β_n is non singular (4) is

$$y'_n = \frac{1}{h}[\beta_n]^{-1}[y_n - \Sigma_n]$$

which can be substituted in (2) to get

$$F(\frac{1}{h}[\beta_n]^{-1}[y_n - \Sigma_n], y_n) = 0 \tag{5}$$

which is an equation for y_n with a solution provided that $h\beta_n F_y + F_{y'}$ is non singular.

The existence of a solution to (5) does not either guarantee a solution to the original DAE, or, if that DAE has a solution, that the numerical solution converges to it as h approaches zero. Unlike ODEs, we need much more information about the DAE before we know whether there are solutions and what types of methods, if any, will compute them.

Consider the simple system

$$y' + \eta z' - z = 0, \tag{6}$$

$$y + \gamma z - t = 0. \tag{7}$$

Clearly, any initial value must satisfy (7). First let η and γ be constants with $\eta \neq \gamma$ and $\gamma \neq 0$. Then the system has solutions through any point lying on the line (7) for a given value of t, so a single initial value, say $y(0)$, is sufficient to determine the unique solution

$$y(t) = t - \gamma + [\gamma + y(0)]e^{-t/(\gamma-\eta)} \tag{8}$$

$$z(t) = (t - y(t))/\gamma. \tag{9}$$

One initial value is necessary to determine a unique solution.

However, if $\gamma = \eta$ in (6) and (7), the nature of the equations changes. By differentiating (7) and substituting in (6) we see that $z = 1$ is determined uniquely. Then, (7) specifies y to be $t - \gamma$, so no initial conditions are required for y or z. Both of these cases can be solved by a number of methods, even by the simple backward Euler method.

If we now chose $\eta = \gamma = \mu t$, $\mu \neq 1$, to get a non-constant coefficient problem, we still do not need any initial values to find the sole solution $z = (1+\mu)^{-1}$, $y = t - \mu(1+\mu^{-1})t$, but this problem cannot be solved by simple methods such as BDF for many values of μ (see [10]).

The purpose of this paper is to give a general introduction to the difficulties that DAEs present beyond ODEs. Many books are available on ODE methods (e.g. [3], [5], [12], and [14]). The best source for further information on DAEs is the new book by Brenan et al[2].

2 Local and Differential Indices

One of the few classes of DAEs for which we can make very precise statements about the nature of solutions are the linear, constant coefficient problems

$$Ay' + By = g(t). \tag{10}$$

For these, there exists a family of solutions[19] if the matrix pencil[4] (A, B) is non singular that is, if $\det(A + \lambda B)$ is non singular for all but a finite set of values of λ (the generalized eigenvalues). In this case, no two solutions pass through any point, so initial values uniquely determine a solution provided that those values lie on one of the solution family (although not all points lie on a solution if A is singular).

A DAE is characterized by its *index*. The word "index" was adopted from the *index of nilpotency* of a matrix pencil. For (10) this quantity determines the structure of the problem. If A or B in (10) are time dependent, the index of nilpotency of the pencil $(A(t), B(t))$ at any time t is called the *local index*. If we have the nonlinear problem (2), then the local index is the that of the pencil $(F_{y'}, F_y)$. However, the local index does not necessarily determine the structure of the problem.

A DAE can be thought of as a system of differential equations coupled with a system of nonlinear ("algebraic") equations. The latter define a manifold which contains the solution. The important sub class, the *semi-explicit* DAEs, illustrate this clearly. A semi-explicit system can be written as

$$y' = f(y, z), \tag{11}$$

$$g(y, z) = 0. \tag{12}$$

The solution clearly lies in the manifold defined by (12). If g_z is non singular, (12) can be solved for $z = z(y)$ and then $y' = f(y, z(y))$ is an ODE for y whose solution determines the trajectory $(y, z(y))$ in the manifold. Initial conditions are needed for $y(0)$ only. Note that in this case, one differentiation of (12) leads to

$$z' = -[g_z]^{-1} g_y f(y, z)$$

which, with (11), is an ODE for y and z. In this case, one differentiation yields the underlying ODE satisfied by the solution. The solution of this ODE is constrained to lie on the manifold (12). We say that the *differential index*, d, is one in this case.

If g_z is singular, (12) does not determine z from y, (12) restricts the values of y as well as those of z. To simplify the discussion, we assume that g is independent of z, although that assumption is not necessary. Differentiating (12) and using (11) we get

$$g_y f(y, z) = 0. \tag{13}$$

Eqs (11) and (13) are a new DAE for y and z, but they are not an implicit ODE: they cannot be solved for y' and z'. Rather, (13) specifies another manifold on which the solution must lie. Thus, the differentiation has "uncovered" a second manifold which also contains the solution. If (13) determines z uniquely in terms of y, that is, if $g_y f_z$ is non singular, then we can differentiate (13) to get

$$z' = -[g_y f_z]^{-1}(g_y f_y f(y, z) + g_{yy} f^2(y, z))$$

which, with (11), gives the underlying ODE of the original DAE. In this case, we differentiated twice to get the underlying ODE, and see that the solution is constrained to lie of two manifolds, the original one, (12), and the hidden one, (13). In this case, we say that the differential index is two. Note that the intermediate DAE, (11) and (13), form an index one DAE. One differentiation reduced the index by one.

In general, each differentiation of a DAE reduces the index by one, and each differentiation either "uncovers" another hidden manifold, or finally yields the underlying ODE. The differential index of a DAE is the number of differentiations needed to yield the underlying ODE, or, equivalently, the number of manifolds on which the solution is constrained to lie, including the first, (12).

The differential index is involved in restricting possible initial values as well as determining the structure of the system. Initial values must lie on each of the manifolds; the initial one which is inherent in the original system and hence is automatically satisfied if $y(0)$ and $y'(0)$ satisfy (2), and the hidden ones if the index exceeds one. These are only uncovered by differentiation. In the case of implicit ODEs (which are also called *index zero* ODEs), (2) evaluated at $y(0)$ and $y'(0)$ must be sufficient to determine the initial values of all components of $y(0)$ and $y'(0)$. In the case of an index one DAE, the initial conditions in (2) alone will either be insufficient to determine all of these values, or some of the initial data in B will be redundant when the differential components are considered. If the initial conditions are not redundant, the additional conditions that must be satisfied are found by differentiating the "algebraic" equations and also satisfying them at the initial point. In successively higher-index problems, the initial values must also satisfy the further derivatives of the algebraic components. (It may be possible to approximate these values numerically without formal differentiation[15].)

In certain cases, we can find the initial values of all of the variables, but not all of the first derivatives, with one less differentiation. For example, consider a semi-explicit, index one problem, that is, (11) and (12) with g_z non singular. If initial values are given for $y(0)$, or for any combination of $y(0)$, $y'(0)$, and $z(0)$ such that (11) and (12) evaluated at $t = 0$ uniquely determine $y(0)$, then (12) can be solved for $z(0)$ and (11) provides $y'(0)$. However, $z'(0)$ cannot be found without a differentiation.

A special type of semi-explicit problem is called the *Hessenberg form*. The index k Hessenberg form is

$$\begin{aligned} g(y_1) &= 0 \\ y_1' &= f_1(y_1, y_2) \\ &\vdots \\ y_{k-1}'Z &= f_{k-1}(y_1, y_2, \cdots, y_k) \end{aligned} \tag{14}$$

where $\frac{\partial g}{\partial y_1}\frac{\partial f_1}{\partial y_2}\cdots\frac{\partial f_{k-1}}{\partial y_k}$ is non singular. This form arises frequently in practice. For example, Euler Lagrange equations with constraints are Hessenberg of index three, and many control problems have a Hessenberg structure.

The index *and* the structure of the problem determine how well various numerical methods cope with the problem. We do not know how to solve problems with no special structure given by (2) if the index exceeds one. If the problem is semi explicit, we can solve it if the index is two or less with BDF methods[8]. If the problem has Hessenberg structure, we can solve it if the index, d, is four or less[13] using generalized BDF methods of order $d-1$ or greater. (The k-step Generalized BDF method has the same structure as the k-step BDF method, but the order is not constrained to be k so that zero-stable methods of order greater than 6 exist.) Numerical evidence suggests that higher index equations can also be solved with the same technique. However, we should note that there is a simple transformation between general and semi-explicit forms that changes the index by one, so the results for semi-explicit and general forms are, in a sense, equivalent. The general form (2) can be converted to a semi-explicit form of one index higher by replacing y' with another variable, say x, and appending the definition of y' to get

$$y' = x$$

$$0 = F(x, y).$$

Conversely, the semi-explicit form (11) and (12) can be changed to a general form by replacing the variable z with a new variable x' to get

$$y' - f(y, x')$$

$$g(y, x') = 0.$$

This has index one lower, but the need to compute the derivative of x to get the desired solution, z, obscures an additional differentiation which increases the index.

There has been interest in the reduction of index of DAES since we cannot solve high index DAEs. We have seen that the index can be reduced by differentiation. Unfortunately, this introduces constants of integration which means that the differentiated system has solutions that are not solutions of the original problem. Even if the solution of the problem is started on the correct initial conditions (for which more values are needed after differentiation), the numerical solution may drift off the desired solution, possibly even unboundedly, as shown by example in [16].

Several approaches to combat this problem have been suggested in the literature. They can be illustrated by considering the index 3 Hessenberg DAE

$$g(y_1) = 0,$$

$$y_1' = f_1(y_1, y_2),$$

$$y_2' = f_2(y_1, y_2, y_3).$$

If we differentiate the first equation, substitute for y_1' from the second, and replace the first equation by the result, $g_{y_1} f_1(y_1, y_2) = 0$, we have an index 2 system which may drift off the solution of the original problem. If we include all of the equations, we have an over determined system, but it has a solution, so some have suggested solving the enlarged system of equations. After the derivatives have been approximated numerically, the resulting system may not have a solution, so use of a least-squares technique has been proposed. Marziglod[17] suggests eliminating the redundant equations from the last two (differential) equations, thus reducing the number of derivative terms present. Gear[6] introduces additional algebraic variables as Lagrange multipliers for the original constraint. Since that constraint is satisfied along the solution, these additional variables are zero, and this fact can be used to simplify the solution process[8]. In the reduction above, the second equation is modified to

$$y_1' = f_1(y_1, y_2) + [g_{y_1}]^T \mu$$

where the superscript T indicates transpose, and the new variables are μ. Unfortunately, all of the techniques require differentiation and inversion of equations, so may not be practical for many problems. The lowest index system that will result has index one since there will always be algebraic equations. (Note that even if the original problem were cast in state variable form, algebraic equations would be needed to specify the desired variables in terms of the state variables, so the index would still be one.)

3 Perturbation Index

In a recent report, Hairer et al [11] define an index of DAEs by considering the effect of perturbations of the equations on the solutions. This index, which we will call the perturbation index, p, is one more than the number of derivatives of the perturbation that must appear in any estimate of the bound of the change in the solution. The perturbation index is the smallest value of the integer p such that the difference between the solution of (2) and the solution of the perturbed equation

$$F(z', z, t) = e(t) \tag{15}$$

can be bounded by an expression of the form

$$\max \|z(t) - y(t)\| \le K[\max(\|E(t)\| + \sum_{j=0}^{p-1} \max(\|e^{(j)}(t)\|)], \tag{16}$$

where

$$E(t) = \int_0^t e(\tau) d\tau.$$

(This definition is a slight modification of that given in [11]; this one permits problems to have index zero.) The perturbation index is important because it indicates the effect of numerical errors on the solution. Since we cannot expect to solve (2) exactly, we expect errors, say ϵ, at each step of size of at least unit round off, usually several times that. If the integration step size is h, the $(p-1)$-st derivative of the error will be of order $\epsilon h^{-(p-1)}$, so significant error amplification can be expected. This naturally raises the question of the relationship between the perturbation index and the differential index. (It should be realized that problems can be stated in a form such that either of both indices may not be defined. For example, the problem

$$y^2 = 0$$

has no perturbation index since (16) does not hold for any p. Its differential index is not well defined either, since if we differentiate we get $yy' = 0$ which has the solutions $y = 0$ and $y' = 0$, the first indicating an index 2 problem, the second indicating an index 1 problem.)

3.1 Integral Form DAEs

In [7] it is shown that $d \leq p \leq d + 1$. The two indices are equal when the DAE has an *integral form*, which means that it can be written as

$$F(y', y) = \frac{da(y)}{dt} + b(y) = 0. \tag{17}$$

Note that F is linear in y'. Any linear, constant coefficient problem has integral form, hence semi-explicit and Hessenberg forms are also integral. (It can also be noted that an ODE has integral form, so that the difference between the solution of $y' = f(y)$ and $z' = f(z) + e(t)$ is $O(\int_0^t e(\tau)d\tau)$.)

The converse, that if $p = d$ then the equation has integral form is not true in general. It is true for index 0 problems, and if $p = d$ in higher index problems, the highest index variables present must be in integral form (but the "highest index algebraic variable" is not a well defined concept, so it is difficult to characterize necessary conditions of $p = d$). The problem arise because we can start with two independent DAEs, one of integral form with $p_1 = d_1$ and the other with non integral form with $p_2 = d_2 + 1$ and we have $di_1 > di_2$, the indices for the union of the two systems will have $p = d = d_1$ although the combined system will not have integral form. For example, the DAE

$$(x')^2 = 1$$

$$y = 1$$

has differential index one (because of the second equation) and perturbation index one because of both equations.

3.2 Integral Algebraic Equations

Integral form DAEs are special cases of a more general form we will call *integral algebraic equations*, or IAEs. The intergal form DAE (17) can be written as

$$a(y) = a(y_0) + \int_0^t b(y(\tau))d\tau.$$

This is a particular case of

$$a(y) = a(y_0) + \int_0^t k(t, \tau, y(\tau))d\tau \tag{18}$$

which is an IAE, and itself a special case of the general IAE

$$a(y) = a(y_0) + \int_0^t K(y(t), y(\tau))d\tau. \tag{19}$$

If $A = a_y$ is such that $\|A^{-1}\| < \infty$ and k is smooth, it is easy to show that (18) has a unique solution using a Picard iteration to define a new iterate for the solution $y(t)$ on the left-hand side in terms of the previous iterate inserted on the right-hand side of (18). In this case, we will call the system an index zero system. The solution of such systems can be approximated using quadrature. For example, if we have computed $\{y_i, i = 1, \cdots, n-1\}$ we can computed y_n by

$$a(y_n) = a(y_0) + \sum_{i=0}^{n} \omega_i k(t_n, t_i, y_i)$$

where the $\{\omega_i\}$ are suitable weights. For small enough ω_n, this will have a solution, and for close enough mesh spacing, ω_n will be small enough. (Of course, this may not be the best approach to a computational approximation.) Note that a similar situation holds for (19) if $A = a_y - \int_0^t K_1(y(t), y(\tau))d\tau$ has a bounded inverse, where K_1 is the partial derivative of $K(y, z)$ with respect to its first argument.

If A is singular, then there is no guarantee that there is a solution, since the system has a structure similar to that of DAEs of index greater than zero. In [7] we give an "index reduction procedure" similar to that in [6] for DAEs which, if it terminates, determines the "index" of the IAE and ensures that there is a solution if the initial values lie on the constraint manifolds implied by the IAE.

References

[1] Brenan, K. E., *Stability and Convergence of Difference Approximations for Higher Index Differential-Algebraic Systems with Applications in Trajectory Control*, PhD thesis, Department of Mathematics, UCLA, 1983

[2] Brenan, K. E., Campbell, S. L., and Petzold, L. R., *The Numerical Solution of Initial Value Problems in Differential-Algebraic Equations*, Elsevier Science Publishing Co, 1989

[3] Butcher, J. C., *The Numerical Analysis of Ordinary Differential Equations: Runge-Kutta and General Linear Methods*, Wiley, New York, 1987

[4] Gantmacher, *The Theory of Matrices, v2*, Chelsea Publishing Co, New York, 1977

[5] Gear, C. W., Numerical Initial Values Problems in Ordinary Differential Equations, prentice Hall, 1971

[6] Gear C. W., Differential-Algebraic Equation Index Transformations, SISSC, **9**, pp39-47, (1988)

[7] Gear, C. W. Differential Algebraic Equations, Indices, and Integral Algebraic Equations, Department of Computer Science Report #1505, University of Illinois at Urbana-Champaign, April, 1989, (submitted to SINUM).

[8] Gear, C. W., Gupta, G., and Leimkuhler, B., Automatic Integration of Euler-Lagrange Equations with Constraints, J. Comp. Appl. Math. **12** & **13**, pp 77-90, 1985.

[9] Gear, C. W., Keiper, G., The Analysis of Generalized BDF Methods Applied to Hessenberg Form DAEs, *in preparation*

[10] Gear C. W., Petzold L., ODE Methods for the Solution of Differential/Algebraic Systems, SINUM, **21**, pp716-728, (1984)

[11] Hairer E., Lubich Ch., Roche M., The Numerical Solution of Differential-Algebraic Systems by Runge-Kutta Methods, Report, Universite de Geneve, Dept. de Mathematiques, Switzerland CH-1211, (1988).

[12] Hairer, E., Norsett, S. P., and Wanner, G., *Solving Ordinary Differential Equations: I. Nonstiff Problems*, Springer-Verlag, Berlin, 1987

[13] Keiper, G., *Generalized BDF Methods Applied to Hessenberg Form DAES*, PhD thesis, Department fo Computer Science, University of Illinois at Urbana-Champaign, 1989.

[14] Lambert, J. D., Computational Methods in Ordinary Differential Equations, Wiley, new York, 1973

[15] Leimkuhler, B., *Approximation Methods for the Consistent Initialization of Differential-Algebraic Equations*, PhD thesis, Department of Computer Science Report #1450, University of Illinois at Urbana-Champaign, Aug, 1988.

[16] Leimkuhler, B., Somes Notes on Perturbations of Differential-Algebraic Equations, Institute of Mathematics Report #A266, Helsinki University of Technology, May, 1989.

[17] Mrziglod, T., *Zur Theorie und Numerischen Realisierung vob Losungsmethoden bei Differentialgleichungen mit Angekoppelten Algebraischen Gleichungen*, PhD thesis, Universitat zu Koln, 1987.

[18] Lotstedt, P., and Petzold, L. R., Numerical Solution of Nonlinear Differential Equations with Algebraic Constraints, I: Convergence Results for Backward Differentiation Formulas, Math. Comp. **46**, pp 491-516, 1986

[19] Sincovec, R. F., Erisman, A. M., Yip, E. L., and Epton, M. A., Analysis of Descriptor Systems using Numerical Algorithms, IEEE Trans. Aut. Control **AC-26**, pp 139-147, (1981)

Methods and Software for Differential-Algebraic Systems

Linda R. Petzold*
Computing and Mathematics Research Division, L-316
Lawrence Livermore National Laboratory
Livermore, California 94550

Abstract

In recent years there has been a great deal of progress in the development of numerical methods and software for the solution of initial value problems in differential-algebraic equations (DAE's). In this paper we review the current state of the development and analysis of numerical methods such as multistep and implicit Runge-Kutta applied to classes of DAE's occuring in applications. We describe some of the available software, giving in particular details on the implementation and use of DASSL and its extensions.

*This work was supported in part by the Applied Mathematical Sciences subprogram of the Office of Energy Research, U. S. Department of Energy by Lawwrence Livermore National Laboratory under contract No. W-7405-Eng-48.

NATO ASI Series, Vol. F 69
Real-Time Integration Methods for Mechanical System Simulation
Edited by E. J. Haug and R. C. Deyo

1 Introduction

In this paper we give an introduction to the solution by numerical ODE methods and software of nonlinear differential-algebraic (DAE) systems of the form

$$0 = F(t, y, y'), \tag{1.1}$$

where $\frac{\partial F}{\partial y'}$ may be singular. Differential-algebraic systems include standard form ODE's as a special case, but they also include problems which are in many ways quite different from ODE's. Initial value problems in DAE's arise in a wide variety of applications, including circuit and control theory, chemical kinetics, modeling of constrained mechanical systems, fluid dynamics and robotics. We explore some classes of initial value problems which can be solved by backward differentiation formulas, and discuss some results on the order of convergence of implicit Runge-Kutta methods applied to DAE systems. We give a description of the algorithms and strategies used in the DAE solver DASSL [30], along with a brief description of how to get started using this code. Finally, we describe some of the extensions to DASSL which have recently been completed or are in progress. Further details on these subjects can be found in [3].

The basic idea of using a numerical method for solving DAE systems was introduced by Gear [16], and consists of replacing y and/or y' in (1.1) by a difference approximation, and then solving the resulting equation for an approximation to y. The simplest example of a numerical ODE method for (1.1) is the backward Euler method. Using this approach, the derivative $y'(t_n)$ at time t_n is approximated by a backward difference of $y(t)$ and the resulting system of nonlinear equations is solved for y_n,

$$0 = F\left(t_n, y_n, \frac{y_n - y_{n-1}}{h}\right), \tag{1.2}$$

where $h = t_n - t_{n-1}$. In this way the solution is advanced from time t_{n-1} to t_n.

This scheme of approximating the solution and/or the derivative in (1.1) and solving the resulting nonlinear equations is quite convenient for the solution of many different problems arising from practical applications. Systems in applications often are written naturally in the form (1.1). If we consider numerical methods for solving these very general systems, there will be no need to rewrite the system to fit into some special form. In addition, even though some DAE systems can be rewritten as standard form ODE's ($y' = f(t, y)$) or in other very special forms, often this is very inconvenient and it sometimes leads to a loss of sparsity in the matrices which are involved in the solution process.

The disadvantage of this quite general formulation is that there are problems which can be written in the form (1.1) which are not solvable by ODE methods. Also there are problems which are solvable by some numerical ODE methods, but we must take very special care in choosing an appropriate method and also in implementing it. To distinguish these classes of problems requires a means of investigating the underlying structure of the DAE's.

2 Structure of DAE Systems

In some sense the simplest class of DAE's is the class of linear constant-coefficient systems of the form

$$Ey' + Fy = g(t). \tag{2.1}$$

When $E + \lambda F$ is singular for all values of λ, then no solutions exist, or infinitely many solutions exist. We are not interested in the solution of these systems. The remaining systems, where $E + \lambda F$ is nonsingular, can be completely understood by transforming the system to *Kronecker canonical form* [36], [15]. These systems are *solvable* in the sense that solutions exist for all sufficiently smooth input functions $g(t)$, and two solutions which have the same initial value are identical. For solvable systems, there exist nonsingular matrices P and Q which decouple the system,

$$\begin{aligned} y_1'(t) + Cy_1(t) &= g_1(t) \\ Ny_2'(t) + y_2(t) &= g_2(t) \end{aligned} \tag{2.2}$$

where

$$Q^{-1}y(t) = \begin{pmatrix} y_1(t) \\ y_2(t) \end{pmatrix}, \quad Pg(t) = \begin{pmatrix} g_1(t) \\ g_2(t) \end{pmatrix}$$

into a "differential" part and a "singular" part. The matrix E is a block diagonal matrix whose blocks have the form

$$\begin{pmatrix} 0 & & & & \\ 1 & 0 & & & \\ & 1 & \ddots & & \\ & & \ddots & 0 & \\ & & & 1 & 0 \end{pmatrix}.$$

The most important concept in classifying these systems is the *index*. The index is the dimension of the largest block of E. The index is zero if there is no "singular" part to the system (that is, if the system is a standard form ODE or a system which can be rewritten as a standard form ODE by multiplying by A^{-1}). In general, the higher the index the more difficulties we are likely to encounter in trying to solve the system by a numerical ODE method.

To put these definitions into perspective, consider a canonical index two problem

$$\begin{aligned} y_1' &= g(t) \\ y_2 &= y_1' \end{aligned}$$

and note that for this system, in contrast to an ODE, the initial values must be consistent with the input function $g(t)$, and the solution is not as smooth as the input.

For nonlinear systems (1.1), we can define the *local index* as the index of the local constant-coefficient system at any given time, or the *global index*, which we will be primarily concerned with here, in terms of the number of differentiations of the system which are necessary to be able to solve for y' uniquely in terms of y and t [10].

Definition 2.1 The global index of a solvable DAE (1.1) is the smallest nonnegative integer m such that F has m continuous derivatives and the nonlinear system

$$\begin{aligned}
F(t,y,y') &= 0 \\
\frac{dF}{dt}(t,y,y',y'') &= \frac{\partial F}{\partial y}y' + \frac{\partial F}{\partial y'}y'' + \frac{\partial F}{\partial t} = 0 \\
&\vdots \\
\frac{d^m F}{dt^m}(t,y,y',y'',\ldots,y^{(m+1)}) &= 0
\end{aligned} \tag{2.3}$$

can be solved for y' uniquely in terms of y and t: $y' = \phi(y,t)$.

There are two important classes of index one systems. The first is the general *fully-implicit* index one system (1.1). If we assume that the rank of $\partial F/\partial y'$ is constant, and that the index is identically equal to one in a neighborhood of the solution, then we will refer to these systems as *uniform index one.* The second class of index one systems is that of *semi-explicit* index one systems. These are systems which are written in the special form

$$\begin{aligned}
0 &= F_1(x,x',y,t) \\
0 &= F_2(x,y,t),
\end{aligned} \tag{2.4}$$

where $\partial F_1/\partial x'$ is nonsingular. The system (2.4) is index one iff $\partial F_2/\partial y$ is nonsingular. These semi-explicit index one systems arise frequently in applications. It is important to distinguish them from the general index one system (1.1) because there are numerical methods which perform well for (2.4) but poorly for (1.1).

For high index systems in the general form (1.1), numerical ODE methods such as the backward Euler method can be unstable for small stepsizes [20]. It is often possible to reduce the index of a semi-explicit system by analytically differentiating the constraints [20]. Campbell [10] has devised an algorithm for solving higher index systems which repeatedly differentiates the entire system and solves the resulting overdetermined system for y' in terms of y and t in the spirit of Definition 2.1. However, in its present form this algorithm is not useful for the solution of most problems in applications because it requires knowledge of the analytic partial derivative matrices of F and time derivatives of these matrices and requires a large degree of smoothness which may not be present in all applications.

Despite the discouraging results on the instability of numerical ODE methods for general high index linear systems, we can identify important subsets of high index nonlinear problems for which we can obtain positive results. These systems arise in the modelling of electrical networks and constrained mechanical systems and in the solution of the equations of fluid flow. For index two, these are semi-explicit DAE systems of the form (2.4). The system is index two if $(\partial F_2/\partial x)(\partial F_1/\partial y)$ is nonsingular. For index three systems, these are semi-explicit systems which can be written in a *triangular form* which includes the class of index three constrained mechanical systems described in the next section.

Gear [17] has noted a simple relationship between the fully-implicit index one system and the semi-explicit index two system with which it is often possible to transfer methods and convergence results from one class of problems to the other.

3 Backward Differentiation Formulas

In this section we explore some results on the solution by BDF methods of nonlinear index one systems and some special index two and three nonlinear systems which occur frequently in practical applications. We find that BDF methods converge with the expected order of accuracy for several large classes of DAE's of practical interest.

To solve (1.1) by a BDF method, we replace $y'(t_n)$ by a k-step backward differentiation formula,

$$\rho y_n = \sum_{i=0}^{k} \alpha_i y_{n-i} \tag{3.1}$$

to obtain the system of nonlinear equations

$$F\left(t_n, y_n, \frac{\rho y_n}{h}\right) = 0. \tag{3.2}$$

Then we have the following result for BDF applied to index one systems [20].

Theorem 3.1 If F is uniform index one and is differentiable with respect to y and y', the solution of (1.1) by the k-step BDF method with fixed stepsize h for $k < 7$ converges to order $O(h^k)$ if all initial values are correct to order $O(h^k)$

An extension of this theorem to variable stepsizes is given in [19].

While the BDF methods converge as expected for index one problems, there are still practical difficulties in implementing these methods for this class of problems [30] [32]. It should be noted that systems whose index is less than or equal to one are the problems that general-purpose codes [30] are designed to handle.

For higher index systems, we have noted earlier that it is not possible to obtain convergence even of backward Euler, in general. However, we can obtain some encouraging results [27] if we restrict our attention to semi-explicit higher index systems (2.4). Systems of this form arise in the solution of constrained mechanical systems of the form

$$\begin{aligned} M(q)q'' &= f(q, q', t) + G(q)\lambda \\ \phi(q) = 0, &\quad \frac{\partial \phi}{\partial q} = G^T, \end{aligned} \tag{3.3}$$

where q are the positions and λ the Lagrange multipliers. The index of the mechanical systems (3.3) is three.

A simple example of a system of form (3.3) is given by the equations describing a pendulum in Cartesian coordinates. Let L denote the length of the bar, λ the force in the bar, and x and y the coordinates of the infinitesimal ball of mass one located at the free end of the bar. Then x, y, and λ solve the DAE system

$$\begin{aligned} x'' &= \lambda x \\ y'' &= \lambda y - g \\ 0 &= \frac{1}{2}(x^2 + y^2 - L^2), \end{aligned}$$

where g is the gravity constant. The index of this sytem is three.

For semi-explicit index two systems and for index three constrained mechanical systems of the form (3.3), the k-step constant-stepsize BDF method converges to order of accuracy $O(h^k)$ if the initial values are sufficiently accurate [27] [4]. Gear et al. [19] generalized this result to show that variable stepsize BDF methods converge for semi-explicit index two systems. Gear and Keiper [18] have recently shown that variable stepsize BDF methods converge for triangular index three systems if the order of the method is greater than one.

It is possible to use a general purpose code based on backward differentiation formulas to solve these special high index nonlinear systems [32]. However, there are some practical difficulties which must be dealt with. It can be shown that for an index m system, the iteration matrix which the code uses in the Newton iteration for solving the nonlinear equation (3.2) has a condition number which is $O(1/h^m)$. This difficulty can be remedied by scaling the equations and the variables. The convergence test and error test must also be modified to allow a variable-stepsize BDF code to solve these types of problems.

4 Implicit Runge-Kutta Methods

In this section we describe some results on the properties of implicit Runge-Kutta Methods applied to index one DAE systems. These methods are potentially advantageous over multistep methods for some systems (for example, for large systems with frequent discontinuities). However, some care must be taken in choosing an implicit Runge-Kutta method which is appropriate for DAE's, as these methods do not in general attain the same order of accuracy for DAE's as they do for ODE's.

An M-stage implicit Runge-Kutta (IRK) method applied to the system of DAE's (1.1) is written as

$$F\left(t_{n-1} + c_i h, y_{n-1} + h \sum_{j=1}^{M} a_{ij} Y_j', Y_i'\right) = 0$$

$$y_n = y_{n-1} + h \sum_{i=1}^{M} b_i Y_i'. \tag{4.1}$$

The method can be written in the shorthand notation which displays the matrix of coefficients,

$$\begin{array}{c|cccc} c_1 & a_{11} & a_{12} & \cdots & a_{1M} \\ c_2 & a_{21} & a_{22} & \cdots & a_{2M} \\ \vdots & \vdots & \vdots & \ddots & \vdots \\ c_M & a_{M1} & a_{M2} & \cdots & a_{MM} \\ \hline & b_1 & b_2 & \cdots & b_M \end{array}$$

We will assume that the matrix $\mathcal{A} = (a_{ij})$ is nonsingular.

We will first give some results on the properties of implicit Runge-Kutta methods applied to different classes of index one systems, and then we will discuss the properties of these methods applied to nonlinear semi-explicit index two systems. First we need to define some terminology.

The Runge-Kutta method will be called *strictly stable* if the difference between a perturbed Runge-Kutta step

$$F\left(t_{n-1}+c_ih, z_{n-1}+h\sum_{j=1}^{M}a_{ij}Z_j'+\delta_n^{(i)}, Z_i'\right)=0 \quad i=1,2,\ldots,M$$

$$z_n=z_{n-1}+h\sum_{i=1}^{M}b_iZ_i'+\delta_n^{(M+1)} \tag{4.2}$$

where $z_0 = y_0 + \delta_0^{(M+1)}$, $\|\delta_n^{(i)}\| \leq \Delta$, and an unperturbed Runge-Kutta step (4.1) satisfies $\|y_n - z_n\| \leq K_0\Delta$, where $0 < h \leq h_0$ and K_0, h_0 are constants depending only on the method and the DAE.

Defining the *stability constant* $r = 1 - b^T\mathcal{A}^{-1}\epsilon_M$, where $\epsilon_M = (1,1,\ldots,1)^T$, it is easy to show for index one DAE's that the IRK method (4.1) is stable iff the method coefficients satisfy the *strict stability condition* $|r| < 1$. This stability condition for DAE's is related to the stability criterion $|R(z)| \leq 1$, $R(z) = 1 + zb^T(I - z\mathcal{A})^{-1}\epsilon_M$, where $z = h\lambda$, for the stiff model problem $y' = \lambda y$ because $\lim_{|z|\to\infty} R(z) = 1 - b^T\mathcal{A}^{-1}\epsilon_M$.

Applying the IRK method (4.1) to a canonical constant-coefficient index one system $u = g(t)$, we find that the method is locally accurate to order $O(h^{k_a+1})$ iff the method coefficients satisfy $A_1(k_a)$, where $A_1(q)$ is defined by

$$A_1(q): \quad b^T\mathcal{A}^{-1}c^j = 1 \qquad j=1,2,\ldots,q \tag{4.3}$$

where $c^j = (c_1^j, c_2^j, \ldots, c_M^j)^T$. If the method satisfies the strict stability condition and the order of the IRK method for purely differential systems is k_d, then it is easy to show that the method is globally accurate to order $O(h^{\min(k_d,k_a+1)})$ for index one constant-coefficient DAE systems.

One class of IRK methods which appears to be particularly promising for the solution of DAE's is that of *stiffly accurate* methods. These are methods whose coefficient matrices satisfy $c_M = 1$, $a_{Mj} = b_j$, $j = 1,\ldots,M$ and $\mathcal{A}$ is nonsingular. For semi-explicit index one systems, these methods have the property which is analogous to BDF that the constraint equations are satisfied exactly at the end of each time step. Griepentrog [21] and Deuflhard et al. [13] have shown that there is no order reduction for stiffly accurate methods applied to semi-explicit index one systems.

For more general implicit Runge-Kutta methods, Roche [33] has derived a set of order conditions which include (4.3) using the theory of Butcher series and rooted trees, for semi-explicit index one systems.

The IRK methods are, in general, even less accurate for fully-implicit nonlinear index one systems than for semi-explicit systems. The additional loss of accuracy comes about because of mixing which can occur between the errors in the differential and singular parts of the system. To state the results, we must first define some terminology.

Defining

$$C(q): \sum_{j=1}^{M}a_{ij}c_j^{k-1} = c_i^k/k, \qquad i=1,2,\ldots,M \quad k=1,2,\ldots,q$$

$$B(q): \sum_{j=1}^{M} b_j c_j^{k-1} = 1/k, \qquad k = 1, 2, \ldots, q \tag{4.4}$$

Then we have the following result, which is shown in [8].

Theorem 4.1 Suppose that (1.1) is uniform index one and linear in y', the Runge-Kutta method satisfies the stability condition $|r| \leq 1$, the errors in the initial conditions are $O(h^G)$ and the errors in terminating the Newton iterations are $O(h^{G+\delta})$, where $\delta = 1$ if $|r| = 1$ and $\delta = 0$ otherwise, and $G \geq 2$. Then the global errors satisfy $||e_n|| = O(h^G)$ where

$$G = \begin{cases} q, & \textit{if } C(q) \textit{ and } B(q) \\ q+1, & \textit{if } C(q),\ B(q+1) \textit{ and } -1 \leq r < 1 \\ q+1, & \textit{if } C(q),\ B(q+1),\ A_1(q+1) \textit{ and } r = 1 \end{cases}$$

It should be noted that implicit Runge-Kutta methods with $|r| = 1$ can be unstable for some classes of fully-implicit index one systems [1]. These results for index one DAE's are in agreement with the order reduction results for stiff ODE's given in [9] in the limit as the stiffness becomes infinite [8].

For nonlinear semi-explicit index two systems, because of the close relationship between fully-implicit index one systems and semi-explicit index two systems, we have that the global error in the "differential" variable x is given by Theorem 4.1. For methods satisfying the strict stability condition, the global errors in the y variable are $O(h^{G_y})$, where G_y is given by [5]

$$G_y = \begin{cases} q & \text{if } C(q),\ B(q),\ A_1(q) \\ q+1 & \text{if } C(q),\ B(q+1),\ A_1(q+1),\ A_2(q+1) \end{cases},$$

where A_2 are the order conditions for Runge-Kutta methods applied to constant-coefficient index two systems and are given by

$$\begin{aligned} A_2(q): \quad & b^T \mathcal{A}^{-1} \epsilon_M = b^T \mathcal{A}^{-2} c \\ & b^T \mathcal{A}^{-2} c^i = i, \quad i = 2, 3, \ldots, q. \end{aligned}$$

In a recent paper by Hairer, Lubich and Roche [23], a complete set of order conditions are given for index one and semi-explicit index two systems. Some preliminary results for index three systems are also discussed.

5 The DAE Solver DASSL

In this section we outline the basic algorithms and strategies used in the DAE solver DASSL [30], along with a brief description of the use of this code. DASSL is a code for solving *index one* DAE systems, although with some modification it can sometimes be used for the solution of higher index systems [32].

Methods and Strategies

The underlying methods in DASSL for solving DAE systems replace the derivative in (1.1) by a difference approximation, and then solve the resulting equation for the solution at the current time t_n using Newton's method. For example, replacing the derivative by the backward difference in (1.1), we obtain the first order formula

$$F\left(t_n, y_n, \frac{y_n - y_{n-1}}{h}\right) = 0. \tag{5.1}$$

This equation is then solved using Newton's method,

$$y_n^{m+1} = y_n^m - \left(\frac{1}{h}\frac{\partial F}{\partial y'} + \frac{\partial F}{\partial y}\right)^{-1} F\left(t_n, y_n^m, \frac{y_n^m - y_{n-1}}{h}\right), \tag{5.2}$$

where m is the iteration index. The algorithms used in DASSL are an extension of this approach. Instead of using the first order formula (5.1), DASSL approximates the derivative using the kth order backward differentiation formula (BDF), where k ranges from one to five. On every step it chooses the order k and stepsize h, based on the behavior of the solution.

Newton's method (5.2) converges most rapidly when the initial guess $y_n^{(0)}$ is accurate. DASSL obtains an initial guess for y_n by evaluating the polynomial which interpolates the computed solution at the last $k+1$ times $t_{n-1}, t_{n-2}, \ldots, t_{n-(k+1)}$, at the current time t_n. An initial guess for y_n' is obtained by evaluating the derivative of this polynomial at t_n. Once $y_n^{(0)}$ is found, Newton's method is used to solve for y_n as in (5.2), except that in general the derivative is approximated by the kth order BDF formula, instead of by the backward difference of y_n. When the stepsize is not constant, there is a choice as to which form of the BDF formula to use. DASSL uses the fixed leading coefficient form of the BDF formula [25].

It is important to solve the nonlinear equation (5.1) efficiently. To simplify notation, we can rewrite this equation as

$$F(t, y, \hat{\alpha}y + \beta) = 0, \tag{5.3}$$

where $\hat{\alpha}$ is a constant which changes whenever the stepsize or order changes, β is a vector which depends on the solution at past times, and t, y, $\hat{\alpha}$, β are evaluated at t_n. This equation is solved in DASSL by a modified version of Newton's method,

$$y^{(m+1)} = y^m - c\left(\alpha\frac{\partial F}{\partial y'} + \frac{\partial F}{\partial y}\right)^{-1} F\left(t, y^m, \hat{\alpha}y^m + \beta\right). \tag{5.4}$$

The iteration matrix $G = \alpha\partial F/\partial y' + \partial F/\partial y$ is computed and factored, and is then used for as many time steps as possible. In general, the value of α when G was last computed is different from the current value of $\hat{\alpha}$. If α is too different from $\hat{\alpha}$, then (5.4) may not converge. The constant c in (5.4) is chosen to speed up the convergence when $\alpha \neq \hat{\alpha}$, and is given by

$$c = \frac{2}{(1 + \hat{\alpha}/\alpha)}. \tag{5.5}$$

The rate of convergence ρ of (5.4) is estimated whenever two or more iterations have been taken by

$$\rho = \left(\frac{||y^{m+1} - y^m||}{||y^1 - y^0||}\right)^{1/m}. \tag{5.6}$$

The norms are scaled norms which depend on the error tolerances specified by the user. The iteration has converged when

$$\frac{\rho}{1-\rho}||y^{m+1} - y^m|| < 0.3. \tag{5.7}$$

If $\rho > 0.9$, or $m > 4$, and the iteration has not yet converged, then the stepsize is reduced, and/or an iteration matrix based on current approximations to y, y' and α is formed, and the step is attempted again.

The linear systems are solved using routines from the LINPACK [14] subroutine package. The matrix can either be dense or have a banded structure. For most problems, the iteration matrix is computed by finite differences. The jth column of G is approximated by incrementing the jth component of y in (5.3), and then forming the finite difference quotient. The choice of the increment is a delicate but important issue. When G is banded, it is computed using the algorithm of Curtis et. al [12] so as to minimize the number of function evaluations required. There is an option available for the user to write a routine to compute G, given t, y, y' and α. For some problems, this can be more efficient than using finite differences to compute the matrix.

After the corrector iteration has converged, an error test is made to determine whether the solution satisfies a local error tolerance specified by the user. The test is satisfied whenever $C\|y_n - y_n^0\| \leq 1$, where C is a constant which depends on the order and recent stepsize history of the method. The constant C is chosen to control both the variable stepsize local truncation error, and the error in interpolated values of y between mesh points. If the error test is satisfied, the code takes another step. Otherwise, the stepsize and/or order are reduced and the step is attempted again.

The stepsize and order for the next step are determined using basically the same strategies as in Shampine and Gordon [34]. The code estimates what the error would have been if the last few steps had been taken at constant stepsize, at the current order k, and at $k-2$, $k-1$, and $k+1$. If these estimates increase as k increases, the order is lowered; if they decrease, it is raised. The new stepsize h_{n+1} is chosen so that the error estimate based on taking constant stepsizes h_{n+1} at order k_{n+1} satisfies the error test.

Using DASSL

DASSL is designed to be as easy to use as possible, while providing enough flexibility and control for solving a wide variety of problems. It is extensively documented in the source code. In this subsection we outline what needs to be done to solve a problem using this code.

The most important information the code needs is how to define and function F in (1.1), which describes the equation to be solved. To define F, the user writes a subroutine RES which takes as input the time T and the vectors Y and YPRIME, and produces as output the vector DELTA, where DELTA = F(T,Y,YPRIME) is the amount by thich the function F fails to be zero for the input values of T, Y, and YPRIME.

To get started, DASSL needs a consistent set of initial values T, Y, and YPRIME. This means that we must have F(T,Y,YPRIME) = 0 at the initial time. There is an option in DASSL to compute the initial YPRIME, in the case where all of the initial values for Y are known. In other cases, where some of the components of Y may not be known and need to be determined using the DAE, there is some recent research [26] which in principle solves this problem, but to our knowledge there is no currently available production code. Sometimes these values can be obtained for specific classes of physical problems.

Additional information which must be supplied to the solver is virtually identical to that needed by standard ODE solvers [35], so we will not discuss it further here.

When DASSL is finished (either successfully or unsuccessfully), it returns to the user's calling program with a flag IDID which indicates what happened. If the flag is positive, the problem was solved successfully. Otherwise, something went wrong. DAE systems are in general quite a bit more complex than ODE systems, and the number of complications which can occur is correspondingly greater. The code documentation gives information about the most likely cause of the problem in the event that a negative IDID is encountered, and diagnostic information is available through the work arrays which DASSL uses for storage.

Extensions to DASSL

Although DASSL is a powerful code which can handle a wide variety of problems, some problems require capabilities which are not implemented in the standard version of DASSL or which can be performed more efficiently with a code based on DASSL but oriented towards a more specific task. These problems include root-finding, sensitivity analysis, and the solution of very large systems of DAE's whose iteration matrices do not fit naturally into a banded structure.

The standard version of DASSL solves a DAE system from time T to time TOUT, where TOUT is specified by the user. In some problems it is more natural to stop the code at the root of some function $g(t, y)$. For example, in computing the trajectory of an object, it does not make sense to continue the solution past the time when the object hits the ground. In other problems, it is necessary to stop the code at the root of g because the function F changes at the roots of g. The code DASSLRT has this capability. A vector of functions $g_i(t, y)$, $i = 1, 2, \ldots, NG$, may be supplied to DASSLRT such that the root of any of the NG functions g_i is desired. If there are several roots in a given output interval, DASSLRT returns them one at a time, in the order in which they occur along the solution. An integer array tells the user which g_i, if any, were found to have a root on any given return. At the present time, a version of DASSLRT exists and is routinely used to solve application problems at several national laboratories. A version for outside release is planned.

A second extension of DASSL has been developed to handle sensitivity analysis for DAE's. Suppose we are given a DAE

$$F(t, y, y', p) = 0, \tag{5.8a}$$

$$y(t_0, p) = y_0(p) \tag{5.8b}$$

where y, $y' \in \mathcal{R}^N$, whose solution depends on a vector of M time independent parameters p. We would like to compute the (N, M) matrix $W(t)$ of sensitivity functions

$$W(t) = \frac{\partial y(t)}{\partial p} \tag{5.9}$$

which describes how the solution components change as a result of changes in the parameters.

The sensitivity matrix satisfies a system of DAE's which can be derived by partial differentiation of equations (5.8) with respect to the parameter vector p

$$\begin{aligned} \frac{\partial F}{\partial y'}W'(t) + \frac{\partial F}{\partial y}W(t) + \frac{\partial F}{\partial t} + \frac{\partial F}{\partial p} &= 0 \\ W(t_0) &= \frac{\partial y_0}{\partial p}. \end{aligned} \tag{5.10}$$

Computationally, the important observation with respect to the sensitivity equations (5.10) is that they are linear and that they have the same iteration matrix as the original system (5.8) if they are solved using the same sequence of methods and stepsizes. Caracotsios and Stewart [11] have written a code DASSAC for solving the sensitivity system which makes use of these observations and is based on DASSL. The code works as follows. The sensitivity equations (5.10) are appended to the original system. The system is solved using a version of DASSL which has been modified to evaluate the iteration matrix on every step, require only one Newton iteration for the linear system (5.10), and make use of the repetitive block diagonal structure of the iteration matrix to save storage and operations in forming the matrix and solving the linear system. The error estimates and stepsize adjustment are based on the entire system (5.10) appended to (5.8). It is to be noted that the sensitivities may not be accurate if the iteration matrix is computed via finite differencing.

One of the obvious deficiencies of the standard DASSL is the lack of options for dealing with Jacobian matrices which do not fit naturally into a dense or banded category. Marquardt [29] has recently implemented a version of DASSL which makes use of the HARWELL sparse direct linear system solver. A version of DASSL which uses the preconditioned GMRES method to solve the linear system at each Newton iteration is currently under development by Brown, Hindmarsh, Petzold and Ulrich, and is expected to be released soon. This code implements many of the strategies described for ODE's in [6]. An alternative to the GMRES method for solving nonsymmetric linear systems is the adaptive Chebyshev method of Manteuffel [28] which has been implemented by Ashby [2]. A version of DASSL which uses the preconditioned Chebyshev method is currently under development by Ashby, Lee, Petzold and Saylor.

Finally, we note that Skjellum et al.[37] have recently implemented a version of DASSL for use on massively parallel computers, called Concurrent DASSL.

References

[1] U. Ascher, *On Symmetric Schemes and Differential-Algebraic Equations*, SIAM J. Sci. Stat. Comp., 10 (1989), pp. 937-949.

[2] S. F. Ashby, *CHEBYCODE - A FORTRAN Implementation of Manteuffel's Adaptive Chebyshev Algorithm*, University of Illinois, Dept. of Computer Science, UIUCDCS-R-85-1203, 1985.

[3] K. E. Brenan, S. L. Campbell and L. R. Petzold, *The Numerical Solution of Initial Value Problems in Differential-Algebraic Equations*, Elsevier Science Publishing Company, 1989.

[4] K. E. Brenan and B. Engquist, *Backward Difference Approximations of Nonlinear Differential-Algebraic Equations*, Math. Comp., 51 (1988), pp. 659-676.

[5] K. E. Brenan and L. R. Petzold, *The Numerical Solution of Higher Index Differential/Algebraic Equations by Implicit Runge-Kutta Methods*, SIAM J. Numer. Anal., 26 (1989), pp. 976-996.

[6] P. N. Brown and A. C. Hindmarsh, *Reduced Storage Matrix Methods in Stiff ODE Systems*, J. Appl. Math. & Comp., (to appear).

[7] K. Burrage, *Efficiently Implementable Algebraically Stable Runge-Kutta Methods*, SIAM J. Numer. Anal. 19 (1982), pp. 245-258.

[8] K. Burrage and L. R. Petzold, *On Order Reduction for Runge-Kutta Methods Applied to Differential/Algebraic Systems and to Stiff Systems of ODEs*, SIAM J. Numer. Anal., (to appear).

[9] K. Burrage, W. H. Hundsdorfer and J. A. Verwer, *A Study of B-Convergence of Runge-Kutta Methods Applied to Stiff Systems*, Computing 36, pp. 17-34 (1986).

[10] S. L. Campbell, *A General Form for Solvable Linear Time Varying Singular Systems of Differential Equations*, SIAM J. Math. Anal., 18 (1987), pp. 1101-1115.

[11] M. Caracotsios and W. E. Stewart, *Sensitivity Analysis of Initial Value Problems with Mixed ODEs and Algebraic Equations,* Computers and Chemical Engineering, 9, (1985), pp. 359-365.

[12] A. R. Curtis, M. J. D. Powell, and J. K. Reid, *On the Estimation of Sparse Jacobian Matrices*, J. Inst. Math. Applic., 15 (1974).

[13] P. Deuflhard, E. Hairer and J. Zugck, *One-Step and Extrapolation Methods for Differential-Algebraic Systems*, Preprint Nr. 318, Universität Heidelberg, Institut für Angewandte Mathematik, 1985.

[14] J. J. Dongarra, J. R. Bunch, C. B. Moler, and G. W. Steward, *LINPACK Users' Guide*, SIAM, Philadelphia (1979).

[15] F. R. Gantmacher, *The Theory of Matrices*, Vol. 2, Chelsea, New York, 1964.

[16] C. W. Gear, *Simultaneous Numerical Solution of Differential/Algebraic Equations*, IEEE Trans. Circuit Theory, CT-18, 1971, pp. 89-95.

[17] C. W. Gear, *Differential-Algebraic Equation Index Transformations*, SIAM J. Sci. Stat. Comp. 9 (1988), pp. 39-47.

[18] C. W. Gear and J. Keiper, personal communication, 1989.

[19] C. W. Gear, B. Leimkuhler and G. K. Gupta, *Automatic Integration of Euler-Lagrange Equations with Constraints*, Journal of Computational and Applied Mathematics 12 and 13 (1985), pp. 77-90.

[20] C. W. Gear and L. R. Petzold, *ODE Methods for the Solution of Differential/Algebraic Systems*, SIAM J. Numer. Anal. 21 (1984), pp. 367-384.

[21] E. Griepentrog, *Initial Value Problems for Implicit Differential Equations Systems*, Humboldt-Universität zu Berlin, reprint, 1984.

[22] E. Griepentrog and R. März, *Differential- Algebraic Equations and their Numerical Treatment*, Teubner-Texte, Leipzig, 1986.

[23] E. Hairer, C. Lubich and M. Roche, *The Numerical Solution of Differential-Algebraic Systems by Runge-Kutta Methods*, Universite de Geneve, September, 1988.

[24] A. C. Hindmarsh, *ODE Solvers for use with the Method of Lines*, Advances in Computer Methods for Partial Differential Equations IV, R. Vichnevetsky and R. S. Stepleman, eds., IMACS, New Brunswick, NJ, 1981, pp. 312-316.

[25] K. R. Jackson and R. Sacks-Davis, *An Alternative Implementation of Variable Step-Size Multistep Formulas for Stiff ODEs*, ACM Trans. on Math. Software 6, No. 3, pp. 295-318, (1980).

[26] B. J. Leimkuhler, L. R. Petzold and C. W. Gear, *Approximation Methods for the Consistent Initialization of Differential-Algebraic Equations*, SIAM J. Numer. Anal., (to appear).

[27] P. Lötstedt and L. Petzold, *Numerical Solution of Nonlinear Differential Equations with Algebraic Constraints I: Convergence Results for Backward Differentiation Formulas*, Mathematics of Computation 46 (1986), pp. 491-516.

[28] T. Manteuffel, *Adaptive Procedure for Estimating Parameters for the Nonsymmetric Tchebychev Iteration*, Numerische Mathematik 31, pp. 183-208, 1978.

[29] W. Marquardt, Universität Stuttgart, personal communication, 1988.

[30] L. R. Petzold, *A Description of DASSL: A Differential/Algebraic System Solver*, IMACS Trans. on Scientific Computation, Vol. 1, R. S. Stepleman, ed., 1982.

[31] L. R. Petzold, *Order Results for Implicit Runge-Kutta Methods Applied to Differential/Algebraic Systems*, SIAM J. Numer. Anal. 23 (1986), pp. 837-852.

[32] L. Petzold and P. Lötstedt, *Numerical Solution of Nonlinear Differential Equations with Algebraic Constraints II: Practical Implications*, SIAM J. Sci. Stat. Comput. 7, (1986), pp. 720-733.

[33] M. Roche, *Runge-Kutta Methods for Differential Algebraic Equations*, SIAM J. Numer. Anal., 26 (1989), pp. 963-975.

[34] L. F. Shampine and M. K. Gordon, *Computer Solution of Ordinary Differential Equations*, W. H. Freeman and Co., 1975.

[35] L. F. Shampine and H. A. Watts, *DEPAC - Design of a User Oriented Package of ODE Solvers*, Sandia National Laboratories report, SAND79-2374, (1980).

[36] R. F. Sincovec, B. Dembart, M. A. Epton, A. M. Erisman, J. W. Manke, and E. L. Yip, *Solvability of Large-Scale Descriptor Systems*, Boeing Computer Services Company, Seattle, Washington, 1979.

[37] A. Skjellum, S. Mattisson, M. Morari, L. Peterson, *Concurrent DASSL: Structure, Application, and Performance*, Proc. Fourth Conf. on Hypercube Concurrent Computers and Applications, Monterey, California, 1989.

PART 2

NEW DAE AND ODE SOLUTION METHODS

A New Class of Generalized Inverses for the Solution of Discretized Euler – Lagrange Equations

C. Führer
Laboratory for Flight Systems Dynamics
German Aerospace Research Establishment (DLR)
D-8031 Oberpfaffenhofen (W.-Germany)

B. Leimkuhler
Institute of Mathematics
Helsinki University of Technology
SF-02150 Espoo 15 (Finland)

Abstract

For a wide class of mechanical systems, so-called *multibody systems*, there are highly developed methods for the automatic generation of the corresponding equations of motion. As these equations can be stated in various, equivalent forms the question which of these forms are best suited for numerical treatment has become an important topic of research in computational mechanics.

The discrete versions of these formulations lead to nonlinear algebraic equations, which, in the presence of truncation error and rounding errors, are not equivalent. In this paper a general framework for comparing these alternative formulations will be given based on identifying with each a certain generalized solution of an overdetermined set of algebraic equations.

1 Equations of Motion of Constrained Multibody Systems

For multibody systems we assume that the mass is entirely concentrated in n rigid or elastic bodies. Their motion can be described by n_p position coordinates p and as many velocity coordinates v. These bodies may be coupled by massless interconnections. Interconnections like springs and dampers cause applied forces acting on the bodies. Others like joints constrain the motion of the bodies relative to each other. For simplicity we consider only holonomic constraints. For this type of system the equations of motion can be written in the form:

$$\dot{p} = v \tag{1.1a}$$

$$M(p)\dot{v} = f(p,v,t) - G^T(p)\lambda \tag{1.1b}$$

NATO ASI Series, Vol. F 69
Real-Time Integration Methods for Mechanical System Simulation
Edited by E. J. Haug and R. C. Deyo

together with the n_λ *position level* constraints

$$0 = g(p) \tag{1.2}$$

with $M(p)$ being an $n_p \times n_p$ regular *mass matrix*, f being the *applied forces*, and λ the n_λ *Lagrange multipliers* or *constraint forces* coupled to the system by the $n_\lambda \times n_p$ *constraint matrix*

$$G(p) := \frac{\partial}{\partial p} g(p).$$

For multibody systems it is also possible to generate the time derivatives of the constraint (1.2), the n_λ constraint equations on *velocity level*

$$0 = G(p)\dot{p} \tag{1.3}$$

and the constraint equations on the *acceleration level*

$$0 = G(p)\dot{v} + \dot{p}^T G_p(p)\dot{p} =: G(p)\dot{v} + z(p, \dot{p}). \tag{1.4}$$

Equation (1.1b) can be solved for $\dot{v}$. The result introduced into (1.4) gives a relation involving the Lagrange multipliers λ, the so-called λ – *constraint*:

$$0 = G(p)M^{-1}(p)f(p, \dot{p}, t) - G(p)M^{-1}(p)G^T(p)\lambda + z(p, \dot{p}). \tag{1.5}$$

It will be assumed in this paper that the systems considered have no redundant constraints, thus

$$H(p) := G(p)M^{-1}(p)G^T(p)$$

is a regular $n_\lambda \times n_\lambda$ – matrix and (1.5) can be solved for the algebraic variable λ:

$$M(p)\ddot{p} = \tilde{f}(p, \dot{p}, t) \tag{1.6}$$

with $\tilde{f}(p, \dot{p}, t) := f(p, \dot{p}, t) - G(p)^T H(p, t)^{-1} \left[G(p)M^{-1}(p)f(p, \dot{p}, t) + z(p, \dot{p})\right]$. This is a regular implicit ODE, while equations (1.1) together with one type of the constraint equations (1.2), (1.3), (1.4), or (1.5) is a system of *differential – algebraic equations* (DAE).

These formulations of the equations of motion are equivalent to each other, in the sense, that they have the same (analytical) solution if initial values are taken satisfying all constraints (1.2), (1.3) and (1.5). These initial values are said to be *consistent* or sometimes *strongly consistent* [Fuh88]. In contrast, the discretized forms of these equations, which are obtained by applying a numerical integration scheme, have quite different properties. These can be explained by using the index – concept in the theory of DAEs. The index of a general DAE $F(\dot{x}, x, t) = 0$ can be defined to be the number of differentiations of the problem with respect to time which are necessary to get a system which is solvable for $\dot{x}$, [BCP89, p. 33]. It can easily be shown, that (1.1),(1.2) is an *index-3 formulation* of the mechanical problem, (1.1),(1.3) an *index-2 formulation* and both, (1.1),(1.4) and (1.1),(1.5) are index-1 formulations.

At the present time there is no reliable numerical method for handling index-3 problems. On the other hand, it has been pointed out that index – reduced problems obtained by differentiating the constraints like (1.1),(1.3) or (1.1),(1.5) do not necessarily have the same stability properties as the original problem. This may cause a solution which drifts away from the position constraint [Bau72] or, even worse, in an unpredictable error growth in the solution itself [CL90,FL89b].

In order to avoid these numerical problems several alternative formulations have been proposed:

In [GGL85] a stabilized index-2 formulation has been suggested, which couples the position constraint (1.2) to the index-2 formulation (1.1), (1.3) by introducing additional *stabilizing Lagrange multipliers* μ:

$$
\begin{aligned}
\dot{p} &= v - G^T(p)\mu && (1.7a)\\
M(p)\dot{v} &= f(p,v,t) - G^T(p)\lambda && (1.7b)\\
0 &= G(p)v && (1.7c)\\
0 &= g(p). && (1.7d)
\end{aligned}
$$

This idea has been also extended to the index-1 problem (1.1), (1.5). Here two additional multipliers μ and η have to be introduced in order to couple the constraints (1.2) and (1.3) to (1.1),(1.5) [FL89b]:

$$
\begin{aligned}
\dot{p} &= v - G^T(p)\mu - \left[v^T G_p(p)\right]^T \eta && (1.8a)\\
M(p)\dot{v} &= f(p,v,t) - G^T(p)\lambda - G^T(p)\eta && (1.8b)\\
0 &= G(p)M^{-1}(p)f(p,v,t) - H(p)\lambda + z(p,v) && (1.8c)\\
0 &= G(p)v && (1.8d)\\
0 &= g(p). && (1.8e)
\end{aligned}
$$

It is worth noting, that in this problem the interesting variables p, v, λ are index-1 variables.

It has been shown in [FL89b] that this formulation is numerically equivalent to the overdetermined DAE

$$
\begin{aligned}
\dot{p} &= v && (1.9a)\\
M(p)\dot{v} &= f(p,v,t) - G^T(p)\lambda && (1.9b)\\
0 &= G(p)M^{-1}(p)f(p,v,t) - H(p)\lambda + z(p,v) && (1.9c)\\
0 &= G(p)v && (1.9d)\\
0 &= g(p), && (1.9e)
\end{aligned}
$$

when solved with a special oblique projection technique, the so-called ssf-iteration. We will discuss this technique in a later section in more detail.

Traditionally stabilization techniques were first introduced for numerically solving systems with invariants, e.g. conservation of energy, and they were first applied to celestial mechanics [Bau72]. In contrast to the above introduction of additional coupling variables, the stabilizing Lagrange multipliers, in these approaches the coupling is performed by constant parameters, sometimes called *Baumgarte-coefficients*. The choice of these coefficients is discussed in detail by *Ostermeier* [Ost90].

The "classical" way of formulating the equations of motion of constrained mechanical systems is based on splitting the coordinates p and v into dependent and independent ones and by eliminating the constraint forces or Lagrange multipliers λ. This can be performed by solving (1.5) for λ and introducing the result into (1.1b). Then the constraint equations (1.2), (1.3) are transformed into equations which are explicit in the dependent coordinates. These are used to transform the differential equations into a reduced set of regular ordinary differential equations, the *state space form* of the problem. Mathematically speaking, the problem is formulated in the local coordinate space of the constraining manifolds given by (1.2), (1.3), and (1.5).

It is important to note, that the explicit forms of the constraint equations may exist in the nonlinear case only locally. This requires a repartitioning of the coordinates into dependent and independent variables if the solution curve leaves a certain region. A numerical method based on the transformation of the equations into state space form and solving them with *Adams – Bashforth – Moulton formulas* is given in [WH82] and a corresponding approach based on *BDF – formulas* for stiff mechanical problems is given in [HY90].

2 Discretized Equations of Motion

All the information we needed in the preceeding section to establish the alternative forms of the equations of motion is contained in the overdetermined DAE (1.9). This set of equations is consistent in the sense that the equations are redundant but not contradictory. Such a statement does not hold for the discretized version of (1.9). Here we will use the implicit *backward differentiation formulas* (BDF) which are most commonly used for numerically integrating stiff ODEs and DAEs.

A typical time step from t_{n-1} to $t_n := t_{n-1} + h$ will be considered:

Applying a BDF-scheme to (1.9) replaces the differentiation operator $\dot{p}(t_n) := Dp(t_n)$ by its corresponding difference operator $\dot{p}_n := \rho p_n$ which is defined by

$$\dot{p}_n := \rho p_n := \frac{\alpha_0}{h} p_n + \underbrace{\frac{1}{h}\sum_{i=1}^{k} \alpha_i p_{n-i}}_{:= \bar{\rho} p_n} \tag{2.10}$$

with α_i being the BDF-coefficients [Gea71]. $\dot{v}(t_n)$ is replaced by $\dot{v}_n$ in a similar way.

By this discretization (1.9) is transformed into a set of nonlinear algebraic equations:

$$\varphi(x_n) := \begin{bmatrix} \rho p_n - v_n \\ M(p_n)\rho v_n - f(p_n, v_n, t_n) + G^T(p_n)\lambda_n \\ G(p_n)M^{-1}(p_n)f(p_n, v_n, t_n) - H(p_n)\lambda_n + z(p_n, v_n) \\ g(p_n) \\ G(p_n)v_n \end{bmatrix} = 0 \tag{2.11}$$

with $x_n^T = \left[p_n^T, v_n^T, \lambda_n^T\right]^T$.

Due to the presence of the discretization error the equations (2.11) will be contradictory in general and (2.11) will have no (classical) solution, so "solving" this nonlinear set of equations requires first the definition of an appropriate generalized solution. We will see in the sequel, that the difference in the alternative formulations of the equations of motion presented in Section 1 can be described in terms of different choices for a generalized solution to (2.11). For some of these generalized solutions we can find some important properties which enable us to relate the formulations to each other.

The definition of generalized solutions can be simplified if we first formally apply Newton's iteration scheme to (2.11). This scheme defines a solution of (2.11) by the limit of a sequence of solutions of linear problems:

$$\varphi'(x_n^{(m)})x_\Delta + \varphi(x_n^{(m)}) = 0 \tag{2.12}$$

with $x_n^{(m+1)} := x_n^{(m)} + x_\Delta$ and $x_n^{(0)}$ being a starting value which is normally obtained by performing a predictor step. In matrix notation equation (2.12) has the following form:

$$\begin{bmatrix} \frac{\alpha_0}{h}I & -I & 0 \\ K & \frac{\alpha_0}{h}M + D & G^T \\ \Gamma_1 & \Gamma_2 & -H \\ G & 0 & 0 \\ \Gamma & G & 0 \end{bmatrix} \begin{bmatrix} p_\Delta \\ v_\Delta \\ \lambda_\Delta \end{bmatrix} + \varphi(x_n) = 0 \tag{2.13}$$

with $K := \dot{v}_n^T M_p(p_n) - f_p(p_n, v_n, t_n) + \lambda_n^T G_p(p_n)$, $M := M(p_n)$, $D := -f_v(p_n, v_n, t_n)$, $G := G(p_n)$, $\Gamma := v_n^T G_p(p_n)$, $\Gamma_1 := \frac{\partial}{\partial p}\left(G(p_n)M^{-1}(p_n)f(p_n, v_n, t_n) - H(p_n)\lambda_n + z(p_n, v_n)\right)$, $\Gamma_2 := \frac{\partial}{\partial v}\left(G(p_n)M^{-1}(p_n)f(p_n, v_n, t_n) - H(p_n)\lambda_n + z(p_n, v_n)\right)$ and the iteration counter m being suppressed for notational simplicity.

Again, the linear problem (2.12) cannot be expected to have a classical solution. A natural choice is to solve this problem in a *least squares sense*. In particular such a solution solves the following problem

$$\varphi'(x_n^{(m)})x_\Delta + \varphi(x_n^{(m)}) = \left[r_1^T, r_2^T, r_\lambda^T, r_p^T, r_v^T\right]^T =: r \tag{2.14}$$

with the residual r being minimal in the Euclidean norm. As corresponding generalized inverse the Moore-Penrose pseudoinverse is taken, [GL83]. For a discussion of this approach see [Sta76,Fuh88]. This solution taken in the Newton-iteration process leads to the *Gauß- Newton iteration* scheme, for which convergence results are well known [DS83].

On the other hand, another generalized solution of (2.12) can uniquely be defined by requiring the residual in (2.14) to have the form

$$r := \left[0, 0, r_\lambda^T, 0, r_v^T\right]^T$$

with arbitrary values for the residuals in the linearized velocity and λ–constraints r_v and r_λ. This is exactly the solution which is obtained in every corrector step when the *index-3 problem* (1.1),(1.2) is solved, as in that formulation only the position constraint enters. Similarly, the solution of a particular corrector step of the *index-2 problem* (1.1),(1.2) is defined by the requirement

$$r := \left[0, 0, r_\lambda^T, r_p^T, 0\right]^T,$$

and for the *index-1 formulation* (1.1),(1.5) by

$$r := \left[0, 0, 0, r_p^T, r_v^T\right]^T.$$

In this way we see that the discretization error is distributed in different ways to the residuals.

3 Discretized State Space Form for a Model Problem

We will restrict ourselves here to a linear *model problem* with linear, time-dependent constraints corresponding to a kinematically driven problem, with its mass matrix being the identity matrix. The latter feature can be obtained by applying a special recursive method for establishing the equations of motion as suggested in [BJO86].

This model problem has the following form:

$$\begin{aligned} \dot{p} &= v && (3.15a)\\ \dot{v} &= -Kp - Dv - G^T\lambda && (3.15b)\\ -GKp - GDv - GG^T\lambda &= \ddot{z}(t) && (3.15c)\\ Gp &= z(t) && (3.15d)\\ Gv &= \dot{z}(t), && (3.15e) \end{aligned}$$

with a constant $n_p \times n_p$ stiffness matrix K, a constant damping matrix D and a constant constraint matrix G. z is assumed to be a twice continously differentiable function describing the kinematic excitation of the problem. If this problem is discretized as in the last section with an implicit BDF–scheme we get corresponding to (2.14) the following overdetermined linear system as corrector problem,

$$\underbrace{\begin{bmatrix} \frac{\alpha_0}{h}I & -I & 0 \\ K & \frac{\alpha_0}{h}I + D & G^T \\ -GK & -GD & -GG^T \\ G & 0 & 0 \\ 0 & G & 0 \end{bmatrix}}_{:=A} \underbrace{\begin{bmatrix} p_n \\ v_n \\ \lambda_n \end{bmatrix}}_{:=x_n} + \underbrace{\begin{bmatrix} \bar{\rho} p_n \\ \bar{\rho} v_n \\ -\ddot{z}(t_n) \\ -z(t_n) \\ -\dot{z}(t_n) \end{bmatrix}}_{:=a} = 0 \qquad (3.16)$$

Again, due to the discretization error involved these equations have no classical solution. Every generalized solution satisfies the equations (3.16) only up to a specific residual vector $r = \left[r_1^T, r_2^T, r_\lambda^T, r_p^T, r_v^T\right]^T$.

We will proceed in this section as follows. First, the problem (3.15) is transformed to state space form (ssf), which is globally defined in that case, and then discretized by the same implicit BDF-scheme. The resulting corrector problems are square linear systems, which can be solved exactly within roundoff. The solution of such a corrector problem, will finally be backtransformed to the full set of variables p, v and λ. For these values, properties of the residual vector will be given.

To transform the above system to state space form the constraints are transformed into explicit form and the *state variables* can be given by the following relations

$$\begin{aligned} p &= G^{\dagger}z(t) + V_1 y_1 && (3.17a)\\ v &= G^{\dagger}\dot{z}(t) + V_1 y_2. && (3.17b) \end{aligned}$$

Here $G^\dagger$ denotes the Moore–Penrose inverse of G. V_1 is defined to be a matrix spanning the nullspace of G, i.e.

$$GV_1 = 0 \tag{3.18}$$

holds.

By premultiplying (3.15a) and (3.15b) by V_1^T and using the relations (3.17) and (3.18) we obtain the state space form of the above model problem:

$$\begin{aligned} V_1^T V_1 \dot{y}_1 &= V_1^T V_1 y_2 & (3.19a)\\ V_1^T V_1 \dot{y}_2 &= -V_1^T (K V_1 y_1 + D V_1 y_2 + K G^\dagger z + D G^\dagger \dot{z} + G^\dagger \ddot{z}). & (3.19b) \end{aligned}$$

After having discretized these equations with implicit BDF – formulas (2.10) we obtain the corrector equations for this problem (n, which indicates the current integration step, is suppressed for notational convenience):

$$\begin{aligned} V_1^T V_1 \rho y_1 - V_1^T V_1 y_2 &= 0 & (3.20a)\\ V_1^T V_1 \rho y_2 + V_1^T (K V_1 y_1 + D V_1 y_2 + K G^\dagger z + D G^\dagger \dot{z} + G^\dagger \ddot{z}) &= 0. & (3.20b) \end{aligned}$$

This is a linear problem which can be solved exactly up to roundoff. After having discretized the state space form of the model problem, we can back-transform to the original set of variables by using the relations (3.17) again. By exploiting the linearity of the difference operator ρ we obtain the following system:

$$\begin{aligned} V_1^T (\rho p - v - G^\dagger (\rho z - \dot{z})) &= 0\\ V_1^T (\rho v + K p + D v - G^\dagger (\rho \dot{z} - \ddot{z})) &= 0. \end{aligned}$$

Due to (3.18) we can add $V_1^T G^T \lambda$ to the left hand side of the second equation. Finally, using $V_1^T G^\dagger = 0$, which is a simple consequence of the definition of V_1 and the Moore–Penrose inverse in the case that G is not rank–deficient, we obtain:

$$\begin{aligned} V_1^T r_1 &= 0 & (3.21a)\\ V_1^T r_2 &= 0. & (3.21b) \end{aligned}$$

Again, from G having full row rank, $\ker(V_1^T) = \text{Range}(G^T)$ follows and we get

$$r_1 \in \text{Range}(G^T) \qquad r_2 \in \text{Range}(G^T). \tag{3.22}$$

For the other components of the residual vector we get from (3.17)

$$r_p = r_v = r_\lambda = 0 \tag{3.23}$$

On the other hand, if we require that the components of the residual r in (3.16) satisfy the conditions (3.22) and (3.23), a solution p, v, λ of (3.16) is uniquely defined. Thus these conditions together with a given stepsize sequence uniquely define the numerical solution of the problem (3.15). To distinguish it from the solutions in the preceeding chapter we will refer to it as the *ssf-solution* of the problem and the special generalized inverse defined by the condition (3.22) and (3.23) is denoted by *ssf–inverse* of matrix A, see Figure 1. In the next section we will give a general definition of this inverse and the corresponding solution.

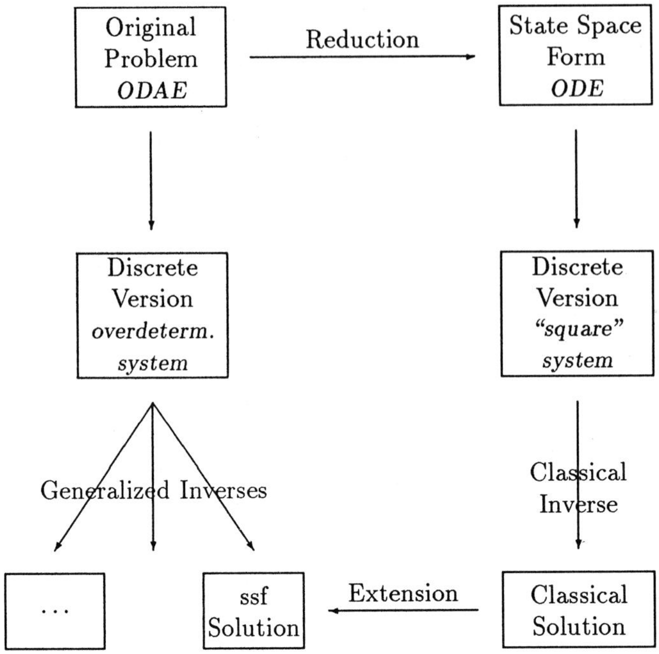

Figurel. Relation between the *ssf-inverse* and the *state space form*

4 The SSF–Solution of General Mechanical Problems

Definition 4.1 *Let the* $n \times m$ *– matrix* A *with* $n > m$ *be partitioned in a square* $m \times m$ *– matrix* A_1 *and a* $n - m \times m$*– matrix* A_2*, then* x *is defined to be the* ssf – solution *of the overdetermined problem*

$$\begin{bmatrix} A_1 \\ A_2 \end{bmatrix} x = \begin{bmatrix} a_1 \\ a_2 \end{bmatrix} \tag{4.24}$$

if the following two conditions are met:

$$A_1 x - a_1 \in Range(A_2^T) \tag{4.25a}$$

$$A_2 x - a_2 = 0. \tag{4.25b}$$

Before showing under what conditions the ssf – solution is well defined, we will give two examples:

Example 4.1 *The matrix* A *in (3.16) can be partitioned as follows:*

$$A_1 := \begin{bmatrix} \frac{\alpha_0}{h} I & -I & 0 \\ K & \frac{\alpha_0}{h} I + D & G^T \\ -GK & -GD & -GG^T \end{bmatrix} \qquad A_2 := \begin{bmatrix} G & 0 & 0 \\ 0 & G & 0 \end{bmatrix}.$$

With this partitioning and a corresponding partitioning of the vector a, it can easily be seen that the above conditions (4.25) are equivalent to those given in the last section (3.22),(3.23).

Example 4.2 *The model problem of the preceeding section can also be formulated in a stabilized form corresponding to (1.8):*

$$\begin{aligned} \dot{p} &= v - G^T\mu \\ \dot{v} &= -Kp - Dv - G^T\lambda - G^T\eta \\ -GKp - GDv - GG^T\lambda &= \ddot{z}(t) \\ Gp &= z(t) \\ Gv &= \dot{z}(t), \end{aligned}$$

After discretizing these equation with an implicit BDF – scheme and using the same notation as in Example 4.1 we obtain:

$$A_1x - a_1 = A_2^T \begin{bmatrix} \mu \\ \eta \end{bmatrix} \tag{4.26a}$$

$$A_2x - a_2 = 0. \tag{4.26b}$$

Thus, the conditions (4.25) are met also the by using the stabilized form. Consequently, for the model problem the stabilized approach (1.8) and the reduction to state space form lead to the same solution, if both forms are discretized with the same scheme.

The ssf – solution is well defined, if (4.25) uniquely defines a vector $x \in \mathcal{R}^n$. A condition for this is given in the following lemma:

Lemma 4.1 *Let V be any $n \times (n-m)$ – matrix spanning the nullspace of A_2, then the ssf - solution of (4.24) is uniquely defined by (4.25), if the $m \times m$ – matrix V^TA_1V is regular.*

Proof: Let us assume $x_1, x_2 \in \mathcal{R}^n$ with $x_1 \neq x_2$ both satisfy (4.25). Then

$$A_1(x_1 - x_2) \in \text{Range}(A_2^T) \tag{4.27a}$$

$$A_2(x_1 - x_2) = 0 \tag{4.27b}$$

By (4.27b) there exists a nonzero vector $\xi \in \mathcal{R}^m$ with $x_1 - x_2 = V\xi$. Inserting this into (4.27a) results in

$$A_1V\xi \in \text{Range}(A_2^T) = \ker(V^T)$$

Thus $V^TA_1V\xi = 0$. By the regularity of V^TA_1V it follows that $\xi = 0$, which is a contradiction to the above assumption. □

It can be easily seen that V^TA_1V is regular for the above model problem. In the general case the regularity also depends on the stepsize h and a general criterion is not known at the present time.

Lemma 4.2 *The ssf-solution of (4.24) is given by either*

$$x_{ssf} = A_2^{\dagger}a_2 + V(V^TA_1V)^{-1}V^T(a_1 - A_1A_2^{\dagger}a_2) \tag{4.28}$$

or, equivalently, with $Q := A_2A_1^{-1}A_2^T$*:*

$$x_{ssf} = A_1^{-1}(I - A_2^TQ^{-1}A_2A_1^{-1})a_1 + A_1^{-1}A_2^TQ^{-1}a_2. \tag{4.29}$$

The matrix $(A_1V)^{ssf} := (V^TA_1V)^{-1}V^T$ *is called the* ssf-inverse *of* A_1V.

Proof: (see [FL89b].) □

The definition of the ssf-solution can be used directly also for solving the discretized corrector step in nonlinear problems. Those problems can only be solved iteratively as shown in Section 2. In every iteration step the linear system (2.13) must be solved. This can be done by taking the ssf-solution given by (4.28) or (4.29) instead of the other approaches discussed at the end of Section 2. For this the matrix A in (2.13) is split into the two submatrices

$$A_1 := \begin{bmatrix} \frac{\alpha_0}{h}I & -I & 0 \\ K & \frac{\alpha_0}{h}M + D & G^T \\ \Gamma_1 & \Gamma_2 & H \end{bmatrix} \qquad A_2 := \begin{bmatrix} G & 0 & 0 \\ \Gamma & G & 0 \end{bmatrix}.$$

For this partitioning V can be taken as

$$V = \begin{bmatrix} V_1 & 0 & 0 \\ -G^{\dagger}\Gamma V_1 & V_1 & 0 \\ 0 & 0 & I \end{bmatrix}$$

and the solution x_{ssf} of a particular iteration step can be computed using (4.28) for example.

This defines the *ssf-iteration* for ODAEs, which is the only numerical method for ODAEs that is equivalent to the reduction to state space form for the model problem.

This iteration has been discussed in detail in [FL89b]. Furthermore it has been shown that the observation in Example 4.2 also holds in the general case: the stabilized formulation (1.8) is equivalent to the BDF-discretized ODAE formulation (1.9) together with the ssf-iteration.

5 Conclusions and Numerical Remarks

We have presented several different formulations of the mechanical equations of motion. Up to the present time there is no theory which can determine which is the best of these formulations under discretization, with respect to stability properties. For example, one of the questions which shoud be asked is which of the formulations (1.7) or (1.8) is more stable and consequently more accurately solvable?

Until some other criteria are found, it appears reasonable to relate all numerical methods to the state space form, which is from the analytical point of view the best ODE form to describe the problem. In this paper we related two DAE formulations, (1.8) and (1.9) to the explicit reduction of the problem to state space form.

The numerical realization of each approach has been worked out to some extent:

- The stabilized approach (1.8) can be implemented by just applying a standard DAE solver, like DASSL [Pet82] without any modification to the code. Clearly, this would be not the most efficient way to implement the method. A more efficient technique, based on partialy decoupling the additional multipliers μ and η from the other variables has been suggested in [GGL85,FL89a].
- The ODAE formulation (1.9) has been realized in an experimental code ODASSL, which is derived from DASSL by replacing the standard Newton corrector iteration by the ssf-iteration described above. For numerical details see [Fuh88]. This code has been implemented in the multibody program SIMPACK [Rul89] . Numerical results for complex closed loop multibody systems can be found in [SR90].
- The third method explicitly computes the state variables by the so – called *generalized coordinate partitioning method* and integrates them with either an ADAMS – scheme or implicit BDF - formulas [HY90,WH82].

A detailed comparison of these three approaches in the environment of a general multibody program is a current project of the authors.

Acknowledgements
The authors would like to thank Professors Haug and Potra as well as Jeng Yen for many fruitful discussions during the NATO Advanced Research Workshop in Snowbird, Utah. Also they are indebted to Professors Nevanlinna and Grübel for their support during the formulations of these ideas.

References

[Bau72] J. Baumgarte. Stabilization of constraints and integrals of motion, in dynamical systems. *Comp. Meth. in Appl. Mechanics*, 1:1 – 16, 1972.

[BCP89] K.E. Brenan, S.L. Campbell, and L.R. Petzold. *The Numerical Solution of Initial Value Problems in Ordinary Differential-Algebraic Equations.* North Holland Publishing Co., 1989.

[BJO86] H. Brandl, R. Johanni, and M. Otter. An Algorithm for the Simulation of Multibody Systems With Kinematic Loops. In *Proc. IFAC/IFIP/IMACS International Symposium on The Theory of Robots, Vienna, Austria*, Dec 1986.

[CL90] S.L. Campbell and B. Leimkuhler. Differentiation of constraints in differential-algebraic equations. In E. Haug and R. Deyo, editors, *NATO Advanced Research Workshop on Real – Time Integration Methods for Mechanical System Simulation*, Springer, Heidelberg, to appear 1990.

[DS83] J.E. Dennis and R.B. Schnabel. *Numerical Methods for Unconstrained Optimization and Nonlinear Equation.* Prentice-Hall, Englewood Cliffs, 1983.

[FL89a] C. Führer and B. Leimkuhler. *Formulation and Numerical Solution of the Equations of Constrained Mechanical Motion.* Technical Report DFVLR-FB 89-08, Deutsche Forschungs- und Versuchsanstalt für Luft- und Raumfahrt (DFVLR), D-5000 Köln 90, 1989.

[FL89b] C. Führer and B. Leimkuhler. Numerical solution of differential-algebraic equations for constrained mechanical motion. *Numerische Mathematik*, submitted for publication 1989.

[Fuh88] C. Führer. *Differential-algebraische Gleichungssysteme in mechanischen Mehrkörpersystemen.* PhD thesis, Mathematisches Institut, Technische Universität München, 1988.

[Gea71] C.W. Gear. *Numerical Initial Value Problems in Ordinary Differential Equations.* Prentice-Hall, 1971.

[GGL85] C.W. Gear, G.K. Gupta, and B.J. Leimkuhler. Automatic integration of the Euler-Lagrange equations with constraints. *J. Comp. Appl. Math.*, 12 & 13:77–90, 1985.

[GL83] G.H. Golub and C.F. Loan van. *Matrix Computations.* The John Hopkins University Press, Baltimore, 1983.

[HY90] E. Haug and J. Yen. Implicit numerical integration of constrained equations of motion via generalized coordinate partitioning. In E. Haug and R. Deyo, editors, *NATO Advanced Research Workshop on Real – Time Integration Methods for Mechanical System Simulation*, Springer, Heidelberg, to appear 1990.

[Ost90] G.P. Ostermeyer. Baumgarte stabilization for differential – algebraic equations. In E. Haug and R. Deyo, editors, *NATO Advanced Research Workshop on Real – Time Integration Methods for Mechanical System Simulation*, Springer, Heidelberg, to appear 1990.

[Pet82] L.R. Petzold. A description of DASSL: a differential/ algebraic system solver. In *Proc. 10th IMACS World Congress, August 8-13 Montreal 1982*, 1982.

[Rul89] W. Rulka. SIMPACK, Ein Rechenprogramm zur Simulation von Mehrkörpersystemen mit grossen Bewegungen. In *Proc. Finite Elemente in der Praxis, Computergestütztes Berechnen und Konstruieren*, pages 206 – 245, T-PROGRAMM GMBH, P.O. Box 1444 D-7410 Reutlingen, 1989.

[SR90] R. Schwertassek and W. Rulka. Aspects of Efficient and Reliable Multibody System Simulation. In E. Haug and R. Deyo, editors, *NATO Advanced Research Workshop on Real – Time Integration Methods for Mechanical System Simulation*, Springer, Heidelberg, to appear 1990.

[Sta76] J.W. Starner. *A Numerical Algorithm for the Solution of Implicit Algebraic-Differential Systems of Equations.* PhD thesis, University of New Mexico, 1976.

[WH82] R.A. Wehage and E.J. Haug. Generalized coordinate partitioning for dimension reduction in analysis of constrained dynamic systems. *J.Mech.Design*, 134:247–255, 1982.

Differential-Geometric Techniques for Solving Differential Algebraic Equations

Florian A. Potra[1] and Werner C. Rheinboldt[2]

Abstract

A differential-geometric approach for the numerical solution of mixed differential-algebraic systems of equations is presented and a general local parametrization for such systems is constructed. Multistep ODE solvers are then applied for obtaining locally a numerical approximation to the solution of the differential-algebraic system. The class of local parametrizations considered in the paper contains as particular cases, the 'tangent space' parametrization and the local parametrization induced by the 'generalized coordinate partitioning'. Applications for the numerical solution of the Euler-Lagrange equations are discussed in detail and computational results for a four-bar linkage mechanism are given.

1. Introduction

Differential-algebraic systems of equations (DAEs) arise in many areas of science and engineering. In particular, the equations of motion for a constrained mechanical system considered in this volume are usually modelled as a second order DAE. In recent years the literature on the numerical solution of such systems has grown rapidly (see e.g. the monographs [1], [4]). However, up to now, existence theories for nonlinear DAEs are available only for a few selected classes of systems.

---

[1]Department of Mathematics, The University of Iowa, Iowa City, Iowa 52242

[2]Dept. of Mathematics and Statistics, University of Pittsburgh, Pittsburgh, PA 15260.
The work of this author was in part supported under ONR-grant N-00014-90-J-1025 and NSF-grant CCR-8907654.

NATO ASI Series, Vol. F 69
Real-Time Integration Methods for Mechanical System Simulation
Edited by E. J. Haug and R. C. Deyo

In [10] a differential-geometric approach was introduced for the analysis of the solution properties of a class of linear DAEs, and in [12] this approach was extended to general, semi-implicit, nonlinear equations of first and second order; that is, to systems with separated algebraic and differential equations. Moreover, it was shown there that these results lead to a general local parametrization approach for the computational solution of these systems.

The differential-geometric approach is based on the observation that, as long as we expect the solution of a DAE to be some smooth path in the space of dependent variables, the system must define a dynamical system in suitable subsets of that space. While this connection with dynamical systems is obvious for ordinary differential equations (ODEs), the same is certainly not true for DAEs. In fact, besides [10], [12] we are only aware of [9] as the only further study that specifically addresses this connection.

This article is intended to be an introductory overview of certain of the cited differential-geometric results and of some of the numerical algorithms that can be developed from them. In order to make the presentation widely accessible, we begin in section 2 with a brief summary of concepts and notations about sub-manifolds of finite-dimensional spaces and their first and second tangent bundles. Then section 3 presents an overview of basic results about dynamical systems in the form needed for our DAE-theory. This is followed in sections 4 and 5 by a presentation of the principal results of [12] on the existence and uniqueness of solutions and the use of local parametrizations. However, in order to avoid some of the technical aspects of the general theory we restrict ourselves, for the most part, to DAEs with certain linearity properties including, in particular, the equations of motion for constrained mechanical system mentioned earlier. In section 6 we discuss the computational implementation of local parametrizations and identify two useful parametrizations induced by the tangent space of the constraint manifold and by a so-called "coordinate partitioning", respectively. Then section 7 presents algorithms based on the application of explicit and implicit multi-step methods to the resulting local dynamical systems and in section 8 versions of these algorithms for the solution of the Euler-Lagrange equations are formulated. These algorithms generalize those previously discussed in [5] and [8]. Finally, in section 9 we give some computational results for a four-bar-linkage mechanism.

2. Differential-Geometric Background

In this section we collect some basic material needed throughout the remainder of the presentation. For further details we refer to standard text on differential geometry such as [6] or [13].

We begin with some standard terminology. If U is an open set of R^n then a mapping $F:U \to R^m$ from U into R^m is of class C^ρ , $\rho \geq 0$, on U if all partial derivatives of F up to and including order ρ exist and are continuous in U. More generally, on an arbitrary set S of R^n a map $F:S \to R^m$ is of class C^ρ if for each $x \in S$ there exists an open set $U \subset R^n$ containing x and a mapping $G:U \to R^m$ of class C^ρ that coincides with F throughout $U \cap S$. A map $F:S \to T$ between the sets $S \subset R^n$ and $T \subset R^m$ is a homeomorphism if F is a one-to-one mapping from S onto T and both F and its inverse $F^{-1}:T \to S$ are continuous. A homeomorphism $F:S \to T$ is a C^ρ-diffeomorphism between S and T and both F and F^{-1} are of class C^ρ.

As usual, $L(R^n,R^m)$ is the space of all linear mappings with domain R^n and range in R^m and by $L^2(R^n,R^m)$ the space of all bilinear maps from R^n to R^m. For any C^1-map $F:U \subset R^n \to R^m$, the derivative of F at $x \in U$ is the linear map DF(x) in $L(R^n,R^m)$ defined by $DF(x)h = \lim_{t \to 0} [F(x+th) - F(x)]$. In other words, DF(x) is the linear map that corresponds to the $m \times n$ matrix of first partial derivatives of F at x. Analogously, if F is of class C^2, then the second derivative of F at x is the bilinear map $D^2F(x) \in L^2(R^n,R^m)$ defined by the second partial derivatives of F at x. Note that when F is a C^1-diffeomorphism between the open sets $U \subset R^n$ and $V \subset R^m$ then n=m and DF(x) is nonsingular at all points $x \in U$.

A subset $M \subset R^n$ is a d-dimensional C^ρ-sub-manifold of R^n if for each point $x \in M$ there exists an open set $U \subset R^n$ containing x such that the neighborhood $U \cap M$ of x on M is C^ρ-diffeomorphic to an open subset V of R^d. Any particular diffeomorphism $F:U \cap M \to V$ is called a chart on $U \cap M$ and its inverse a local coordinate system on $U \cap M$.

Note that by this definition any open subset U of R^n is an n-dimensional C^∞-sub-manifold of R^n. The tangent space T_xU of this manifold U at any point $x \in U$ is the n-dimensional linear space $\{x\}\times R^n$ and the first and second tangent bundles TU and T^2U of U are the 2n- dimensional and 4n-dimensional submanifolds $U\times R^n$ of $(R^n)^2$ and $U\times(R^n)^3$ of $(R^n)^4$, respectively[3].

The classical example of a 2-dimensional C^∞-sub-manifold of R^3 is, of course, the unit sphere $S^2 = \{ (\xi,\eta,\zeta) \in R^3;\ \xi^2 + \eta^2 + \zeta^2 = 1 \}$. More generally, let $F:E \subset R^n \to R^m$, n >m, be some mapping of class C^ρ ,ρ≥1, on the open set E of R^n. A point $x \in E$ is a regular point of F if dim $DF(x)R^n = m$; that is, if the derivative DF(x) has full rank m. A point $b \in R^m$ is a regular value of F if the inverse image $F^{(-1)}(b) = \{ x \in E, F(x) = b\}$ consists only of regular points. Then the following result holds:

Theorem 1: Let $F:E \subset R^n \to R^m$, n > m, be a mapping of class C^ρ ,ρ≥1, on the open set E of R^n. Then for any regular value $b \in R^m$ the inverse image $F^{(-1)}(b)$ is either empty or an (n-m)-dimensional C^ρ-sub-manifold of R^n.

From now on, let $F:E \subset R^n \to R^m$, d=n-m > 0, be a given mapping of class C^ρ ,ρ≥3, on the non-empty open set E of R^n such that $DF(x)R^n = R^m$ for $x \in E$. Then each member of the family of sets

$$M_b = \{ x \in E, F(x) = b\},\quad b \in F(E) \tag{2.1}$$

is a non- empty d-dimensional C^ρ-sub-manifold of R^n. Clearly, any point $x_0 \in E$ belongs to exactly one of these manifolds, namely that for $b = F(x_0)$; we shall call this the manifold of the family through the point x_0.

For any point $x \in M_b$ the tangent space T_xM_b of M_b at x is defined by

$$T_xM_b = \{ (x,p) \in T_xR^n;\ DF(x)p = 0 \}. \tag{2.2}$$

[3]We use here the notation $(R^n)^k = R^n\times R^n \ldots \times R^n$ (k-times).

Clearly, T_xM_b is a d-dimensional linear subspace of the n-dimensional linear space $T_xR^n = \{x\}\times R^n$. The tangent bundle TM_b of M_b is the disjoint union of all tangent spaces T_xM_b for $x \in M_b$; that is,

$$TM_b = \{ (x,p) \in TE;\ F(x) = b,\ DF(x)p = 0 \}. \tag{2.3}$$

In other words, the points $(x,p) \in TM_b$ are the zeroes of the mapping

$$H: E\times R^n \to R^m \times R^m;\ H(x,p) = \begin{pmatrix} F(x) - b \\ DF(x)p \end{pmatrix},\ \forall\ (x,p) \in E\times R^n$$

Since DF(x) was assumed to have full rank on E it follows that the derivative

$$DH(x,p) = \begin{pmatrix} DF(x) & 0 \\ D^2F(x)p & DF(x) \end{pmatrix}$$

has full rank on TE and hence, by Theorem 1, that the tangent bundle is a non-empty, 2d-dimensional $C^{\rho-1}$-sub-manifold of TR^n. Therefore, TM_b itself has a tangent bundle, namely, the 4d-dimensional $C^{\rho-2}$-sub-manifold $T(TM_b) = T^2M_b$ of the 4n-dimensional product space T^2R^n defined by

$$T^2M_b = \{((x,y),(p,q)) \in T^2E;\ F(x)=b,\ DF(x)p = 0,\ DF(x)q+D^2F(x)(y,p)=0 \}. \tag{2.4}$$

3. <u>Vectorfields</u>

A C^σ-vectorfield, $\sigma \geq 1$, on some open subset E_0 of R^n is a C^σ-mapping on E_0 such that

$$\pi:\ E_0 \to TE_0\ ;\ \pi(x) = (x,\ \theta(x)),\ \ \forall\ x \in E_0\ . \tag{3.1}$$

An integral curve of π through a point $x_0 \in E_0$ is any C^σ-path ξ: $J \to E_0$, defined on some open interval $J \subset R^1$ containing $0 \in J$, for which $(\xi(t),\xi'(t)) = \pi(\xi(t))$ for $t \in J$ and $\xi(0) = x_0$; that is, which solves the initial value problem

$$x' = \theta(x), \ x \in E_0, \ x(0) = x_0. \tag{3.2}$$

As before, let $F:E \subset R^n \to R^m$, d=n-m > 0, be a given mapping of class C^ρ, $\rho\geq 3$, on the non-empty open set E of R^n such that $DF(x)R^n = R^m$ for $x \in E$, and consider the family (2.1) of d-dimensional C^ρ-sub-manifolds of R^n. We call the vectorfield (3.1) tangential to this family of manifolds (2.1) if $\pi(x) \in T_xM_b$ for all $x \in E_0 \cap M_b$. Since $x \in M_b$, $b=F(x)$, for any $x \in E_0 \cap E$, this requires that

$$DF(x)\theta(x) = 0, \ \forall \ x \in E_0 \cap E. \tag{3.3}$$

Thus, for any integral curve $\xi: J \to E_0 \cap E$ of π through $x_0 \in E_0 \cap E$ it follows that $DF(\xi(t))\xi'(t) = 0$, $t \in J$. Since $\xi(J)$ is a connected subset of the open set $E_0 \cap E$, the integral mean-value theorem guarantees that

$$F(\xi(t)) - F(\xi(0)) = \int_0^t DF(\xi(s))\xi'(s)ds = 0, \ \forall t \in J.$$

In other words, the path $\xi: J \to E_0 \cap E$ remains on the manifold M_b, $b = F(x_0)$, through the initial point x_0, and (3.3) implies that $(\xi(t), \xi'(t)) \in TM_b$, for $t \in J$.

From this and the standard theory of ODEs (see e.g. [6] or [13]) we obtain now the following existence and uniqueness result:

Theorem 2: Let (3.1) be a C^σ-vectorfield, $\sigma \geq 1$, on the (non-empty) open subset E_0 of R^n. Then the following results hold:

(i) There exists a C^σ-integral curve $\xi: J \to E_0$ of π through each $x \in E_0$ defined on an open interval J containing 0. Moreover, any two such curves are equal on the intersection of their domains.

(ii) If π is tangential to the family (2.1) and $E_0 \cap E$ is non-empty, then any integral curve $\xi:J \to E_0 \cap E$ of π through $x_0 \in E_0 \cap E$ satisfies $(\xi(t), \xi'(t)) \in TM_b$, $b=F(x_0)$, for all $t \in J$.

(iii) The union of the domains of all integral curves of π through a point $x \in U_0$ is an open, possibly unbounded interval $J_x = (\tau_-(x), \tau_+(x))$. There exists a C^σ-integral curve $\xi^*:J_x \to E_0$, of π through x, and J_x is the largest interval on which such an intergal curve exists.

(iv) If $\tau_+(x) < \infty$ for some $x \in E_0$, then for any compact set $C \subset E_0$ there exists a $\delta > 0$ such that $\xi^*(t) \notin C$ for $t > \tau_+(x)-\delta$. A corresponding result holds when $\tau_-(x) > -\infty$.

(v) The set $D(\pi) = \{(t,x) \in R^1 \times U_0;\ t \in J_x\}$ is open in $R^1 \times E_0$ and contains $\{0\} \times U_0$. Moreover, the global flow $\gamma: D(\pi) \to E_0$, $\gamma(t,x)=\xi^*(t)$, $t \in J_x$, of π is of class C^σ on $D(\pi)$.

Consider now a second order initial value problem $x'' = \theta(x,x')$, $x \in E_0$, $x(0)=x_0$, $x'(0)=y_0$, which, of course, may be written in the first order form

$$x' = y,\ \ y' = \theta(x,y),\ x \in E_0,\ x(0) = x_0,\ x'(0) = y_0. \tag{3.4}$$

Thus, we encounter in this case a vector-field of the form

$$\pi: E_\pi = E_0 \times Y \subset TE_0 \to T^2E_0\ ;\ \pi(x,y) = ((x,y),(y,\theta(x,y))),\ \ \forall\ (x,y) \in E_0 \times Y \tag{3.5}$$

on a subset of the tangent bundle TE_0 of E_0. Note that the second and third component of the image vector are identical. In other words, (3.5) represents a sub-class of the vector fields on E_π called the vector fields on E_π that are consistent with a second order ODE. We assume always that the domain E_π of π is some open subset of TE_0.

An integral curve of (3.5) through a point $(x_0, y_0) \in E_\pi$ is now a C^σ-path $\xi: J \to E_0$, defined on some open interval $J \subset R^1$ containing $0 \in J$, for which

$$\begin{aligned} &(\xi(t),\ \xi'(t)) \in E_\pi\ ,\ \xi(0)=x_0,\ \xi'(0)=y_0 \\ &((\xi(t),\xi'(t)),(\xi'(t),\xi''(t))) = \pi(\xi(t),\xi'(t)),\ \forall\ t \in J; \end{aligned} \tag{3.6}$$

that is, which is a solution of the initial value problem (3.4).

As before, the vectorfield (3.5) is called tangential to the family of tangent bundles TM_b, $b \in F(E)$, of (2.1) if $\pi(x,y) \in T_{(x,y)}(TM_b)$ for $(x,y) \in E_\pi \cap TM_b$; that is, if

$$DF(x)\theta(x,y) + D^2F(x)(y,y) = 0,\ \forall\ (x,y) \in E_\pi \cap (E \times \ker DF(x)) \tag{3.7}$$

Then, for any integral curve $\xi:J \to E_0 \cap E$, of π through $(x_0,y_0) \in E_\pi \cap TM_b$ such that $DF(\xi(t))\xi'(t) = 0$, $t \in J$, the integral mean-value theorem provides that

$$DF(\xi(t))\xi'(t)-DF(x_0)y_0 = \int_0^t [DF(\xi(s))\xi''(s)+D^2F(\xi(s))(\xi'(s),\xi'(s))]ds = 0, \quad \forall\, t \in J$$

Hence, the path $\xi:J \to E_0 \cap E$ remains on the tangent bundle TM_b, $b = F(x_0)$, corresponding to x_0 and (3.7) implies that $((\xi(t),\xi'(t)),(\xi'(t),\xi''(t))) \in T^2M_b$, for $t \in J$.

Again an existence and uniqueness result of the form of Theorem 2 holds. We note here only the following shortened version.

Theorem 3: Let (3.5) be a C^σ-vectorfield, $\sigma \geq 2$, on the (non-empty) open subset $E_\pi \subset TE_0 \subset TR^n$. Then there exists an integral curve $\xi: J \to U_0$ of π through each $(x,y) \in E_\pi$ defined on an open interval J containing 0. Moreover, any two such curves are equal on the intersection of their domains. If π is tangential to the family (2.1) and $E_0 \cap E$ is non-empty, then any integral curve $\xi:J \to E_0 \cap E$ of π through $(x_0,y_0) \in E_\pi \cap TM_b$, $b=F(x_0)$, for which $DF(\xi(t))\xi'(t) = 0$ for t in J, satisfies $((\xi(t),\xi'(t)),(\xi'(t),\xi''(t))) \in T^2M_b$, for all $t \in J$.

4. A Class of First and Second Order DAEs

In this section we begin with the autonomous, first order DAE

$$F_1(x) = b$$
$$F_2(x, x', z) = 0 \tag{4.1}$$

for which we assume that

$F_1: E_x \subset R^n \to R^r$ and $F_2: E_2 = E_x \times E_p \times E_z \subset (R^n)^2 \times R^m \to R^s$ are of class C^ρ, $\rho \geq 3$, on their domains, where $E_x \subset R^n$, $E_p \subset R^n$, and $E_z \subset R^m$, are non-empty open sets, and $r<n\leq r+s=n+m$; (4.2a)

and for each $(x,p,z) \in E_2$ the matrix

$$\begin{pmatrix} DF_1(x) & 0 \\ D_pF_2(x,p,z) & D_zF_2(x,p,z) \end{pmatrix}$$

is non-singular (4.2b)

From (4.2b) it follows that $DF_1(x)R^n = R^r$ for all $x \in E_x$ and hence, as we saw in section 2, that each member of the family of sets

$$M_b = \{ x \in E_x, F_1(x) = b\}, \quad b \in F_1(E_x), \tag{4.3}$$

is a non- empty (n-r)-dimensional C^ρ-sub-manifold of R^n. For any $x_0 \in E_x$ we call the unique manifold (4.3) with $b = F_1(x_0)$ the constraint manifold through that point.

For given $b \in F_1(E_x)$ a C^σ-solution, $1 \le \sigma \le \rho-1$, of (4.1) consists of two C^σ-paths $x: J \to E_x$ and $z: J \to E_z$, defined on some open interval J of R^1, such that

$$(x(t),x'(t),z(t)) \in E_2\,,\ F_1(x(t)) = b,\ \ F_2(x(t),x'(t),z(t)) = 0,\ \ \forall\, t \in J. \tag{4.4}$$

This necessitates that $DF_1(x(t))x'(t) = 0$, $\forall\, t \in J$. Hence, if $(x_0,p_0,z_0) \in E_2$ is any point on a solution (4.4); that is, if $x(t_0) = x_0$, $x'(t_0) = p_0$, $z(t_0) = z_0$ for some $t_0 \in J$, then we must have $DF_1(x_0)p_0 = 0$, and $F_2(x_0,p_0,z_0) = 0$, while, of course, automatically $x_0 \in M_b$ for $b=F_1(x_0)$.

This suggests the definition of the <u>initial data map</u>

$$H: E_2 \to R^r \times R^s, \quad H(x,p,z) = \begin{pmatrix} DF_1(x)p \\ F_2(x,p,z) \end{pmatrix}, \ (x,p,z) \in E_2\,. \tag{4.5}$$

Evidently, for any given $(x,p,z) \in E_2$, the partial derivative $D_{p,z}H$ of H with respect to p and z is the matrix in (4.2b). By Theorem 1 this implies that

$$K = \{ (x,p,z) \in E_2\,;\ H(x,p,z) = 0 \} \tag{4.6}$$

is a n-dimensional $C^{\rho-1}$-submanifold of $(R^n)^2 \times R^m$, the <u>initial data manifold</u> of the problem.

A general existence and uniqueness theory for (4.1) was given in [12] and requires a closer analysis of the relationship between the initial data manifold K and the constraint manifolds (4.3) utilizing the theory of covering spaces. For the applications considered here it suffices to restrict attention to the case when F_2 is linear in p and z; that is, when (4.1) has the special form

$$\begin{aligned} &F_1(x) = b \\ &A(x)x' + B(x)z + G(x) = 0, \end{aligned} \tag{4.7}$$

Here (4.2a) requires that F_1: $E_x \subset R^n \rightarrow R^r$, A:$E_x \rightarrow L(R^n,R^s)$, B: $E_x \rightarrow L(R^n,R^s)$, and G: $E_x \rightarrow R^s$ are of class C^ρ, $\rho \geq 3$, on the open non-empty set $E_x \subset R^n$, and that $r<n\leq r+s=n+m$. Moreover, condition (4.2b) is equivalent with the assumption that for each $x \in E_x$ the matrix

$$\begin{pmatrix} DF_1(x) & 0 \\ A(x) & B(x) \end{pmatrix} \tag{4.8}$$

is non-singular.

Hence, in this case the equation H(x,p,z) = 0 has for each $x \in E_x$ a unique solution

$$\begin{pmatrix} p \\ z \end{pmatrix} = \begin{pmatrix} \eta(x) \\ \zeta(x) \end{pmatrix} = \begin{pmatrix} D_1F(x) & 0 \\ A(x) & B(x) \end{pmatrix}^{-1} \begin{pmatrix} 0 \\ -G(x) \end{pmatrix} \tag{4.9}$$

Then

$$\pi: E_x \rightarrow TE_x, \quad \pi(x) = (x, \eta(x)), \quad x \in E_x \tag{4.10}$$

defines a C^ρ-vectorfield on the open set E_x which by definition of the initial data manifold K is tangential to the family of constraint manifolds (4.3).
Now, consider (4.7) together with the initial condition $x(0) = x_0 \in E_x$ and set $p_0=\eta(x_0)$, $z_0=\zeta(x_0)$ which implies that $(x_0, p_0, z_0) \in K$. Then Theorem 3 holds and there exists an integral curve ξ:J $\rightarrow E_x$ of π through x_0 for which $(\xi(t),\xi'(t))\in TM_b$, $b=F(x_0)$, for all $t \in J$. In other words, the paths x:J$\rightarrow E_x$, z:J$\rightarrow E_z$, defined by $x(t)=\xi(t)$, $z(t)=\zeta(\xi(t))$, $t\in J$, constitute a solution of (4.7).

Instead of repeating all of Theorem 3 we summarize this result only as follows:

Theorem 5: If (4.2a/b) holds for (4.7), then, for any given $x_0 \in E_x$, there exists a unique, maximally extended C^r-solution $x: J \to E_1$ and $z: J \to E_z$, of (4.7) which satisfies the initial conditions $x(0) = x_0$, $x'(0) = p_0 = \eta(x_0)$, $z(0) = z_0=\zeta(x_0)$.

As noted, a corresponding result for the general equation (4.1) was proved in [12]. There the theory was also extended to the second order system

$$\begin{aligned} &F_1(x) = b \\ &F_2(x, x', x'', z) = 0 \end{aligned} \tag{4.11}$$

subject to the conditions

$F_1: E_x \subset R^n \to R^r$
$F_2: E_2 = E_x \times E_y \times E_q \times E_z \subset (R^n)^3 \times R^m \to R^s$ are of class C^ρ, $\rho \geq 4$, on their domains where $E_x, E_y, E_z \subset R^n$, and $E_z \subset R^m$, are non-empty open sets and $r<n\leq r+s=n+m$;
(4.12a)

for each $(x,y,q,z) \in E_2$ the matrix

$$\begin{pmatrix} DF_1(x) & 0 \\ D_qF_2(x,y,q,z) & D_zF_2(x,y,q,z) \end{pmatrix}$$

is non-singular. (4.12b)

As before we see that each member of the family of sets (4.3) is a non-empty (n-r)-dimensional C^ρ-sub-manifold of R^n, the constraint manifold of (4.11) through x_0.

It is natural to reduce (4.11) to the first order system:

$$\begin{aligned} &F_1(x) &&= b \\ &x' - y &&= 0 \\ &F_2(x, y, y', z) &&= 0. \end{aligned} \tag{4.13}$$

With the combination (x,y) as new differential variable, this constitutes a DAE of the form (4.1) for which (4.2a) turns out to be valid. However, (4.2b) does not hold since the corresponding matrix

$$\begin{pmatrix} DF_1(x) & 0 & 0 \\ I_n & 0 & 0 \\ 0 & D_qF_2(x,y,q,z) & D_zF_2(x,y,q,z) \end{pmatrix}$$

is singular. This failure of (4.2b) is hardly surprising since we should expect (4.11) to induce a vector field on the tangent bundle TE_x that is consistent with a second order equation.

For any $b \in F_1(E_x)$ a C^σ-solution, $1 \le \sigma \le \rho-2$, of (4.1) consists of C^σ- paths $x: J \to E_x$ and $z:J \to E_z$, defined on some open interval J of R^1, such that

$$(x(t),x'(t),x''(t),z(t)) \in E_2,\ F_1(x(t)) = b,\ \ F_2(x(t),x'(t),x''(t),z(t)) = 0,\ \ \forall\, t \in J. \quad (4.14)$$

This implies that $DF_1(x(t))x'(t) = 0$, $DF_1(x(t))x''(t) + D^2F_1(x)(x'(t),x'(t))=0$, for all t in J, which means that $\gamma{:}J \to T^2M_b$, $\gamma(t) = ((x(t),x'(t)),(x'(t),x''(t))$, $t \in J$, is a path on T^2M_b. In analogy to the first order case, this suggests the definition

$$\begin{aligned} &H{:}E_2 \subset (R^n)^3 \times R^m \to R^{r+s} \\ &H(x,y,q,z) = (DF_1(x)q + D^2F_1(x)(y,y),\ F_2(x,y,q,z))\ ,\ \forall\ (x,y,q,z) \in E_2 \qquad (4.15) \end{aligned}$$

for the initial data map of (4.11). Once again, (4.12b) implies that the solution set

$$K = \{\ (x,y,q,z) \in E_2\ ;\ H(x,y,q,z) = 0\ \} \qquad (4.16)$$

is an n-dimensional $C^{\rho-2}$-submanifold of $(R^n)^3 \times R^m$, called the initial data manifold of (4.11).

As before, we shall not present here the general theory but restrict ourselves to the linear case

$$F_1(x) = b$$
$$A(x,x')x'' + B(x,x')z + G(x,x') = 0, \tag{4.17}$$

Then (4.12a) requires that the maps $F_1: E_x \subset R^n \to R^r$, $A: E_x \times E_y \to L(R^n,R^s)$, $B: E_x \times E_y \to L(R^m,R^s)$ and $G: E_x \times E_y \to R^s$ are of class C^ρ, $\rho \geq 4$, on their domains where $E_x, E_y \subset R^n$ are non-empty open sets and $r<n\leq r+s=n+m$. Moreover, (4.12b) is equivalent with the assumption that the matrix

$$\begin{pmatrix} DF_1(x) & 0 \\ A(x,y) & B(x,y) \end{pmatrix} \tag{4.18}$$

is non-singular for all $(x,y) \in E_x \times E_y$.

Then, as in the first order case, the equation $H(x,y,q,z) = 0$ has for each (x,y) in $E_x \times E_y$ a unique solution

$$\begin{pmatrix} q \\ z \end{pmatrix} = \begin{pmatrix} \eta(x,y) \\ \zeta(x,y) \end{pmatrix} \equiv -\begin{pmatrix} DF_1(x) & 0 \\ A(x,y) & B(x,y) \end{pmatrix}^{-1} \begin{pmatrix} D^2F_1(x)(y,y) \\ G(x,y) \end{pmatrix} \tag{4.19}$$

and hence

$$\pi: E_\pi = E_x \times E_y \subset TE_x \to T^2E_1, \quad \pi(x) = ((x,y),(y,\eta(x,y))), \quad (x,y) \in E_\pi \tag{4.20}$$

defines a $C^{\rho-1}$-vectorfield on the open set E_π of the tangent bundle TE_x. Clearly, by definition of the initial data manifold K, this vectorfield is tangential to the family of tangent bundles TM_b, $b \in F_1(E_x)$ of the constraint manifolds (4.3) of (4.17); that is,

$$DF_1(x)\eta(x,y) + D^2F_1(x)(y,y) = 0, \ \forall\ (x,y) \in E_x \times (E_y \cap \ker DF_1(x)) \tag{4.21}$$

Now, consider (4.17) together with the initial condition

$$x(0) = x_0\,,\ y(0) = y_0\,,\ (x_0,y_0) \in E_x \times (E_y \cap \ker DF_1(x_0)) \tag{4.22}$$

and set $q_0=\eta(x_0,y_0)$, $z_0=\zeta(x_0,y_0)$ which implies that $(x_0,y_0, q_0, z_0) \in K$. Thus by Theorem 3 there exists an integral curve $\xi: J \to E_x$ of π for which (3.6) holds. By definition of π we have $((\xi(t),\xi'(t)),(\xi'(t),\xi''(t))) \in K$, $t \in J$, and hence, in particular $DF_1(\xi(t))\xi'(t) = 0$, $t \in J$. Thus it follows that $((\xi(t),\xi'(t)),(\xi'(t),\xi''(t))) \in T^2M_b$, $b=F_1(x_0)$, and therefore that the paths $x:J\to E_x$, $z:J\to E_z$, defined by $x(t)=\xi(t)$, $z(t)=\zeta(\xi(t))$, $t\in J$, constitute a solution of (4.7).

Once again, instead of repeating all of Theorem 4 we summarize this result only in the brief form:

Theorem 6: If (4.12a/b) holds for (4.17), then, for any given initial data (4.22), there exists a unique, maximally extended C^p-solution $x: J \to E_x$, $z: J \to E_z$, of (4.17) which satisfies the initial conditions $x(0) = x_0$, $x'(0) = y_0$, $x''(0)=\eta(x_0,y_0)$, $z(0) = \zeta(x_0,y_0)$.

For a corresponding result for the general equations (4.11) see again [12].

5. Local Parametrizations

As shown in [12] the results about the semi-implicit DAEs (4.1) and (4.11) lead to a general local parametrization approach for the numerical solution of these systems. Once again, we shall restrict our discussion here to the linear systems (4.7) and (4.17).

Consider first the system (4.7), and suppose that we are in the setting of Theorem 5. Thus, we wish to compute a numerical approximation of the unique C^p-solution $x: J \to E_x$, $z: J \to E_z$ of (4.7) which satisfies the initial conditions $x(0) = x_0$, $p_0 = \eta(x_0)$, $z_0 = \zeta(x_0)$ for given $x_0 \in E_x$. Here $\eta:E_x \to E_p$ and $\zeta:E_x \to E_z$ are the mappings (4.9). As we saw, the problem of solving (4.7) in E_x then reduces to that of solving the explicit initial value problem

$$x'= \eta(x),\ x \in E_x,\ x(0) = x_0. \tag{5.1}$$

Since the desired solution $x: J \to E_0$ of (5.1) through x_0 remains on the tangent bundle TM_b of the constraint manifold M_b , $b =F_1(x_0)$, through x_0 it is natural to work with a local coordinate system on M_b.

Consider any point $x_c \in M_b$, on the manifold M_b through x_0. The subscript 'c' indicates here that x_c will later represent a 'current' (approximate) point on the solution. Now choose a linear subspace $T \subset R^n$, dim $T = n-r$, such that $T^{\perp} \cap \ker DF_1(x_c) = \{0\}$. Then it follows from the implicit function theorem that there exist open neighborhoods V of the origin in T and S_x of x_c in R^n, respectively, as well as a C^{ρ}-map $w: V \to T^{\perp} \subset R^n$ with $w(0) = 0$, such that $M_b \cap S_x = \Psi(V)$ where Ψ is the local coordinate map

$$\Psi: V \to R^n, \ \Psi(t) = x_c + t + w(t), \ t \in V. \tag{5.2}$$

In practice it is often useful to work with local coordinate mappings that correspond to the tangent spaces of M_b; that is, to choose $T=\ker DF(x_c)$. Note that then $Dw(0) = 0$, (see, e.g., [11]).

For the computation we introduce orthonomal bases

$$\begin{aligned} &Q_1 \in L(R^{n-r}, R^n), \ Q_2 \in L(R^r, R^n), \\ &Q_1 R^{n-r} = T, \ Q_2 R^r = T^{\perp} \\ &Q_1^* Q_1 = I_{n-r}, \ Q_2^* Q_2 = I_r, Q_2^* Q_1 = 0 \end{aligned} \tag{5.3}$$

for T and $T^{\perp}$. Then we have the transformed local coordinate map

$$\Phi: U = Q_1^{-1} V \to R^n, \ \Phi(u) = x_c + Q_1 u + Q_2 \omega(u), \ u \in U \subset R^{n-r} \tag{5.4}$$

where $\omega(u) = (Q_2|T^{\perp})^{-1} w((Q_1|T)^{-1} u)$, $u \in U$, is again of class C^{ρ} and satisfies $\omega(0)=0$. From $F_1(\Phi(u)) = 0$ we find that $D\Phi(u)R^{n-r} \subset \ker DF_1(\Phi(u))$ for $u \in U$ and, by (5.3), that

$$Q_1^* D\Phi(u) = Q_1^*[Q_1 + Q_2 D\omega(u)] = I_{n-r} \tag{5.5}$$

whence, by a dimensionality argument,

$$D\Phi(u) R^{n-r} = \ker DF_1(\Phi(u)), \ \forall \ u \in U. \tag{5.6}$$

This implies that for any $u \in U$ and $c \in \ker DF_1(\Phi(u))$ the equation $D\Phi(u)a=c$ has a solution $a \in R^{n-r}$ for which $a = Q_1^* c$ and hence which is unique.

In our local coordinate system we obtain for the ODE (5.1) the local representation

$$D\Phi(u)u' = \eta(\Phi(u)),\ u \in U \tag{5.7a}$$

which, because of $\eta(\Phi(u)) \in \ker DF_1(\Phi(u))$, can be written in the form of the (n-r)-dimensional explicit system

$$u' = Q_1^*\ \eta(\Phi(u)),\ u \in U. \tag{5.7b}$$

Obviously, with $p = Q_1\eta_1 + Q_2\eta_2$, $\eta_1 \in R^{n-r}$, $\eta_2 \in R^r$, the equation $H(x,p,z) = 0$ becomes the non-singular, linear system

$$\begin{pmatrix} DF_1(x)Q_1 & DF_1(x)Q_2 & 0 \\ A(x)Q_1 & A(x)Q_2 & B(x) \end{pmatrix} \begin{pmatrix} \eta_1 \\ \eta_2 \\ z \end{pmatrix} = \begin{pmatrix} 0 \\ -G(x) \end{pmatrix} \tag{5.8}$$

Hence, if, for given $x = \Phi(u)$, $u \in U$, the solution of (5.8) has been found then we have $Q_1^*\ \eta(\Phi(u)) = \eta_1$ and $\zeta(\Phi(u)) = z$.

This local parametrization can also be carried over to the second order system (4.17). As before, suppose that we are in the setting of Theorem 6. Thus, we wish to compute a numerical approximation of the unique $C^{\rho-1}$-solution $x: J \to E_x$, $z: J \to E_z$ of (4.17) which satisfies the initial conditions $x(0)=x_0$, $x'(0)=y_0$, $x''(0)=\eta(x_0,y_0)$, $z(0)=\zeta(x_0,y_0)$ where $(x_0,y_0) \in E_x \times E_y \cap TM_b$, $b=F_1(x_0)$, are given and $\eta: E_\pi = E_x \times E_y \to E_q$, $\zeta: E_x \times E_y \to E_z$, are the mappings (4.19). As we saw, the problem of solving (4.17) reduces to that of solving the explicit system

$$x' = y,\ y' = \eta(x,y),\quad (x,y) \in E_\pi,\ x(0)=x_0,\ y(0)=y_0, \tag{5.9}$$

Since the desired solution $x: J \to E_x$ of (5.1) through x_0 remains on the second tangent bundle T^2M_b of the constraint manifold M_b through x_0 we are led to working with a local coordinate system on TM_b.

Once again let x_c be a 'current' point on the manifold M_b through x_0 and choose a linear subspace $T \subset R^n$, dim T = n-r, such that $T^{\perp} \cap \ker DF_1(x_0) = \{0\}$. Then, with basis maps Q_1, Q_2 satisfying (5.3), the local coordinate map (5.4) is well defined and

$$\Theta: U \times R^{n-r} \to TM_b,\ \Theta(u,v) = (\Phi(u), D\Phi(u)v),\quad u \in U,\ v \in R^{n-r} \tag{5.10}$$

defines a local coordinate system on TM_b. Clearly, we can choose some neighborhood S_0 of the origin of $U \times R^{n-r}$ such that $\Theta(u,v)$ belongs to E_π for all (u,v) in S_0.

Thus with $x = \Phi(u)$ and $y = D\Phi(u)v = Q_1v+Q_2D\omega(u)v$, the differential equations (5.9) assume the local form

$$\begin{aligned} &D\Phi(u)u' = Q_1v+Q_2D\omega(u)v \\ &D\Phi(u)v' + D^2\Phi(u)(u',v) = \eta(\Phi(u), Q_1v+Q_2D\omega(u)v). \end{aligned} \tag{5.11}$$

Recall that for any $d \in \ker DF_1(\Phi(u))$ the unique solution of $D\Phi(u)a = d$ is $a=Q_1^*d$. Hence, since $Q_1v+Q_2D\omega(u)v \in \ker DF_1(x)$, the first equation reduces simply to $u'= v$ and, with this, the second equation can be written as

$$D\Phi(u)v' = \eta(x,y) - D^2\Phi(u)(v,v)\ ,\ x = \Phi(u),\ y = Q_1v+Q_2D\omega(u)v.$$

From $DF_1(\Phi(u))D\Phi(u) = 0$, it follows, together with (4.21) and (5.9), that

$$\begin{aligned} 0 &= DF_1(x)D^2\Phi(u)(v,v) + D^2F_1(x)(D\Phi(u)v, D\Phi(u)v) \\ &= DF_1(x)D^2\Phi(u)(v,v) + D^2F_1(x)(y,y) \\ &= DF_1(x)[D^2\Phi(u)(v,v) - \eta(x,y)]\quad,\ \forall\ (u,v) \in S_0 \end{aligned} \tag{5.12}$$

and, therefore that, as desired, $\eta(x,y) - D^2\Phi(u)(v,v) \in \ker DF_1(x)$.

With this we have shown now that on S_0 the equations (5.11) can be reduced to the explicit form

$$u' = v$$
$$v' = Q_1^* [\eta(\Phi(u),Q_1v+Q_2D\omega(u)v) - D^2\Phi(u)(v,v)]. \tag{5.13}$$

From (5.5) it follows that $Q_1^*D^2\Phi(u)=0$, so that (5.13) reduces to

$$u'=v$$
$$v'=Q_1^*\eta(\Phi(u),Q_1v+Q_2D\omega(u)v) = Q_1^*\eta(\Phi(u),D\Phi(u)v) \tag{5.14}$$

Now , with $\eta(x,y)=Q_1\eta_1 + Q_2\eta_2$, $\eta_1 \in R^{n-r}$, $\eta_2 \in R^r$, the equation $H(x,y,q,z) = 0$ becomes the non-singular, linear system

$$\begin{pmatrix} DF_1(x)Q_1 & DF_1(x)Q_2 & 0 \\ A(x,y)Q_1 & A(x,y)Q_2 & B(x,y) \end{pmatrix} \begin{pmatrix} \eta_1 \\ \eta_2 \\ z \end{pmatrix} = -\begin{pmatrix} D^2F_1(x)(y,y) \\ G(x,y) \end{pmatrix} \tag{5.15}$$

Hence, if, for given $x = \Phi(u)$, $y = D\Phi(u)v$, $(u,v) \in S_0$, a solution of (5.15) has been obtained then $v' = Q_1^*\eta(\Phi(u),D\Phi(u)v) = \eta_1$ and $z =\zeta(\Phi(u),D\Phi(u)v)$.

6. Computational Implementation of the Local Parametrization

In the previous section we have used the local coordinate map (5.4) to reduce the semi-implicit DAEs (4.7) and (4.17) to the explicit systems of ODEs (5.7b) and (5.14), respectively. Theoretically any ODE solver can be applied to these ODE systems to obtain a local solution of the original DAE. Before discussing this in more detail, we consider first how the local coordinate map Φ of (5.4) at the current point x_c of the constraint manifold M_b, $b = F_1(x_0)$, may be implemented and how we might choose the matrices Q_1 and Q_2 that define this local parametrization.

By definition, for any given $u \in U$, the point $x = \Phi(u)$ on M_b is the solution of the augmented system

$$\begin{pmatrix} F_1(x) \\ Q_1^*(x - x_c) \end{pmatrix} = \begin{pmatrix} b \\ u \end{pmatrix} \tag{6.1}$$

Here, of course, the matrices Q_1, Q_2 are assumed to satisfy (5.3) and the subspace $T=Q_1R^{n-r}$ has to induce a local parametrization of M_b at x_c; that is, we have

$$(Q_1 R^{n-r})^{\perp} \cap \ker DF_1(x_c) = \{0\}. \tag{6.2}$$

It is readily seen that (6.2) holds if and only if the Jacobian

$$\begin{pmatrix} DF_1(x) \\ Q_1^* \end{pmatrix} \tag{6.3}$$

of the mapping on the left side of (6.1) is nonsingular at x_c which, in turn is equivalent with the nonsingularity of $DF_1(x_c)Q_2$.

As proved, for instance, in [7], under this nonsingularity assumption there exists an open set $U_1 \subset U$ containing the origin, such that for any u in U_1 Newton's method applied to (6.1) and started from $y^{(0)} = x_c + Q_1u$ produces a sequence of points $\{y^{(k)}\}$ that converges Q-quadratically to $x=\Phi(u)$. A step of this process here has the algorithmic form:

(1) Evaluate $a_1 = F_1(y^{(k)}) - b$, $a_2 = Q_1^*(y^{(k)} - x_c)$;
(2) solve the linear system

$$\begin{pmatrix} DF_1(y^{(k)}) \\ Q_1^* \end{pmatrix} s = \begin{pmatrix} a_1 \\ a_2 \end{pmatrix};$$

(3) set $y^{(k+1)} = y^{(k)} - s$.

Observe that for our choice $y^{(0)} = x_c + Q_1u$ of the starting point the iterates $y^{(k)}$ remain in the affine subspace $x_c + Q_2R^r$.

Let $s_1 = Q_1^*s$, $s_2 = Q_2^*s$, then, by (5.3), we have $s = Q_1s_1 + Q_2s_2$ and we obtain the solution of the linear system in step (2) by setting $s_1=a_2$ and solving the (n-r)-dimensional linear system

$$[DF_1(y^{(k)})Q_2]\, s_2 = a_1 - DF_1(y^{(k)})\, Q_1 a_2 . \qquad (6.4)$$

Thus, when the Jacobian of $F_1(x)$ is readily available, then Newton's method provides an efficient numerical procedure for implementing the local coordinate map (5.4).

We turn now to the construction of the matrices Q_1, Q_2 for which (5.3) and (6.2) are satisfied . Two choices appear to be particularly useful in practice. The first one was already mentioned in the previous section and defines the parametrization by using the space $T = \ker DF_1(x_c)$ corresponding to the tangent space of M_b at x_c. In this case the matrices Q_1, Q_2 may be obtained, for instance, by performing a QR-factorization of the transposed Jacobian of F_1

$$DF_1(x_0)^* = Q \begin{pmatrix} R \\ 0 \end{pmatrix} \qquad (6.5)$$

where Q is an $n \times n$ unitary matrix and R an $r \times r$ upper triangular matrix which, by (4.2b) is non-singular. In fact, it follows easily that then the local parametrization is defined by the matrices

$$Q_2 = Q(e_1, \ldots, e_r)\,,\ Q_1 = Q(e_{r+1}, \ldots, e_n) \qquad (6.6)$$

formed from the first r and last n-r columns of Q, respectively. Here $e_1, \ldots, e_n$ denote the natural basis vectors of R^n.

This "tangent space" parametrization may be somewhat costly to use. To reduce the cost it is advantageous to choose a local coordinate space T which is spanned by n-r suitably selected natural basis vectors of R^n. If, say,

$$T^{\perp} = \text{span}\,\{ e_{j_1}, \ldots, e_{j_r} \},\ \ T = \text{span}\,\{ e_{j_{r+1}}, \ldots, e_{j_n} \} \qquad (6.7)$$

then the condition $T^{\perp} \cap \ker DF_1(x_c) = \{0\}$ requires that we select the indices $j_1, \ldots, j_r$ such that the corresponding columns of $DF_1(x_c)$ are linearly independent. It is well-known that such a choice may be derived, for instance, from a Jordan factorization with row and column pivoting, or from a singular value decomposition (SVD) of $DF_1(x_c)$ (see.e.g. [3]). The matrices of the local parametrization induced by (6.6) are

$$Q_1 = (e_{j_{r+1}}, \ldots, e_{j_n}), \quad Q_2 = (e_{j_1}, \ldots, e_{j_r}) \tag{6.8}$$

and satisfy (5.3) by construction.

The choice of the permutation $[j_1,\ldots,j_n]$ in (6.7) and (6.8) "partitions" the components of any vector x into a vector $\xi_1 = Q_1{}^*x$ of " independent coordinates " and a vector $\xi_2 = Q_2{}^*x$ of "dependent coordinates ". Thus it is natural to call (6.8) a local parametrization by "coordinate partitioning".

7. Explicit and Implicit Multistep Methods

Consider again the first-order DAE (4.7) under the assumptions (4.2a/b) which, by Theorem 5, guarantee the existence of a solution $x{:}J \to E_x$, $z{:}J \to E_z$ that satisfies the initial conditions $x(0) = x_0$, $x'(0) = p_0 = \eta(x_0)$, $z(0) = z_0 = \zeta(x_0)$ corresponding to the given point $x_0 \in M_b$ on the constraint manifold.

Suppose that $x_c = x(t_c) \in M_b$ is a 'current' point on this solution where a local parametrization (5.4) has been constructed. In some region near x_c we wish to compute a sequence of approximation

$$x_i \cong x(t_i),\ z_j \cong z(t_i),\ t_i = t_c + ih\ ,\ i=1,2,\ldots,N \tag{7.1}$$

of points $x(t_k)$ along the solution. More precisely, we suppose that the constants h and N are chosen such that the points $x(t_k)$ belong to the neighborhood of x_c where the local parametrization (5.4) is valid Then, if u is the solution of (5.7b) satisfying the initial condition $u(t_c)=0$, it follows that

$$x(t_k) = \Phi(u(t_k)) \quad k=1,2,\ldots,N,\ \ x(t_c) = \Phi(u(t_c)) = x_c. \tag{7.2}$$

For the approximate solution of (5.7b) we consider a multistep method of the general form

$$u_k = \sum_{j=1}^{p} \alpha_j u_{k-j} + h \sum_{j=0}^{p} u'_{k-j} \, , \; u'_{k-j} = Q_1^* \eta(\Phi(u_{k-j})) \tag{7.3}$$

which is assumed to be consistent; that is,

$$\sum_{i=1}^{p} \alpha_i = 1, \tag{7.4}$$

as well as convergent of order $\upsilon \geq 1$. Assume that for some k, $1 \leq k \leq N$, the approximations

$$u_j \cong u(t_j) \, , \; x_j \cong \Phi(u_j) \, , \; j=0,1,...k-1, \tag{7.5}$$

have already been computed. Then the next point $u_k \cong u(t_k)$ along the solution of (5.7b) is specified by (7.3) and, by solving the equation (6.1) with $u = u_k$, we obtain $x_k = \Phi(u_k)$ as the next approximation of the solution of (4.7).

As shown in section 5, the vectors u'_{k-i} of (7.3) are the solutions of a linear system of the form (5.8). We consider first the case $\beta_0 = 0$ of explicit integration. Since the local coordinate map (5.4) is defined by the matrices Q_1, Q_2 we have, by (6.1),

$$u \; = \; Q_1^*(x-x_c) \tag{7.6}$$

In other words, we may assume that the computed approximations (7.4) satisfy

$$u_j = Q_1^*(x_j-x_c), \quad j = 1,2,...,k-1 \tag{7.7}$$

Together with (7.6) this implies that when u_k is determined by the multistep method (7.3) then, instead of using (6.1) with $u = u_k$, we may obtain $x_k = \Phi(u_k)$ as a solution of the nonlinear system

$$\begin{pmatrix} F_1(x) - b \\ Q_1^* \left(x - \sum_{j=1}^{p} [\alpha_j x_{k-j} + h\beta_j \eta(x_{k-j})] \right) \end{pmatrix} = 0 \qquad (7.8)$$

This leads to the following algorithm for computing from the last p known approximations

$$x_{k-j} \cong x(t_{k-j}),\ z_{k-j} \cong z(t_{k-j}),\ w_{k-j} \cong \eta(x_{k-j}),\ j = 1,2,\ldots,p \qquad (7.9)$$

a next approximate point on the desired solution of (4.7):

<u>Algorithm 1.</u>

(1) Evaluate $a_k = Q_1^*(\sum_{i=1}^{p} \alpha_i x_{k-i} + h\sum_{i=1}^{p} \beta_i w_{k-i})$

(2) Compute the solution x_k of the nonlinear system

$$\begin{pmatrix} F_1(x) - b \\ Q_1^* x - a_k \end{pmatrix} = 0$$

(3) With $x = x_k$ solve the linear system (5.8) to obtain $w_k = Q_1\eta_1$ and $z_k = z$.

This algorithm may be applied as long as the computed points do not leave the region of validity of the local parametrization at x_c defined by Q_1 and Q_2. To determine when the points leave this region is a very delicate problem and requires special attention. In our numerical implementation we decide to change the local parametrization when the estimated condition number of the Jacobian of the system in step (2) becomes too large or when the number of Newton steps required for solving this system exceeds a certain bound . Of course, if the multistep method (7.3) has order υ then one should solve the systems in step (2) and (3) with an error not exceeding $O(h^{\upsilon+1})$.

A further delicate problem is the initialization of the overall process. One approach is to obtain $u_1,u_2,\ldots,u_p$ by means of some known start-up process for the multistep method (7.3) applied to the ODE (5.7b) and then to set

$$x_i = \Phi(u_i)\,,\quad w_i = \eta(x_i)\,,\ i = 1,2,\dots,p$$

by solving the corresponding systems (6.1) and (5.8) . Numerical experience indicates that no reinitialization is necessary when passing from one local parametrization to another.

In the case $\beta_0 \equiv 0$ the new point is implicitely defined by both (7.3) and (5.8); that is, the systems in step (2) and (3) of algorithm 1 can no longer be solved separately. Thus, in this case the algorithm has to be modified as follows:

Algorithm 2.

(1) Evaluate $a_k = Q_1^*(\sum_{i=1}^{p} \alpha_i x_{k-i} + h\sum_{i=1}^{p} \beta_i w_{k-i})$

(2) Obtain $x_k = x$, $z_k = z$, $w_k = w$ as the numerical solution of the nonlinear system

$$\begin{pmatrix} F_1(x) - b \\ Q_1^*(x - h\beta_0 w) - a_k \\ DF_1(x)Q_1 w + DF_1(x)Q_2 v \\ A(x)Q_1 w + A(x)Q_2 v + B(x)z + G(x) \end{pmatrix} = 0$$

The comments following algorithm 1 apply again; in particular, the nonlinear system in step (2) has to be solved with an error not exceeding $O(h^{\upsilon+1})$.

These results can be readily carried over to second order systems of the form (4.17). For this we assume now that the hypotheses of Theorem 6 are satisfied and hence that the existence of a solution $x\colon J \to E_x$, $z\colon J \to E_z$ of (4.17) is guaranteed which satisfies the initial conditions $x(0) = x_0$, $x'(0) = y_0$, $x''(0)=\eta(x_0,y_0)$, $z(0) = \zeta(x_0,y_0)$ for a given point $(x_0,y_0) \in E_x \times (E_y \cap \ker DF_1(x_0))$.

As above, let $x_c = x(t_c) \in M_b$, $b=F_1(x_0)$, be a current point on this solution where we construct a local parametrization (5.4) defined by the linear maps Q_1,Q_2. In section 5 we saw that in some neighborhood of x_c, where this parametrization is valid , the functions

$$u = Q_1^*(x-x_c), \quad v = Q_1^*x' . \tag{7.10}$$

satisfy the ODE (5.14).

In the second order case, the multistep method (7.3) now reads

$$u_k = \sum_{j=1}^{p}\alpha_j u_{k-j} + h\sum_{j=0}^{p}\beta_j u'_{k-j}, \quad v_k = \sum_{j=1}^{p}\alpha_j v_{k-j} + h\sum_{j=0}^{p}\beta_j v'_{k-j} \tag{7.11a}$$

where

$$v'_i = Q_1^*\eta(\,\Phi(u_i), D\Phi(u_i)v_i\,). \tag{7.11b}$$

As we saw at the end of section 5, v_i' is obtained by solving the linear system (5.15).

We begin again with the case $\beta_0 = 0$ and use the same notation and assumptions as before. In particular, let

$$x_i \cong x(t_i),\ \ y_i \cong x'(t_i),\ w_i \cong \eta(x_i, y_i\,),\ \ z_i \cong z(t_i)\ ,\ i = 1,2,\ldots,k-1 \tag{7.12}$$

be known approximations. Then we obtain the following the explicit-integration algorithm for computing from the last p points of this sequence the next approximate point:

<u>Algorithm 3.</u>

(1) Evaluate $a_k = Q_1^*(\sum_{i=1}^{p} \alpha_i x_{k-i} + h\sum_{i=1}^{p} \beta_i y_{k-i})$, $a'_k = Q_1^*(\sum_{i=1}^{p} \alpha_i y_{k-i} + h\sum_{i=1}^{p} \beta_i w_{k-i})$

(2) Solve the nonlinear system

$$\begin{pmatrix} F_1(x) - b \\ Q_1^* x - a_k \\ Q_1^* y - a'_k \\ DF_1(x)y \end{pmatrix} = 0$$

to obtain $x_k = x$, $y_k = y$.

(3) With $x = x_k$, $y = y_k$ obtain $w_k = Q_1\eta_1$ and $z_k = z$ as solutions of the linear system (5.15).

When $\beta_0 \neq 0$ then, analogous to algorithm 2, we can implement the multistep method (7.11a/b) for the numerical solution of (4.17) as follows:

<u>Algorithm 4.</u>

(1) Evaluate a_k, a'_k as in step (1) of algorithm 3.
(2) Solve the nonlinear system

$$\begin{pmatrix} F_1(x) - b \\ Q_1^*(x - \beta_0 hy) - a_k \\ Q_1^*(y - \beta_0 hw) - a'_k \\ DF_1(x)y \\ DF_1(x)Q_1\eta_1 + DF_1(x)Q_2\eta_2 + D^2F_1(x)(y,y) \\ A(x,y)Q_1\eta_1 + A(x,y)Q_2\eta_2 + B(x,y)z + G(x,y) \end{pmatrix} = 0$$

to obtain $x_k = x$, $y_k = y$, $w_k = Q_1\eta_1$, $z_k = z$.

Obviously the comments made immediately following algorithm 1 apply again to both algorithm 3 and 4.

8. Application to the Euler-Lagrange Equations.

A classical example for second order DAEs of the form (4.17) are, of course, the equations arising in constrained multibody dynamics. These equations have the general form

$$\begin{aligned} &\Psi(q,t) = 0, \\ &M(q,t)\, q'' + D_q\Psi(q,t)^T z + K(q,q',t) = 0, \end{aligned} \tag{8.1}$$

and are subsumed under the special case of (4.17) when both A and B depend only on x. In fact, we need to set only $x=(q,t)$ and define

$$F_1(x) = \Psi(q,t),\ A(x)=\begin{pmatrix} M(q,t) & 0 \\ 0 & 1 \end{pmatrix},\ B(x) = \begin{pmatrix} D_q\Psi(q,t)^T \\ 0 \end{pmatrix},\ G(x,x')=\begin{pmatrix} K(q,q',t) \\ 0 \end{pmatrix} \tag{8.2}$$

Suppose that in (8.1) the mappings $\Psi: R^{n-1}\times R^1 \to R^r$, $K:(R^{n-1})^2\times R^1 \to R^{n-1}$, and $M:R^{n-1}\times R^1 \to L(R^{n-1},R^{n-1})$, $r < n-1$, satisfy, for all (q,t) under consideration, the smoothness conditions corresponding to (4.12a). Evidently, (4.12b) is here equivalent with

$$\operatorname{rank} D_q\Psi(q,t) = r, \quad a^T M(q,t) a \neq 0,\ \forall\, a \in \ker D_q\Psi(q,t); \tag{8.3}$$

that is, with the assumptions that the algebraic constraints are independent and that the mass matrix M is definite on the nullspace of $D_q\Psi$. Thus, Theorem 6 applies to (8.1). Note also that now the defining relations (4.19) for the mappings $\eta:(R^{n-1})^2 \times R \to R^{n-1}$, $\zeta: (R^{n-1})^2 \times R \to R^r$, have the form

$$\begin{pmatrix} \eta(q,q',t) \\ \zeta(q,q',t) \end{pmatrix} = -\begin{pmatrix} M(q,t) & D_q\Psi(q,t)^T \\ D_q\Psi(q,t) & 0 \end{pmatrix}^{-1} \begin{pmatrix} K(q,q',t) \\ D^2_{qq}\Psi(q,t)(q',q')+2D^2_{qt}\Psi(q,t)q'+D^2_{tt}\Psi(q,t) \end{pmatrix} \tag{8.4}$$

We reduce (8.1) to a system of ODEs by using a local parametrizations of the type considered in section 6. However in doing so care should be taken not to modify the "special" variable t . By (8.2) we have

$$DF_1(x) = (D_q\Psi(q,t),\ D_t\Psi(q,t)) \tag{8.5}$$

and because of (8.3) there exist always r linearly independent columns among the first n-1 columns of $DF_1(x)$. Hence, when we construct a local parametrization by "coordinate partitioning" at a current point $x_c = (q_c,t_c)$ then we can always choose a permutation $j_1,\ldots,j_{n-1}$ of the set $\{1,2,\ldots,n-1\}$ such that the matrices

$$Q_1 = (e_{j_{r+1}}, \ldots, e_{j_{n-1}}, e_n) = \begin{pmatrix} P_1 & 0 \\ 0 & 1 \end{pmatrix}, \quad Q_2 = (e_{j_1}, \ldots, e_{j_r}) = \begin{pmatrix} P_2 \\ 0 \end{pmatrix} \tag{8.6}$$

satisfy (5.3) and (6.2) and hence define the desired parametrization. Evidently, in (8.6) the (n-1)×r matrix P_1 and the (n-1)×(n-1-r) matrix P_2 consist of the basis vectors of R^{n-1} with indices $j_1,\ldots,j_r$ and $j_{r+1},\ldots,j_{n-1}$, respectively. In other words, we construct the parametrization (8.6) by working only with the r×(n-1) matrix $D_q\Psi(q_c,t_c)$ rather than with the r×n matrix $DF_1(x_c)$.

Analogously we can implement a "tangent space parametrization " by performing a QR-factorization of $D_q\Psi(q_c,t_c)^*$ rather than of $DF_1(x_c)^*$. More specifically, if

$$D_q\Psi(q_c,t_c)^* = P\begin{pmatrix} R \\ 0 \end{pmatrix} \tag{8.7}$$

where P is an (n-1)-dimensional unitary matrix while R is again r×r upper-triangular, then, corresponding to (6.6), the matrices

$$Q_1 = \begin{pmatrix} P & 0 \\ 0 & 1 \end{pmatrix}(e_{r+1}, \ldots, e_{n-1}, e_n) = \begin{pmatrix} P_1 & 0 \\ 0 & 1 \end{pmatrix},\ Q_2 = \begin{pmatrix} P & 0 \\ 0 & 1 \end{pmatrix}(e_1, \ldots, e_r) = \begin{pmatrix} P_2 \\ 0 \end{pmatrix} \tag{8.8}$$

satisfy (5.3) and (6.2) and hence define the desired parametrization. In (8.8), P_2 is the (n-1)×r matrix consisting of the first r columns of P, and the remaining (n-1-r) columns of P make up the (n-1)×(n-1-r) matrix P_1.

Now, the algorithms 3 and 4 of section can be applied. However since the matrices Q_1 ,Q_2 of (8.6) or (8.8) have a special form some simplifications are possible. Moreover, it should be taken into account that in many applications involving the equations (8.1) the accelerations

$$x'' = \begin{pmatrix} q'' \\ 0 \end{pmatrix} = \eta(x, x') \tag{8.9}$$

are explicitly required.

Suppose again that the approximate points

$$x_i = (q_i, t_i),\ \ y_i = (q'_i, 1),\ \ w_i = (q''_i, 0),\ \ z_i\ ,\ t_i = ih,\ \ i=0,1,\ldots,k-1$$

are already known and that $x_c = (q_c, t_c)$ is the current point for the local parametrization. Note that the multistep method (7.11a/b) was assumed to be consistent so that, besides (7.4), the coefficients must satisfy

$$-\sum_{j=1}^{p} j\alpha_j + \sum_{j=0}^{p} \beta_j = 1$$

Hence, in step (2) of algorithm 3 and 4, the last equation of $Q_1^* x = a_k$ reduces to t = kh while the last equation of $Q_1^* y = a'_k$ is trivially satisfied. Thus, the explicit algorithm 3 can be simplified as follows:

<u>Algorithm 5.</u>

(1) Evaluate $a_k = P_1^*(\sum_{i=1}^{p} \alpha_i q_{k-i} + h\sum_{i=1}^{p} \beta_i q'_{k-i}),\ \ a'_k = P_1^*(\sum_{i=1}^{p} \alpha_i q'_{k-i} + h\sum_{i=1}^{p} \beta_i q''_{k-i})$

(2) Obtain $q_k = q$, $q'_k = q'$ as solutions of the nonlinear system

$$\begin{pmatrix} \Psi(q,t_k) \\ P_1^* q - a_k \\ P_1^* q' - a'_k \\ D_q\Psi(q,t_k)q' + D_t\Psi(q,t_k) \end{pmatrix} = 0$$

(3) With $q=q_k$, $q'=q'_k$ solve the linear system (8.4) to obtain $q''_k = q''$, and $z_k = z$

For the implicit algorithm, it is useful to introduce the abbreviation

$$\gamma(q,q',t) = D^2_{qq}\Psi(q,t)(q',q') + 2D^2_{qt}\Psi(q,t)q' + D^2_{tt}\Psi(q,t)\,.$$

Then, with the acceleration (8.9), the last equations in the nonlinear system of step 2 of algorithm 4 can be written in the form

$$\begin{aligned} &D_q\Psi(q,\, t_k)q'' = -\,\gamma(q,\, q',\, t_k) \\ &M(q,\, t_k)q'' + D_q\Psi(q,\, t_k)^T z \ + K(q,\, q',\, t_k) = 0 \end{aligned}$$

Evidently, the first of these equations can also be obtained formally by differentiating the first equation of (8.1) twice.

With these observations , algorithms 4 reduces to the following algorithm:

<u>Algorithm 6</u>.

(1) Evaluate a_k, a'_k as in step (1) of algorithm 5.

(2) Obtain $q_k=q$, $q'_k=q'$, $q''_k= q''$, $z_k=z$ as solution of the nonlinear system

$$\begin{pmatrix} \Psi(q, t_k) \\ P_1^*(q-\beta_0 hq') - a_k \\ P_1^*(q'-\beta_0 hq'') - a'_k \\ D_q\Psi(q, t_k)q' + D_t\Psi(q, t_k) \\ D_q\Psi(q, t_k)q'' + \gamma(q,q',t_k) \\ M(q,t_k)q''+D_q\Psi(q, t_k)^T z + K(q,q',t_k) \end{pmatrix} = 0$$

The numerical solution of the nonlinear system (9.23) represents a significant computational challenge. However, in a separate paper it shall be shown that when proper care is taken to exploit its special structure, then the computational complexity of this problem can be reduced greatly.

9. A numerical example

A frequently encountered basic mechanisms is the four-bar system shown schematically in Figure 1. To model this system, each of the four links and the ground are considered as a body and marked by the integers 1, 2, 3, 4. A frame is fixed for each body with the origin at its centroid. For each body the coordinates of the centroid are given in Table 1. This identifies also the initial position of the system as it is sketched in Figure 1. Table 2 lists the mass and moment of inertia for each body. All the joints of the mechanism are revolute joints, they are marked by the letters A, B, C, D. Table 3 identifies the two bodies connected at each joint and gives the coordinates of the common point in the coordinate frame of each body. . The mechanism is subject to no applied force other than gravity. The initial velocity of each generalized coordinate is assumed to be equal to zero.

Body #	1	2	3	4
x	0.0	2.0	6.0	12.0
y	0.0	2.0	4.0	4.0
θ	0.0	π / 4	0.0	π / 4

Table 1 . Body centroids

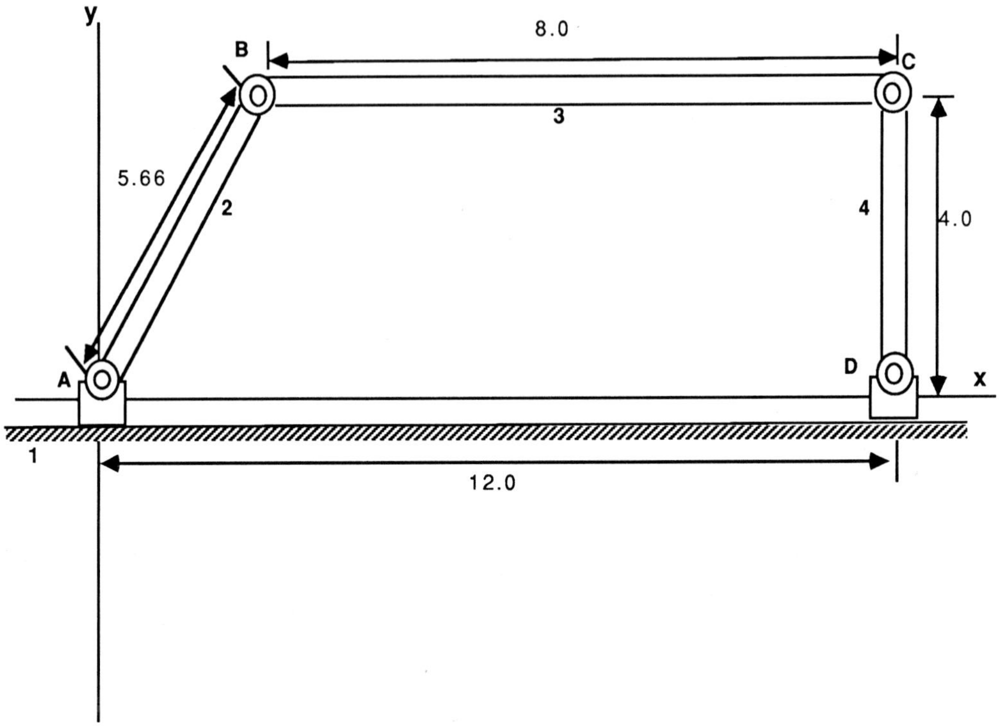

Figure1. Fourbar-Linkage

Body #	1	2	3	4
Mass (kg)	1.0	200.0	300.0	100.0
Inertia $(kgm)^2$	1.0	200.0	300.0	100.0

Table 2. Masses and Moments of Inertia

Joint	A	B	C	D
Body i	1	2	3	4
$x_i(P)$	0.0	2.828	4.0	2.0
$y_i(P)$	0.0	0.0	0.0	0.0
Body j	2	3	4	1
$x_j(P)$	-2.828	-4.0	-2.0	12.0
$y_j(P)$	0.0	0.0	0.0	0.0

Table 3. Joint data at the common point P

The constrained equations of motion for this system have been solved using the algorithms discussed in Section 9. At the same time, as a check the model was also analyzed by means of DADS, a general purpose code for mechanical design [2].

The numerical experiments were carried out with the implicit as well as the explicit algorithm. The second order BDF-formula was chosen as the implicit method and the second order PECE- (Adams -Bashforth - Moulton)-formula as the explicit method. In each case, fixed-stepsizes h=0.01, and h=0.0025 were applied. The nonlinear systems were solved by a chord Newton method. As indicated earlier, the local parametrization was changed whenever the estimated condition number of the linear systems exceeded a specific bound or when the nonlinear solver failed to converge in a given number of steps. In Figures 2-4 we show the position, velocity, and acceleration of the x-coordinate of the centroid of body 2 for the tangent space parametrization.

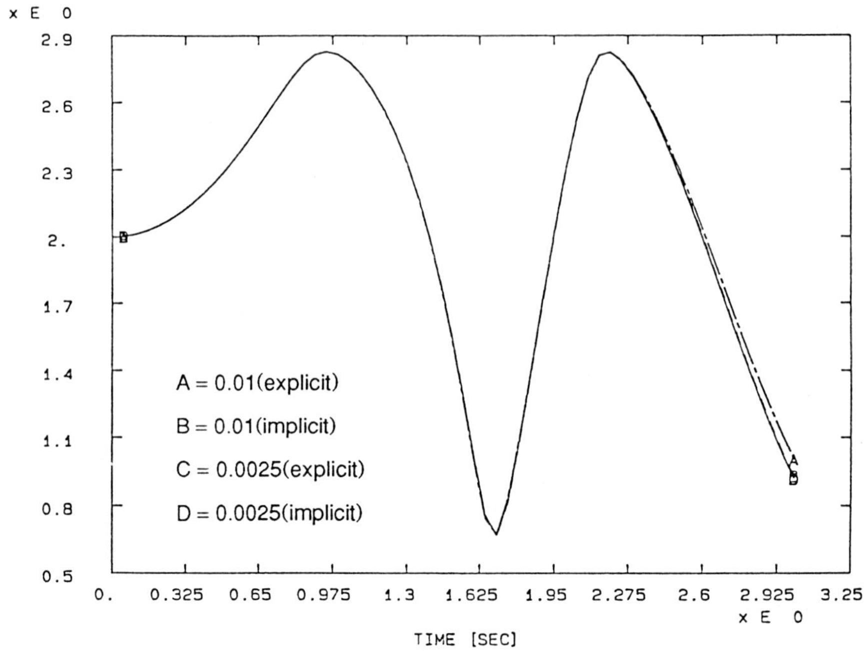

Figure 2. Position of the x-coordinate of the centroid of body 2

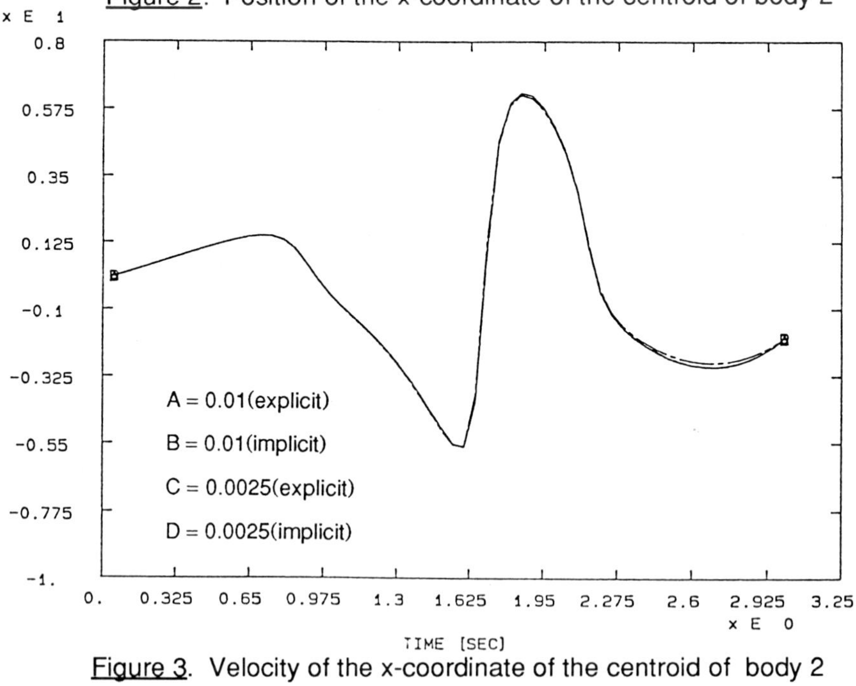

Figure 3. Velocity of the x-coordinate of the centroid of body 2

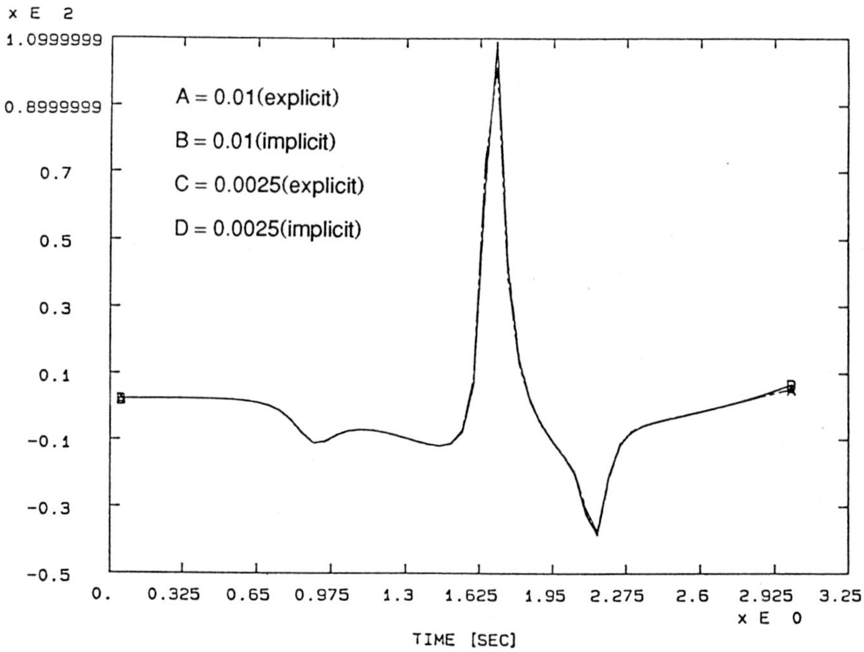

Figure 4. Acceleration of the x-coordinate of the centroid of body 1

The numerical solutions obtained with the implicit method are accurate to four decimal digits throughout the time interval [0,3] and hence, in the figures, they cannot be distinguished from the solutions given by DADS. On the other hand, the solutions obtained with the explicit method are drifting away for $t > 2.5$ sec. (see Fig 2, 3, 4) when the the stepsize is increased.

The computations were also carried out with the local parametrization, induced by "coordinate partitioning " and they agree to three significant digits with the result for the "tangent space" parametrization. Table 4 provides some statistical information about the total number of function and Jacobian evaluations as well as about the number of re-parametrizations for the two choices of local parametrizations when the step-size $h = 0.01$ was used. In the table, TG and GCP stands for the tangent space and coordinate partitioning parametrization, respectively.

	Explicit Method		Implicit Method	
	TG	GCP	TG	GCP
Function Eval.	989	1021	1456	1520
Jacobian Eval.	56	65	134	153
Re-Parametr.	6	6	15	19

Table 4 . Performance Statistics

Acknowledgement: We would like to thank Mr. Jeng Yen for helping us with many of the numerical experiments.

References

[1] K.Brennan, S.Campbell, L.Petzold, Numerical Solution of Initial-Value Problems in Differential-Algebraic Equations,North-Hollond,New-York,1989.

[2] DADS User's Manual , Rev. 4.0, Computer Aided Design Software, Inc., Oakdale, Iowa,1987.

[3] G.H.Golub, C.F.VanLoan, Matrix Computations, Johns Hopkins Univ. Press, Baltimore,MD 1983.

[4] E. Griepentrog, R. Maerz, Differential-Algebraic Equations and Their Numerical Treatment, B.G.Teubner Verlag, Leipzig, 1986.

[5] E.J.Haug,J.Yen, Implicit Numerical Integration of Constrained Equations of Motion via Generalized Coordinate Partitioning , Univ. of Iowa, Ctr. for Simulation and Design Optim. of Mech. Systems, Tech. Rep. R-39, Feb. 1989.

[6] S.Lang, Introduction to Differentiable Manifolds, Wiley , New York, NY, 1962.

[7] J.M. Ortega, W.C.Rheinboldt, Iterative Methods for Nonlinear Equations in Several Variables, Academic Press, New York, 1970.

[8] F.A.Potra, J.Yen, Implicit Numerical Integration for Euler-Lagrange Equations via Tangent Space Parametrization, Univ. of Iowa, Ctr. for Simulation and Design Optim. of Mech. Systems, Tech. Rep. R-56, June 1989.

[9] S.Reich, Beitraege zur Theorie der Algebrodifferentialgleichungen, Ph.D. Dissertation (Electronics), Techn. Univ. Dresden, Spring 1988.

[10] W. C. Rheinboldt, Differential-Algebraic Systems as Differential Equations on Manifolds, Math. of Comp. 43, 1984, 473-482.

[11] W.C. Rheinboldt, Numerical Analysis of Parametrized Nonlinear Equations, John Wiley and Sons, New York, 1986.

[12] W.C.Rheinboldt, On the Existence and Computation of Solutions of Nonlinear Semi-Implicit Algebraic Equations, University of Pittsburgh, Inst. f. Comp. Math. and Appl., Tech. Rep. ICMA-89-139, August 1989; SIAM J. Num. Anal., submitted.

[13] M Spivak, A Comprehensive Introduction to Differential Geometry, Vol 1-5, Publish or Perish, Inc. Boston, MA 1970.

On Baumgarte Stabilization for Differential Algebraic Equations

Georg-P. Ostermeyer
Volkswagen AG
Postfach
3180 Wolfsburg
Germany

Abstract. Baumgarte's method uses analytical reformulations of constraint forces in mechanical systems to handle differential algebraic equations with every standard integration routine. This stabilization technique for inner and outer constraints is easy to use.

This paper deals with control theoretic aspects to explain the effects of Baumgarte's method and to give some rules for choosing the parameters in his technique. In addition the construction of new stabilizing procedures is described and some optimal formulas are listed at the end of this paper.

1. Introduction

A multibody system with n degrees of freedom, see fig. 1a, may be described in the following way for shortness:

Let t be the time and $\mathbf{q} = \mathbf{q}(t) = (q_1, q_2, \ldots, q_n)^t$ a vector of n generalized coordinates. With the system's Lagrangian L

$$L = L(\dot{\mathbf{q}}, \mathbf{q}, t) = T(\dot{\mathbf{q}}, \mathbf{q}, t) - V(\mathbf{q}, t) \quad , \qquad \dot{\mathbf{q}} := \frac{d}{dt}\mathbf{q} \; ,$$

and the vector of generalized nonpotential forces $\mathbf{Q}$:

$$\mathbf{Q} = \mathbf{Q}(\dot{\mathbf{q}}, \mathbf{q}, t) = (Q_1, Q_2, \ldots, Q_n)^t ,$$

the equations of motion are computed in the form

$$\frac{d}{dt}\left(\frac{\partial}{\partial \dot{\mathbf{q}}} L\right) - \frac{\partial}{\partial \mathbf{q}} L = \mathbf{Q},$$

or, for shortness,

$$[\ L\ ]_{\mathbf{q}} = \mathbf{Q}, \tag{1.1}$$

where the bracket $[]_{\mathbf{q}}$ denotes the Eulerian operator

$$[\ .\ ]_{\mathbf{q}} := \frac{d}{dt}\left(\frac{\partial}{\partial \dot{\mathbf{q}}}(.)\right) - \frac{\partial}{\partial \mathbf{q}}(.) \ .$$

Let us assume, that there is installed an additional constraint

NATO ASI Series, Vol. F 69
Real-Time Integration Methods for Mechanical System Simulation
Edited by E.J. Haug and R.C. Deyo

in the system (1.1) , described by a scalar diffentiable

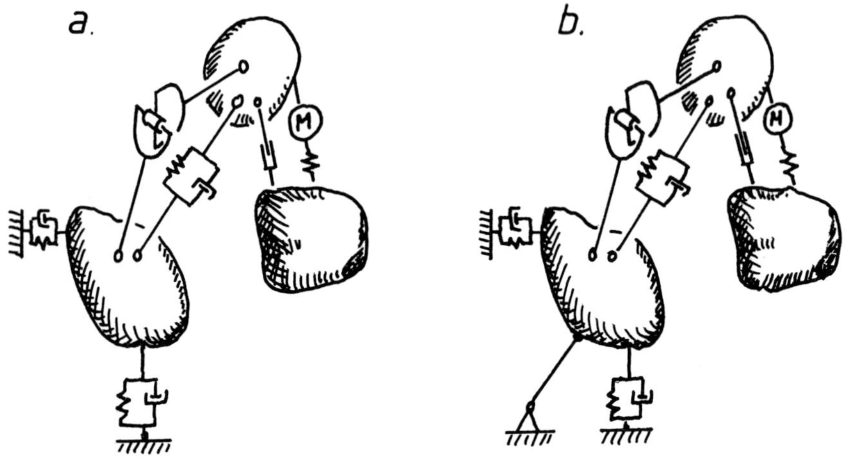

Figure 1. *a) multibody system with b) an additional constraint.*

equation $f = f(\mathbf{q},t) = 0$. It forms a manifold in the configuration space $\mathbf{q}$ of (1.1) the system has to move on. Two ways are possible to take care of this additional holonomic contraint in the equations of motion:

a) Choose a new set of n-1 generalized variables $\bar{\mathbf{q}}(t)$ with $f(\bar{\mathbf{q}},t) \equiv 0$. The resulting equations of motion are then n-1 differential equations (DE's) of second order:

$$[\ L\ ]_{\bar{\mathbf{q}}} = \left(\frac{\partial}{\partial \bar{\mathbf{q}}}\mathbf{q}\right)^t \mathbf{Q}. \tag{1.2}$$

b) Introduce constraint forces $\mathbf{Q}^{\mathbf{z}} := [-\lambda f]_{\mathbf{q}}$, where the Lagrangian multiplier λ has to be calculated in such a way, that solutions of (1.3) lay on the manifold $f(\mathbf{q},t) = 0$.

$$[\ L\ ]_{\mathbf{q}} = \mathbf{Q} + \lambda \frac{\partial}{\partial \mathbf{q}} f \quad , \tag{1.3a}$$

$$0 = f(\mathbf{q},t). \tag{1.3b}$$

The equations (1.3) are differential algebraic equations.

The usual procedure to solve (1.3) is to differentiate the algebraic equation (1.3b) twice with respect to time. This equation is linear then in the accelerations $\ddot{\mathbf{q}}$ just like the differential equations (1.3a). Inserting the accelerations of (1.3a) leads to a single equation, linear in the Lagrangian

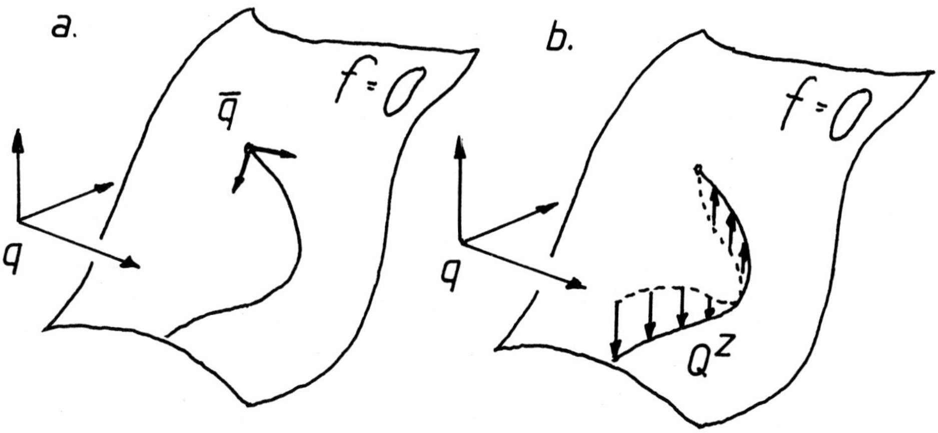

Figure 2. *The system with an additional holonomic constraint f. a) generalized coordinates, b) contraint forces.*

multiplier λ, which can be computed as function of coordinates, velocities and time:

$$[\,L\,]_{\mathbf{q}} = \mathbf{Q} + \lambda \frac{\partial}{\partial \mathbf{q}} f \,, \qquad \lambda = \lambda(\dot{\mathbf{q}},\mathbf{q},t). \tag{1.4}$$

From mechanical point of view the solutions of (1.2) and (1.4) are exactly the same, when the initial conditions of both systems describe the same point and direction in the manifold f. It is wellknown, that the numerical solution may differ in a significant way.

The mathematical pendulum is used in the following as simple example of a mechanical system with a holonomic contraint. The Lagrangian L is $L = \frac{1}{2}\, m\, (\dot{x}^2 + \dot{y}^2) - mgy$, the constraint equation has the form $2\,f = (x^2 + y^2 - l^2) = 0$. There are no forces $\mathbf{Q}$ in the system.

A generalized coordinate is the angle φ with $x = l\,\sin\varphi$ and $y = -l\,\cos\varphi$, leading to the well known equation

$$\ddot{\varphi} + \frac{g}{l}\sin\varphi = 0. \tag{1.5}$$

Formulated with a constraint force the equations of motion are computed as

$$m\ddot{x} = + \lambda x, \qquad m\ddot{y} = -mg + \lambda y, \qquad \lambda = \frac{\dot{x}^2 + \dot{y}^2 - gy}{x^2 + y^2} \quad . \tag{1.6}$$

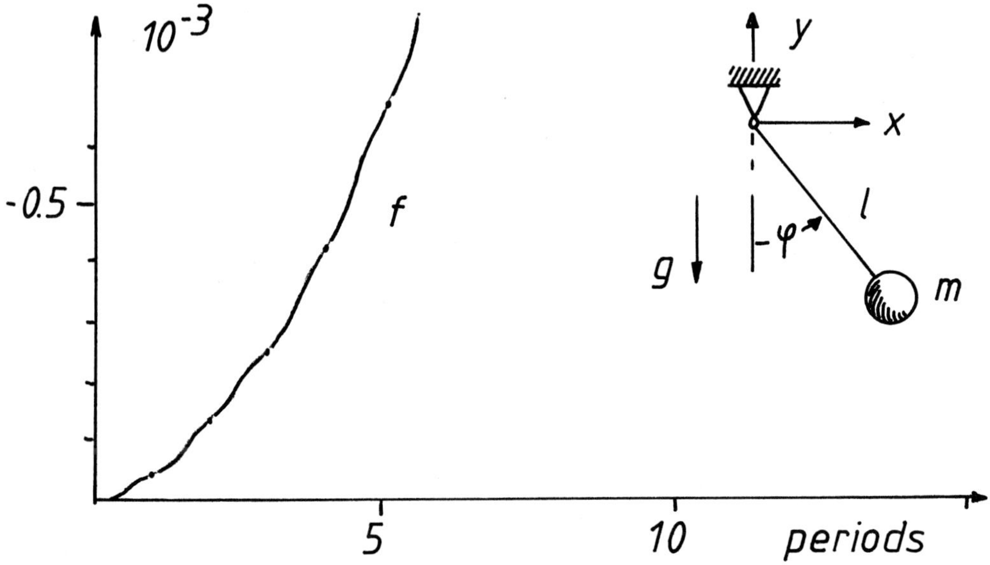

Figure 3. *Scheme of numerical solution of the pendulum equation with respect to the holonomic contraint using a Runge Kutta integration routine.*

The numerical solution of (1.6) violates the constraint equation quadratically in time. After a few periods of pendulum motion this solution may be useless.

Another constraint type occuring in MBS are nonholonomic constraints of the form $g = g(\dot{\mathbf{q}},\mathbf{q},t) = 0$. The resulting equations of motion are

$$[\ L\ ]_{\mathbf{q}} = \mathbf{Q} + \mu \frac{\partial}{\partial \dot{\mathbf{q}}} g \ , \tag{1.7a}$$

$$0 = g(\dot{\mathbf{q}},\mathbf{q},t) \ . \tag{1.7b}$$

For solving these equations the nonholonomic constraint is differentiated once with respect to time. Inserting the equations (1.7a) leads again to an algebraic solution for the

Lagrangian multiplier μ.

The equations (1.3b) and (1.7b) are called "outer" constraints. Inner constraints are integrals of motion $I = I(\dot{\mathbf{q}},\mathbf{q},t) = 0$, for example the energy of system (1.5) or (1.6). The system equations are:

$$[\ L\ ]_{\mathbf{q}} = \mathbf{Q}\ , \tag{1.8a}$$

$$0 = I(\dot{\mathbf{q}},\mathbf{q},t)\ . \tag{1.8b}$$

No explicit constraint force appears in (1.8a) for an inner constraint.If (1.8b) would be treated as nonholonomic constraint (1.7b), the resulting Lagrangian multiplier μ is computed to be zero.

If the equations (1.7b), (1.8b) are not taken into account by choosing suitable generalized velocities in the system, the numerical solution violates the constraint equations linear with respect to time.

In view of the numerical solution the best way of treating additional constraints in a system (1.1) is the reduction of order of the equations of motion. But it is not always possible to choose one set of generalized variables, characterising the system globally. To avoid a switching of the set of variables during the system motion the introduction of constraint forces is usefull. In practice there are many other reasons to deal with DAE's in mechanics. If, for instance,two complex subsystems have to be coupled, the concept of constraint forces avoid the entirely new generation of equations of motion.

2. Baumgarte's method for DAE's

One of the first papers dealing with the numerical integration of differential algebraic equations in mechanics is that of Baumgarte [1]. His aim was not the construction of new codes of integration routines but a suitable analytical computation of constraint forces. He introduced so called "stabilizing Gaussian constraints". As described above, the lagrangian multipliers are computed with the once or twice differentiated constraint equations usually. By the Baumgarte method

$$[\,L\,]_{\mathbf{q}} = Q + \lambda \frac{\partial}{\partial \mathbf{q}} f, \tag{2.1}$$

$$0 = \ddot{f} + 2\alpha\dot{f} + \beta\, f^2 \qquad \Rightarrow [\,L\,]_{\mathbf{q}} = Q + Q^{z} + (2\alpha\dot{f} + \beta^2 f)\hat{Q}^{z}$$

$$[\,L\,]_{\mathbf{q}} = Q + \mu \frac{\partial}{\partial \dot{\mathbf{q}}} g \tag{2.2}$$

$$0 = g + \delta g \qquad \Rightarrow [\,L\,]_{\mathbf{q}} = Q + Q^{z} + \delta g\, \hat{Q}^{z}$$

$$[\,L\,]_{\mathbf{q}} = Q + \nu \frac{\partial}{\partial \dot{\mathbf{q}}} I \tag{2.3}$$

$$0 = I + \delta I \qquad \Rightarrow [\,L\,]_{\mathbf{q}} = Q + Q^{z} + \delta I\, \hat{Q}^{z}$$

the Lagrangian multiplier λ in (1.3) is computed with the differential equation $0 = \ddot{f} + 2\alpha\dot{f} + \beta^2 f$. The resulting constraint force contain the classical term Q^{z}, computed by $\ddot{f} = 0$, and in addition so called stabilizing terms, see (2.1).

These additional terms vanish for the exact solution where $\dot{f} \equiv 0$ and $f \equiv 0$. During the numerical solution these terms control the error behaviour, whenever the constraint equations are violated. Baumgarte deals with nonholonomic constraints (2.2) and inner constraints (2.3) too. By his method the resulting constraint force for integrals of motion is not zero but consists on control terms, so these inner constraints can be stabilized !

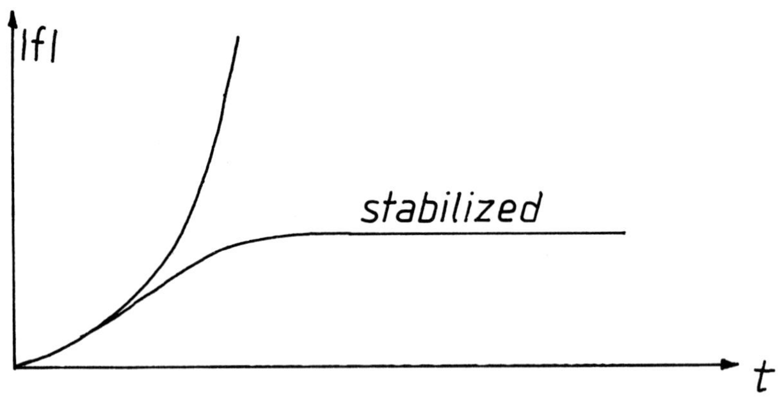

Figure 4. *Scheme of the effect of Baumgarte's stabilization for holonomic constraints.*

The principle effect of these stabilization procedures is bounding the numerical errors with respect to the constraint equations. The problem is a suitable choice of the parameters α, β and γ. There are very different experiences to be found in literature. Some papers choose very small values for these parameters (e.g. [5]), other papers suggest very large values to get a nice error behaviour (e.g. [3]). Some authors show, that Baumgarte's method stabilizes the constraint equations to the wrong value or even destabilizes the numerical solution (e.g. [4]).

There are several ways to interpretate Baumgarte's method.

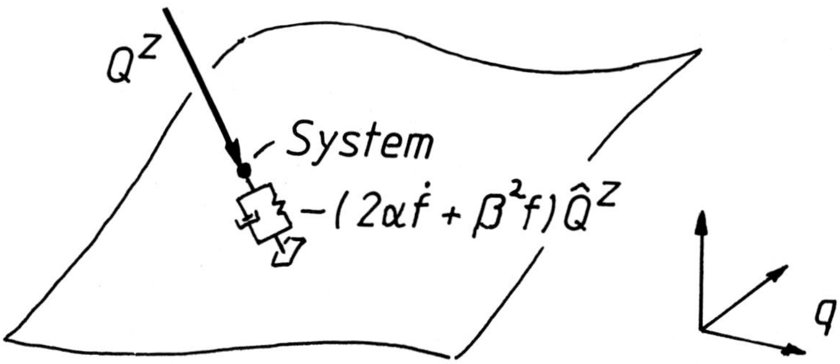

Figure 5. *Interpretation of Baumgarte's method from mechanical point of view.*

a) The additional terms in the constraint force (2.1) form a spring-damper, which can move free on the manifold $f(\mathbf{q},t) = 0$. whenever the classical constraint force $\mathbf{Q}^{\mathbf{z}}$ is computed erroneous and the system leave the manifold, the spring -damper force pull the system back to $f(\mathbf{q},t) = 0$.

b) Baumgarte's stabilization can be seen as a special way of regularization of DAE's:

$$[\ L\ ]_{\mathbf{q}} = \mathbf{Q} + \lambda \frac{\partial}{\partial \mathbf{q}} f \ ,$$

$$-\varepsilon_2 \ddot{f} - \varepsilon_1 \dot{f} = f, \qquad 0 < \varepsilon_1, \varepsilon_2.$$

For more details on regularization see [11].

c) The additional control terms computed by Baumgarte's method removes the double eigenvalue zero, caused by $\ddot{f} = 0$, to the left side of the complex plane.

These control theroretic aspects are discussed in the next chapter in more detail.

3. Controlling of constraint forces.

One aim of control theory is to control the output of a process under perturbations, which are known only qualitative. With help of a controller the difference of output and wanted output is used to modify the process input for minimizing this difference.

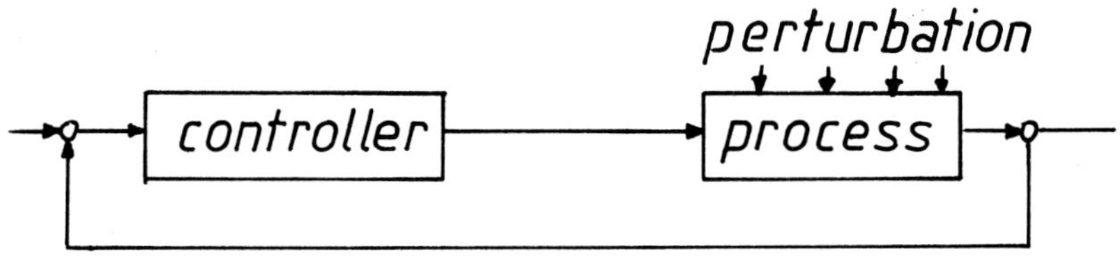

Figure 6. *A control circuit.*

The computation of constraint forces can be described by a characteristic process, shown in fig. 7.

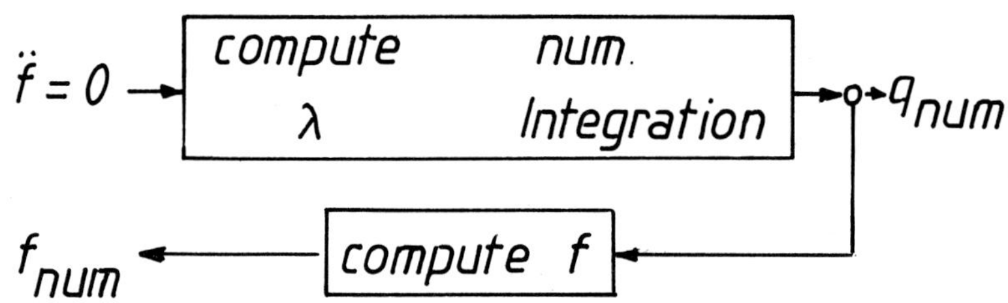

Figure 7. *Process : treatment of DAE's for holonomic constraints*

There the twice differentiated holonomic holonomic constraint $\ddot{f}$ = 0 enter the process by computing the Lagrangian multiplier. The output of the process is the actual numerical value of f. In a first approximation step this process can be idealized by a double integrator.

The qualitative behaviour of perturbations is described by

$$z(t) = \text{const.} + \Sigma\, c_j\, e^{i\omega_j t} \qquad (3.1)$$

The constant part causes the typical meanvalue behaviour of the error devellopement. The second part of (3.1) describes additional oscillatory errors, which are characteristic for the mechanical system.

For nonholonomic constraints and integrals of motion the related process is a single integrator. the perturbations are of the same form (3.1) too.

A classical controller for the holonomic constraint process is a PD-controller (see fig. 8).

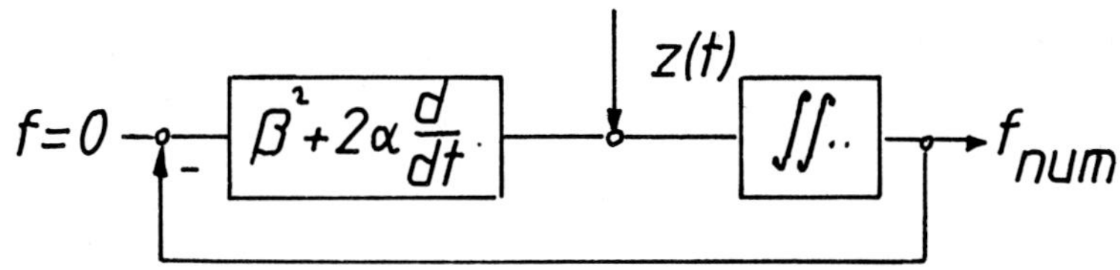

Figure 8. *PD-controller for holonomic constraints.*

In this closed loop there is no longer the equation $f = 0$ at the input of process, bat the equation $f = - 2\alpha f - \beta^2 f$. This is exactly the Baumgarte stabilization method! So his method can be interpretated as a virtual controller build in the equations of motion with respect to the constraint equation.

One way to describe the effect of the controller on the perturbed system is the Bode diagram, see fig. 9a. There is

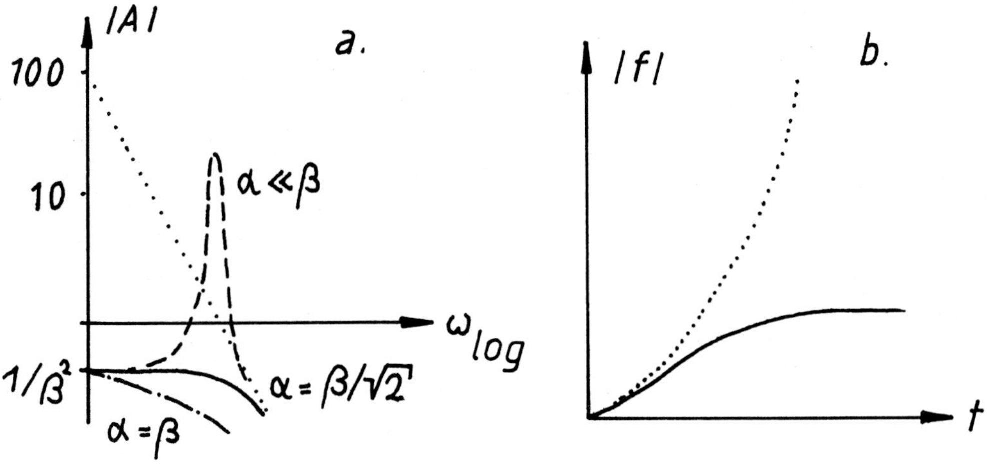

Figure 9. *a) Bode diagram b) process output for holonomic constraints.*

shown the maximal amplitude of the stationary answer of the system over the frequence of perturbation with amplitude 1. The dotted line is the answer of the uncontrolled process.

The constant part of perturbation ($\omega \to 0$) causes a bounded answer of the controlled process. So the polynomial order of the mean value of numerical errors with respect to a holonomic constraint is reduced by two orders, independent of the choosen magnitude of β. With respect to the periodic parts of perturbation β controlles the limit frequency of the controller. For frequencies larger than β the Baumgarte stabilization shows no effects. The parameter α controlles the answer of the process in the near of the frequency β. A small parameter value α causes high amplitudes of system answer near the eigenfrequency. For large values α the change of amplitudes is very small. In control theory the value $\alpha = \beta/\sqrt{2}$ is seen as good choice.

If the user want to have bounded constraint errors with respect to the numerical integration, he has to choose small parameters, when he want to control the periodic parts of perturbation too, the parameters have to be large.

In addition to the frequencies of the mechanical system, the controller introduces the frequency β. When β is larger then the highest system frequency, some integration routines choose small stepsizes controlled by β but not by the system. So the numerical error behaviour sometimes seems to be better, but some integration routines will fail in this case, especially when the user has choosen a constant stepsize (see [4]).

The Bode diagramm shows, that there is left a constant value by PD-controllers proportional to $1/\beta^2$ with respect to the constraint equation.

Analogous conclusions can be done for nonholonomic constraints and integrals of motion. Even this very simple idealization of the process "treatment of DAE's" in mechanical systems with the controll loop "Baumgarte stabilization" give nice answers on the effect of stabilization. In addition, this idealization contain the possibility to construct new stabilization procedures, using the experience of control theory.

In control theory it is known, that controllers must have integrators too, to get a exact stationary answer of the process in mind for constant perturbations. A controll circuit for nonholonomic constraints and integrals of motion is shown in fig. 10a. The effect of a socalled PI-controller is characterised by the Bode diagram in fig. 10b.

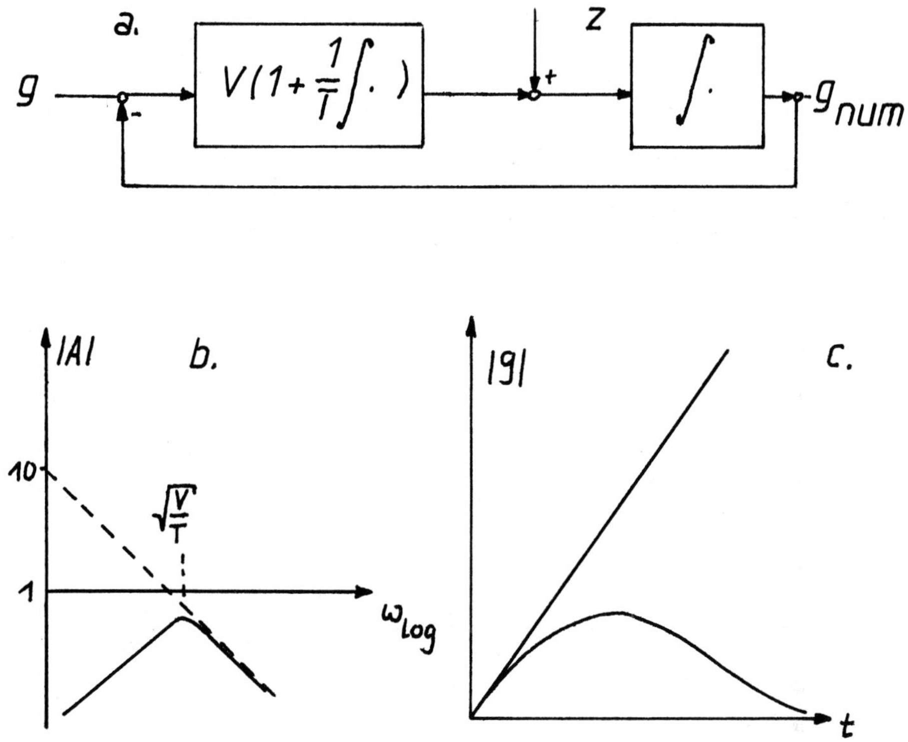

Figure 10. *a) PI-controller b) Bode diagram c) schematic answer of the process.*

The constraint force is computed via the equations:

$$
\begin{aligned}
[\;L\;]_{\mathbf{q}} &= \mathbf{Q} + \mu \frac{\partial}{\partial \dot{\mathbf{q}}} g \;, \\
\dot{q}_{n+1} &= g(\dot{\mathbf{q}}, \mathbf{q}, t)\,, \qquad\qquad (3.2) \\
0 &= \dot{g} + V\,(\,g + \frac{1}{T}\, q_{n+1})\,.
\end{aligned}
$$

The order of system is increased by 1, the new variable q_{n+1} is the integral of the constraint equation. For $1/T \rightarrow 0$ the system (3.2) is reduced to system (2.2). For $V \rightarrow 0$ the classical form of a system with a nonholonomic constraint is described.

The following system (e.g. [4]) describing quaternions is an example with an inner constraint , $I = \mathbf{x}^2 - 1 = 0$:

$$\dot{\mathbf{x}} = \frac{1}{2}\,\mathbf{\Omega}\,\mathbf{x} \;, \qquad \mathbf{\Omega} = \begin{bmatrix} 0 & -\omega_1 & -\omega_2 & -\omega_3 \\ \omega_1 & 0 & \omega_3 & -\omega_2 \\ \omega_2 & -\omega_3 & 0 & \omega_1 \\ \omega_3 & \omega_2 & -\omega_1 & 0 \end{bmatrix}$$
$$0 = \mathbf{x}^2 - 1 \;,$$

The stabilization with a PI-controller leads to the system

$$\begin{aligned} \dot{\mathbf{x}} &= \frac{1}{2}\,\mathbf{\Omega}\,\mathbf{x} + 2\,\nu\,\mathbf{x}, \\ y &= \mathbf{x}^2 - 1, \\ 0 &= 2\,\dot{\mathbf{x}}\,\mathbf{x} + V(\,\mathbf{x}^2 - 1 + \frac{1}{T}\,y). \end{aligned} \tag{3.3}$$

The Lagrangian multiplier ν consists on control terms only

$$\nu = -\frac{V^2}{4\mathbf{x}^2}(\mathbf{x}^2 - 1 + \frac{1}{T}\,y),$$

and is equal to zero on the exact solution.

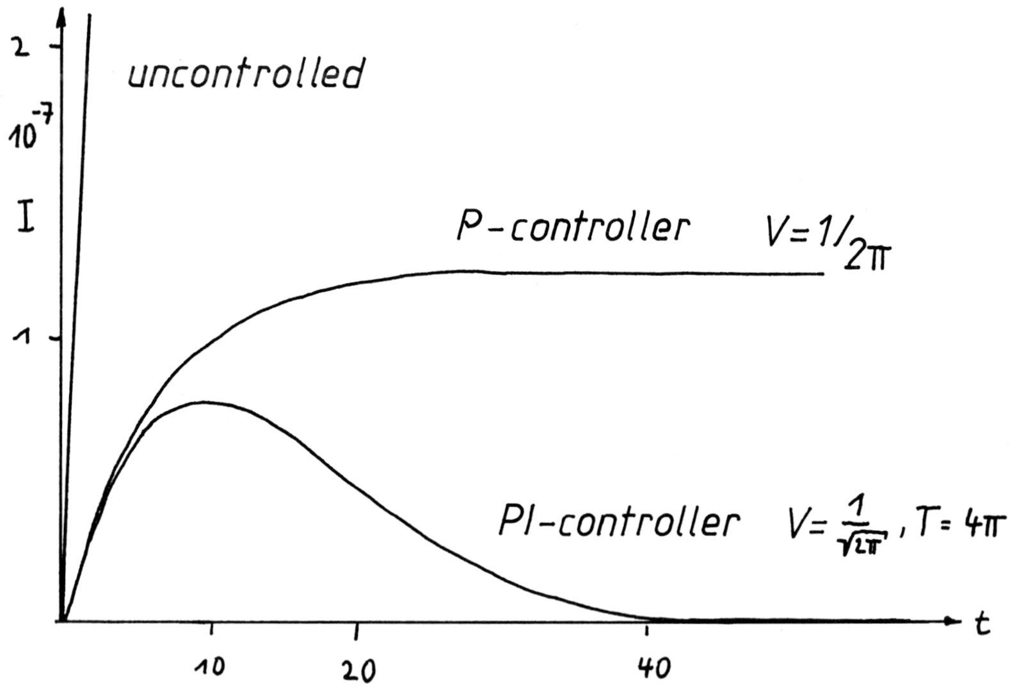

Figure 11. *Numerical errors of (3.3) with respect to integral I (Integration routine: RKF 7(8) with stepsize control).*

Other aspects from control theory, usefull for building up

new stabilization procedures, are [6] :

- Introduction of PID-controllers.
- Introduction of additional timeparameters T*, to describe the process in more details.
- Introduction of optimum criteria to compute the stabilization parameters.

With respect to the "symmetrical optimum" the new stabilizing Gaussian constraints in the holonomic case are:

$$\ddot{f} + \frac{1}{2T^*} \left(4 \dot{f} + \frac{1}{T^*} f + \frac{1}{16T^{*2}} \int_{t_0}^{t} f \, d\tau \right) = 0, \tag{3.3}$$

and for nonholonomic constraints and integrals of motion the resulting equation is:

$$\dot{g} + \frac{1}{2T^*} \left(g + \frac{1}{4T^*} \int_{t_0}^{t} g \, d\tau \right) = 0. \tag{3.4}$$

In these equations only one parameter is left (= T*). Even this parameter can be computed via an adaptive stabilization T* = T*(h), where h denotes the actual stepsize of the program.

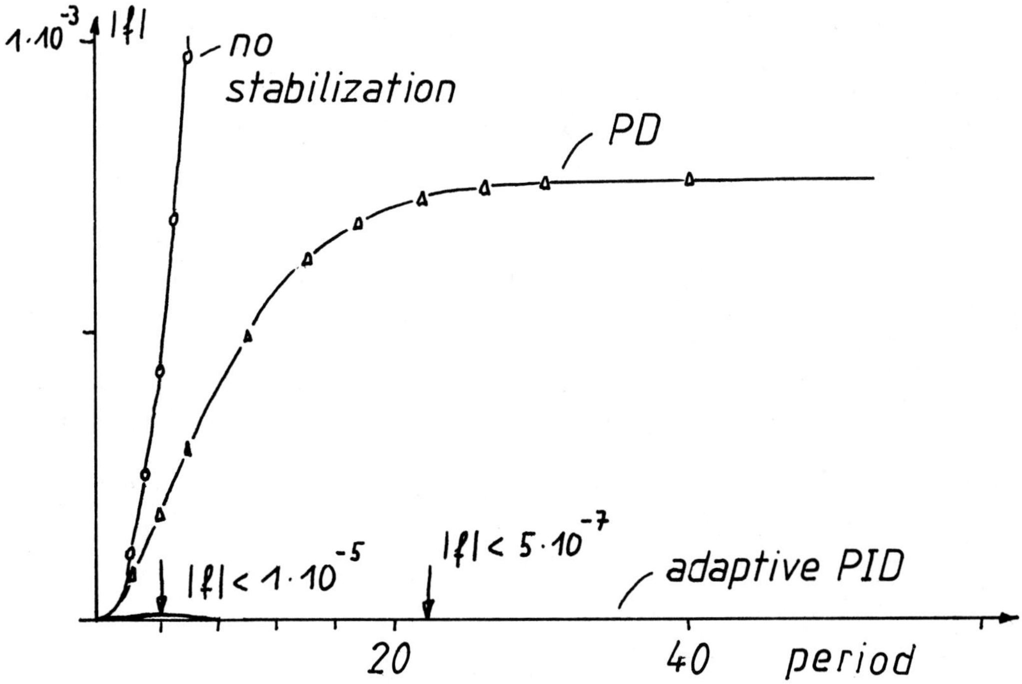

Figure 12. *Constraint errors in system: mathematical pendulum.*

This function is characteristic for the special integration routine, the user has choosen. Fig. 12 shows the effect of an adaptive stabilization via (3.3) for the pendulum system (1.6). The physical parameters are : m = 1 [kg], l = 1 [m], g = 10 [m/s²], the integration routine is a RKF7(8) code, the tolerance was set to 10^{-5}. The initial conditions $x = 0$, $y = -1$, $\dot{x} = 4$, $\dot{y} = 0$, set the period of oscillatory motion to 2.25 seconds.

4. Conclusions

Here only linear controllers are taken into acount. But there are some ways to construct nonlinear controllers. Usually they are simpler to implement and give as nice results as linear controllers. Another way to deal with DAE's is in contrast to the search of proper controllers the change of the type of process [6],[8]. Reports on these aspects will be done elsewhere.

Baumgarte's method is a very simple and cheep way to take care of DAE's without bounding the set of types of integration codes, the user want to compute with. The results are very satisfactury. There are a lot of questions coming up with Baumgarte's method. For instance : is it possible to choose a controller for the constraints, which makes it unnecessary to compute Lagrangian multipliers algebraically. Such a controller would make the automatic computation of constraint forces very easy.

References

1. Baumgarte, J.: Stabilization of constraints and integrals of motion in dynamical systems. Comp. Meth. in Appl. Mech. and Eng. 1 (1972), 1 - 16.
2. Roberson, R.E.: Constraint stabilization for rigid bodies: an extension of Baumgarte's method, IUTAM Symp. on Dynamics of multibody systems, Munich 29.8.-3.9.77,Berlin Springer Verlag 1978, S. 274-290.
3. Grünhagen, W.v.: Zur Stabilisierung der numerischen Integration von Bewegungsgleichungen. Diss. TU Braunschweig, DFVLR - FB79 - 41.
4. Geiger, W.: Numerische Instabilität und Stabilisierung der kinematischen Quaternionengleichung. ZAMM 59 (1979),T118-T120

5: Wittenburg, J.: Dynamics of multibody systems, IUTAM Symp. on Theor. and appl. Mechanics, Toronto 17.8. - 23.8. 1980, North Holland Publ. Comp. 1981, S 11-22.
6. Ostermeyer, G.P.: Mechanische Systeme mit beschränktem Konfigurationsraum, Diss. TU Braunschweig 1983.
7. Nikravesh, P.E.: Some methods for dynamic analysis of constrained mechanical systems: a survey. In E. Haug (ed.), Computer aided analysis and optimization of mechanical system dynamics, Springer-Verlag 1984.
8. Baumgarte,J., Ostermeyer, G.P.: Quasigeneralisierte Variable. ZAMM 65 (1985) 10, 417 - 478.
9. Petzold, L.R., Lötstedt,P.: Numerical solution of nonlinear differential equations with algebraic constraints II:Practical Implications. SIAM J. Sci. Stat. Comput., 7,3,1986, S.720-733
10.Führer, C.: Differential - algebraische Gleichungssysteme in mechanischen Mehrkörpersystemen, Theorie, num.Ansätze und Anwendungen., Diss. TU München, 1988.
11.Knorrenschild, M.: Regularisierung von Differentiell-algebraischen Systemen - theoretische und numerische Aspekte. Diss. TH Aachen, 1988.

A Stabilization Method for Kinematic and Kinetic Constraint Equations

Dae-Sung Bae and Sung-Mo Yang‡

Mechanical Engineering Department
The University of Kansas
Lawrence, KS

ABSTRACT

A method that decides the optimal stabilization constant of the constraint stabilization method is developed for both the real time constant step integration and the variable order, variable step integration methods. The stability theory for multistep integration formulas is applied to determine the stability region of the stabilized constraint equations. An algorithm that maintains error control of the constraint equations as well as the system integration variables is developed. The proposed algorithm is implemented on the variable step, variable order DE algorithm [1]. A kinetic constraint equation is formulated, based on the energy conservation theorem. Violation of the kinetic constraint equation is corrected by stabilizing the equations of motion. Application of the proposed methods to the real time simulation is discussed. Several examples are solved to demonstrate the effectiveness of the proposed methods.

---

‡) The Chunbuk National University, Chunju, Korea

NATO ASI Series, Vol. F 69
Real-Time Integration Methods for Mechanical System Simulation
Edited by E. J. Haug and R. C. Deyo

1. Introduction

The equations of motion for a constrained mechanical system are formulated as a differential algebraic equation (DAE). There are several solution methods in solving the DAE. A stiff gear algorithm was used to form a set of substituted equations of motion in Ref. 2. The equations of motion are substituted into the backward difference formula and solved simultaneously with algebraic constraint equations that represent the kinematic joints of a system. Since the error control on the velocity constraints that are obtained by differentiating the position constraint equations is not considered in this solution method, the velocity constraint violation may gradually grow.

A Generalized Coordinate Partitioning method was presented by Wehage in Ref. 3. The generalized coordinates are partitioned into the independent and dependent coordinates. The independent generalized coordinates are integrated and the dependent coordinates are recovered by solving the constraint equations. Even though this method is mathematically rigorous, it is difficult to choose the independent coordinates.

Since the algebraic constraint equation introduces so many difficulties in solving the DAE, a set of null space methods that numerically eliminate the constraint were proposed in Refs. 4, 5, and 6. The null space of constraint Jacobian matrix is generated by numerical methods, such as Gram-Schmidt process or QR decomposition. A set of new generalized coordinates that are tangent to the constraint hyper-plane are defined. Since the null space of the constraint Jacobian is tangent to the constraint hyper-plane, the new generalized coordinates are not subjected to any constraint equations. The equations of motion are then transformed from the constrained differential equations to unconstrained differential equations. However, it is computationally expensive procedure to regenerate the null space numerically at every integration time step.

A constraint stabilization method was developed, based on a linear feedback control theory in Ref. 7. The method is applied to the Hamiltonian equations of motion in Ref. 8. The position and velocity constraint violations are feeded back to the acceleration constraint equations. Chang tried to find the optimal stabilization constants α and β in Ref. 9. The constraint violation at the next time step is estimated by the Taylor expansion of the constraint equation and higher order terms are neglected. Since the error propagation of the constraint is nonlinear, the negligence of the higher order terms may predict the actual constraint violation at the next time step inaccurately. The stabilization algorithm was combined with the generalized coordinate partitioning algorithm in Ref. 10. The advantages of the both methods are exploited.

In order to improve the constraint stabilization method, a method that determines the optimal stabilization constants α and β is presented in this paper. The Cartesian equations of motion are derived in Section 2. The constraint stabilization methods are explained in Section 3. Section 4 presents the method that determines the optimal stabilization constant for both constant and variable step integration algorithms. Formulation and stabilization of a kinetic constraint equation are discussed in Section 5. Numerical examples and discussions are presented in Section 6.

2. Equations of Motion

The variational form of equations of motion in the Cartesian space is given in Ref. 11 as

$$\delta \mathbf{q}^T (\mathbf{M}\ddot{\mathbf{q}} + \Phi_{\mathbf{q}}^T \lambda - \mathbf{Q}_e) = \mathbf{0} \tag{1}$$

where

$\mathbf{q}$	= Generalized coordinate vector
$\ddot{\mathbf{q}}$	= Acceleration vector
$\mathbf{M}$	= Mass matrix
$\mathbf{Q}_e$	= Generalized external force vector
Φ	= Constraint equation vector
$\Phi_{\mathbf{q}}$	= Constraint jacobian matrix
λ	= Lagrange multiplier vector

Since the $\delta\mathbf{q}$ is arbitrary in Eq. 1, its coefficient must be zero, which yields

$$\mathbf{M}\ddot{\mathbf{q}} + \Phi_{\mathbf{q}}^T \lambda = \mathbf{Q}_e \tag{2}$$

Equation 2 comprises less equations than unknowns. Therefore, the acceleration constraint equations must be appended to Eq. 2 to form the following augmented equations of motion:

$$\begin{bmatrix} \mathbf{M} & \Phi_{\mathbf{q}}^T \\ \Phi_{\mathbf{q}} & \mathbf{0} \end{bmatrix} \begin{bmatrix} \ddot{\mathbf{q}} \\ \lambda \end{bmatrix} = \begin{bmatrix} \mathbf{Q}_e \\ \gamma \end{bmatrix} \tag{3}$$

where

$$\begin{aligned} \gamma &= \Phi_{\mathbf{q}}\ddot{\mathbf{q}} \\ &= -(\Phi_{\mathbf{q}}\dot{\mathbf{q}})_{\mathbf{q}}\dot{\mathbf{q}} - 2\Phi_{\mathbf{q}t}\dot{\mathbf{q}} - \Phi_{tt} \end{aligned} \tag{4}$$

Taken with the initial conditions $\mathbf{q}(0)$ and $\dot{\mathbf{q}}(0)$ that satisfy $\Phi(\mathbf{q}(0),0)=\mathbf{0}$ and $\dot{\Phi}(\mathbf{q}(0),\dot{\mathbf{q}}(0),0)=\mathbf{0}$, Eq. 3 can be solved for $\ddot{\mathbf{q}}$ and λ.

3. The Constraint Stabilization Method

If Eq. 3 is solved for $\ddot{q}$ and λ and then $\dot{q}$ and $\ddot{q}$ are integrated for q and $\dot{q}$ at the next time step, the position and velocity constraints at the next time step may not be satisfied:i.e.,

$$\Phi\,(\,q(t_i),t_i\,) \neq 0$$

$$\dot{\Phi}\,(\,q(t_i),\dot{q}(t_i),t_i\,) \neq 0 \qquad (5)$$

In order to overcome this drawback, Baumgate proposed a constraint stabilization method [7]. The linear feedback control theory is adopted to form the following stabilized acceleration constraint equation:

$$\ddot{\Phi} + 2\alpha\dot{\Phi} + \beta^2\Phi = 0 \qquad (6)$$

where α and β are the stabilization constants and Φ and $\dot{\Phi}$ are the position and velocity constraint violations, respectively. If Eq. 6 is augmented to Eq. 2 instead of Eq. 4, the augmented equations of motion becomes

$$\begin{bmatrix} M & \Phi_q^T \\ \Phi_q & 0 \end{bmatrix}\begin{bmatrix} \ddot{q} \\ \lambda \end{bmatrix} = \begin{bmatrix} Q_e \\ \gamma - 2\alpha\dot{\Phi} - \beta^2\Phi \end{bmatrix} \qquad (7)$$

The solution procedures of the stabilization method are as follows:

1) Solve Eq. 7 for $\ddot{q}$ and λ with known q and $\dot{q}$.

2) Integrate $\dot{q}$ and $\ddot{q}$ from t_i to t_{i+1} to get q and $\dot{q}$, respectively.

3) If t_{i+1} has reached the final time, stop. Otherwise go to step 1 with $t=t_{i+1}$.

As an integration proceeds, the position and velocity constraints may be violated due to the local truncation error of the integration. In such case, the amount of violations are amplified by the stabilization constants of 2α and β^2 and feeded back to Eq. 7. This process slightly changes the direction of accelerations so as to satisfy the position and velocity constraint equations at the next time step.

4. Determination of the Optimal Stabilization Constants

4.1 Relationship Between α and β

Equation 6 is a second order linear differential equation of Φ. The critical damping is achieved when $\alpha = \beta$. It was hoped in Ref. 10 that the constraint violations were stabilized quickly by using the critical damping condition. However, the constraint violations Φ and $\dot{\Phi}$ are evaluated by the generalized coordinates and velocities that are obtained by an integration and the error propagation behavior of the constraints is nonlinear. Therefore, the error propagation behavior of the constraints seems not quite sensitive to the critical damping condition that comes from the linear differential equation of Eq. 6.

The coefficients of Φ and $\dot{\Phi}$ in Eq. 6 may be considered as the weighting factors of the penalty functions for the position and velocity constraint violations. In this sense, the critical damping condition of $\alpha = \beta$ imposes more weighting on position constraint violation than velocity constraint violation if $\alpha > 1$. Figure 1 shows the position and velocity constraint violations for a five body open chain that will be explained in Section 6 with the critical damping condition of $\alpha = \beta = 5$. It can be observed that the velocity constraint violation is much larger than the position constraint violation. Since the velocity constraint violation is as important as the position constraint violation, the weighting factors for the both position and velocity constraints are taken to be same. The resulting augmented acceleration constraint is

$$\ddot{\Phi} + \alpha\dot{\Phi} + \alpha\Phi = 0 \tag{8}$$

The magnitude of α represents the weighting factor of the penalty functions for the position and velocity constraint violations. As the magnitude of α increases, the weighting of the penalty term becomes heavier. Therefore, a large α will maintain the position and velocity constraint violations to be smaller than a small α.

4.2 Constant Step Integration

The real time simulation provides dynamic solutions for a motion platform within real time. To achieve this real time goal, a constant step integration must be used. The accuracy and stability of an integration must be preserved throughout an integration. The accuracy can be controlled only by varying the integration stepsize. Therefore, the constant integration stepsize must be small enough to maintain the truncation error to be small.

Even if a stepsize h is chosen to be stable and accurate for the integration variables of the generalized coordinates and velocities, it does not guarantee that the stability and accuracy requirements of the algebraic constraint equation are satisfied. Since the accuracy of the integration is controlled only by changing the stepsize, it is difficult to control the accuracy of the constraint by changing the magnitude of α in the constant step integration. However, the characteristic equation of Eq. 8 affects the stiffness of the system, the stability of the constraint can be controlled by varying the magnitude of α. The stability theory of the multi-step methods is used to find the stability region of the algebraic constraint equation.

The characteristic equation of Eq. 8 is given as

$$D^2 + \alpha D + \alpha = 0 \tag{9}$$

The roots of the characteristic equation are

$$D = -\frac{\alpha}{2} \pm \sqrt{\left(\frac{\alpha}{2}\right)^2 - \alpha} \tag{10}$$

The roots of the characteristic equation of the stabilized acceleration constraint must be within the stability region of the integration method employed. The absolute stability region of the Adams-Bashforth method of order k was drawn in Ref. 12 as in Fig. 2. Note in Fig. 2 that the region of the stability becomes smaller as the order of the method increases. Since the roots of the characteristic equation are real numbers for $\alpha > 4$, the root with larger magnitude must satisfy the following condition:

$$h\left(\frac{\alpha}{2} + \sqrt{\left(\frac{\alpha}{2}\right)^2 - \alpha}\right) < ST_k \tag{11}$$

where ST_k is the absolute value of the minimum of the stability region of order k on the real axis. The ST_k values for the Adams-Bashforth predictors are listed in Table 1. Since the behaviors of Φ and $\dot{\Phi}$ are nonlinear, slightly smaller value of ST_k than the one on the boundary of the stability region is used to guarantee the stability. Solving Eq. 11 for α gives

order k	1	2	3	4	5	6	7
ST_k	1.6	0.8	0.4	0.2	0.1	0.05	0.005

Table 1 ST_k Values for the Adams-Bashforth Methods

$$\alpha < \frac{ST_k^2}{(ST_k\, h - h^2)} \tag{12}$$

Since h is generally so small, the h^2 term can be neglected, which yields

$$\alpha < \frac{ST_k}{h} \tag{13}$$

It is indicated in Section 4.1 that a large stabilization constant α keeps the constraint violations to be smaller than a small α. As a result, the optimal stabilization constant α^* is taken to be the greatest number that satisfies the inequality of Eq. 13 as

$$\alpha^* = \frac{ST_k}{h} \tag{14}$$

As an example, the α^* for stepsize $h = 0.001$ and the Adams-Bashforth third order method is obtained from Eq. 14 and Table 1 as $\alpha^* = ST_3 / h = 0.4 / 0.001 = 400$.

4.3 Variable Order, Variable Stepsize Integration

The order and stepsize of a variable step, variable order integration algorithm continue to change throughout the integration, based on the error estimation of the integration variables. As the stepsize and order change, the optimal stabilization constant α^* continues to change at every time step. Drastic change of the α^* introduces another stiffness into the integration. In other words, the magnitude of $\partial \dot{\alpha}^*/\partial \alpha^*$ is large. Therefore, the α^* had better be constant throughout the integration.

In order not to disturb the stability of any steps from a starting time to an ending time, the most unstable step must be considered in selecting α^*. The most unstable step for the α^* occurs when the stepsize and order are the largest step size and the maximum order, respectively. Because, the stability region of a higher order method is smaller than that of a lower method. As a result, the α^* for a variable step, variable order method is determined by

$$\alpha^* = \frac{ST_{k\,max}}{h_{max}} \tag{15}$$

where k_{max} and h_{max} are the maximum order and stepsize allowed in a variable order, variable step algorithm.

The stepsize of a variable order, variable step integration algorithm for the ordinary differential equations is determined by checking the error estimation of the integration variables. Since the DAE has the algebraic constraint equations in addition to the differential equations, the error propagation of the constraint equations as well as that of the integration variables must be controlled and considered in determining the integration step size. Combining the error estimation theory of the integration variables and the error propagation behavior of the constraints may be complicated.

A simple algorithm that considers the error estimation of the integration variables and error propagation of the constraint separately is proposed as follows:

1) Determine a stepsize and order by checking the error estimations of the integration variables [1].
2) Check if the constraint violations grow fast. The following expression is used as a criterion in detecting the growth of the constraint violations

$$(\|\Phi\| + \|\dot{\Phi}\|)_t - (\|\Phi\| + \|\dot{\Phi}\|)_{t-h} < \varepsilon \tag{16}$$

where ε in Eq. 16 is an error tolerance. If Eq. 16 is satisfied, the stepsize selected in Step 1 is accepted. Otherwise, the stepsize is reduced by $h = \theta\, h$ for $0.5<\theta<1$.

5. Formulation and Stabilization of the Kinetic Constraint Equation

Define a system energy H as

$$H = T + U \tag{17}$$

where the kinetic energy T and the potential energy U including the velocity potential are defined by

$$T = \frac{1}{2}\dot{q}^T M \dot{q} \tag{18}$$

and

$$\begin{aligned} U &\equiv \int (-Q_e + \Phi_q^T \lambda)^T dq \\ &= \int (-Q_e + \Phi_q^T \lambda)^T \dot{q}\, dt \end{aligned} \tag{19}$$

The H for a conservative system becomes the total energy of the system.

Differentiation of H in Eq. 17 becomes

$$\dot{H} = \dot{q}^T(M\ddot{q} - Q_e + \Phi_q^T\lambda) \qquad (20)$$

Substitution of Eq. 2 into Eq. 20 yields $\dot{H} = 0$. The H must be preserved throughout the integration. As a result, the following kinetic constraint equation is formulated:

$$\Psi = H(t) - H(t_0) = H - H_0 = 0 \qquad (21)$$

$$\dot{\Psi} = 0$$

If Eq. 21 is violated, the violation can be damped out by stabilizing $\Psi = 0$ as

$$\dot{\Psi} = -\alpha\Psi \qquad (22)$$

or

$$\dot{H} = -\alpha(H - H_0) \qquad (23)$$

where α is the stabilization constant that is determined by methods presented in the previous sections. Substitution of Eq. 20 into 23 yields

$$\dot{q}^T(M\ddot{q} - Q_e + \Phi_q^T\lambda) = \frac{\dot{q}^T\dot{q}}{\dot{q}^T\dot{q}}(-\alpha)(H - H_0) \qquad (24)$$

Equation 24 may be simplified to obtain the following stabilized equations of motion:

$$M\ddot{q} + \Phi_q^T\lambda = Q_e + \frac{\dot{q}}{\dot{q}^T\dot{q}}(-\alpha)(H - H_0) \tag{25}$$

for arbitrary $\dot{q}$. Appending the acceleration constraint equation in Eq. 8 to Eq. 25 yields the following augmented equations of motion:

$$\begin{bmatrix} M & \Phi_q^T \\ \Phi_q & 0 \end{bmatrix}\begin{bmatrix} \ddot{q} \\ \lambda \end{bmatrix} = \begin{bmatrix} Q_e + \frac{\dot{q}}{\dot{q}^T\dot{q}}(-\alpha)(H - H_0) \\ \gamma - \alpha\dot{\Phi} - \alpha\Phi \end{bmatrix} \tag{26}$$

The potential energy U in Eq. 19 can be computed analytically, if Q_e and Φ are the simple functions of q. Otherwise, the U must be obtained by numerical integration of dU/dt $= \dot{q}^T(\Phi_q{}^T\lambda - Q_e) = -(\Phi_t{}^T\lambda + \dot{q}^TQ_e)$.

6. Numerical Examples

Three examples are solved to show the effectiveness of the method presented in the previous sections.

Example 1. Simple Pendulum

The simple pendulum shown in Fig. 3 consists of the ground and the body that is connected to the ground by a revolute joint. The ground is not considered as a body. Therefore, three generalized coordinates are assigned for the body and two algebraic constraint equations are formulated from the revolute joint. The system has one degree of freedom.

The second order Adams-Bashforth predictor is used to integrate the generalized coordinates and velocities with a constant integration stepsize of 0.002. The ST_2 for the Adams-Bashforth method is given as 0.8 in Table 1. The optimal stabilization constant α^* is computed from Eq. 13 as $\alpha^* = 0.8/0.005 = 160$. Dynamic analysis of the simple pendulum is carried out for 3 sec with $\alpha = 1$, 100, 160, and 220. The x coordinate of the pendulum is shown in Fig. 4. It is expected that as the α increases up to about 160, the constraint violation decreases and starts to diverge shortly after 160. Figure 5 shows the additions of the second norms of the position and velocity constraints with the different α values. As expected, it can be observed in Fig. 5 that the constraint violation becomes smaller with the greater α values and the integration becomes unstable with the α greater than the α^*.

Example 2. High Mobility Multi-Purpose Vehicle(HMMWV)

Real time simulation of the HMMWV vehicle shown in Fig. 6 was attempted in Ref. 13. The system consists of four double A-arm suspension subsystems and the chassis. The resulting degree of freedom is ten. Rotational equations of motion for the wheels are decoupled from the equations of motion for the rest of subsystems by ignoring the gyroscopic coupling effects. Empirical tire deformation and slip model is used to model the interaction between the tire and the ground. The steering motion of the vehicle is modeled as a rack and pinion mechanism.

The Recursive Equations of Motion [13] were derived and implemented on the Alliant FX/8 parallel processor. The Generalized Coordinate Partitioning Method [3] was adopted to solve the DAE for the vehicle system. The same recursive equations of motion with the stabilized acceleration constraint equations for the vehicle model are used to evaluate the performance of the constraint stabilization method with the different α values.

There are several advantages of the constraint stabilization method over the Generalized Coordinate Partitioning Method as long as the stabilization method maintains the constraint violation to be small. First, the Newton-Raphson iterations for the position analysis and the velocity analysis become obsolete. Second, elimination of these procedures removes several synchronization points in the parallel task graph shown in Fig. 16 of Ref. 13. This elimination will reduce the computing time significantly.

The dynamic analysis is carried out for 8 sec with the initial velocity of 30 m/sec. The steering input for the relative rack position with respect to the chassis is given as $u(t) = 0.008\sin(2\pi(t-2)/3)$. The steering input gives a typical lane change maneuver of the vehicle. The lateral position of the vehicle is shown in Fig. 7. Since the time derivative of the steering input is $\dot{u}(t) = 0.016\pi\cos(2\pi(t-2)/3)$ and has a velocity jump at t=2 sec from 0 to 0.016π, the constraints at t=2.0 sec are expected to be violated suddenly. The Adams-Bashforth 3rd order predictor is employed for integration with the stepsize of 0.001.

The optimal stabilization constant α^* is obtained from Eq. 14 as $\alpha^* = ST_3 / h = 0.4/0.001 = 400$. The second norms of the constraint violation with $\alpha = 10, 50, 400$, and 600 are drawn in Fig. 8. As expected, the constraint violation with the greater α is smaller than this with the smaller α and the integration becomes unstable with the α value greater than the optimal stabilization constant α^*.

Example 3. Five Body Open Kinematic Chain

The chain shown in Fig. 9 consists of six bodies including the ground. Each body is connected to its preceding body with a revoulte joint. Three translational and four Euler parameter generalized coordinates are assigned for each body and five constraints are formulated for each revolute joint Therefore, the chain has five degrees of freedom. Since there is no damping element and time dependent constraint, the chain system is a conservative system.

Dynamic analysis of the chain is carried out for 3 sec. Variable order, variable step DE integration algorithm [1] is employed for integration. The Adams-Bashforth predictor and Adams-Moulton corrector are used in the algorithm. The stability region of the predictor-corrector algorithm are drawn in Ref. 1. The maximum order allowed in the current DE algorithm is seven and the ST_7 for the predictor-corrector algorithm is 0.5. Integration error tolerance and ε in Eq. 16 are 0.0001 and 0.001 for the current simulation, respectively. The maximum stepsize allowed for the integration is given as 0.01. The optimal stabilization constant α^* is obtained from Eq. 14 as $\alpha^* = ST_7 / h_{max} = 0.5/0.01 = 50$.

The Z acceleration of body 6 is shown in Fig. 10. Note that the chain experiences extremely wild motion. The first dynamic analysis is done with the critical damping condition. The second simulation is carried out with $\alpha = 50$ and the stepsize determination algorithm described in Section 4.3. The average stepsizes for the first and second simulations are 0.0034 and 0.003, respectively. The norms of the constraint violation are drawn in Fig. 11 for the both simulations. The constraint violation of the second simulation is much smaller than this of the first simulation with slightly shorter stepsize.

Next, the kinetic constraint of Eq. 26 is imposed on the dynamic equations of motion. The $\alpha = 50$ is used for the stabilization of the kinetic constraint. The total energies of the system with and without the kinetic constraint stabilization are shown in Fig. 12. The total energy deviation with the stabilization of the kinetic constraint is more stable than this without stabilization.

References

1. Shampine, L. F. and Gordon, M. K.: Computer Solution of Ordinary Differential Equations: The Initial Value Problem, W. J. Freeman, San Frncisco, CA, 1975.

2. Orlandea, N., Chace, M. A., and Calahan, D. A.: " A Sparsity Oriented Approach to the Dynamic Analysis and Design of Mechanical Systems", J. of Engineering for Industry, 1977, pp. 773-784.

3. Wehage, R. A., and Haug, E. J.: "Generalized Coordinate Partitioning for Dimension Reduction in Analysis and Design of Constrained Dynamic Systems", J. of Mechanical Design, Vol. 104, 1982, pp. 247-255.

4. Kim, S. S. and Vanderploeg, M. J.: "A General and Efficient Method for Dynamic Analysis of Mechanical Systems Using Velocity Transformations", J. of Mechanisms, Transmissions, and Automation in Design, Vol. 108, 1986, pp. 176-182.

5. Mani, N. K., Haug, E. J., and Atkinson, K. E.: "Application of Singular Value Decomposition for Analysis of Mechanical System Dynamics", ASME Paper No. 84-DET-89.

6. Liang, C. G. and Lance, G. M.: "A Differential Null Space Method for Constrained Dynamic Analysis, ASME Paper No. 85-DET-86.

7. Baumgarte, J.: "Stabilization of Constraint and Integrals of Motion in Dynamical Systems", Computer Methods in Applied Mechanics and Engineering, 1972, pp. 1-16.

8. Baumgarte, J. W.:"A New Method of Stabilization for Holonomic Constraints", J. of Applied Mechanics, Vol. 50, 1983, pp. 869-870.

9. Chang, C. O.: "Dynamic Analysis and Optimization of Mechanical Systems With Constraint Violation Stabilization Method", Ph. D. Dissertation, The University Iowa, Iowa City, Iowa, 1984.

10. Park, T. W.: "A Hybrid Numerical Integration Method for Machine Dynamic Simulation", J. of Mechanisms, Transmissions, and Automation in Design, Vol. 108, pp. 211-216.

11. Bae, D. S. and Haug, E. J.: "A Recursive Formulation for Constrained Mechanical System Part II-Closed Loop", Mechanics of Structures and Machines, Vol. 15, No. 4, 1987.

12. Atkinson, K. E.: An Introduction to Numerical Analysis, John Wiley & Sons, New York, 1978.

13. Hwang, R. S., Bae, D. S., Haug, E. J. and Kuhl, J. G.: "Parallel Processing for Real-Time Dynamic System Simulation", J. of Mechanisms, Transmissions, and Automation of Design, submitted January, 1988.

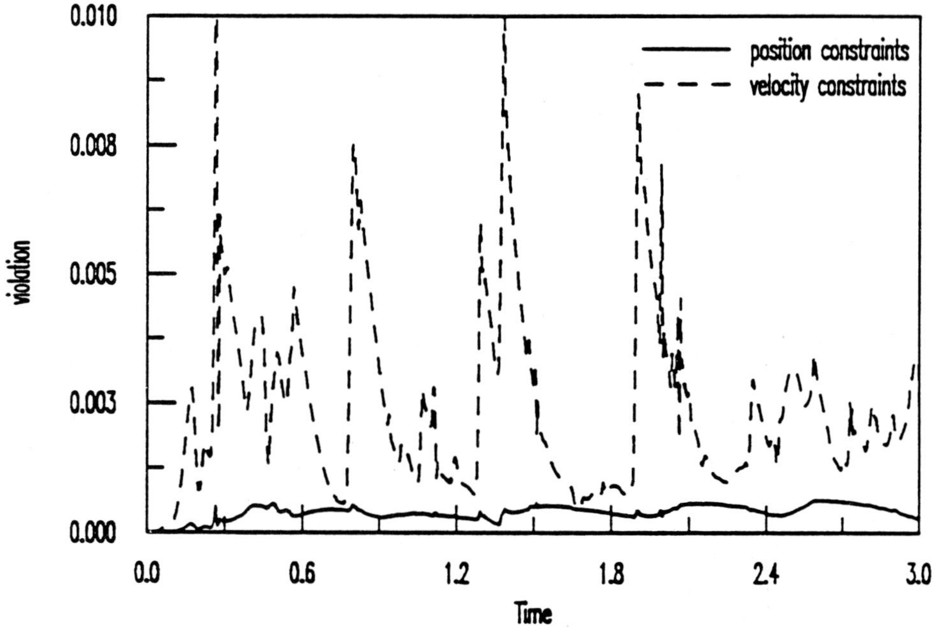

Figure 1 Norms of Constraint Violations for An Open Chain

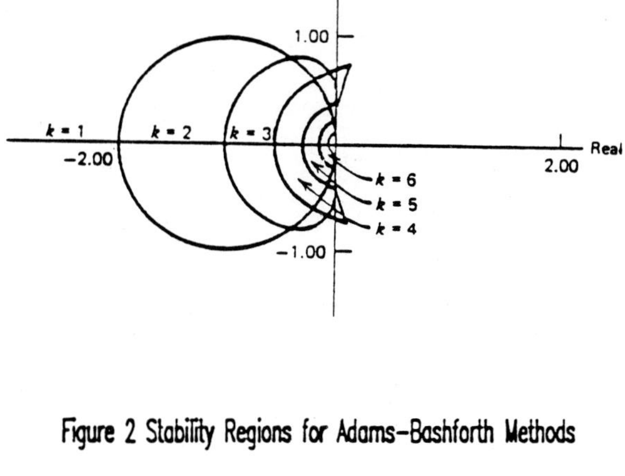

Figure 2 Stability Regions for Adams-Bashforth Methods

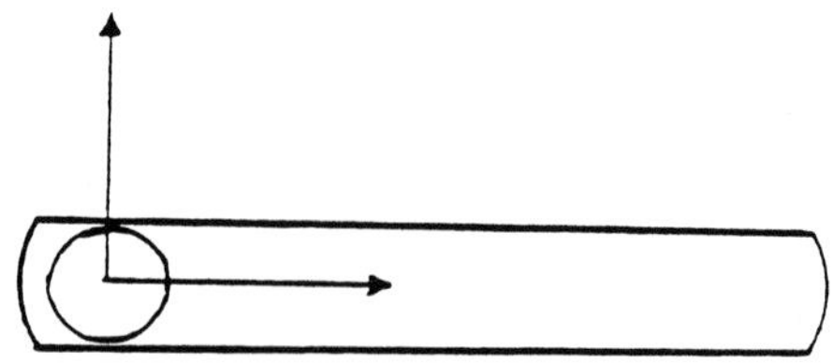

Figure 3 A Single Pendulum

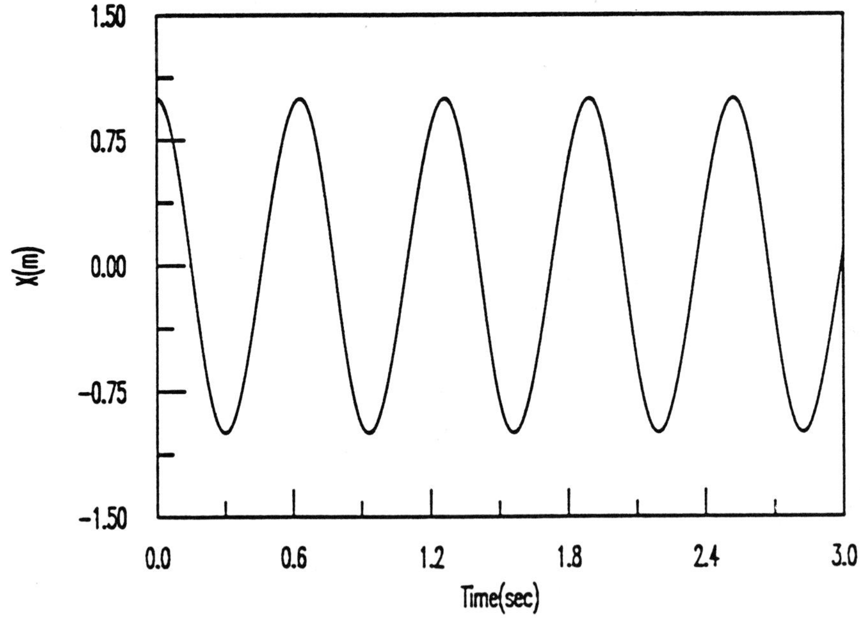

Figure 4 X Coordinate of Pendulum

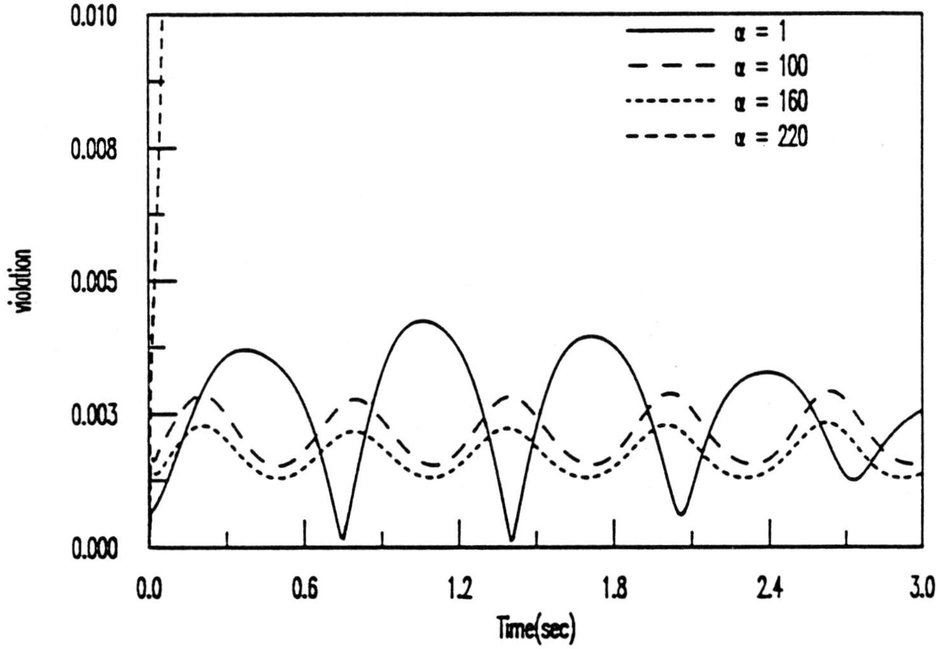

Figure 5 Constraint Violations for the Pendulum

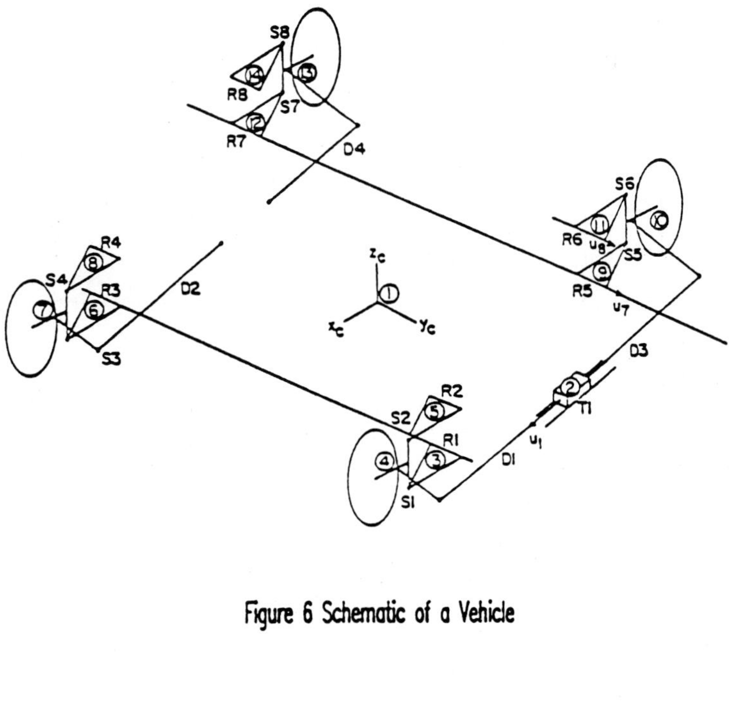

Figure 6 Schematic of a Vehicle

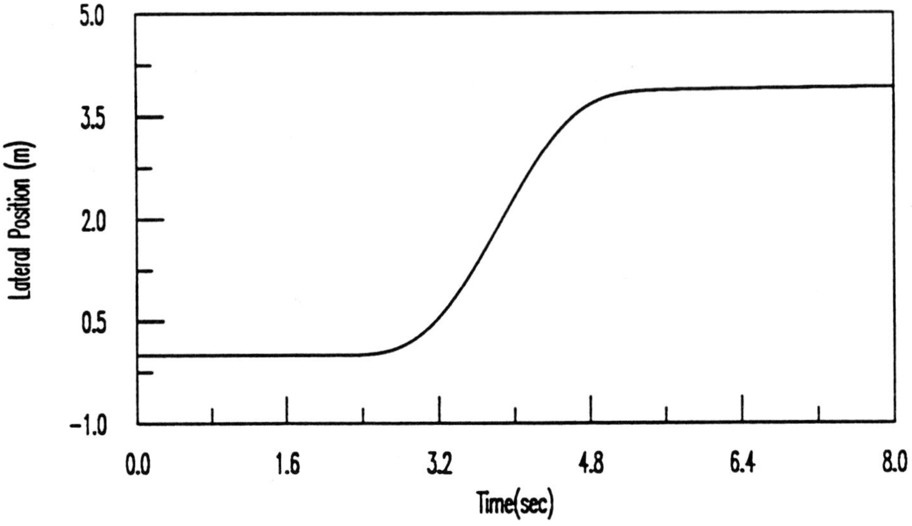

Figure 7 Lateral Position of the Chassis

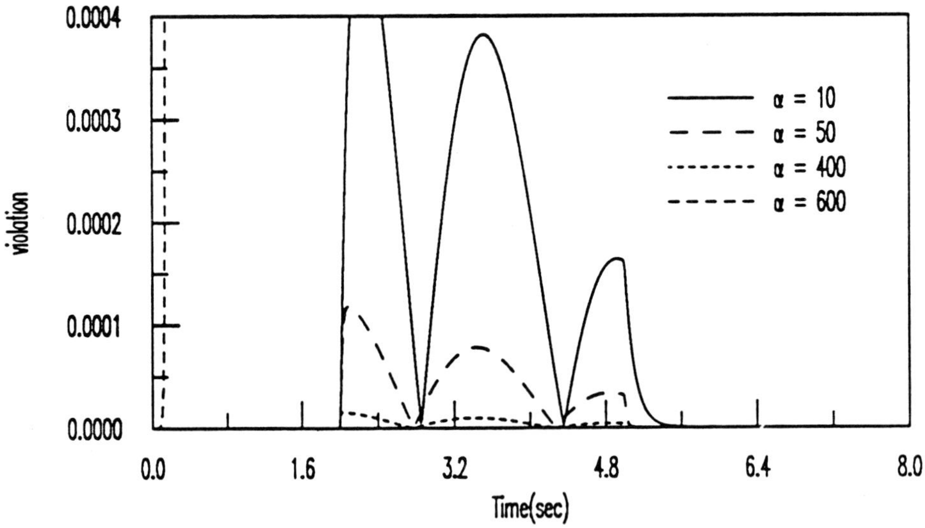

Figure 8 Constraint Violations of the Vehicle

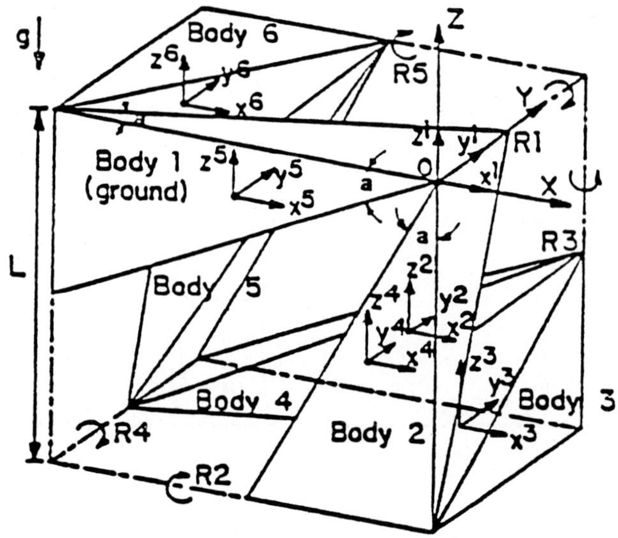

Figure 9 An Open Kinematic Chain

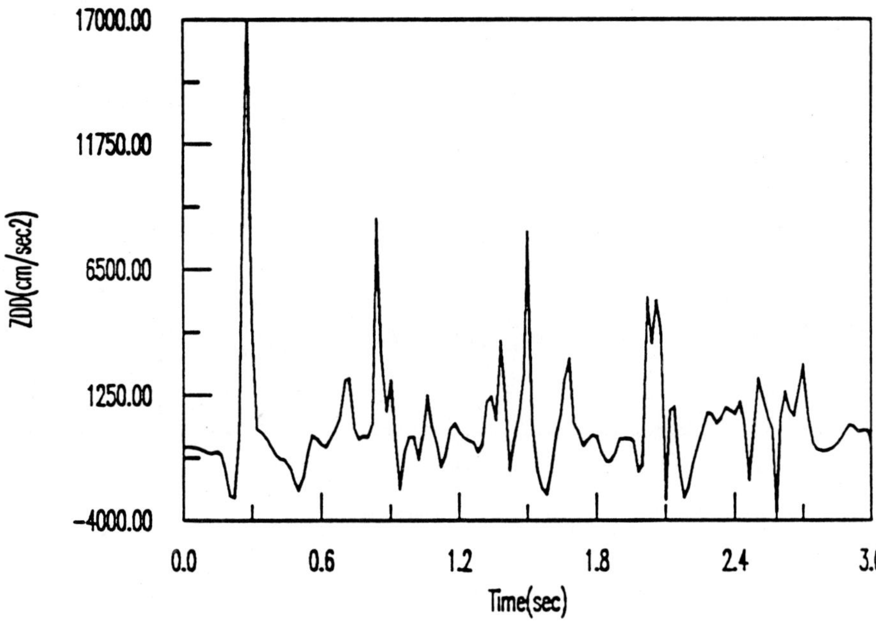

Figure 10 Z Acceleration of Body 6

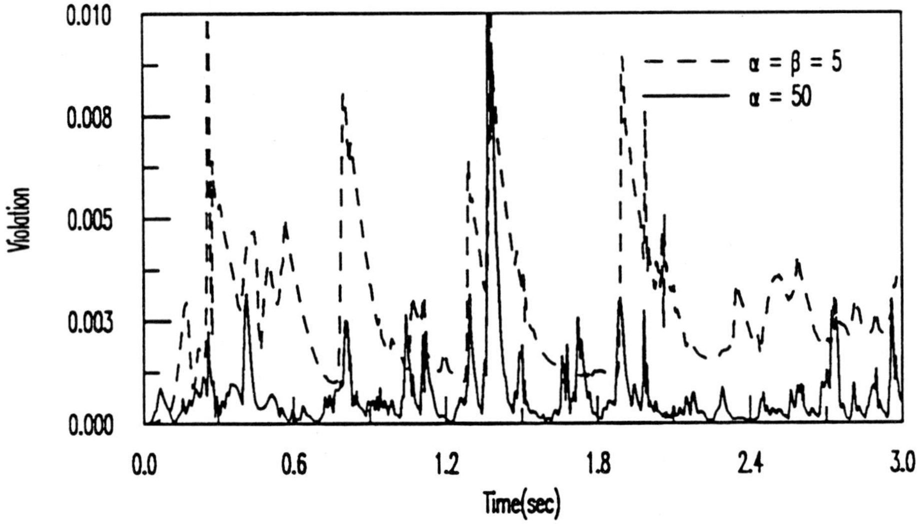

Figure 11 Constraint Violations of the Open Chain

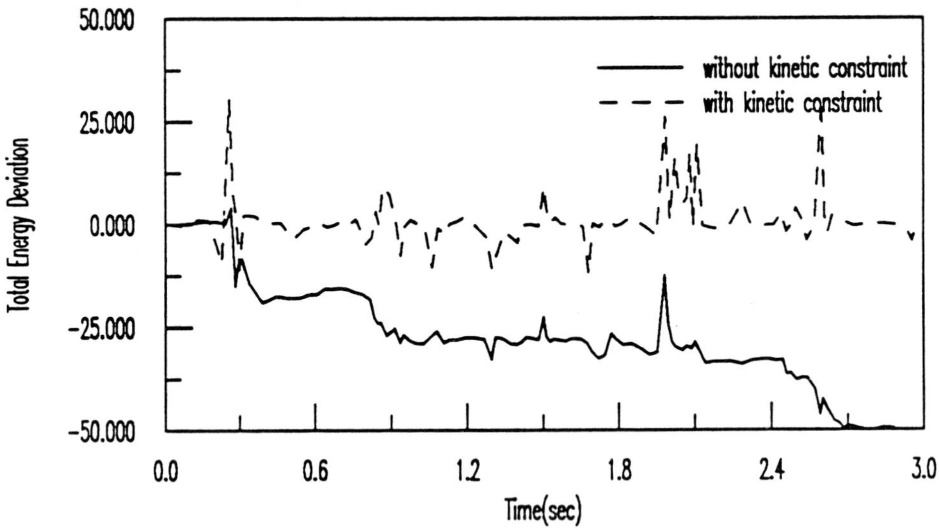

Figure 12 Total Energy Deviation of the Open Chain

Parallel Solution of ODEs

C. W. Gear*
Department of Computer Science
University of Illinois at Urbana-Champaign

Abstract

This talk examines the factors that will limit the application of parallel methods to ordinary differential equations (ODEs). Two primary classes of methods have been discussed in the literature: *parallelism across time*, also called *parallelism across the method*, in which different processors are used to handle different points in time (or different parts of the method); and *parallelism across space*, also called *equation segmentation* or *parallelism across the system*, in which different groups of equations are integrated on different processors. The latter class of methods is suitable and often proposed for real time applications, while both are suitable for non-real time applications. However, in both classes, the factor that limits the speed of the method is the inherent communication in the problem that must be represented in the method. In parallelism across time, the natural flow of information in the increasing time of an initial value problem is a limiting factor. It will be shown that it does not appear possible to achieve a speed of better than logarithmic in the number of time points, and reasons will be given why even that may be extremely difficult. In parallelism across space, the natural flow of information from one part of space to another in the simulated system maps into flow of information between processors. We examine the amount of information that must be transmitted. In a real time application, the time required for the information to flow across several processors may be the limiting factor.

1 Introduction

How much parallel computation is possible in the solution of differential equations due to the physical nature of the underlying problem? In this paper we speculate on the maximum parallelism that can be achieved in initial value problems if the concern is utilization of (possibly massive) parallelism to achieve high speed rather than efficiency. (This paper does not discuss the large range of methods that have been proposed, a modest survey can be found in [2].) In parallelism across space we assign different processors to each equation or subset of equations. Can we come close to execution speeds that are independent of the number of equations, given

*Work supported in part by US DOE under grant DOE DEFG02-87ER25026 and by NSF under grant DMS 87-03226

NATO ASI Series, Vol. F 69
Real-Time Integration Methods for Mechanical System Simulation
Edited by E. J. Haug and R. C. Deyo

sufficient processors? Can we use more processors to increase speed in the case of real-time problems? In parallelism across time we assign different processors to different points in time. Can we come close to execution speeds that are independent of the number of time points to be computed, given sufficient processors?

It will be convenient to study the system of ordinary differential equations (ODEs)

$$y' = \frac{dy}{dt} = f(y,t)$$

or

$$\frac{dy_p}{dt} = f_p(\{y_q\},t).$$

For ODEs derived from PDEs, either $y_p(t) = y(x_p,t)$ (finite differences) or $y_p(t)$, is a *local* aggregate of properties near x_p (finite elements), in either case known as the method of lines (MOL). In both cases, the variables represent information at a particular point or small region of space. (When spectral methods are used to discretize the problem spatially, individual variables are "global" in the sense that they represent information over the whole spatial region. Systems of ODEs derived this way may not be subject to the limitations we will discuss below.)

The relationship between a variable and a spatial position is obvious for ODEs derived by the MOL. The same relationship holds for many other ODEs describing physical systems because they are frequently describing "lumped circuit" models of what are really infinite-dimensional problems properly described by PDEs. For example, an electrical network is usually described in terms of discrete elements such as gates and interconnections. The elements could be modeled by a set of PDEs with complex boundary conditions. However, the external behavior of the element can be approximated by a small set of ODEs. The variables in these ODEs are aggregates of local quantities such as charge.

2 Parallelism Across Time

Information in initial value problems flows naturally in increasing time. Until we have an approximate value for $y(t_n)$ we cannot compute $f(y(t_n))$ to get an approximation to $y'(t_n)$, and the only way we can get the first good approximation to $y(t_n)$ is by extrapolation from nearby, earlier points. Hence, the problem seems inherently serial. However, there are some special cases in which other options are possible.

First, consider the quadrature case in which $f = f(t)$ is independent of y. In that case, we can evaluate all $f(t_n)$ in parallel and then compute

$$y(t_n) = y(t_0) + \sum_{i=0}^{n} \omega_i f(t_i)$$

where the ω_i are suitable quadrature coefficients. This can be computed for all $n = 1,\cdots,N$ in $O(\log(N))$ time on N processors. We cannot add N terms in less than $O(\log(N))$ time, so this is lower limit on speed of parallelism across time for ODEs. The major question is can we even come close to $O(\log(N))$ for ODEs?

2.1 Linear Problems

In the case of linear problems the answer is "yes." If $f(y,t)$ is linear in y, then knowledge of $f(\hat{y},t_n)$ for some $\hat{y}$ and of $\partial f/\partial y$ provides full knowledge of the system at t_n. The details are straightforward: Let the system be

$$y' = A(t)y + g(t).$$

By superposition, the solution is

$$y(t) = \Phi(t,t_m)y(t_m) + z(t,t_m) \tag{1}$$

where $z(t,t_m)$ satisfies

$$\frac{d}{dt}z(t,t_m) = A(t)z(t,t_m) + g(t); \qquad z(t_m,t_m) = 0$$

and the transition matrix Φ satisfies

$$\frac{d}{dt}\Phi(t,t_m) = A(t)\Phi(t,t_m); \qquad \Phi(t_m,t_m) = I.$$

Superposition also implies that

$$z(t,t_m) = \Phi(t,t_j)z(t_j,t_m) + z(t,t_j). \tag{2}$$

If we define

$$z_{nm} = z(t_n,t_m), \qquad m > 0,$$

$$z_{n0} = y(t_n),$$

and

$$s_{nm} = \Phi(t_n,t_m)$$

then (1) and (2) imply

$$z_{nm} = s_{nj}z_{jm} + z_{nj}$$

while the definition of Φ implies that

$$s_{nm} = s_{nj}s_{jm}.$$

This leads to the following algorithm:

1 Divide the interval $[0,T]$ into N subintervals of length H with $t_n = nH$.

2 Compute all $z_{n,n-1}$ and $s_{n,n-1}$ in parallel by solving the ODEs

$$z' = A(t)z + g$$

and

$$\Phi(t,t_{n-1})' = A(t)\Phi(t,t_{n-1})$$

over $[t_{n-1},t_n]$, $n = 1,2,\cdots,N$ from suitable starting conditions (the identity for Φ, and zero for z to compute $z_{n,n-1},n$ for $n > 0$ and y_0 for z to compute z_{10}).

3 Solve the difference equation

$$y_n - s_{n,n-1} y_{n-1} = z_{n,n-1}$$

as a linear equation by odd-even reduction. This can be done in $O(\log(N))$ time using $O(N)$ processors. It is illustrated for the case $N = 8$ below.

Original problem:

$$\begin{bmatrix} 1 & 0 & 0 & 0 & 0 & 0 & 0 & 0 \\ -s_{21} & 1 & 0 & 0 & 0 & 0 & 0 & 0 \\ 0 & -s_{32} & 1 & 0 & 0 & 0 & 0 & 0 \\ 0 & 0 & -s_{43} & 1 & 0 & 0 & 0 & 0 \\ 0 & 0 & 0 & -s_{54} & 1 & 0 & 0 & 0 \\ 0 & 0 & 0 & 0 & -s_{65} & 1 & 0 & 0 \\ 0 & 0 & 0 & 0 & 0 & -s_{76} & 1 & 0 \\ 0 & 0 & 0 & 0 & 0 & 0 & -s_{87} & 1 \end{bmatrix} \begin{bmatrix} y_1 \\ y_2 \\ y_3 \\ y_4 \\ y_5 \\ y_6 \\ y_7 \\ y_8 \end{bmatrix} = \begin{bmatrix} z_{10} \\ z_{21} \\ z_{32} \\ z_{43} \\ z_{54} \\ z_{65} \\ z_{76} \\ z_{87} \end{bmatrix}$$

First reduction uses the odd-numbered rows to eliminate from the next higher-numbered rows in parallel to get

$$\begin{bmatrix} 1 & 0 & 0 & 0 & 0 & 0 & 0 & 0 \\ 0 & 1 & 0 & 0 & 0 & 0 & 0 & 0 \\ 0 & -s_{32} & 1 & 0 & 0 & 0 & 0 & 0 \\ 0 & -s_{42} & 0 & 1 & 0 & 0 & 0 & 0 \\ 0 & 0 & 0 & -s_{54} & 1 & 0 & 0 & 0 \\ 0 & 0 & 0 & -s_{64} & 0 & 1 & 0 & 0 \\ 0 & 0 & 0 & 0 & 0 & -s_{76} & 1 & 0 \\ 0 & 0 & 0 & 0 & 0 & -s_{86} & 0 & 1 \end{bmatrix} \begin{bmatrix} y_1 \\ y_2 \\ y_3 \\ y_4 \\ y_5 \\ y_6 \\ y_7 \\ y_8 \end{bmatrix} = \begin{bmatrix} z_{10} \\ z_{20} \\ z_{32} \\ z_{42} \\ z_{54} \\ z_{64} \\ z_{76} \\ z_{86} \end{bmatrix}$$

The second step uses row 2 to eliminate from rows 3 and 4, and row 6 to eliminate from rows 7 and 8 to get

$$\begin{bmatrix} 1 & 0 & 0 & 0 & 0 & 0 & 0 & 0 \\ 0 & 1 & 0 & 0 & 0 & 0 & 0 & 0 \\ 0 & 0 & 1 & 0 & 0 & 0 & 0 & 0 \\ 0 & 0 & 0 & 1 & 0 & 0 & 0 & 0 \\ 0 & 0 & 0 & -s_{54} & 1 & 0 & 0 & 0 \\ 0 & 0 & 0 & -s_{64} & 0 & 1 & 0 & 0 \\ 0 & 0 & 0 & -s_{74} & 0 & 0 & 1 & 0 \\ 0 & 0 & 0 & -s_{84} & 0 & 0 & 0 & 1 \end{bmatrix} \begin{bmatrix} y_1 \\ y_2 \\ y_3 \\ y_4 \\ y_5 \\ y_6 \\ y_7 \\ y_8 \end{bmatrix} = \begin{bmatrix} z_{10} \\ z_{20} \\ z_{30} \\ z_{40} \\ z_{54} \\ z_{64} \\ z_{74} \\ z_{84} \end{bmatrix}$$

Note that the first four equations are now "solved," while the last four depend only on the value of y_4 which by now is known as z_{40}. The third step ($3 = \log_2 N$ for $N = 8$) gives the result after row 4 is used to eliminate the non-diagonal elements from rows 5, 6, 7, and 8.

Thus, a linear ODE can be solved in $O(\log(N))$ time, although it must be noted that this is an expensive process, especially if the ODE is a system of M equations, because the s_{nm} components are $M \times M$ matrices which have to be multiplied at each step. Although in principal each multiplication can be done with sufficiently many processors in $O(\log(M))$ to get a total time of $O(\log(N)\log(M))$, the number of processors, at $O(NM^3)$, becomes prohibitive!

2.2 Nonlinear Problems: Waveform Methods

What about nonlinear ODEs? The obvious approach is to linearize and use iteration. Iteration is the basis of the *waveform methods* which can be written as

$$y^{(m+1)} - G(y^{(m+1)}, y^{(m)}) = f(y^{(m)}) - G(y^{(m)}, y^{(m)}) \tag{4}$$

where G is any suitable smooth function chosen to make the integration of (4) for the next iterate $y^{(m+1)}$ inexpensive. In the waveform Newton method we set

$$G = f_y(y^{(m)})(y^{(m+1)} - y^{(m)}) \tag{5}$$

to reflect the linear behavior of f about the current solution $y^{(m)}$). Since (4) plus (5) gives a linear ODE, the method described above can be used to integrate it. Hence the cost is $O(Q\log(N))$, where Q is the number of iterations. However, the number of iterations depends on N (except for linear problems). If N is increased to lengthen the interval of integration, convergence will be slowed because, under exact integration, each iteration increases the order of the power series approximation being developed by the method (see Juang[3] and Juang and Gear[4]). If N is increased to reduce stepsize over a constant interval so as to increase integration accuracy, more iterations will be needed to increase iteration accuracy correspondingly. The nature of the dependence of Q on N cannot be determined easily. If we assume, for the constant interval case, that the iteration is linearly convergent, we can make the following argument (in which equality is to be interpreted as "order of"): suppose we want an accuracy of ϵ and want equal errors from truncation and iteration. If a pth order method is used, we have $h^p = \epsilon$. Since $N = 1/h$ we have $N^p = 1/\epsilon$. If the convergence rate is $r < 1$, then to obtain an iteration error ϵ we must iterate until $r^Q = \epsilon$ or

$$Q = O(\log(\epsilon)/\log(r)) = O(\log(N)).$$

This would yield an overall speed of $O(\log^2(N))$, but the assumptions are questionable. Alternatively, consider N being increased to increase the interval of integration. Here we need a different assumption on convergence. Suppose the iteration error after Q iterations is $O(N^Q/Q!)$. This leads to a Q which is larger than $O(N)$. Again, the assumptions are questionable, but these estimates suggest that this iteration will not be valuable for massive parallelism. (The waveform methods are popular for classes of problems, particularly nonlinear electrical network models, but the reasons for their success seem to be due to considerations to do with ease of implementation for highly adaptive methods, effective use of paging from secondary memory, and their ability to reap benefits from the special structure of such problems that leads to the one way flow of much information.)

2.3 A Blended Waveform Method

This leaves open the question whether or not there are other methods that can come close to $O(\log(N))$ speed in parallelism across time. We have been experimenting with a new method that might be useful for some classes of problems. It is based on the following observation:

There are two types of problems for which parallelism is easy: quadrature and nonlinear equations. For the former we have already seen that integration can be performed in $O(\log(N))$ time with N processors. The latter, namely solving the problem $f(y,t) = 0$ for N different values of t, can be done in $O(1)$ time with N processors. These two problems are, in a sense, limiting cases of an ODE when the stiffness changes from zero to infinity. Consider the class of problems $y' = Jf(y,t) + g(t)$ for variable J. Assume that f is "well behaved" in the sense that its Jacobian has a reasonable condition number and norm. As J tends to zero, the stiffness of the problem goes to zero and we get the infinitely nonstiff problem $y' = g(t)$ which is the quadrature problem. As all eigenvalues of J become infinite, we tend to the infinitely stiff problem, $f(y,t) = 0$.

An ODE lies somewhere between these extremes, so below we propose a method that uses a blended combination of methods that would be good for the two extremes in the spirit of the blended methods of Skeel and Kong[8] although the methods proposed are very different in significant ways. As in Skeel and Kong, the blend is determined by the Jacobian $\partial f/\partial y$ of the system, and the underlying methods proposed are the BDF methods for stiff problems and the Adams methods for nonstiff problems. However, they are applied in such a way that the majority of the computation can be performed in parallel, even on SIMD/vector architectures.

2.3.1 The Method

The stiff components of a problem can be computed using a backward differentiation formula (BDF). In the conventional use of BDF-based methods, the formula is applied iteratively to the points computed in prior steps, making the algorithm serial. For infinitely stiff problems, the prior values do not affect the current value since the problem reduces to the solution of $f(y,t) = 0$. Hence, even if we use past values from a previous iteration, we will get the correct answer for the infinitely stiff components in one iteration.

Suppose we have a discrete approximation $y_n^{(m-1)}$, $n = k, k+1, \cdots, N$ and some starting values y_j, $j = 0, \cdots, k-1$. (Usually, $k = 1$ since a variable-order, variable-step method is used and the order starts at $k = 1$.) For the initial approximation, we usually choose $y_n^{(0)} = y_{k-1}$ for $n \geq k$. We can compute a BDF approximation, $z_n^{(m)}$, using

$$z_n^{(m)} = \Sigma_B y_n^{(m-1)} + h\beta_0^B f(z_n^{(m)}) \tag{6}$$

where

$$\Sigma_B w_n = \sum_{i=1}^{k} \alpha_i^B w_{n-i},$$

and β_0^B and the $\{\alpha_i^B\}$ are the BDF coefficients of order k. Since this in general is a nonlinear equation, it might be approximated by

$$z_n^{(m)} = \Sigma_B y_n^{(m-1)} + h\beta_0^B[f(y_n^{(m-1)}) + J_1(z_n^{(m)} - y_n^{(m-1)})] \tag{7}$$

where J_1 is an approximation to the Jacobian chosen in part for its convenience in solving the linear equations. (We could solve (6) by iterating a form of (7) to convergence.) Note that all z values can be computed in parallel because they are mutually independent. (Since the calculations for all $z_n^{(m)}$ are identical, they could be done on an SIMD or vector architecture.)

Equation (7) should be chosen when the system is large and it is desirable to partition the equations across different processors. In that case, J_1 would be chosen as an approximation to the Jacobian of f that is zero in blocks representing information that is expensive to communicate. J_1 should also be chosen so that $J_1 x = b$ is easy to solve.

The extremely stiff parts are computed very accurately by either (6) or (7). At the same time, the derivatives of the extremely nonstiff components are also computed extremely accurately when $f(z_n^{(m)})$ is evaluated because, in that case, f does not depend on the value of z to any great extent.

The nonstiff components are best calculated by a quadrature formula. Standard nonstiff integration formulas such as Adams formulas are good for quadrature, so it seems reasonable to use

$$y_n^{A,(m)} = y_{n-1}^{(m)} + h\Sigma_A \tilde{f}(z_n^{(m)}) \tag{8}$$

where

$$\Sigma_A w_n = \sum_{i=0}^{k} \beta_i^A w_{n-i},$$

the β_i^A are the Adams-Moulton coefficients, and

$$\tilde{f}(z_n^{(m)}) = f(y_n^{(m-1)}) + J_1(z_n^{(m)} - y_n^{(m-1)}),$$

i.e., $\tilde{f}$ is the approximation used for the derivative in (7). (We should use $\tilde{f} = f$ if (6) is used.) We would like to combine the two solutions $z_n^{(m)}$ and $y_n^{A,(m)}$ so that we select the stiff components from $z_n^{(m)}$ and the non stiff components from $y_n^{A,(m)}$. To do this we combine them using

$$\begin{aligned} [I - h\gamma J_2]y_n^{(m)} &= y_n^{A,(m)} - h\gamma J_2 z_n^{(m)} \\ &= y_{n-1}^{(m)} + h\sum_A \tilde{f}(z_n^{(m)}) - h\gamma J_2 z_n^{(m)} \end{aligned} \tag{9}$$

This uses a blended combination of the two solutions based on the size of the matrix J_2. In practice, J_2 is an approximation to the Jacobian chosen for its sparsity and the ease of solving linear equations involving J_2. It may or may not be the same approximation as the J_1 used in (7). The coefficient γ will be chosen to obtain desirable stability properties for $y_n = \lim_{m\to\infty} y_n^{(m)}$ and rate of convergence as $m \to \infty$.

Although equation (9) with (8) is a linear recurrence relation, N steps of it can be solved simultaneously in $\log N$ time, as shown earlier, because all coefficients and the inhomogeneous term can be evaluated in parallel. A number of questions have to be asked about this proposed method. These include

Does the iteration converge?

To what ODE method does the iteration converge?

Is that method zero stable and consistent?

What are its large-h stability properties?

The brief answers, elaborated in the next subsection, are that the iteration converges provided only that J_1 is close enough to the system Jacobian, and the limit of the iteration is a stable and consistent method (at least for some choices of the underlying methods) with reasonable properties such as stiff stability.

2.3.2 Convergence and Stability

To study the stability and convergence of this method, we study the convergence of the iteration as $m \to \infty$ separately from the convergence as $h \to 0$. If the iteration converges, it converges to the solution of

$$z_n = \Sigma_B y_n + h\beta_0^B[f(y_n) + J_1(z_n - y_n)] \tag{10}$$

and

$$[I - h\gamma J_2]y_n = y_{n-1} + h\Sigma_A \tilde{f}(z_n) - h\gamma J_2 z_n. \tag{11}$$

Convergence of the iteration is studied by comparing the solution of (7) and (9) to that of (10) and (11). Define

$$e_n^{(m)} = y_n^{(m)} - y_n, \qquad d_n^{(m)} = z_n^{(m)} - z_n$$

Subtracting (10) and (11) from (7) and (9) we get

$$[I - h\beta_0^B J_1]d_n^{(m)} = \Sigma_B e_n^{(m-1)} + h\beta_0^B[f_y - J_1]e_n^{(m-1)}$$

$$[I - h\gamma J_2]e_n^{(m)} = e_{n-1}^{(m)} + h\Sigma_A[(f_y - J_1)e_n^{(m-1)} + J_1 d_n^{(m)}] - h\gamma J_2 d_n^{(m)})$$

where f_y is the Jacobian of f with each entry evaluated at possibly different points in the neighborhood of the solution. Let $\Delta = f_y - J_1$ (the "error" in the Jacobian approximation J_1). Also define

$$W = [I - h\beta_0^B J_1]^{-1},$$

$$V = [I - h\gamma J_2]^{-1},$$

$$E = W\Delta,$$

$$F = V\Delta.$$

We have

$$d_n^{(m)} = W\Sigma_B e_n^{(m-1)} + h\beta_0^B E e_n^{(m-1)}$$

$$e_n^{(m)} = Ve_{n-1}^{(m)} + hF\Sigma_A e_n^{(m-1)} + hV[J_1\Sigma_A d_n^{(m)} - \gamma J_2 d_n^{(m)}]$$

or

$$\begin{aligned} e_n^{(m)} &= Ve_{n-1}^{(m)} + hF\sum_{j=0}^{k}\beta_j^A e_{n-j}^{(m-1)} \\ &+hV[J_1\sum_{j=0}^{k}\beta_j^A(W\sum_{i=1}^{k}\alpha_i^B e_{n-j-i}^{(m-1)} + h\beta_0^B E e_{n-j}^{(m-1)}) \\ &\qquad -\gamma J_2(W\sum_{i=1}^{k}\alpha_i^B e_{n-i}^{(m-1)} + h\beta_0^B E e_n^{(m-1)})]. \end{aligned}$$

This has the form

$$e_n^{(m)} - Ve_{n-1}^{(m)} = h\sum_{j=0}^{2k} P_j e_{n-j}^{(m-1)} \tag{12}$$

where

$$\begin{aligned} P_0 &= \beta_0^A F + hV(J_1E\beta_0^A\beta_0^B - J_2E\beta_0^B\gamma) \\ P_j &= \beta_j^A F + V(J_1W\textstyle\sum_{i=1}^{j}\beta_{j-i}^A\alpha_i^B - J_2W\gamma\alpha_j^B) + hVJ_1E\beta_j^A\beta_0^B, \quad 1 \le j \le k \\ P_j &= VJ_1W\textstyle\sum_{i=j-k}^{k}\beta_{j-i}^A\alpha_i^B, \quad k+1 \le j \le 2k. \end{aligned}$$

This iteration converges if $\|hP_0\| < 1$. This situation occurs when J_1 is close to the system Jacobian f_y since Δ is then small. In fact, it is necessary only that hE and hF be small, which means that hJ_1 need only be close to hf_y in the spaces corresponding to the eigenvectors of the small eigenvalues of of J_1 and J_2 because of the terms $[I - h\beta_0^B J_1]^{-1}$ and $[I - h\gamma_0 J_2]^{-1}$ in E and F, respectively.

An important case arises when the BDF is solved essentially exactly at each step using (6). In that case, no error from $y_n^{(m-1)}$ is propagated into $y_n^{(m)}$ so that the error amplification matrix is nilpotent and we have unconditional convergence (although it could be slow if the other matrix elements are large).

The stability of the comparison method, (10) and (11), also needs to be studied. The linear error analysis will yield an equation similar to (12) with the iteration superscripts in m removed, namely

$$0 = \sum_{j=0}^{2k} R_j e_{n-j} \tag{13}$$

where

$$\begin{aligned} R_0 &= -I + hP_0 \\ R_1 &= V + hP_1 \\ R_j &= hP_j, \qquad 2 \le j \le 2k. \end{aligned}$$

The method is zero stable since, for $h = 0$, (13) reduces to $e_n = e_{n-1}$. The usual definition of the region of absolute stability is found by considering the case $J_1 = J_2 = f_y = J$, or $\Delta = 0 = E = F$, and determining the region in which the difference equation has roots inside the unit disk. This leads to equation (13) with

$$\begin{aligned} R_0 &= -I \\ R_1 &= V + hVJW[\beta_0^A\alpha_1^B - \gamma\alpha_1^B], \\ R_j &= hVJW[\textstyle\sum_{i=1}^{j}\beta_{j-i}^A\alpha_i^B - \gamma\alpha_j^B], \quad 2 \le j \le k \\ R_j &= hVJW\textstyle\sum_{i=j-k}^{k}\beta_{j-i}^A\alpha_i^B, \quad k+1 \le j \le 2k. \end{aligned} \tag{14}$$

Since V, J, and W have the same eigenspace, stability can be studied by considering the eigenvalues, λ, of J and computing the values of λ for which the roots of (13) with (14) are $e^{i\theta}$ to get a locus which includes the boundary of the region of absolute stability.

The result is the quadratic in $h\lambda = \mu$:

$$0 = \sum_{j=0}^{2k} c_j(\mu)e^{i\theta(2k-j)}$$

where

$$\begin{aligned} c_0 &= -(1-\beta_0^B\mu)(1-\gamma\mu) \\ c_1 &= (1-\beta_0^B\mu) + \mu[\beta_0^A\alpha_1^B - \gamma\alpha_1^B], \\ c_j &= \mu[\textstyle\sum_{i=1}^{j}\beta_{j-i}^A\alpha_i^B - \gamma\alpha_j^B], \quad 2 \le j \le k \\ c_j &= \mu\textstyle\sum_{i=j-k}^{k}\beta_{j-i}^A\alpha_i^B, \quad k+1 \le j \le 2k \end{aligned}$$

Since c_0 is the only term quadratic in μ, the method is stable and damping at infinity. Initial plots of the regions of absolute stability indicate that they are stiffly stable for $k \le 3$ and $\gamma = 1$. Other cases remain to be studied. Figure 1 shows the locus in the μ plane for the case $k = 3$ (3rd-order BDF, 4th-order Adams Moulton) and $\gamma = 1$. The box encompasses the region $-0.637 \le x \le 11.572, |y| \le 7.427$. The method is damping at infinity, so, by a continuity argument, the exterior of the locus is absolutely stable.

3 Parallelism Across Space

Parallelism across space is a natural form of parallelism, especially on SIMD machines or hypercubes, for time-dependent PDEs. It was used in codes for the Illiac IV, one of the first large-scale parallel computers. It is good for large-scale parallelism when there are many equations (or spatial mesh points); its major limitation seems to be communication.

We consider the underlying physical problem to understand the amount of communication needed. In hyperbolic problems, communication is limited to nearby neighbors—no information can travel faster than the local speed of sound (along characteristics). Consequently, as problem size increases, communication does not increase relative to computation. Although communication may be expensive relative to computation (as in most hypercube architectures), its volume relative to computation can be reduced by handling a large number of equations in each processor.

On the other hand, in parabolic problems some information travels arbitrarily far in any time step, no matter how small. It is not surprising that similar problems arise in stiff ODEs since the semi-discretization of parabolic equations leads to stiff equations.

3.1 Parabolic Problems and Stiff ODEs

If we have a system of ODEs

$$y' = f(y),$$

the structure of the Jacobian matrix $A = \partial f/\partial y$ indicates the direct spatial communication present in the problem. If $\partial f_p/\partial y_q$ is non-zero, the variable y_q directly influences y_p, that is to say, there is direct communication between these two spatial points. However, it is important to realize that communication may be required between other pairs of points. Consider a stiff ODE $y' = Ay$. The stiffness of the problem implies that

1 We must use an implicit method.

2 We must solve (nonlinear) equations at each step.

3 There must be complete interprocessor communication unless the problem partially decouples.

The first two facts follow directly from stiffness [7]. The third can be seen by considering an implicit method such as the backward (implicit) Euler, which is $[I - hA]y_{n+1} = y_n$ for $y' = Ay$, or

$$y_{n+1} = [I - hA]^{-1} y_n.$$

We claim (and demonstrate below) that unless the problem can be decoupled into subproblems that can be solved serially, every element of $[I - hA]^{-1}$ is non zero (except for fortuitous cancellation). Hence, each element of y_{n+1} depends on *all* elements of y_n, suggesting that each processor will have to obtain information from every other processor at every time step.

This claim follows from the theorem: If $(I - hA)$ is *irreducible* then $[I - hA]^{-1}$ is *structurally full.* Irreducible means that $I - hA$ cannot be permuted to block lower triangular form—*i.e.* there does not exist an independent subsystem of ODEs which can be solved first. Structurally full means that every element is nonzero for *almost all* values of the nonzeros in A. This is proved in ([1]).

If this amount of communication is really required, it seems to impose a serious limit on the amount of parallelism possible, since, as the number of equations, N, grows, the apparent communication increases like N^2 However, we will show below that the communication needed may not grow that rapidly. To do this, we consider a simple example, the heat equation in one dimension:

$$u_t = u_{xx}.$$

If we have the solution at a given time, $u(x,t)$, the solution at time $t + h$ is given by

$$u(t+h, x) = \frac{1}{2\sqrt{\pi h}} \int_{-\infty}^{+\infty} e^{-s^2/4h} u(t, x+s) ds. \tag{15}$$

Suppose we wish to compute $u(t+h,x)$ from (15) to an accuracy of ϵ relative to $\max|u|$. This is to be done in the processor handling the spatial point x. How much information must be transmitted from other points, that is, from other processors. Let us suppose that we approximate $u(t,x+s)$ in (15) by $\hat{u}(t,x+s)$ such that the error is $2^{-b(s)}\max|u|$. (For simplicity, we will take $\max|u|$ to be one below.) This means that we can effectively use $b(s)$ bits of information to represent $\hat{u}(t,x+s)$. From this we compute the approximation y given by

$$y(t+h,x)=\frac{1}{2\sqrt{\pi h}}\int_{-\infty}^{+\infty}e^{-s^2/4h}\hat{u}(t,x+s)ds. \tag{16}$$

Note that the integral in (16) can be computed from $-w$ to $+w$, where w is such that $b(s)<0$ for $|s|>|w|$. Let us suppose that the cost of transmitting b bits of information a distance s is $c(b,s)$. Then we wish to minimize

$$\int_{-w}^{+w}c(b,s)ds$$

subject to the error being bounded by ϵ. This condition is found by subtracting (16) from (15) to get

$$\frac{1}{2\sqrt{\pi h}}[\int_{-w}^{+w}e^{-s^2/4h}2^{-b(s)}ds+2\int_{-\infty}^{-w}e^{-s^2/4h}ds]\le\epsilon. \tag{17}$$

The minimum occurs when

$$\frac{\partial c}{\partial b}=\lambda e^{-s^2/4h}2^{-b(s)},$$

where λ is a constant. If we assume a cost function of the form $c(b,s)=(A+Bb)d(s)$, $b>0$, and $c(0,s)=0$ (likely values of $d(s)$ are 1, $\log s$, or s) we get

$$2^{-b(s)}=d(s)e^{(s^2-w^2)/4h}/d(w). \tag{18}$$

Since likely $d(s)$ have a much smaller variation with respect to s than the exponential term in (18), we see that

$$b(s)\approx(w^2-s^2)/(4h\log 2). \tag{19}$$

The important points shown above are that, for a given accuracy, information need not be transmitted further than a certain distance, $w(\epsilon)$, nor need information be transmitted to full accuracy. (However, the total amount of information transmitted is not much larger, nor is the cost much larger, if we transmit all values within this range to the maximum accuracy required by the most accurate.)

How does w depend on ϵ? From (17) and (19) we get

$$\frac{1}{2\sqrt{\pi h}}[\int_{-w}^{+w}e^{-w^2/4h}ds+2\int_{-\infty}^{-w}e^{-s^2/4h}ds]\le\epsilon,$$

or

$$\frac{1}{\sqrt{\pi h}}e^{-w^2/4h}[w+\int_{-\infty}^{-w}e^{(w^2-s^2)/4h}ds]\le\epsilon,$$

which is satisfied if

$$e^{-w^2/4h}[w\frac{1}{\sqrt{\pi h}}+1]\le\epsilon.$$

From this we see that

$$w = 2\sqrt{h\log(1/\epsilon)} + o(h\log(1/\epsilon)). \tag{20}$$

Since the number of mesh points, N_w, in the span of w is $w/\Delta x$, we see that, if we use a spatial order of q and a time order of p so that $h = O(\epsilon^p)$ and $\Delta x = O(\epsilon^q)$, the the number of mesh points from which information is needed is

$$N_w = O(\epsilon^{p/2-q}(-\log\epsilon)^{1/2}). \tag{21}$$

This shows that we do not have to have complete processor intercommunication to achieve a finite accuracy if we can construct a method to use information just from N_w points. Direct evaluation of the integral in (16) is not a reasonable approach: although it would work for problems in which we knew an explicit integral form, most problems are not in that class.

3.1.1 A Numerical Method

We start with any implicit numerical method for the given problem (to avoid the usual stability limitation of explicit methods). For the purposes of presentation we take the heat equation solved by the fully implicit (backward Euler) method which yields

$$u_{n+1} = u_n + \mu A u_{n+1} \tag{22}$$

where u_n is a vector of the components of $u(t_n, x)$ at the set of mesh points x_i, $\mu = h/(\Delta x)^2$, and A is the usual tridiagonal matrix, diag(1,-2,1). The i-th processing node could solve this equation for $u_{n+1,i}$ by obtaining the values of u_n from its neighbors to the required precision if they are within w of node i, substituting 0 for the other values of u_n and solving the linear system. As it stands, this means that each processor is solving a full problem—hardly a saving over one processor solving the problem in the first place! However, the size of the problem on each processor can be reduced by introducing artificial boundaries at a distance w from node i. These have to be selected according to the problem. For the heat equation, the artificial boundary can be von Neuman—namely open ends at which we impose $u_{n+1,i\pm(w+1)} = u_{n,i\pm(w+1)}$.

This amounts to a type of domain decomposition method[5]. Each processor handles one domain and solves for a single point. In practice, the efficiency will improve if each processor solves for several points. For example, if each processor handles w points, there will be a need only for nearest neighbor communication because the points within distance w will be in the processors immediately adjacent.

It is interesting to look at the case $w = 1$ (implying a large error). If the fully implicit method (backward Euler) is used, each node uses the difference equation

$$(1+2\mu)u_{n+1,k} = \mu(u_{n,k-1} + u_{n,k+1}) + u_{n,k}.$$

This is unconditionally stable. However, it is not convergent as a difference formula because, as h and Δx shrink to increase accuracy, w, measured in x-mesh points, should also have been increased to involve more points to allow sufficient accuracy to the integral approximation.

As accuracy increases (which decreases Δx) in either finite difference methods, domain decomposition methods, or this method, we see the following differences:

Finite difference method The *stencil* is fixed as the number of mesh points increases. Hence, h will have to shrink rapidly to satisfy (20) for the specified w (which is shrinking because $w = N_w \Delta x$ where N_w is the fixed number of points in the stencil "reaching out" to other processors).

Domain decomposition The regions (and their number) are fixed, so as total number of mesh points increases, the number in each region increases. If each domain is handled by a single processor, the amount of parallelism does not increase.

Proposed method The number of regions increases, but so does the number of points spanned by w to maintain the accuracy needed. Thus, communication costs increase, but, in principal, the cost of the computation, which is to greater accuracy and requires more bits, also increases. In practice, the computer has sufficiently large fixed precision and the computation costs don't increase.

It appears that greater parallelism is possible by these sort of techniques than by domain decomposition, and that, even for parabolic problems, the number of processors can increase with problem size without increase in computation time if the increase in problem size is solely to cover a larger region. If it is used to increase accuracy, additional communication costs will be incurred. A similar scheme is discussed by Kuznetsov[6].

3.2 Real-time Problems

Equation segmentation has been proposed for real-time problems since many models of the types of systems solved in real-time naturally decompose into subsystems. For example, an aircraft simulation system might have subsystems for the engine dynamics, control system dynamics, control surface dynamics, and aircraft dynamics, each being a closely coupled set of ODEs more loosely coupled to other subsystems. At first sight, this seems a natural application for parallelism across space. However, on further study we see that there are potential problems when this method is used to simulate a system with external feedback. If an integration time step of δt is used, each integrator will get its input (at, say time t_n) from the the original input or an integrator of a prior subsystem on another processor, and compute its output for the time t_{n+1}. Hence there is a delay of δt for any information passing through the integrator. If there are N integrators in series, there is a minimum delay of $N\delta t$ from the input of any information to the system until its effect is felt on the output, as shown in Figure 2. If the external feedback from the output to the input (given, say, by a real pilot flying the simulator) is important to the control or stability of the system, this delay will cause the simulated system to be uncontrollable or unstable. The solution to this difficulty does not appear to be simple unless the system is nearly linear. In that case, the Jacobian of each subsystem can be precomputed and the effect of the input on the output can be approximated from a linearized formula. This effect can be considered in the integration formula for the next subsystem.

References

[1] Duff, I. S. et al, Some Remarks on Inverses of Sparse Matrices, AERE Harwell Report CSS 17, (1985).

[2] Gear, C. W., Parallel Methods for Ordinary Differential Equations, Department of Computer Science Report #1369, University of Illinois at Urbana Champaign, Aug, 1987.

[3] Juang, F., Accuracy Increase in Waveform Relaxation, Dept of Computer Science Report #1466, University of Illinois at Urbana Champaign, 1988

[4] Juang, F., Gear, C. W., Accuracy Increase in Waveform Gauss Seidel, Dept of Computer Science Report #1518, University of Illinois at Urbana Champaign, June, 1989.

[5] Lions, P. L., On the Schwartz Alternating Method. I., in Domain Decomposition Methods for Partial Differential Equations, ed. Glowinski et al, SIAM, Philadelphia, 1988

[6] Kuznetsov, Y. A., *New Algorithms for Approximate Realization of Implicit Difference Schemes*, Sov. J. Numer. Anal. Math. Modeling, **3**, #2, pp 99-114, 1988.

[7] Shampine, L., Gear, C. W., A User's View of Solving Stiff Ordinary Differential Equations, SIAM Review, **21**, #1, pp 1-17, Jan, 1979.

[8] Skeel, R. D. and Kong, K-Y., Blended Linear Multistep Methods, ACM Trans. Math. Software, Dec 1977, pp326-345.

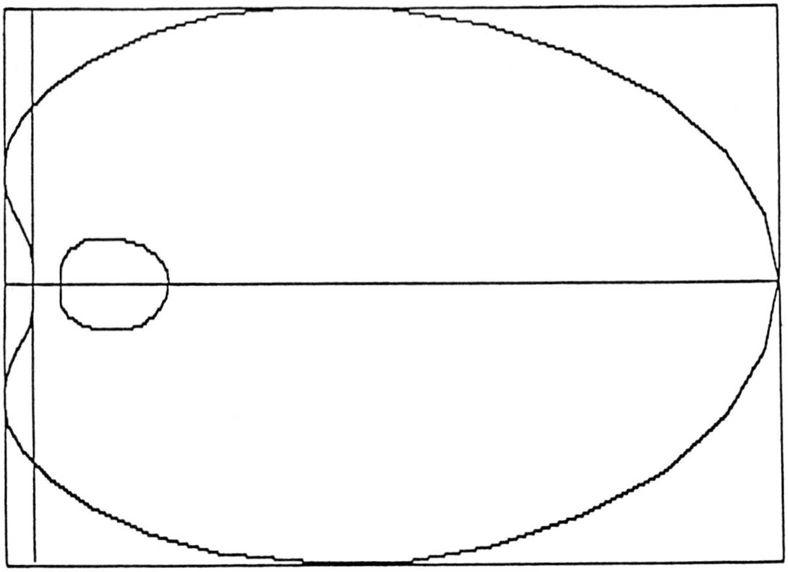

Figure 1. Stability Region for $k = 3$.

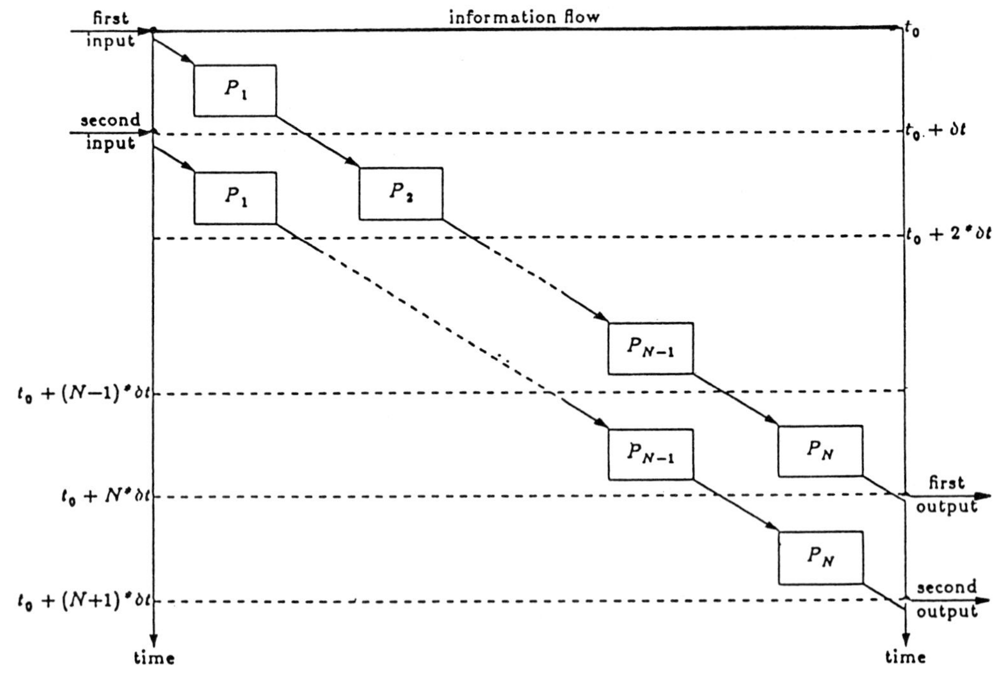

Figure 2. Delay in Real-time Parallelism.

SUBCYCLING APPLIED TO ORDINARY DIFFERENTIAL EQUATIONS

W.E.M. Bruijs[*], C.J.L. Florie[**], P.J.A. de Coo[***], A.A.H.J. Sauren[*]

* Eindhoven University of Technology
Faculty of Mechanical Engineering
P.O. Box 513
5600 MB Eindhoven
The Netherlands

ABSTRACT

An important application of explicit integration methods is to find the solution of a set of ordinary differential equations which is obtained using the finite element method. In many engineering applications, the finite element mesh consists of areas where large deformations are expected and areas where only small deformations are expected. In the areas where large deformations are expected, a fine mesh is necessary, while in the other areas a coarse grid is sufficient. The Courant criterion states that the time step must be smaller than the characteristic length of the element divided by the dilatational wave speed. Due to this Courant criterion, in the fine grid a small time step is necessary to ensure a stable solution. In the coarse grid, a much larger time step is allowed for the integration. If subcycling is applied, different time steps are allowed in the same mesh. This means that the smaller elements can be integrated with smaller time steps than the larger elements. This will lead to a decrease of the number of element calculations and hence to a decrease of the computer time.

** PISCES International bv
Groningenweg 6
2803 PV Gouda
The Netherlands

*** TNO Road–Vehicles Research Institute
P.O. Box 237
2600 AE Delft
The Netherlands

NATO ASI Series, Vol. F 69
Real-Time Integration Methods for Mechanical System Simulation
Edited by E. J. Haug and R. C. Deyo

In this paper, the subcycling algorithm is presented. A case study is used to derive the stability of the algorithm. An algorithm which automatically divides a finite element mesh into groups of elements that are treated with different time steps will be discussed. This algorithm chooses the group division in such a way that the simulation costs are minimal. The subcycling method will be applied to some test cases. The results of these test cases will be presented. It will be shown for the test cases that application of subcycling yields substantial computer time savings. The loss of accuracy due to the application of subcycling is acceptable for many engineering applications.

INTRODUCTION

Basically two different methods for the numerical integration of a set of ordinary differential equations (ODE's) can be distinguished: implicit and explicit methods. If the set of ODE's is obtained after spatial discretization of a structure with the finite element method, the mass matrix can be lumped (Krieg & Key, 1973), resulting in a diagonal mass matrix. If the mass matrix is diagonal, the application of an explicit method implies that no sets of equations have to be solved during a time step, so the calculations are very efficient. In exchange for this, explicit methods are only conditionally stable. The time step used for the integration is bounded by the Courant criterion (Courant, Friedriechs & Lewy, 1928), which states that the time step must be smaller than a characteristic length of the element divided by the dilatational wave speed in the material. An advantage of implicit methods is that they often are unconditionally stable. This implies that the time step is not bounded by stability considerations, but can be chosen based on accuracy demands only. The disadvantage of implicit methods is the necessity to solve a set of equations during each cycle. Computational costs and core storage for the solution of a set of equations increase dramatically for larger numbers of degrees of freedom.

It depends on the characteristics of the set of ODE's that must be solved which integration method is most suited. However, in many engineering applications, none of the methods by itself is very efficient. For example, if a crash simulation of a vehicle structure is performed, the number of degrees of freedom is huge. So the application of an implicit method is not very efficient for this problem. On the other hand, the large deformations that are to be expected in some parts of the vehicle structure require some very small elements in that area. This means that, due to stability conditions, a very small time step must be applied, if an explicit method is used. Explicit methods are thus not particularly efficient for this problem as well.

In this paper, a method is described that allows different time steps for the solution of a set of coupled ODE's. This technique – often called subcycling – is applied in combination with an explicit integration scheme, the central difference method. Each equation of the set of ODE's is integrated with a time step that is close to the maximum stable time step for that equation. For the example of the crash simulation of the vehicle structure, this implies that the smaller elements will be treated with a smaller time step than the larger elements. So for the larger elements, the number of calculations per element will decrease and thus the computer time will decrease.

SUBCYCLING

Consider a set of ODE's resulting from spatial discretization of a structure with the finite element method:

$$\underline{M}\ddot{\underline{x}} = \underline{f}_{ext}(t) - \underline{f}_{int}(t,\underline{x}) \qquad {}^{*)} \qquad (1)$$

where $\underline{M}$ is the lumped mass matrix, $\ddot{\underline{x}}$ the column containing the nodal accelerations, $\underline{f}_{ext}$ the column containing the nodal external forces that are a function of time t, and $\underline{f}_{int}$ the column containing the internal nodal forces that are a function of the column containing the nodal displacements $\underline{x}$ and time t.

Equation (1) can be integrated with the central difference method:

$$\dot{\underline{x}}_{n+1/2} = \dot{\underline{x}}_{n-1/2} + \Delta t \ddot{\underline{x}}_n \qquad {}^{**)} \qquad (2)$$

$$\underline{x}_{n+1} = \underline{x}_n + \Delta t \dot{\underline{x}}_{n+1/2} \qquad (3)$$

---

*) In this paper, an underlined upper case symbol denotes a matrix and an underlined lower case symbol a column. A superposed dot stands for the time derivative.

**) A subscript denotes that the quantity is considered at a certain point of time, e.g. $\underline{x}_{n+1}$ denotes the column of the nodal displacements at time $(n+1)\Delta t$.

If (1) is considered at time $n\Delta t$, the accelerations can be calculated at this time:

$$\ddot{\underline{x}} = \underline{M}^{-1}\left[\underline{f}_{ext}(t_n) - \underline{f}_{int}(t_n, \underline{x}_n)\right] \tag{4}$$

It is assumed that the mass matrix is lumped, so the inversion of $\underline{M}$ is trivial due to the diagonal form of $\underline{M}$. Substitution of $\ddot{\underline{x}}_n$ in (2) yields $\dot{\underline{x}}_{n+1/2}$ and substitution of the latter in (3) yields $\underline{x}_{n+1}$.

Because of the conditional stability, the time step used for the integration must satisfy (Courant, Friedriechs & Lewy, 1928):

$$\Delta t < d/c \tag{5}$$

where d is a characteristic length of an element and c is the dilatational wave speed, which is dependent on the material parameters.

When subcycling is used, the ODE's are integrated with different time steps. For reasons of simplicity, the case for which only two different time steps are used for the integration, is considered. The set of ODE's will be split up into two partitions, denoted by the superscripts a and b.:

$$\begin{bmatrix} \underline{M}^a & \underline{0} \\ \underline{0} & \underline{M}^b \end{bmatrix} \begin{bmatrix} \ddot{\underline{x}}^a \\ \ddot{\underline{x}}^b \end{bmatrix} = \begin{bmatrix} \underline{f}^a_{ext}(t) \\ \underline{f}^b_{ext}(t) \end{bmatrix} - \begin{bmatrix} \underline{f}^a_{int}(t, \underline{x}^a, \underline{x}^b) \\ \underline{f}^b_{int}(t, \underline{x}^a, \underline{x}^b) \end{bmatrix} \tag{6}$$

Eq. (6) can be regarded as two coupled sets of ODE's. Partition a will be integrated with time step $\alpha\Delta t$ and partition b with time step Δt. The parameter α is the ratio between the time steps and must be a positive integer number. A calculation with a time step $\alpha\Delta t$ is called a cycle, an update with the time step Δt is called a subcycle. During a cycle the following computations have to be performed:

– Updates for partition a:

$$\ddot{\underline{x}}^a_n = \underline{M}^{a^{-1}}\left[\underline{f}^a_{ext}(t_n) - \underline{f}^a_{int}(t_n, \underline{x}^a_n, \underline{x}^b_n)\right] \tag{7}$$

$$\dot{\underline{x}}^a_{n+\alpha/2} = \dot{\underline{x}}^a_{n-\alpha/2} + \alpha\Delta t\ddot{\underline{x}}^a_n \tag{8}$$

$$\underline{x}^a_{n+\alpha} = \underline{x}^a_n + \alpha\Delta t\dot{\underline{x}}^a_{n+\alpha/2} \tag{9}$$

– Updates for partition b

$$\ddot{\underline{x}}^b_n = \underline{M}^{b^{-1}}\left[\underline{f}^b_{ext}(t_n) - \underline{f}^b_{int}(t_n,\underline{x}^a_n,\underline{x}^b_n)\right] \tag{10}$$

$$\dot{\underline{x}}^b_{n+1/2} = \dot{\underline{x}}^b_{n-1/2} + \Delta t\ddot{\underline{x}}^b_n \tag{11}$$

$$\underline{x}^b_{n+1} = \underline{x}^b_n + \Delta t\dot{\underline{x}}^b_{n+1/2} \tag{12}$$

$$\ddot{\underline{x}}^b_{n+1} = \underline{M}^{b^{-1}}\left[\underline{f}^b_{ext}(t_{n+1}) - \underline{f}^b_{int}(t_{n+1},\underline{x}^a_{n+1},\underline{x}^b_{n+1})\right] \tag{13}$$

$$\dot{\underline{x}}^b_{n+3/2} = \dot{\underline{x}}^b_{n+1/2} + \Delta t\ddot{\underline{x}}^b_{n+1} \tag{14}$$

$$\underline{x}^b_{n+2} = \underline{x}^b_{n+1} + \Delta t\dot{\underline{x}}^b_{n+3/2} \tag{15}$$

upto:

$$\ddot{\underline{x}}^b_{n+\alpha-1} = \underline{M}^{b^{-1}}\left[\underline{f}^b_{ext}(t_{n+\alpha-1}) - \underline{f}^b_{int}(t_{n+\alpha-1},\underline{x}^a_{n+\alpha-1},\underline{x}^b_{n+\alpha-1})\right] \tag{16}$$

$$\dot{\underline{x}}^b_{n+\alpha-1/2} = \dot{\underline{x}}^b_{n+\alpha-3/2} + \Delta t\ddot{\underline{x}}^b_{n+\alpha-1} \tag{17}$$

$$\underline{x}^b_{n+\alpha} = \underline{x}^b_{n+\alpha-1} + \Delta t\dot{\underline{x}}^b_{n+\alpha-1/2} \tag{18}$$

For partition a, the displacements are only known at times $0, \alpha\Delta t, 2\alpha\Delta t$, etc. But for the calculation of the accelerations of partition b at intermediate points of time, the displacements of partition a must be known at these intermediate points of time. This is due to the fact that $\underline{f}^b_{int}$ is not a function of $\underline{x}^b$ only, but also depends on $\underline{x}^a$. In Bruijs, et al. (1988), different methods to find an approximation of the intermediate values of $\underline{x}^a$

are compared with respect to numerical stability, accuracy and computer time consumption. It was concluded that a linear interpolation of the displacements is the best alternative. In order to complete the list of calculations that have to be performed during a cycle, the linear interpolation of $\underline{x}^a$ must be added to the updates of partition a:

$$\underline{x}^a_{n+\alpha-j} = (\alpha-j)\underline{x}^a_{n+\alpha}/\alpha - (j\underline{x}^a_n)/\alpha, \text{ for } j = 1,2,\ldots,\alpha-1 \tag{19}$$

This equation completes the subcycling algorithm. In fig. 1 a schematic overview of the computations is given.

STABILITY

The subcycling algorithm has been implemented in the PISCES–3DELK code for triangular constant strain membrane elements. A case study on the stability of the subcycling algorithm of a simple system (fig. 2) is performed. Node 1 is integrated with the time step Δt and node 2 with the time step $\alpha\Delta t$. Only displacements in the plane of the drawing are considered. The equations of motion can – in case of linear material behaviour – be written in the form:

$$\underline{M}\ddot{\underline{x}} + \underline{K}\underline{x} = \underline{0} \tag{20}$$

with $\underline{M}$ the lumped mass matrix, $\underline{K}$ the stiffness matrix and $\underline{x}^T = [x_{1x}\ x_{1y}\ x_{2x}\ x_{2y}]$, where x_{1x} is the displacement of node 1 in x–direction etc. If the subcycling algorithm described in the previous section is applied to (20), the result can be written in the form:

$$\underline{A}\underline{y}^{n+1} = \underline{B}\underline{y}^n \tag{21}$$

with $\underline{y}^n = [x^{n+\alpha}_{2x} \ldots x^{n-\alpha+1}_{2x}, x^{n+\alpha}_{2y} \ldots x^{n-\alpha+1}_{2y}, x^{n+\alpha}_{1x} \ldots x^{n}_{1x}, x^{n+\alpha}_{1y} \ldots x^{n}_{1y}]^T$ and **A** and **B** are square matrices of dimension $6\alpha+2$. Furthermore, $\underline{A}$ is a regular matrix. Eq. (21) can be rewritten in the form:

$$\underline{y}^{n+1} = \underline{A}^{-1}\underline{B}\underline{y}^n \tag{22}$$

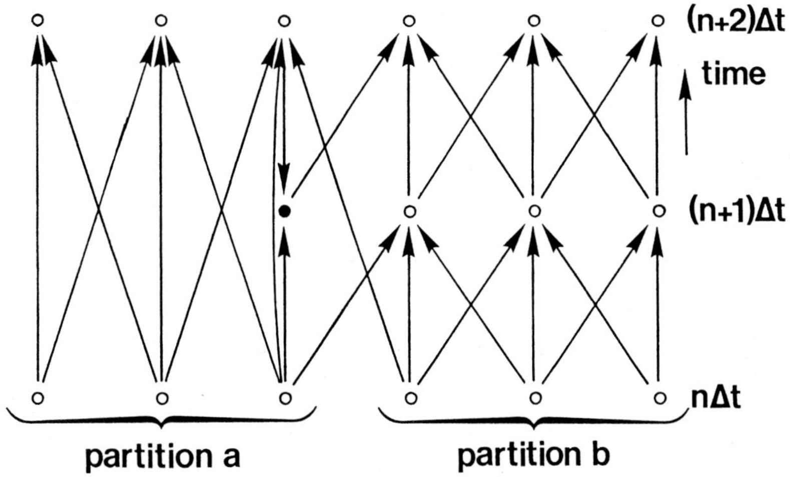

Fig. 1. A schematic overview of the computations.
Partition a is integrated with 2Δt and partition b with Δt. A point represents a node at a certain time. An arrow pointing from one point to another indicates that the displacements and accelerations of the former point must be known to calculate these quantities of the latter point. For the calculation of the displacements of the bold point, only the displacements of the points from which the arrows start are necessary. The calculation of the velocities is not shown in this diagram.

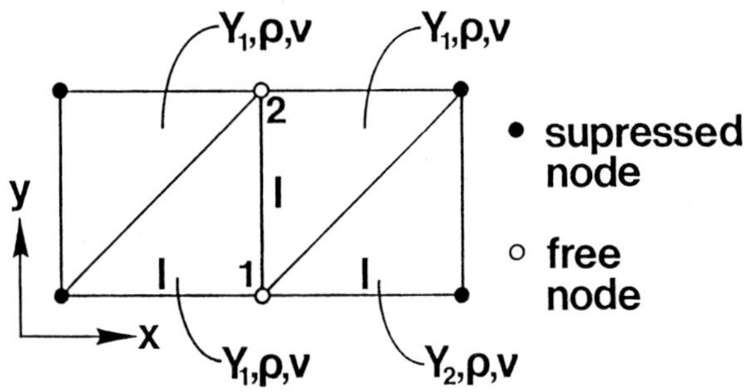

Fig. 2. The system for which the stability is derived.
Y: Youngs modulus, ρ: density, ν: Poisson ratio, l: side length
• supressed node o free node

where $\underline{A}^{-1}\underline{B}$ is the so–called amplification matrix. The integration method is stable if the spectral radius ρ_s of the amplification matrix $\underline{A}^{-1}\underline{B}$, defined by $\rho_s(\underline{A}^{-1}\underline{B}) = \max |\lambda_i|$ with λ_i the ith eigenvalue of $\underline{A}^{-1}\underline{B}$, satisfies (Hughes, 1983):

$$\rho_S(\underline{A}^{-1}\underline{B}) \leq 1 \tag{23}$$

The eigenvalues of the amplification matrix have been calculated numerically for different values of α and Δt. Using the results of these calculations, the maximum stable time steps can be determined. In fig. 3, the maximum stable time steps are given as a function of α.

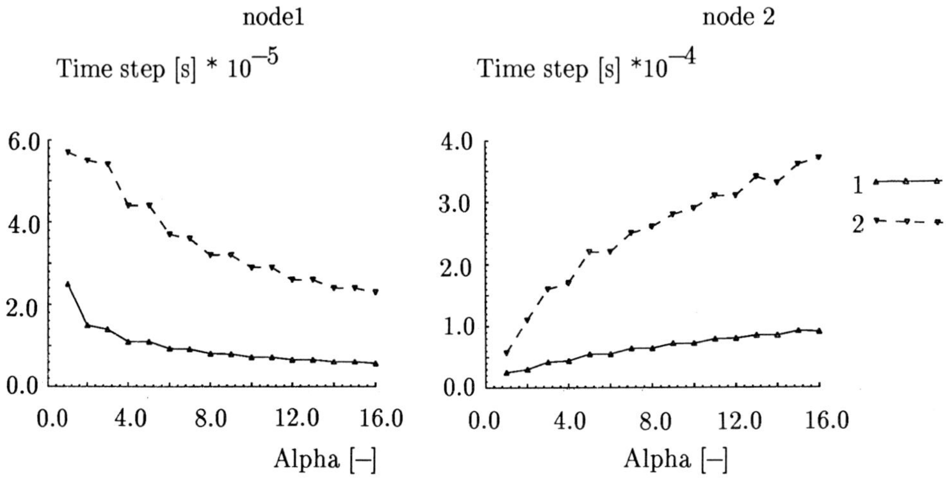

Fig. 3. The maximum stable time step as a function of the time step ratio.
$\rho = 10^3$ [kg m^{-3}], $\nu = 0.3$ [–], l = 0.1 [m], thickness = 0.01 [m]
1: $Y_1=10^{10}$ [Nm^{-2}] $Y_2=10^{10}$ [Nm^{-2}], 2: $Y_1=6.25\ 10^8$ [Nm^{-2}] $Y_2=10^{10}$ [Nm^{-2}]

It is concluded that the subcycling method is conditionally stable. The maximum stable time steps are larger than the time steps that follow from (5). This is due to the fact that (5) is determined for a free element. In the system of fig. 2, degrees of freedom have been suppressed. This changes the maximum frequency when compared to free elements.

PARTITIONING OF ELEMENTS IN GROUPS

For the description of the subcycle algorithm, only two different time steps were used. For calculations with the PISCES–3DELK code much more time steps are allowed, but they must satisfy the condition that all time steps are integer multiples of each other, although this condition is in general too severe. To start, for all elements the maximum stable time step is calculated. Then the elements are splitted up into groups. Group 1 contains elements with a time step satisfying $\Delta t_{min} \leq \Delta t < 2\Delta t_{min}$, group 2 elements with $2\Delta t_{min} \leq \Delta t < 3\Delta t_{min}$ etc., with Δt_{min} the minimum time step of the mesh. Group 1 can be treated with the time step Δt_{min}, group 2 with $2\Delta t_{min}$, group 3 with $3\Delta t_{min}$ etc. However, this group division does not satisfy the above condition. Therefore an algorithm has been developed that automatically finds that group division, satisfying the above condition, with minimal simulation costs. The user only has to specify whether subcycling must be applied. The algorithm finds the best group division and returns the expected computer time savings.

As mentioned before, the condition that all time steps have to be integer multiples of each other is too severe. Only the time steps of two neighbouring element groups have to be integer multiples of each other. But, because the difference in savings for the severe condition and the weak condition are small (about 2%) and the fact that it is very difficult to check whether the weak condition is satisfied for a specific group division, it is chosen to satisfy the severe condition.

TEST EXAMPLES

The first test problem is the plate shown in fig. 4. The left side of the plate is clamped and the velocity of the right side of the plate is prescribed to be 0.1 $[ms^{-1}]$. In this figure also the time steps used are given. Nodes on the boundary lines are integrated with the largest time step of the groups the line separates. The displacement histories of some nodes – indicated in fig. 4 – are given for a calculation with and without subcycling in fig. 5.

The generation algorithm predicted a computer time saving of 53%. The actual saving was 44%. The difference between the predicted and the achieved saving is caused by the fact that the generation algorithm does not take into account the overhead costs of subcycling and the fact that the algorithm presumes that the updates of the internal forces consume much more computer time than the updates of the nodes. In case of the relatively simple membrane elements this is not true.

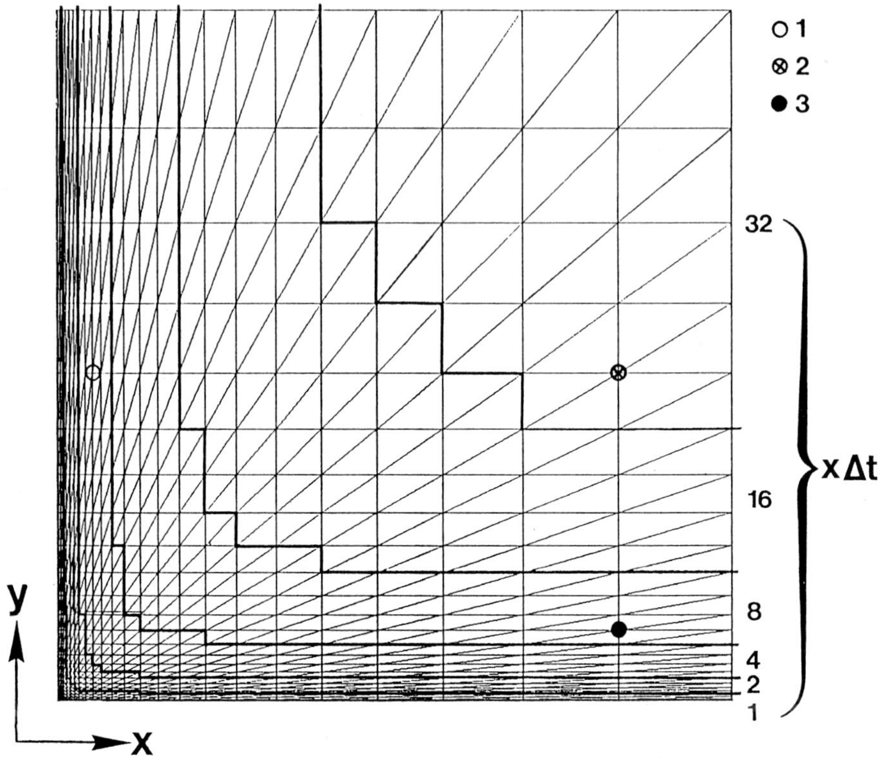

Fig. 4. The mesh for the calculation with the plate.
Y = 3.06 10^8 [Nm^{-2}], ρ = 691.617 [kg m^{-3}], ν = 0.3 [–], Thickness = 0.0005 [m], length = 10 [m], width = 10 [m].

The second test problem is the cylinder shown in fig. 6. This problem has been chosen in order to check whether the use of different time steps would not yield displacements of the centre of gravity of the cylinder. For this reason, no kinematic boundary conditions were specified. The cylinder is loaded with a jump in the internal pressure of 6000 [Nm^{-2}] at time zero. Four different time steps were used (fig. 6).

The displacements of the centre of mass in y–direction varied between 0 and 24 10^{-6} [m] for the calculation with subcycling and between 0 and 21 10^{-6} [m] for the calculation without subcycling.

In fig. 7, the displacement histories of two nodes are given for a calculation with and without subcycling. No significant differences are found.

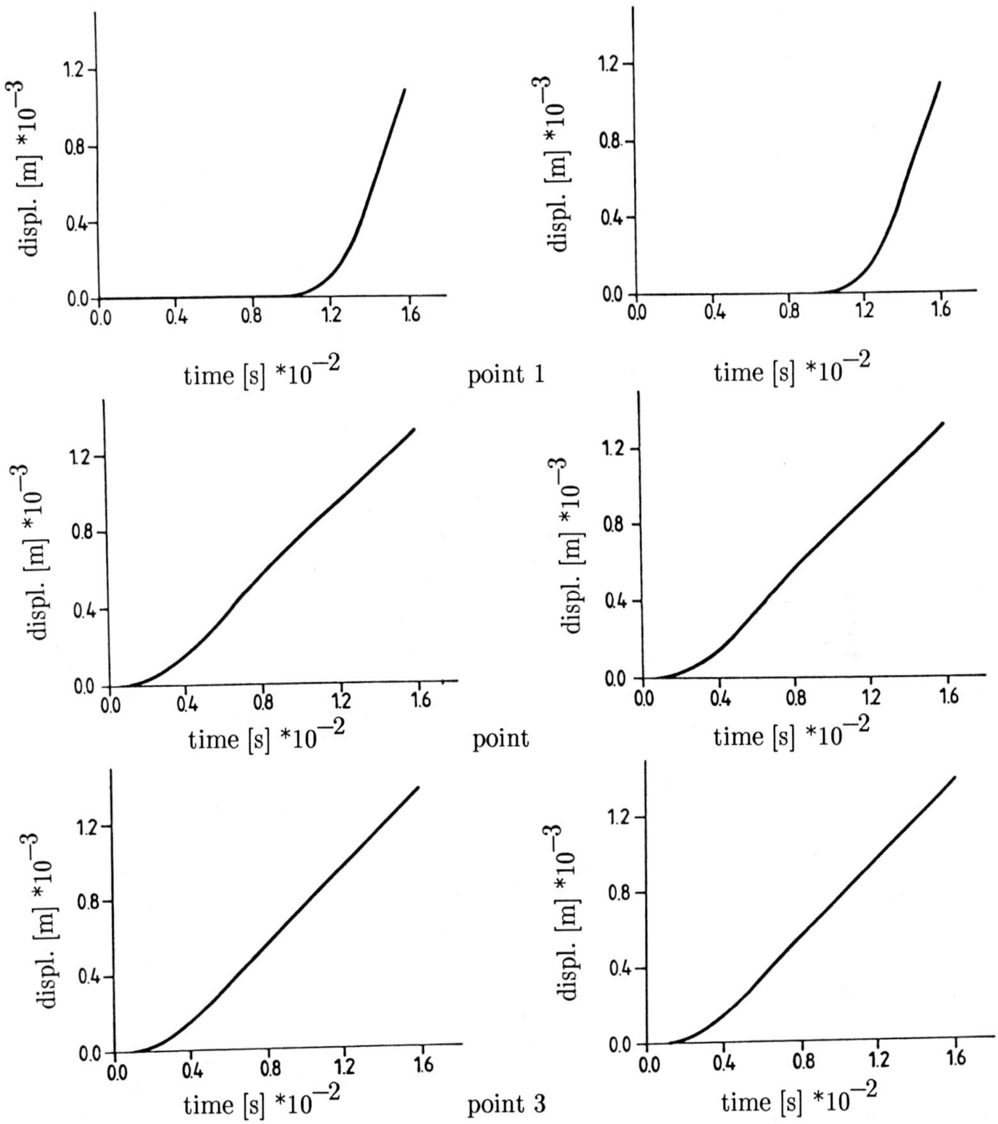

Fig. 5. Displacements histories for the plate. The left column is the result of a calculation with subcycling, the right column of a calculation without subcycling.

The predicted saving was 52%. The achieved saving was only 35%. This is larger than the difference in predicted and achieved savings for the plate. This difference is caused by the two reasons mentioned for the plate and the fact that the calculation of the external forces is not subcycled.

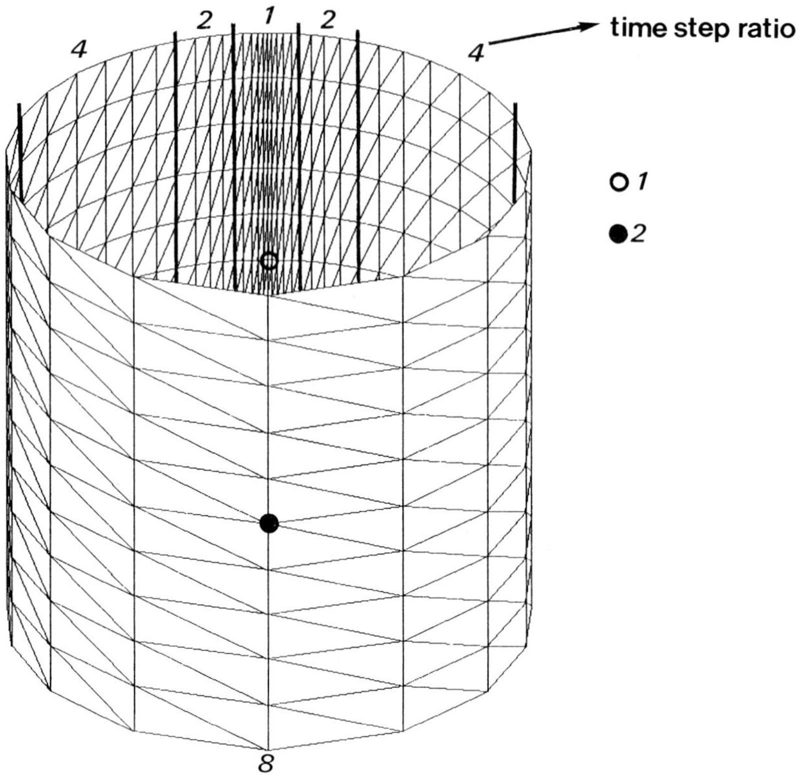

Fig. 6. The mesh for the calculation with the cylinder.
$Y = 3.06\ 10^8$ [Nm^{-2}], $\rho = 691.617$ [kg m^{-3}], $\nu = 0.3$ [–], Thickness = 0.001 [m], Diameter = 1 [m], Length = 1 [m].

CONCLUSION AND FINAL REMARKS

Subcycling indeed yields substantial computer time savings. The loss of accuracy is acceptable for many engineering applications.

In the future, the algorithm will be adjusted in order to allow impact between different meshes.

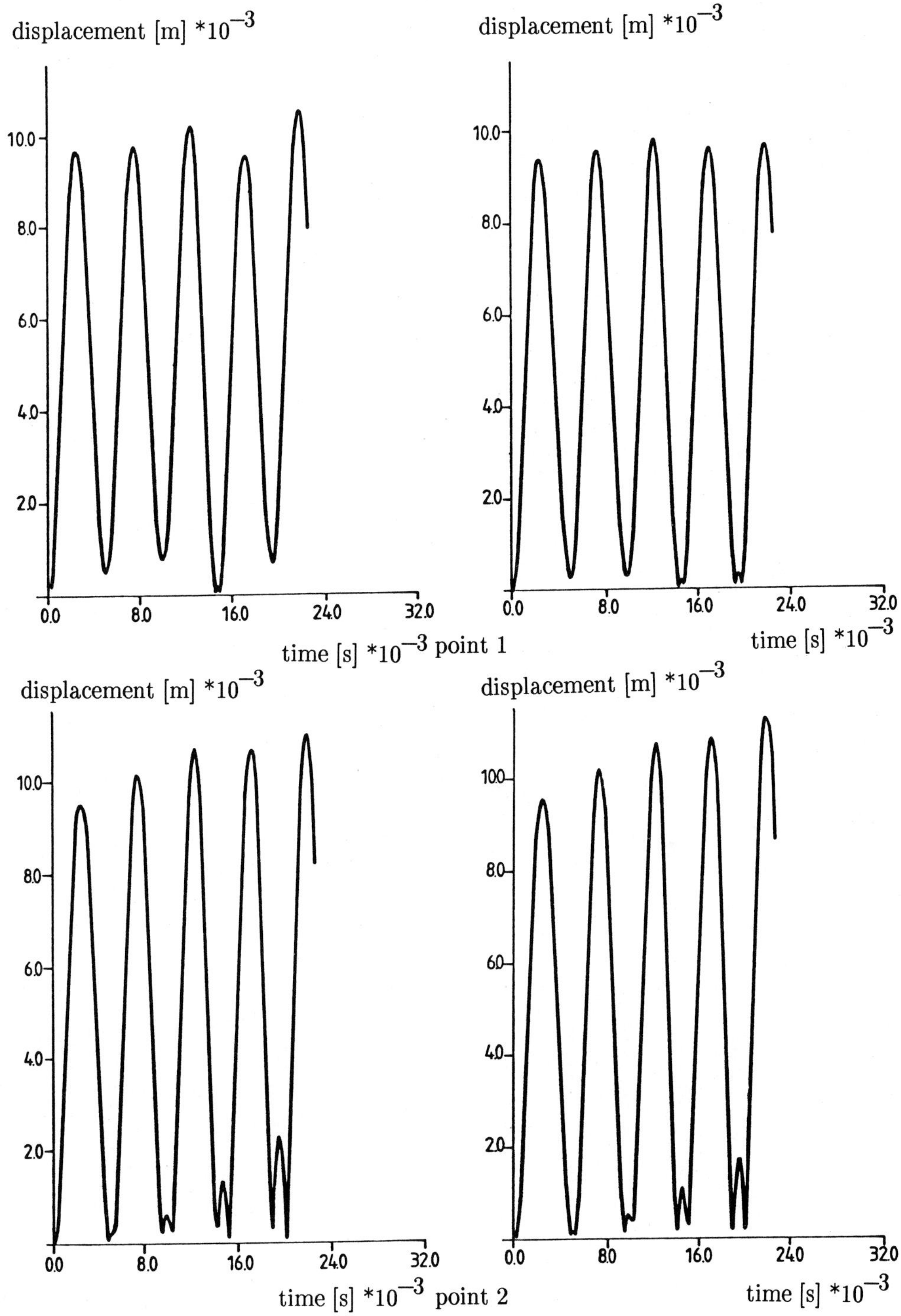

Fig. 7. Displacements histories for the cylinder. The left column is the result of a calculation with subcycling, the right column of a calculation without subcycling.

ACKNOWLEDGEMENTS

This work is partly sponsored by the Netherlands Organization for Applied Scientific Research – TNO

REFERENCES

Bruijs, W.E.M., Brekelmans, W.A.M., van Campen, D.H., de Coo, P.J.A., van der Heijden, A.M.A. & Janssen, J.D.: Computer Time Reduction by Subcycling with an Application to Numerical Crash Analysis. In: Supercomputer Applications in Automotive Research and Engineering Development (C. Marino, ed.). pp. 347–371. Minneapolis, Minnesota: Cray Research, Inc. 1988

Courant, R., Friedriechs, K. & Lewy, H.: On the Partial Differential Equations of Mathematical Physics. Math. Ann. 100, 32–74 (1928)

Hughes, T.J.R.: Analysis of Transient Algorithms with Particular Reference to Stability Behaviour. In: Computational Methods for Transient Analysis (T. Belytschko & T.J.R. Hughes, eds.). pp. 67–155. North Holland 1983

Krieg, R.D. & Key S.W.: Transient Shell Response by Numerical Time Integration. International Journal of Numerical Methods in Engineering. 7, 273–286 (1973)

PART 3

ADVANCED DAE APPLICATIONS

REAL TIME SIMULATION OF COMPLEX 3-D MULTIBODY SYSTEMS WITH REALISTIC GRAPHICS

J. García de Jalón, J.M. Jiménez, A. Avello, F. Martín and J. Cuadrado

Escuela Superior de Ingenieros Industriales (University of Navarra)

Centro de Estudios e Investigaciones Técnicas de Guipúzcoa (CEIT)
Barrio de Ibaeta sn, 20009, San Sebastián, SPAIN

1. ABSTRACT

In the last few years a new method for kinematic and dynamic simulation of multibody problems has been developed by the authors at CEIT and University of Navarra. The most distinctive feature of this method is the use of a fully cartesian set of dependent coordinates; instead of describing the spatial position of a rigid body through the cartesian coordinates of a point and Euler angles or Euler parameters, this method uses the cartesian coordinates of two or more points and the cartesian components of one or more unit vectors rigidly attached to the body. Points and vectors can be shared between contiguous elements, keeping the number of variables moderate and contributing to the definition of pair constraints. With these coordinates the formulation has important advantages: constant mass matrix in the global reference frame, absence of Coriolis and centrifugal inertia forces in the dependent coordinates and a jacobian matrix much more easy to evaluate. The result is a very general and very efficient dynamic formulation.

In addition to this a new formulation has been developed to obtain a further increasing of speed and to get the program more suitable for multiprocessor architectures. As in other formulations, the mechanism is first converted onto a tree structure opening the closed loops by removing the appropriate constraints that are introduced later on through Lagrange multipliers. Then a vector basis for the space of allowable motions is constructed for each branch (each vector can be computed recursively and in parallel with the others). Next the constant mass matrix is projected onto the joint coordinates space. This operation is carried out with a double product of matrices, operation very easy to parallelize. For a 6R branch this method needs only a 15% more arithmetic operations than the composite inertia method of Walker and Orin, but gives more information (absolute position of every link in the branch) and gives much more opportunities for parallelization.

NATO ASI Series, Vol. F 69
Real-Time Integration Methods for Mechanical System Simulation
Edited by E. J. Haug and R. C. Deyo

This method is being implemented on a Silicon Graphics Power Iris 240 GTX superworstation that integrates four 3.9 Megaflops CPUs with a very powerful graphic subsystem.

2. THE GENERAL PURPOSE METHOD

The kinematic and dynamic analysis of 3-D complex multibody systems presents a great interest in many areas of mechanical engineering, such as robotics, ground vehicles, spacecraft, machinery, biomechanics, etc. In the last two decades a great deal of research has been done, most of them summarized in refs. [1] and [2]. As a result, some general purpose programs such as IMP, ADAMS, DADS, NEWEUL, ... have been used successfully in industrial projects.

In the last few years, a great emphasis has been put on the efficiency of the methods of analysis. Kinematic simulation interactivity is a very desirable capability of any program, and in the dynamic case large systems of nonlinear differential equations must be integrated as fast as possible, even in real time [3].

Looking for this improved efficiency, several authors [4], [5] have developed symbolical formalisms to obtain the motion differential equations in closed form. When applicable, these formalisms have better performance than the fully numerical formulations, but until now the latter remain the only approach to a truly general dynamic simulation, able to deal with mechanisms of changing topology and with special factors such as Coulomb friction, backlash, impacts, etc.

The method described in this paper is based on a particularly simple, general and efficient original idea [6]-[9].

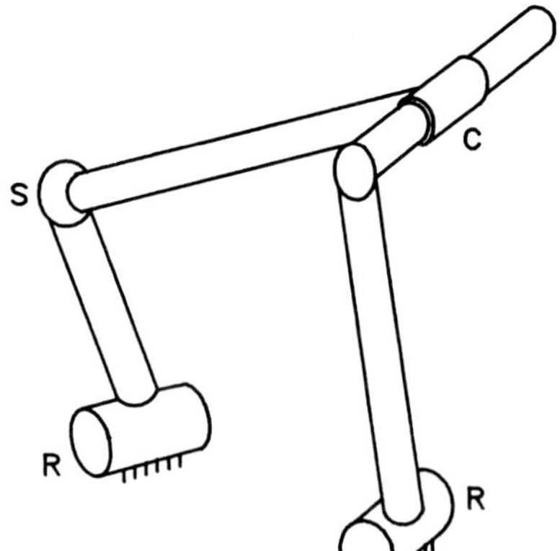

Figure 1 . RSCR 1 d.o.f. Mechanism

In figure 1 a three-dimensional four bar (RSCR) mechanism with 1 degree of freedom is presented as an example. In order to analyze this mechanism it is necessary to choose a set of parameters (dependent coordinates) that unequivocally describe the position of the three moving links. This can be done in several ways, with different kinds of dependent coordinates. The first possibility is to use relative coordinates, that describe the position of a link relative to another link joined by a pair, using the coordinates of relative motion allowed by that pair. Another possibility is to describe the spatial position of each body with the cartesian coordinates of one of its points (usually the center of gravity) and with three of four parameters that describe the angular orientation (usually Euler angles or Euler parameters).

The dependent coordinates are related through the *constraint equations*. The partial derivatives of the constraint equations with respect to the dependent coordinates constitute the *jacobian matrix*. The jacobian matrix is very important because it determines in practice both the kinematic and the dynamic equations.

With relative coordinates the constraint equations arise from the closure condition of kinematic loops. With reference point coordinates the constraint equations arise from the limitations in relative motion between contiguous elements imposed by the pair that joins them.

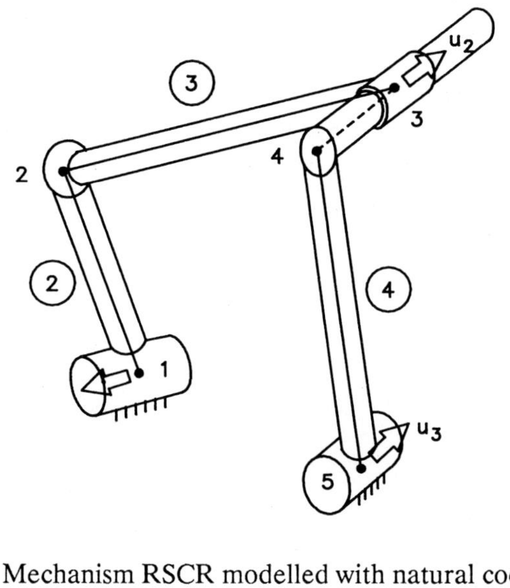

Figure 2. Mechanism RSCR modelled with natural coordinates

In the method described in this paper a new kind of dependent coordinates has been used: the position of a body is determined by the cartesian coordinates of at least two of its points and the cartesian components of at least one unit vector rigidly attached to this body. In figure 2 the modellization of the RSCR mechanism of figure 1 with these fully cartesian coordinates, that originally [6] were called *natural coordinates*, is shown.

The example of figure 2 requires 4 relative coordinates, 18 (21) reference point coordinates with Euler angles (Euler parameters), and 12 natural coordinates. What first makes natural coordinates very attractive, in addition to their immediate geometrical meaning, is the simplicity of the constraint equations that relate them, and, as a consequence, the simplicity of the jacobian matrix. For the example of Figure 2 the jacobian matrix with reference point coordinates and Euler parameters, evaluated according with reference [10], has 128 non-zero elements and requires nearly one thousand floating point operations; with natural coordinates the jacobian matrix has 57 non-zero elements and requires only twelve arithmetic operations.

2.1. Constraint Equations

The ultimate reason for the efficiency of natural coordinates can be found in the kind of constraint equations they determine. For instance, in the RSCR mechanism of figure 2 (and in most cases) the constraint equations arise in a double way. First, it is necessary that the points and vectors that belong to the same link move according to the rigid body condition. Secondly, it is necessary that points and vectors belonging to contiguous elements move according to the degrees of freedom of relative motion allowed by the pair that joins them.

Rigid body constraint equations can be introduced very easily. For instance, element 4 of the mechanism of figure 2 has two points (4 and 5) and two unit vectors (u_2 and u_3). There are 12 coordinates and 6 degrees of freedom, so 6 constraint equations must be found:

$$(x_4-x_5)^2 + (y_4-y_5)^2 + (z_4-z_5)^2 - C_1 = 0 \tag{1}$$

$$(x_4-x_5)u_{2x} + (y_4-y_5)u_{2y} + (z_4-z_5)u_{2z} - C_2 = 0 \tag{2}$$

$$(x_4-x_5)u_{3x} + (y_4-y_5)u_{3y} + (z_4-z_5)u_{3z} - C_3 = 0 \tag{3}$$

$$u_{2x}\, u_{3x} + u_{2y}\, u_{3y} + u_{2z}\, u_{3z} - C_4 = 0 \tag{4}$$

$$u_{2x}^2 + u_{2y}^2 + u_{2z}^2 - 1 = 0 \tag{5}$$

$$u_{3x}^2 + u_{3y}^2 + u_{3z}^2 - 1 = 0 \tag{6}$$

Eq. (1) corresponds to a constant distance condition between points 4 and 5; eqs. (2), (3) and (4) correspond to constant angle conditions between segment 3-4 and vectors u_2 and u_3; eqs. (5) and (6) correspond to the unit module condition for vectors u_2 and u_3

(in fact, eq. (6) is in this case unnecessary because u_3 is a fixed vector and so its components are known).

An interesting feature of natural coordinates is that points and unit vectors can be shared among two contiguous elements, contributing to the definition of the position of both and so keeping the total number of coordinates moderate. In addition to this, introduction of the constraint equations due to the pairs is strongly simplified, when not eliminated at all. For instance, the spherical pair in the mechanism of figure 2 does not introduce any equation because it is automatically introduced when links 2 and 3 share point 2. In the same way, as points 1 and 5 and vectors u_1 and u_3 are fixed and located on the axis of revolute pairs, both pairs neither introduce any constraint equation. On the other hand elements 3 and 4 share vector u_2; to introduce the constraint equations corresponding to pair C it is enough to impose the condition that points 3 and 4 (belonging respectively to links 3 and 4) remain permanently aligned with vector u_2. Analytically this can be introduced through the vector product of vectors:

$$\{u_2\} \wedge [\{r_3\} - \{r_4\}] = \{0\} \tag{7}$$

(only two of these three equations are independent).

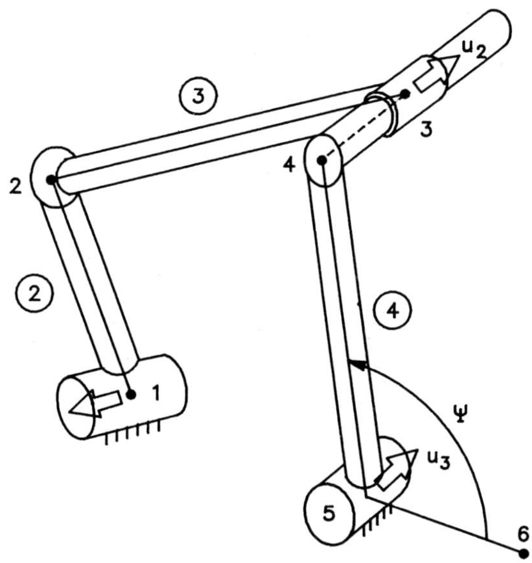

Figure 3. Mechanism RSCR with a driving angle

With natural coordinates angles are never necessary to describe the spatial position of a rigid body. However, sometimes the definition of an angle in a revolute joint can be very useful, for instance if the value of this angle need to be controlled by an actuator. In figure 3 the same RSCR mechanism of figure 2 is presented adding the angle ψ rotated by element 4. A new fixed point has been included. In order to include ψ among the dependent coordinates, the following new constraint equation, originated by the dot product of vectors, must be added,

$$(x_6-x_5)(x_4-x_5) + (y_6-y_5)(y_4-y_5) + (z_6-z_5)(z_4-z_5) - C_5 \cos\Psi - C_6 = 0 \tag{8}$$

If the value of angle ψ is near $(n\pi)$ radians $(n=0,1, ...)$ the dot product must be replaced by a component of the vector product of vectors.

With natural coordinates the constraint equations are always quadratic equations. As a consequence, the elements of the jacobian matrix are linear functions of natural coordinates; this is the reason of the extraordinary simplicity and efficiency of this formulation.

2.2. Kinematic Analysis

The constraint equations of a particular mechanism, both rheonomic and scleronomic, can be formulated shortly as:

$$\{\Phi(\{q\},t)\} = \{0\} \tag{9}$$

where $\{q\}$ is the vector of natural coordinates.

The initial position (assembly) problem and the finite displacement problem, can be solved from the Newton-Raphson iterative scheme,

$$[\Phi_q(\{q\}_i,t)][\{q\}_{i+1} - \{q\}_i] = -\{\Phi(\{q\}_i,t)\} \tag{10}$$

from which a better approximation $\{q\}_{i+1}$ is obtained. $[\Phi_q]$ is the jacobian matrix.

For velocity and acceleration analysis it is enough to differentiate eq. (9) with respect to the time,

$$[\Phi_q(\{q\},t)]\{\dot{q}\} = -\{\Phi_t\} \equiv \{b\} \tag{11}$$

$$[\Phi_q(\{q\},t)]\{\ddot{q}\} = -\{\dot{\Phi}_t\} - [\dot{\Phi}_q]\{\dot{q}\} \equiv \{c\} \tag{12}$$

In eqs. (10)-(12) the importance of the jacobian matrix for kinematic analysis is very clear.

2.3. Dependent and Independent Coordinates

For reasons that will be made evident later, it is very useful to formulate the dynamic equations in terms of a reduced set of F independent coordinates {z} (F is the number of degrees of freedom of the mechanism). In this section the relationship between dependent {q} and independent {z} coordinates will be exposed.

A large family of methods [8], [11], [12] use as independent velocities $\{\dot{z}\}$ the projection of the dependent ones $\{\dot{q}\}$ on the rows of a constant (F x N) matrix [B].

$$[B]\ \{\dot{q}\} = \{\dot{z}\} \tag{13}$$

Putting together eqs. (11) and (13):

$$\begin{bmatrix} [\Phi_q] \\ [\ B\ ] \end{bmatrix} \{\dot{q}\} = \begin{Bmatrix} \{b\} \\ \{\dot{z}\} \end{Bmatrix} \tag{14}$$

If matrix [B] is chosen in such a way that its rows are linearly independent of the rows of $[\Phi_q]$, it can be written:

$$[\dot{q}] = \begin{bmatrix} \{\Phi_q\} \\ [B] \end{bmatrix}^{-1} \begin{Bmatrix} \{b\} \\ \{\dot{z}\} \end{Bmatrix} \equiv [\,[S][R]\,] \begin{Bmatrix} \{b\} \\ \{\dot{z}\} \end{Bmatrix} = [S]\{b\} + [R]\{\dot{z}\} \tag{15}$$

This is a very important result and it can be taken as a definition of matrices [S] and [R]. Eq.(14) establishes that $\{\dot{q}\}$ is the sum of a particular solution of eq. (11) plus the general solution of the homogeneous velocity equation. If the constraint equations are not time dependent, {b} = {0}, then only the second term of eq. (15) exists.

The matrix [R] defined in eq. (15) has great importance for the methods of dynamic analysis described in this paper. It can easily be seen that the column space of [R] is orthogonal to the row space of $[\Phi_q]$ and, as long as these columns are also linearly independent, they can be taken as a basis of the nullspace of $[\Phi_q]$, that is the space of allowable velocities with non time-dependent constraints. The independent velocities $\{\dot{z}\}$ are the components of $\{\dot{q}\}$ on the columns of [R], that are the basis vectors of the nullspace of $[\Phi_q]$.

For accelerations a similar result follows. Putting together eq. (12) and the derivative of eq. (13):

$$\begin{bmatrix} [\Phi_q] \\ [\,B\,] \end{bmatrix} \left\{ \ddot{q} \right\} = \left\{ \begin{matrix} (c) \\ (\ddot{z}) \end{matrix} \right\} \tag{16}$$

inverting the matrix of this expression:

$$\{\ddot{q}\} = \begin{bmatrix} [\Phi_q] \\ [\,B\,] \end{bmatrix}^{-1} \left\{ \begin{matrix} (c) \\ (\ddot{z}) \end{matrix} \right\} = [S](c) + [R](\ddot{z}) \tag{17}$$

This result is very useful in dynamic analysis. It is now necessary to describe the way in which the matrix [B] introduced in expression (13) can be chosen. According to eqs. (13) and (14) the only condition to be fulfilled by this constant matrix is that its rows be independent of the rows of the jacobian matrix $[\Phi_q]$. There are three main possibilities:

a) Mani, Haug and Atkinson [11] use the Singular Value Decomposition (SVD) of $[\Phi_q]$ in a previous position so as to compute an orthogonal basis of the nullspace of $[\Phi_q]$ in this position. This basis is taken as matrix [B] (nullspace in a previous position) and it is expected that it remains independent of the row space of $[\Phi_q]$ for a large motion range.

b) Kim and Vanderploeg [12] make a similar approach to a) using the QR decomposition, that is cheaper than SVD. These authors compute matrices [S] and [R] by an updating technique.

c) García de Jalón and coworkers [7], [8] use for matrix [B] a boolean matrix that simply extracts some elements of $\{\dot{q}\}$ as independent velocities $\{\dot{z}\}$. The elements of $\{\dot{q}\}$ to be taken as independent are chosen after a Gaussian decomposition of $[\Phi_q]$ with total pivoting. This is the simplest method and it is also very efficient because with a boolean matrix [B] in eq. (15) the computation of matrices [S] and [R] is simpler. This is the standard method used in this paper.

2.4. Dynamic Analysis

In the context of natural coordinates virtual power is the most straightforward way to establish the motion differential equations. The virtual power of inertia forces of a link containing two points and two non coplanar unit vectors will be formulated next.

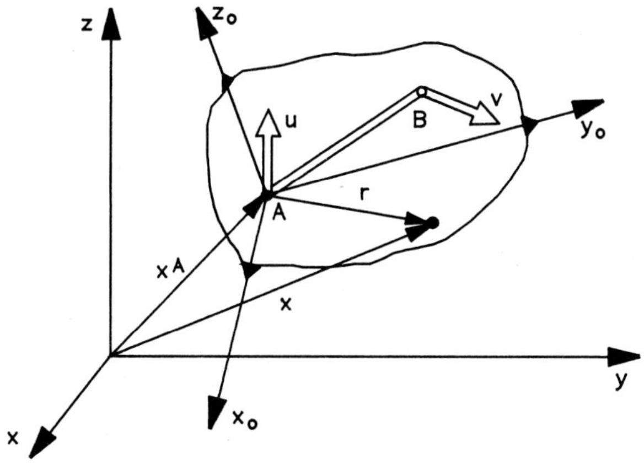

Figure 4. Inertia forces of a link with two points and two vectors

Consider the element of figure 4. The virtual power of this element can be expressed as:

$$W_{in} = \int_v \text{trace}\left(\{\ddot{x}\}\,\{\dot{x}'\}^T\right) dm \tag{18}$$

where $\{\ddot{x}\}$ is the acceleration vector and $\{\dot{x}'\}$ is the vector of virtual velocities. Vector $\{x\}$ can be expressed as:

$$\{x\} = \{x^A\} + [T]\,\{r\} \tag{19}$$

$[T]$ being the rotation matrix. The inertial components of vectors (u), (v) and segment (AB) can be expressed in the form:

$$\left[X\right] = [T]\,[X_0] \tag{20}$$

where $[X]$ is a (3x3) matrix whose columns are:

$$\left[X\right] \equiv \left[\left(\{x^B\}-\{x^A\}\right)\ \{u\}\ \{v\}\right] \tag{21}$$

According to eq. (19) the velocities and accelerations can be expressed as:

$$\{\dot{x}\} = \{\dot{x}^A\} + [\dot{T}]\,\{r\} \tag{22}$$

$$\{\ddot{x}\} = \{\ddot{x}^A\} + [\ddot{T}]\,\{r\} \tag{23}$$

matrices [T] and [T] can be obtained differentiating eq. (20) and taking into account that matrix $[X_0]$ is constant (it contains the coordinates of A, B, {u} and {v} in the moving frame),

$$\left[\dot{T}\right] = \left[\dot{X}\right]\left[X_0\right]^{-1} \tag{24}$$

$$\left[\ddot{T}\right] = \left[\ddot{X}\right]\left[X_0\right]^{-1} \tag{25}$$

Substituting eqs. (22)-(25) in eq. (18), after some algebraic manipulation, it is possible to arrive at the following result:

$$W_{in} = \{\dot{q}'^{e}\}^{T}\,[M^{e}]\,\{\ddot{q}^{e}\} \tag{26}$$

where $\{\dot{q}'^{e}\}$ and $\{\ddot{q}^{e}\}$ are respectively the natural virtual velocities and natural accelerations of the element. For instance, vector $\{\ddot{q}^{e}\}$ has the form:

$$\{\ddot{q}^{e}\}^{T} \equiv \left[\{\ddot{x}^{A}\}^{T}, \{\ddot{x}^{B}\}^{T}, \{\ddot{u}\}^{T}, \{\ddot{v}\}^{T}\right] \tag{27}$$

and matrix $[M^e]$ is the inertia matrix of the element. It is constant (independent of the element position) and has the following expression:

$$[M^{e}] = \begin{bmatrix} (z_{11} + 2s_1 + M)[I] & -(s_1+z_{11})[I] & (s_2+z_{12})[I] & (s_3+z_{13})[I] \\ & z_{11}[I] & -z_{12}[I] & -z_{13}[I] \\ & & z_{22}[I] & z_{23}[I] \\ \text{symmetric} & & & z_{23}[I] \end{bmatrix} \tag{28}$$

In this expression [I] is the (3x3) unit matrix and,

$$\{S\} = (s_1\; s_2\; s_3)^{T} = M\,[X_0]^{-1}\,\{r^{G}\} \tag{29}$$

$$[Z] = [X_0]^{-1}\,[J]\,[X_0]^{-T} \tag{30}$$

$$[J] = \int_{v}\{r\}\,\{r\}^{T}dm \tag{31}$$

M is the mass of the element, $\{r^G\}$ the position vector of the center of gravity and [J] the inertia tensor. Vector {S} plays the role of a linear momentum and [Z] is a transformed inertia tensor.

There are two very important points that need to be emphasized about these results: the first one is that the inertia forces are formulated in the inertial frame through a constant inertia matrix, allowing an increased efficiency in the solution of the dynamic equations; the second is that there aren't velocity dependent inertia forces, further improving the efficiency and simplifying the formulation.

The virtual power theorem applied to the whole mechanism leads to the expression:

$$\{\dot{q}'\}^T \Big([M]\{\ddot{q}\} - \big\{Q\big(\{q\}, \{\dot{q}\}\big)\big\} \Big) = 0 \qquad (32)$$

where {Q} is the vector of external or internal forces that are position or velocity dependent (springs, dampers, friction, etc.) and [M] is the constant mass matrix of the whole mechanism, obtained from the element matrices $[M^e]$ through an assembly process similar to the one used in the finite element method. The virtual velocity vector $\{\dot{q}'\}$ must satisfy the homogeneous constraint equation for velocities,

$$[\Phi_q]\,\{\dot{q}'\} = \{0\} \qquad (33)$$

Transposing this equation, multiplying it by a vector $\{\lambda\}$ of Lagrange Multipliers and adding it to eq. (32) the following equation is obtained:

$$\{\dot{q}'\}^T \Big([M]\{\ddot{q}\} + [\Phi_q]^T\{\lambda\} - \{Q\} \Big) = 0 \qquad (34)$$

now, for an arbitrary vector $\{\dot{q}'\}$ it is always possible to find a vector $\{\lambda\}$ that makes null the parenthesis of eq. (34). Putting this parenthesis together with eq. (12) the following equation is obtained:

$$\begin{bmatrix} [M] & [\Phi_q]^T \\ [\Phi_q] & [0] \end{bmatrix} \begin{Bmatrix} \{\ddot{q}\} \\ \{\lambda\} \end{Bmatrix} = \begin{Bmatrix} \{Q\} \\ \{c\} \end{Bmatrix} \qquad (35)$$

This is perhaps the dynamic formulation most often found in the bibliography. Remember that natural coordinates make it specially appropriate because matrix [M] is constant, matrix $[\Phi_q]$ is particularly easy to evaluate and there are not Coriolis or centrifugal inertia forces.

It is possible to derive another expression for the dynamic equations in which Lagrange multipliers do not appear. Using eq. (15) to introduce independent virtual velocities in eq.(32):

$$\{\dot{z}'\}^T [R]^T \left(\{M\}\{\ddot{q}\} - \{Q\} \right) = 0 \tag{36}$$

Now virtual velocities $\{\dot{z}'\}$ are independent and can be eliminated. Putting this equation together with eq. (12):

$$\begin{bmatrix} [\Phi_q] \\ [R]^T [M] \end{bmatrix} \{\ddot{q}\} = \begin{Bmatrix} \{c\} \\ [R]^T \{Q\} \end{Bmatrix} \tag{37}$$

This is an alternative equation to eq. (35). Both equations can suffer a lack of stability in the fulfillment of constraint equations. This problem can be solved either using the Baumgarte stabilization method [13], integrating a mixed system of algebraic-differential equations, or formulating and integrating the motion differential equations in independent coordinates. This is the approach most currently used with this method.

Substituting in eq. (37) the expression for $\{\ddot{q}\}$ defined in eq. (17) the following equation is obtained:

$$[R]^T[M][R]\{\ddot{z}\} = [R]^T\{Q\} - [R]^T[M][S]\{c\} \tag{38}$$

In order to apply this equation it is necessary to compute matrix [R] from eq. (15) but not matrix [S], because this matrix is never used separately but multiplied by vector {c}. From eq. (17) the term ([S]{c}) can be computed as the vector of dependent accelerations $\{\ddot{q}\}$ when the independent accelerations $\{\ddot{z}\}$ are taken to be zero. Eq. (16) allows the computation of $\{\ddot{q}\}$ with this condition.

2.4. Dynamic examples solved with the general purpose formulation

In figure 5 three mechanisms are shown. The first one is a 1 d.o.f, closed loop, over-constrained system known as Bricard mechanism. The second one is similar to the first one but releasing one of the boundary points, then obtaining a 5 d.o.f., open loop pendulum. The third example is a 3 d.o.f., closed loop robot.

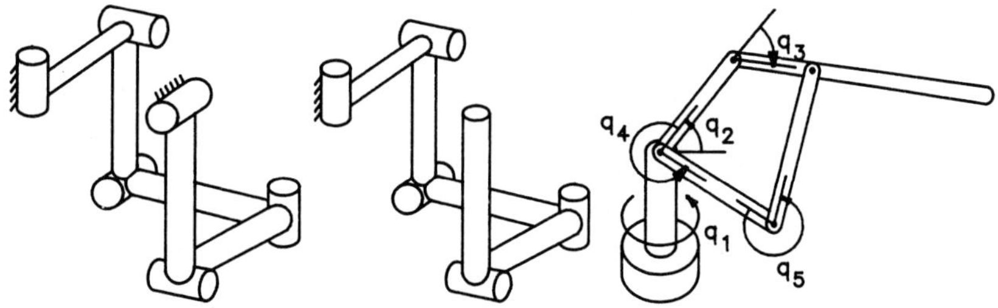

Figure 5

The mechanisms in figure 5 are very different in kinematic and dynamic structure (No. of dependent coordinates, No. of degrees of freedom, open or closed loops, etc), and it is most interesting to study how the general purpose formulation of eq. (38) perfom in these cases. To do this the profile utility of UNIX has been used, measuring the total CPU time per integration step and the CPU percentage spent in each part of the integration step. A Silicon Graphics IRIS 4D/240 workstation has been used (only 1 processor).

The results are shown in Table 1 .

Operation	Bricard	5R pend.	Robot
- Form the jacobian $[\Phi q]$	5.23%	3.13%	5.21%
- L-U factorization of $[\Phi q]$	56.68%	39.54%	17.23%
- Form matrix [R] (forw. and backw. subs)	12.22%	30.32%	28.81%
- Compute $\{\dot{q}\} = [R]\{\dot{z}\}$	0.96%	0.90%	1.20%
- Compute the term ([S]{c})	11.80%	6.65%	14.09%
- Compute [R]T [M]	4.41%	5.21%	11.21%
- Compute ([R]T[M])[R]	1.10%	8.56%	10.36%
- Compute [R]T{Q}-[R]T[M][S]{c}={f}	2.25%	2.35%	5.48%
- Solve $[R]T[M][R]\{\ddot{z}\}=\{f\}$	---	0.20%	---
- Integrate $\{\ddot{z},\dot{q}\}_t \to \{\dot{z},q\}_{t+\Delta t}$	5.00%	3.14%	6.41%
- No. of dependent coordinates	29	35	15
- No. of degrees of freedom	1	5	3
- CPU msec/step	7.33	23.01	6.67

Table 1

It is very interesting to raise some points about the results shown in Table 1:

1. Good CPU times per integration step have been obtained. In the cases of the Bricard and d.o.f. robot the results obtained are already suitable for real time simulation.

2. In all cases most of the CPU time is spent in the jacobian factorization and in the subsequent forward and backward substitutions necessary to compute matrix [R].

3. The products of matrices necessary to project the inertia matrix take a relatively small percentage of the total CPU time.

4. It is three times more expensive to compute the open loop pendulum than the closed loop Bricard. The reason is the mechanism number of degrees of freedom, that determines the number of columns of matrix [R].

It can be concluded that the bottleneck of this formulation is the jacobian factorization and the subsequent forward and backward substitutions. In addition to this it can be concluded too that this formulation is not very suitable for multiprocessor architectures such as the IRIS 4D/240 one, because matrix factorization is an operation much more difficult to parallelize than the product of matrices.

In the following Section a new dynamic formulation that provides much better results will be described.

3. IMPROVED METHOD FOR REAL TIME DYNAMIC SIMULATION

In the last years a great effort has been made to improve the efficiency of the dynamic formulation of complex 3-D multibody problems. In this context it is necessary to comment on the big influence of the work of Amstrong [14] and Featherstone [15], who first developed recursive formulations for serial manipulators that compute the link accelerations with a number of arithmetic operations that depend linearly on the number of links. However, these formulations are not necessarily the most efficient ones, if the number of links is not very large. In addition to this, the recursive character of these formulations prevents their efficient implementation in modern multiprocessor superminicomputers or superworkstations.

The most important contributions to the improvement of standard dynamic formulations have been made by the Iowa group [16]-[20]. Bae and Haug [16]-[17] and Wehage [18] use fully recursive formulations propagating backward inertias, external forces and closure loops constraints and propagating forward joint and link accelerations. This can be very good for a single processor computer but not for a multiprocessor one.

The algorithms that take advantage of multiprocessor architectures are described in refs. [19]-[20]. In these papers some improvements with respect to the previous ones have been introduced. First of all, a generalized velocity state vector is used so as to simplify the resulting mathematical expressions. Secondly, the joint and base body accelerations are not computed recursively but all at once, constructing a generalized mass matrix. The formulation of this mass matrix and the solution of the corresponding system of linear equations are easy to parallelize. In ref. [20] many other useful ideas for parallelization are presented, for example the non simultaneous integration of velocities and accelerations corresponding to time (t).

The development described in this paper shares many ideas with references [19]-[20] as for instance the opening of closed loops. However, the formulation presented here is strongly based on the characteristics of natural coordinates and it is simpler because it is more based on numerical analysis than in analytical expressions. However, a very good numerical efficiency has been achieved.

3.1. Open Loops: Basis of the Subspace of Allowable Velocities

The formulation presented in the first part of this paper states the equations of motion with a set of independent coordinates $\{z\}$, as indicated in equation (38). Notice that matrix [R] (defined in equation (15)) plays a fundamental role.

As it has been pointed out, the columns of matrix [R] constitute a basis of the nullspace of the jacobian matrix $[\Phi_q]$. Assuming that the constraint equations are independent of time (vector, $\{b\} = \{0\}$ in equation (14)), any set of velocities $\{\dot{q}\}$, compatible with the constraints of the mechanism, can be expressed as a linear combination of the columns of matrix [R]. Therefore, this matrix represents a basis of the subspace of allowable velocities of the mechanism. The coefficients of this linear combination are the independent velocities $\{\dot{z}\}$.

As it has been shown with the results in Table 1, the computation of matrix [R] is the most time consuming step, because it requires a Gaussian decomposition with as many forward and backward reductions as degrees of freedom the mechanism has. However, for open kinematic chains, using "natural coordinates" as dependent coordinates $\{q\}$ and relative coordinates defined in each joint as independent coordinates $\{z\}$, an expression for matrix [R] can be found explicitely.

The i-th column of matrix [R] defined in equation (38) represents the dependent velocities of the mechanism when $\dot{z}_i = 1$ and $\dot{z}_j = 0$, $j = i$. With this choice of dependent and independent coordinates, the i-th column can be seen as the velocities of all the points and unit vectors when the i-th joint has a unit angular velocity (revolute joint) or a unit linear velocity (prismatic joint). Notice that only the points and unit vectors between the i-th joint and the end of the branch have non-zero velocity. Then, the columns of matrix [R] can be computed in the following way:

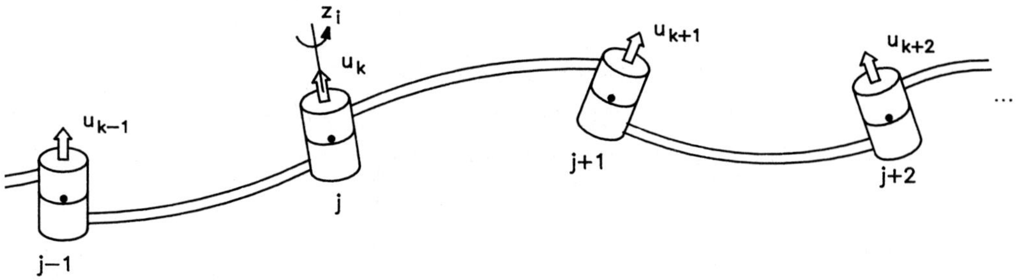

Figure 6. Unit angular velocity in a revolute pair

* **Revolute joint** (Figure 6)

$\dot{r}_p = 0$	$p = 1, \ldots, j$	(39a)
$\dot{r}_p = \dot{r}_{p-1} + u_k \wedge (r_p - r_{p-1})$	$p = j+1, \ldots, n$	(39b)
$\dot{u}_p = 0$	$p = 1, \ldots, k$	(40a)
$\dot{u}_p = u_k \wedge u_p$	$p = k+1, \ldots, m$	(40b)

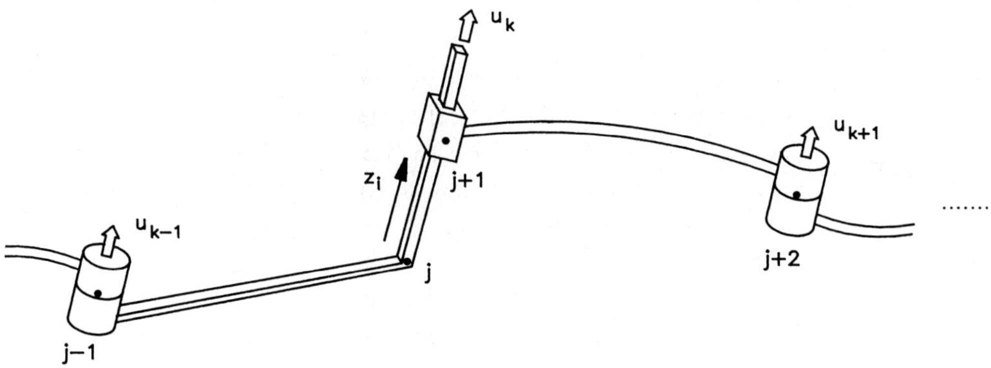

Figure 7. Unit velocity in a prismatic pair

* **Prismatic joint** (Figure 7)

$$\dot{r}_p = 0 \qquad p = 1, \ldots, j \tag{41a}$$

$$\dot{r}_p = u_k \qquad p = j+1, \ldots, n \tag{41b}$$

$$\dot{u}_p = 0 \qquad p = 1, \ldots, m \tag{42}$$

where (n) is the number of points and (m) is the number of unit vectors that define the mechanism. From the point of view of computational efficiency a few things can be pointed out:

- The vector of differences $(r_p - r_{p-1})$ needs to be calculated only once, just before the computation of matrix [R].
- Each column does not depend on the others, so the whole computation of matrix [R] can be easily parallelized.
- If the points and unit vectors are properly numbered matrix [R] is sparsely structured, which is an important point for the triple product $[R]^T[M][R]$ that appeared in equation (38).

3.2. Projection of the mass matrix

The mass matrix [M] of the whole mechanism is obtained by assembling the mass matrices $[M^e]$ of each link, given by equation (28). As matrices $[M^e]$ are constant, matrix [M] is also constant and it needs to be computed only once. Matrix [M] is symmetric and positive definite and can be decomposed as a product of a lower triangular matrix and its transpose,

$$[M] = [\bar{M}]\,[\bar{M}]^T \tag{43}$$

This decomposition is carried out at the beginning of the computation and, as it will be seen, greatly simplifies the projection of the mass matrix onto the subspace of allowable velocities

$$[R]^T[M][R] = [R]^T[\bar{M}][\bar{M}]^T[R] = [\bar{R}]^T[\bar{R}] \tag{44}$$

where,

$$[\bar{R}] = [\bar{M}]^T[R] \tag{45}$$

Using eq. (44) the number of arithmetic operations necessary to project the mass matrix, can be approximately halved.

3.3. Projection of forces

If vector {Q} in equation (38) is decomposed in a vector $\{\tau\}$ of motor forces (i.e. torques at revolute joints and linear forces at prismatic joints), and a vector {F} of applied forces (i.e.: gravity, damping, friction, etc.) the equations of motion can be rewritten as follows:

$$[R]^T[M][R]\{\ddot{z}\} = [R]^T(\{F\}-[M][S]\{c\}) + \{\tau\} \tag{46}$$

The term $[R]^T(\{F\}-[M][S]\{c\})$ represents the projection of the applied forces and the inertia forces that depend on the velocities onto the subspace of allowable velocities. Its computation can be done through equation (17), to compute vector [S]{c}, and then by forming the term ([M][S]{c}) and premultiplying it by $[R]^T$. Remember that [M] is a band matrix and [R] has sparse form, what can be taken into account to avoid unnecessary floating point operations.

Another way of computing the term $[R]^T(\{F\}-[M][S]\{c\})$ consists in solving the inverse dynamic problem with a zero fictitious acceleration: $\{\ddot{z}^*\} = 0$. Substituting into equation (45) one obtains:

$$\{\tau^*\} = [R]^T(\{F\} - [M]\,[S]\,\{c\}) \tag{47}$$

where $\{\tau^*\}$ are the motor forces corresponding to the acceleration $\{\ddot{z}^*\} = \{0\}$. The well known and very efficient Newton-Euler recursive formulation, with natural coordinates, is proposed in this paper to compute $\{\tau^*\}$. The expressions for the outward iterations to compute the accelerations of the points and unit vectors with $\{\ddot{z}^*\} = \{0\}$ are,

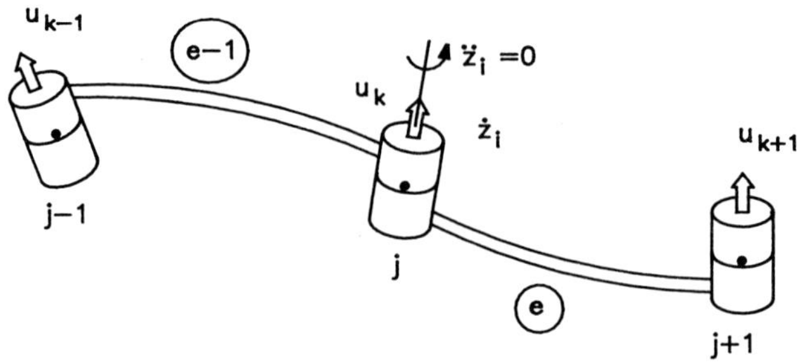

Figure 8. Motion propagation in a revolute pair

*** Revolute joint** (Figure 8)

$$\{w_e\} = \{w_{e-1}\} + \dot{z}_i \{u_k\} \tag{48}$$

$$\{\dot{w}_e\} = \{\dot{w}_{e-1}\} + \dot{z}_i \{\dot{u}_k\} \tag{49}$$

$$\{\dot{u}_{k+1}\} = \{w_e\} \Lambda \{u_{k+1}\} \tag{50}$$

$$\{\ddot{r}_{j+1}\} = \{\ddot{r}_j\} + \{\dot{w}_e\} \Lambda \{r_{j+1}-r_j\} + \{w_e\} \Lambda \left(\{w_e\} \Lambda \{r_{j+1}-r_j\}\right) \tag{51}$$

$$\{\ddot{u}_{k+1}\} = \{\dot{w}_e\} \Lambda \{u_{k+1}\} + \{w_e\} \Lambda \{\dot{u}_{k+1}\} \tag{52}$$

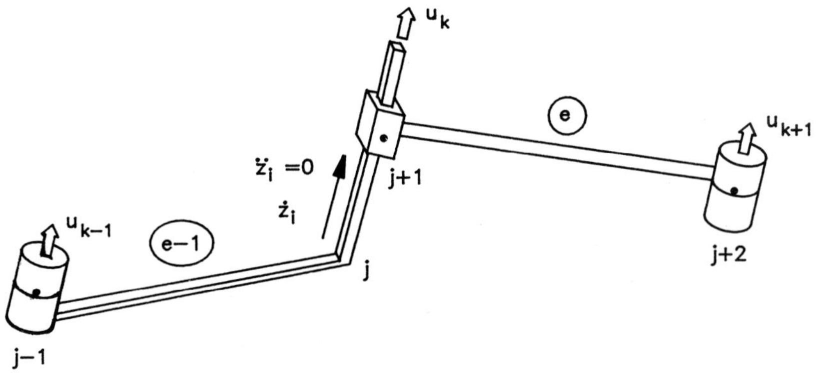

Figure 9. Motion propagation in a prismatic pair

* **Prismatic joint** (Figure 9)

$$\{w_e\} = \{w_{e-1}\} \tag{53}$$

$$\{\dot{w}_e\} = \{\dot{w}_{e-1}\} \tag{54}$$

$$\{\dot{u}_{k+1}\} = \{w_e\} \wedge \{u_{k+1}\} \tag{55}$$

$$\{\ddot{r}_{j+1}\} = \{\ddot{r}_j\} + \{\dot{w}_e\} \wedge \{r_{j+1}-r_j\} + \{w_e\} \wedge \big(\{w_e\} \wedge \{r_{j+i}-r_j\}\big) + 2\{w_e\} \wedge \dot{z}_i\{u_k\} \tag{56}$$

$$\{\ddot{r}_{j+2}\} = \{\ddot{r}_{j+1}\} + \{\dot{w}_e\} \wedge \{r_{j+2}-r_{j+1}\} + \{w_e\} \wedge \big(\{w_e\} \wedge \{r_{j+2}-r_{j+1}\}\big) \tag{57}$$

$$\{\ddot{u}_{k+1}\} = \{\dot{w}_e\} \wedge \{u_{k+1}\} + \{w_e\} \wedge \{\dot{u}_{k+i}\} \tag{58}$$

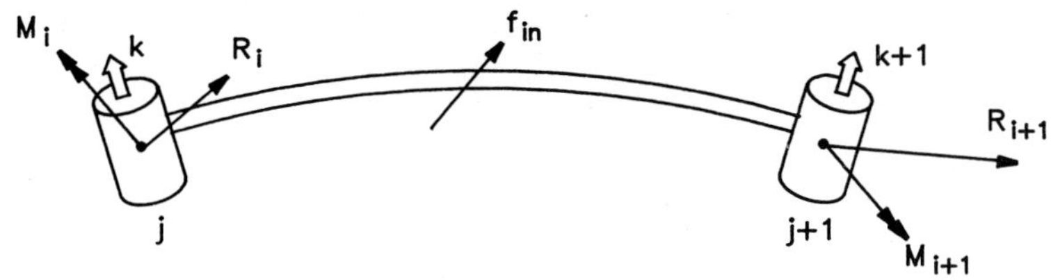

Figure 10. Propagation of forces in an element

Once the fictitious accelerations with $\{\ddot{z}^*\} = \{0\}$ have been obtained, the inertia forces of each element are computed, and the equations of dynamic equilibrium for each element can be stated in the following way. The inertia forces for link (e) are:

$$\begin{Bmatrix} f_{in}^{j} \\ f_{in}^{j+i} \\ f_{in}^{k} \\ f_{in}^{k+1} \end{Bmatrix} = \begin{bmatrix} M^e \end{bmatrix} \begin{Bmatrix} \ddot{r}_j \\ \ddot{r}_{j+1} \\ \ddot{u}_k \\ \ddot{u}_{k+1} \end{Bmatrix} \tag{59}$$

The equilibrium of forces and torques in element (e),

$$R_i = -(f_{ext})^e - (f_{in}^{j})^e - (f_{in}^{j+1})^e - R_{i+1} \tag{60}$$

$$M_i = -(M_{ext})^e - (r_{j+1}-r_j) \wedge \left[(f_{in}^{j+1})^e + R_{i+1} \right] -$$

$$-u_k \wedge (f_{in}^{k})^e - u_{k+1} \wedge (f_{in}^{k+1})^e - M_{i+1} \tag{61}$$

where R_i and M_i are the reaction force and reaction torque that link (e) apply on link (e-1) in point (j).

Notice that in equations (48)-(58) the terms $(r_{j+1}-r_j)$ need not to be computed because they were saved from a previous step (computation of matrix [R]).

3.4. Computation algorithm

According to the described formulation a new algorithm for the dynamic simulation is presented. Assume that the values of positions and velocities in time (t) are known, i.e. $\{q_t\}$ and $\{\dot{z}_t\}$. The following steps can be carried out:

1. Compute matrix [R] with expressions (39)-(42)

2. Compute the matrix product $[\bar{R}] = [M]^T [R]$

3. Compute $[R]^T[M][R]$ by multiplying $[\bar{R}]^T[\bar{R}]$

4. Solve the inverse dynamics using the recursive Newton-Euler formulation with fictitious accelerations $\{\ddot{z}^*\} = \{0\}$ to compute $\{\tau^*\}$

5. Solve for $\{\ddot{z}_t\}$ in the set of linear equations given by,

$$[R]^T[M][R]\{\ddot{z}_t\} = \{\tau\} - \{\tau^*\}$$

6. Compute $\{\dot{q}_t\}$ from $\{\dot{z}_t\}$

7. Numerically integrate $\{\ddot{z}_t\}$ and $\{\dot{q}_t\}$ to obtain $\{\dot{z}_{t+\Delta t}\}$ and $\{q_{t+\Delta t}\}$

8. $t = t + \Delta t$

9. Repeat from step 1.

3.5. Closed loop systems

Usually, closed loops are converted into open loops by removing a joint. Using natural coordinates joints are modelled with points and vectors that can be shared between contiguous elements, so to remove a joint implies to duplicate the variables shared at this joint. Because of this, with natural coordinates it is better to open a closed loop by removing a link, i.e., by removing the constraint equations that guarantee that the points and vectors of this link move according with the rigid body condition. According to fig. 11 the constant distance condition between points (i) and (i+1) and the three constant angle conditions between segment (i-i+1) and vectors $\{u_j\}$ and $\{u_{j+1}\}$ must be released.

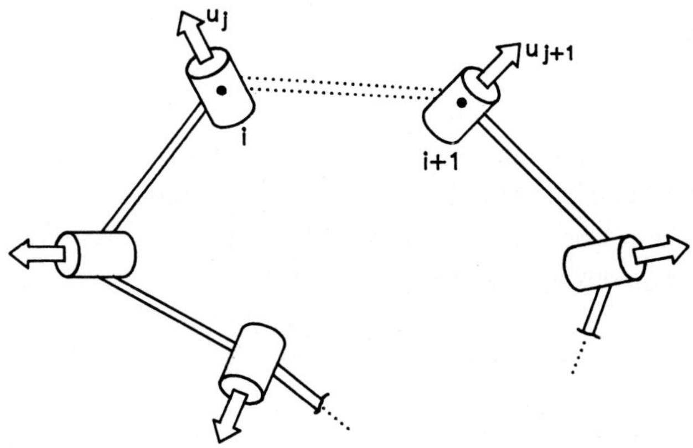

Figure 11. Elimination of a link in a closed loop

Denoting as $[\Phi^1_q]$ the jacobian matrix of the constraint equations corresponding to the open tree, and $[\Phi^2_q]$ the jacobian matrix of the loop closure constraints, eq.(35) can be written in the form,

$$\begin{bmatrix} [M] & [\Phi^1_q]^T & [\Phi^2_q]^T \\ [\Phi^1_q] & [\ 0\ ] & [\ 0\ ] \\ [\Phi^2_q] & [\ 0\ ] & [\ 0\ ] \end{bmatrix} \begin{Bmatrix} \{\ddot{q}\} \\ \{\lambda^1\} \\ \{\lambda^2\} \end{Bmatrix} = \begin{Bmatrix} \{Q\} \\ \{c^1\} \\ \{c^2\} \end{Bmatrix} \tag{62}$$

According to the method explained in 3.1. a matrix $[R^1]$ can be constructed that relates the dependent natural coordinates $\{q\}$ with the (also dependent in this case) joint coordinates $\{z\}$ can be constructed very easily. Then, eq. (17) transforms in,

$$\{\ddot{q}\} = [R^1]\{\ddot{z}\} + [S^1]\{c^1\} \tag{63}$$

Introducing eq.(63) into eq.(62), premultiplying by $[R^1]^T$ and taking into account that the columns of $[R^1]$ are orthogonal to the rows of $[\Phi^1_q]$, it is obtained:

$$\begin{bmatrix} [R^1]^T[M][R^1] & [R^1]^T[\Phi^2_q]^T \\ [\ \Phi^2_q\ ][\ R^1\ ] & [\quad 0 \quad] \end{bmatrix} \begin{Bmatrix} \{\ddot{z}\} \\ \{\lambda^2\} \end{Bmatrix} = \begin{Bmatrix} [R^1]^T\{Q\}-[R^1]^T[M][S^1]\{c^1\} \\ \{\ c^2\ \} - [\ \Phi^2_q\ ][\ S^1\ ]\{\ c^1\ \} \end{Bmatrix} \tag{64}$$

This equation is analogous to eq.(46) but with the loop closure constraints projected onto the space of open loop allowable velocities. The loop closure Lagrange multipliers $\{\lambda_2\}$ can also be eliminated projecting eq.(64) onto a basis $[R^2]$ of the nullspace of matrix $([\Phi^2_q]\ [R^1])$, but it is better to solve eq.(64) directly. It is convenient to consider that matrix $[\Phi^2_q]$ has non zero columns only in the positions corresponding to the points and vectors belonging to the eliminated link. On the other hand, the columns of $[R^1]$ contain non zero elements in the rows corresponding to the eliminated link, only if the columns corresponds with unit angular velocities in the joints of the loop that has been opened. It is very easy to take advantage of this sparsity and to formulate eq.(64) with a minimum number of arithmetic operations.

3.6. Dynamic examples solved with the improved formulation

The dynamic simulation of the 5R pendulum and 3 d.o.f. robot shown in Figure 5 has been carried out again using the new formulation. The results for the CPU time per integration step and the CPU time percentages are shown in Table 2.

Operation	5R pend.	Robot
- Form matrix $[R^1]$	3.33%	2.55%
- Compute $\{\dot{q}\}=[R^1]\{\dot{z}\}$	3.39%	5.95%
- Compute $[S^1]\{C^1\}$	4.28%	4.17%
- Compute $[R^1]^T(\{Q\}-[M][S^1]\{C'\})$	9.28%	20.36%
- Compute $[R^1]^T[M][R^1]$	48.98%	30.93%
- Compute $[\Phi_q]\ [R^1]$	---	5.57%
- Compute $\{C^2\}-[\Phi_q][S^1]\{C'\}$	---	---
- Solve $\begin{bmatrix} R^{1T}MR^1 & R^{1T} & \Phi^{2T} \\ \Phi_Q^2\ R^1 & & 0 \end{bmatrix}\begin{Bmatrix}\ddot{z}\\ \lambda^2\end{Bmatrix}=\begin{Bmatrix}Q\\ c\end{Bmatrix}$	1.70%	4.71%
- Integrate $\{\ddot{z},\dot{q}\}\rightarrow\{\dot{z},q\}_{t+\Delta t}$	29.04	25.76
CPU msec/step	2.05	1.65
CPU msec/step general purpose formulation	(23.01)	(6.67)

Table 2

The results contained in Table 2 show that a very important improvement in CPU times per integration step has been obtained with the new formulation. The new CPU figures are quite suitable for real-time dynamic simulation. Another very important point regarding to these results it that the bottleneck of the jacobian factorization and subsequent forward and backward substitutions has been removed; now most of the CPU time is spent in the product of matrices and in the inverse dynamic problem with zero independent accelerations. These operations are much more suitable for parallelization.

A further remark with respect to the time spent in the numerical integration: in these examples the DE routine of Shampine and Gordon has been used. This routine contains a variable order, variable step size Adams Moulton integrator with automatic error control. With the improved dynamic formulation the computations are so fast that the DE routine takes a very important percentage (more than a 25%) of the CPU time.

It is very likely that using a simpler integrator more suitable for real time simulation (such as an Adams-Moulton fixed formula) the CPU time per integration step will be reduced again.

4. CONCLUSIONS

A new kind of dependent fully cartesian coordinates has been described. The general purpose formulation based on these coordinates is very simple and efficient because the mass matrix is constant in the inertial reference frame, the jacobian matrix is very easy to evaluate and there are not velocity dependent inertia forces. Several general purpose dynamic formulations have been described. In order to get a further increasing in numerical efficiency the method has been modified according to the usual practice of removing constraints from the closed loops to open them and by developing a method efficient and easy to parallelize for the open loop system.

The new dynamic formulation has shown a very good numerical efficiency, far beyond the limits of real time behaviour. In addition to this the formulation fully maintains the simplicity, appealing and easy implementation of the standard formulation, with which keeps full compatibility.

5. ACKNOWLEDGMENTS

The authors acknowledge the support of the NATO Scientific Affairs Division under the Research Grant No. 0877/87

6. REFERENCES

1 Paul, B. "Analytical Dynamics of Mechanisms - A Computer Oriented Overview", Mechanism and Machine Theory, vol. 10, pp. 481-507, 1975.

2 Haug, E.J. (ed.). "Computer Aided Analysis and Optimization of Mechanical System Dynamics", Springer-Verlag, 1984.

3 Bae, D.-S., Hwang, R.S. and Haug, E.J., "A Recursive Formulation for Real-Time

Dynamic Simulation", ASME Conference on Advances in Design Automation, 1988.

4 Schiehlen, W.O., "Dynamics of Complex Multibody Systems", SM Archives, vol. 9, pp.159-195, 1984.

5 Rosenthal, D.E. and Sherman, M.A., "High Performance Multibody Simulations Via Symbolic Equation Manipulation and Kane's Method", The Journal of the Astronautical Sciences, vol. 34, pp. 223-239, 1986.

6 Vilallonga, G., Unda, J. and García de Jalón, J., "Numerical Kinematic Analysis of Three-Dimensional Mechanism Using a Natural System of Dependent Coordinates", ASME Paper No. 84-DET-199, 1984.

7 García de Jalón, J., Unda, J. and Avello, A., "Natural Coordinates for the Computer Analysis of Three-Dimensional Multibody Systems", Computer Methods in Applied Mechanics and Engineering, vol. 56, pp. 309-327, 1986.

8 García de Jalón, J., Unda, J., Avello, A. and Jiménez, J.M., "Dynamic Analysis of Three-Dimensional Mechanisms in Natural Coordinates", ASME J. on Mechanisms, Transmissions and Automation in Design, vol. 109, pp. 460-465, 1987.

9 Unda, J., García de Jalón, J., Losantos, F. and Emparantza, R., "A Comparative Study on Some Different Formulations of the Dynamic Equations of Constrained Mechanical Systems", ASME J. of Mechanisms, Transmissions and Automation in Design, vol. 109, pp. 466-474, 1987.

10 Nikravesh, P.E., "Computer-Aided Analysis of Mechanical Systems", Prentice-Hall, 1988.

11 Mani, N.K., Haug, E.J. and Atkinson, K.E., "Application of Singular Value Decomposition for Analysis of Mechanical System Dynamics", ASME J. on Mechanisms, Transmissions and Automation in Design, vol. 107, pp. 82-87, 1985.

12 Kim, S.S. and Vanderploeg, M.J., "QR Decomposition for State Space Representation of Constrained Mechanical Dynamic Systems", ASME J. on Mechanisms, Transmissions and Automation in Design, vol. 108, pp. 176-182, 1986.

13 Baumgarte, J., "Stabilization of Constraints and Integrals of Motion in Dynamical Systems", Computer Methods in Applied Mechanics and Engineering, vol. 1, pp. 1-16, 1972.

14 Armstrong, W.W., "Recursive Solution to the Equations of Motion of an N Link Manipulator", proc. 5th World Congress on the Theory of Machines and Mechanisms, pp. 1343-46, Montreal, July, 1979.

15 Featherstone, R., "Robot Dynamics Algorithms", Kluwer Academic Publishers, 1987.

16 Bae, D.-S. and Haug, E.J. "A Recursive Formulation for Constrained Mechanical Systems Dynamics: Part I. Open Loop Systems", Mech. Struct. and Mach., vol. 15, pp. 359-382, 1987.

17 Bae, D.-S. and Haug, E.J., "A Recursive Formulation for Constrained Mechanical Systems Dynamics: Part II. Closed Loop Systems", Mech. Struct. and Mach., vol. 15,

pp. 481-506, 1988.

18 Wehage, R.A., "Application of Matrix Partitioning and Recursive Projection to 0(n) Solution of Constrained Equations of Motion", Trends and Developments in Mechanisms, Machines and Robotics, vol. Two, ASME, pp. 221-230, 1988.

19 Bae, D.-S., Hwang, R.S. and Haug, E.J., "A Recursive Formulation for Real-Time Dynamic Simulation", Advances in Design Automation, ASME, pp. 499-508, 1988.

20 Hwang, R.S., Bae, D.-S., Haug, E.J. and Kuhl, J.G., "Parallel Processing for Real-Time Dynamics System Simulation", Advances in Design Automation, ASME, pp. 509-518, 1988.

On the GAUSS Principle in the Numerical Integration of Mechanical Systems

S. Sparschuh and P. Hagedorn
Institut für Mechanik, TH Darmstadt
West Germany

1 Introduction: The GAUSS Principle

Here we consider mechanical systems with their configuration described by the in general non-minimal coordinates $q_1, q_2, \ldots, q_n$, which we arrange in a column matrix as $\mathbf{q} := (q_1, q_2, \ldots, q_n)^T$. The system is subjected to constraints of the form

$$c_i(\mathbf{q}, \dot{\mathbf{q}}, t) = 0, \quad i = 1, 2, \ldots, m \tag{1}$$

which we also write as

$$\mathbf{c}(\mathbf{q}, \dot{\mathbf{q}}, t) := (c_1, c_2, \ldots, c_m)^T = \mathbf{0}. \tag{2}$$

If the constraints do not depend on $\dot{\mathbf{q}}$, differentiation of (1) with respect to the time t leads to

$$\mathbf{b}_i^T(\mathbf{q}, t)\,\dot{\mathbf{q}} + b_{oi}(\mathbf{q}, t) = 0, \quad i = 1, 2, \ldots, m, \tag{3}$$

and an additional differentiation gives

NATO ASI Series, Vol. F 69
Real-Time Integration Methods for Mechanical System Simulation
Edited by E. J. Haug and R. C. Deyo

$$\mathbf{b}_i^T(\mathbf{q},\ t)\ \ddot{\mathbf{q}} + \dot{\mathbf{q}}^T \frac{\partial \mathbf{b}_i}{\partial \mathbf{q}} \dot{\mathbf{q}} + \left[\frac{\partial \mathbf{b}_i^T}{\partial t} + \frac{\partial b_{oi}}{\partial \mathbf{q}} \right] \dot{\mathbf{q}} + \frac{\partial b_{oi}}{\partial t} = 0, \quad i=1,2,\ldots,m. \tag{4}$$

If $\dot{\mathbf{q}}$ is contained in (1) (this holds particularly for nonholonomic systems) we assume that this function is linear in $\dot{\mathbf{q}}$, i.e. it is of the type (3) and we again arrive at (3), (4).

We now compare different vectors $\ddot{\mathbf{q}}$ compatible with the constraint (4) and corresponding to the same values of $\mathbf{q}$, $\dot{\mathbf{q}}$ and t. If they differ by $\Delta\ddot{\mathbf{q}}$ we have from (4)

$$\mathbf{b}_i^T \Delta\ddot{\mathbf{q}}_i = 0, \quad ,i = 1,\ 2,\ldots,m. \tag{5}$$

With $\mathbf{f}^*$ as the vector of the *generalized active forces*, i.e. all the forces but the forces of constraint, we define the function

$$G := \frac{1}{2}\ (\ \mathbf{f}^* - \mathbf{M}\ddot{\mathbf{q}}\ )^T\ \mathbf{M}^{-1}\ (\ \mathbf{f}^* - \mathbf{M}\ddot{\mathbf{q}}\ ), \tag{6}$$

where $\mathbf{M}$ is the inertia matrix, possibly depending on $\mathbf{q}$. GAUSS showed in 1829 that the function G is minimized with respect to $\ddot{\mathbf{q}}$ for the true motion of the system if $\mathbf{q}$, $\dot{\mathbf{q}}$ and t are unchanged and only changes $\Delta\ddot{\mathbf{q}}$ satisfying (5) are taken into account. The *GAUSS principle* was originally proved for systems of point masses, the matrix $\mathbf{M}$ then being diagonal and constant, but it can easily be generalized to a much larger class of systems.

We now show that one indeed recovers the NEWTON-EULER equations from GAUSS' principle. The change in G is given by

$$\Delta G := \frac{1}{2} \left[\mathbf{f}^* - \mathbf{M} \left(\ddot{\mathbf{q}} + \Delta\ddot{\mathbf{q}} \right) \right]^T \mathbf{M}^{-1} \left[\mathbf{f}^* - \mathbf{M} \left(\ddot{\mathbf{q}} + \Delta\ddot{\mathbf{q}} \right) \right]$$
$$- \frac{1}{2} \left[\mathbf{f}^* - \mathbf{M} \ddot{\mathbf{q}} \right]^T \mathbf{M}^{-1} \left[\mathbf{f}^* - \mathbf{M} \ddot{\mathbf{q}} \right] \tag{7}$$

or

$$\Delta G = \frac{1}{2} (\Delta\ddot{\mathbf{q}})^T \mathbf{M} \Delta\ddot{\mathbf{q}} - \left[\mathbf{f}^* - \mathbf{M} \ddot{\mathbf{q}} \right]^T \Delta\ddot{\mathbf{q}}. \tag{8}$$

If ΔG assumes a minimum with respect to $\Delta\ddot{\mathbf{q}}$, one must have

$$\left[\mathbf{f}^* - \mathbf{M} \ddot{\mathbf{q}} \right]^T \Delta\ddot{\mathbf{q}} = 0, \quad \forall \Delta\ddot{\mathbf{q}}, \quad \mathbf{b}_i^T \Delta\ddot{\mathbf{q}} = 0, \quad i = 1, 2, \ldots, m. \tag{9}$$

The expression in brackets on the left hand side of (9) being orthogonal to the $\Delta\ddot{\mathbf{q}}$ which is orthogonal to the $\mathbf{b}_i$, $i=1,2,\ldots,m$, must itself be in the span$(b_1, b_2, \ldots, b_m)$, so that one has

$$\mathbf{f}^* - \mathbf{M} \ddot{\mathbf{q}} = - \mathbf{f}_c \tag{10}$$

with

$$\mathbf{f}_c = \lambda_1 \mathbf{b}_1 + \lambda_2 \mathbf{b}_2 + \ldots + \lambda_m \mathbf{b}_m. \tag{11}$$

The coefficents $\lambda_1, \lambda_2, \ldots, \lambda_m$ are the well known *LAGRANGE multipliers* and $\mathbf{f}_c$ represents the forces of constraint. From (10) one recovers the NEWTON-EULER equations

$$\mathbf{M} \ddot{\mathbf{q}} = \mathbf{f}^* + \mathbf{f}_c. \tag{12}$$

2 Time discretization in the GAUSS principle

The GAUSS principle can not only be used to generate the equations of motion, which can then be numerically integrated, but a discretization can also be performed directly in the function G, leading to an efficient numerical scheme for the computation of the motion, without making use of the equations of motion. In what follows we outline this idea in its simplest form. First the time t is discretized as

$$t = k\,\Delta t, \qquad k \in \mathbb{Z} \tag{13}$$

and similarly the coordinates and the active forces are written in discretized form as

$$\mathbf{q}_k := \mathbf{q}(k\,\Delta t), \qquad \mathbf{f}_k^* := \mathbf{f}^*(k\,\Delta t). \tag{14}$$

A TAYLOR series expansion gives

$$\mathbf{q}_k = \mathbf{q}_{k+1} - \Delta t\,\dot{\mathbf{q}}_{k+1} + \frac{1}{2}(\Delta t)^2\,\ddot{\mathbf{q}}_{k+1} - \ldots, \tag{15a}$$

$$\mathbf{q}_{k-1} = \mathbf{q}_{k+1} - 2\,\Delta t\,\dot{\mathbf{q}}_{k+1} + \frac{1}{2}(2\,\Delta t)^2\,\ddot{\mathbf{q}}_{k+1} - \ldots, \tag{15b}$$

and solution with respect to $\dot{\mathbf{q}}_{k+1}$ leads to

$$\dot{\mathbf{q}}_{k+1} \approx \frac{1}{2\,\Delta t}(3\mathbf{q}_{k+1} - 4\mathbf{q}_k + \mathbf{q}_{k-1}). \tag{16a}$$

In a similar manner one also obtains

$$\ddot{\mathbf{q}}_{k+1} \approx \frac{1}{(\Delta t)^2}(\mathbf{q}_{k+1} - 2\mathbf{q}_k + \mathbf{q}_{k-1}). \tag{16b}$$

Note that a non-central difference quotient was used in (16a) in order that $\dot{\mathbf{q}}_{k+1}$ not depend on $\mathbf{q}_{k+2}$. With (16b) the discretized form of (6) is

$$G := \frac{1}{2}\,\mathbf{q}_{k+1}^T \mathbf{M}\,\mathbf{q}_{k+1} - \mathbf{q}_{k+1}^T\left[\mathbf{M}\,(2\mathbf{q}_k - \mathbf{q}_{k-1}) + (\Delta t)^2\,\mathbf{f}_k^*\right] \tag{17}$$

and for given $\mathbf{q}_{k-1}$, $\mathbf{q}_k$ the value of $\mathbf{q}_{k+1}$ can be obtained by solving the minimization problem

$$\min_{q_{k+1}} G \quad c(q_{k+1}, q_k, q_{k-1}, k+1) = 0. \tag{18}$$

With the definition

$$C := \frac{\partial c}{\partial q_{k+1}}, \tag{19}$$

where C is a mxn matrix, this leads to

$$q_{k+1} = q_k + \left[M^{-1} - M^{-1}C^T(CM^{-1}C^T)^{-1}CM^{-1} \right] \left[M\,(q_k - q_{k-1}) + (\Delta t)^2 f_k^* \right] \tag{20}$$

if the equations of constraint are linearized in q_{k+1}. In the special case of an unconstrained system this simplifies to the elementary formula

$$q_{k+1} = 2q_k - q_{k-1} - M^{-1}(\Delta t)^2 f_k^*. \tag{21}$$

3 An example

Consider the simple example of the mathematical pendulum depicted in Fig.1, with n=2 and the constraint

$$c(q, t) = q^T q - l^2 = 0. \tag{22}$$

This leads to

$$q^T \dot{q} = 0 \tag{23}$$

in the time derivative of **q**. In the numerical integration given by (20) the motion is decribed by an elementary step along the tangent to a circle during

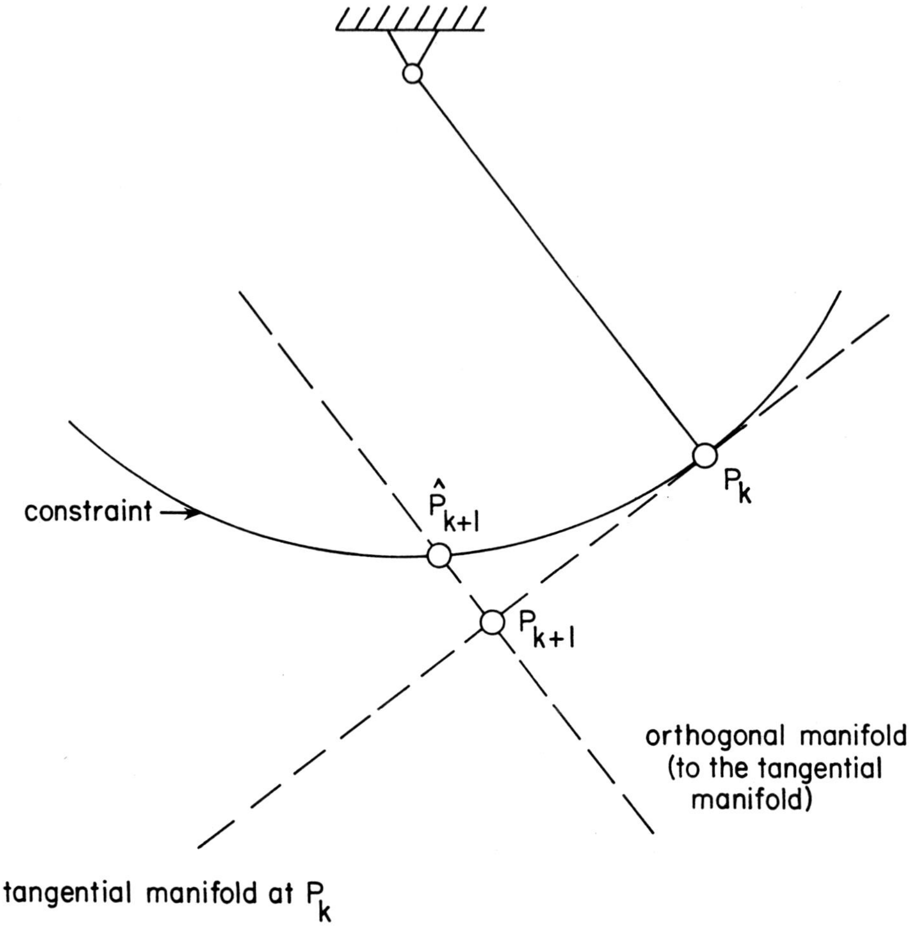
constraint
$\hat{P}_{k+1}$
P_k
P_{k+1}
orthogonal manifold
(to the tangential
manifold)
tangential manifold at P_k

Figure 1

each time interval Δt and these errors may accumulate and lead to an inadmissible large deviation from the constraint (22), originally given in the coordinates and not in the velocities. For the general case this can be seen directly from (20) by multiplying with $\mathbf{C}$. This results in $\mathbf{C}(\mathbf{q}_{k+1}-\mathbf{q}_k)=0$, which means that the motion from $\mathbf{q}_k$ to $\mathbf{q}_{k+1}$ is in the space tangential to $\mathbf{c}(\cdot)=0$. It is therefore convenient after each step given by (18), where the point in Fig.1 moves *perpendicularly to the vector* $\mathbf{q}$, to add a step in which the point moves *in the direction of* $\mathbf{q}$ so as to bring the particle back to the circle of radius l:

$$\hat{q}_{k+1}= q_{k+1}+ v\, q_{k+1}. \tag{24}$$

The value of v is determined by the requirement that $\hat{\mathbf{q}}_{k+1}$ fullfill the constraint $\hat{\mathbf{q}}^T_{k+1}\hat{q}_k-l^2=0$, i.e.

$$\hat{q}^2_{k+1} + 2v\, \hat{q}^2_{k+1}+ v^2\hat{q}^2_{k+1}- l^2= 0. \tag{25}$$

Linearization with respect to v gives

$$v = (l^2 - q^2_{k+1}) \;/\; 2q^2_{k+1}. \tag{26}$$

Numerical tests with the pendulum and with other examples showed that this correction gives excellent results.

In the general case (24) is substituted by

$$\hat{q}_{k+1}= q_{k+1}+ C^T(q_{k+1})\; \mathbf{v}, \tag{27}$$

which, substituted in the constraint equations gives

$$\mathbf{c}\;[\, q_{k+1}+ C^T(q_{k+1})\; \mathbf{v}\,] = 0. \tag{28}$$

Linearization now leads to

$$\mathbf{c}(\mathbf{q}_{k+1}) + C(\mathbf{q}_{k+1})\, C^T(q_{k+1})\, \mathbf{v} + o(\mathbf{v}) = 0, \tag{29}$$

finally giving

$$\hat{q}_{k+1} = \mathbf{q}_{k+1} - C^T (\, C\, C^T)^{-1} c(\mathbf{q}_{k+1}). \tag{30}$$

In the determination of the motion of a constrained system each integration step of the type (20) should be followed by a correction step (30), which is similar to a NEWTON-EULER step for the determination of the zeroes of a given funtion. In contrast to the NEWTON-EULER algorithm here propagation is restricted to the orthogonal space (by means of the non-quadratic matrix **C**).

4 Conclusions

In this note we discussed the possibility of using a time discretization before applying the GAUSS principle, which is particularly suitable for systems containing costraints of the implicit type. In particular, also systems of rigid bodies of a non-tree structure can be treated in this manner. Each time step along the tangent to the constraint manifold is followed by a step orthogonal to this manifold, in order to assure the fullfillment of the constraint equations. The algorithm is extremely simple if non-minimal coordinates are used. Of course also some of the constraints can be used beforehand to eliminate some of the coordinates. In this case only the function G has to be expressed accordingly. In place of the simple finite difference quotients used in this note, also more elaborate quotients can of course be applied. The authors believe that such direct methods of obtaining the motion of constrained mechanical systems can be quite useful in solving problems of rigid body dynamics.

Simultaneous Derivation of Control Laws and of Dynamical Model Equations for Controlled Mechanisms

M. Cotsaftis

UGRA
CEN-FAR BP No 6
92260 Fontenay aux Roses, France

C. Vibet

Laboratoire de Robotique Industrielle
22 Allee J. Rostand
91011 Evy Cedex, France

Abstract

This report introduces generating rules for direct derivation from the Lagrangian of mechanisms of the nonlinear control algorithms which lead to output decoupling and feedback linearization of the dynamics. No derivative with respect to the time is needed. Examples are provided and it is shown that the mechanical dynamical model can also be derived from the nonlinear control laws.

Keywords

Decoupling method, Lagrange's formalism, control law generation.

INTRODUCTION

In today's available codes devoted to computer analysis of mechanical system dynamics [1-3], the dynamical model is used to derive the convenient feedback laws to be implemented in the controlled system [1,4-9]. In Robotics, the Nonlinear Decoupling Method is usually implemented to do that, but both large amounts of symbolic computations and costly running programs result while there is no simple physical meaning for the designer in such a process. In an alternate design strategy, this paper shows how the nonlinear feedback laws to be implemented in a controlled mechanical system can be directly derived from the Lagrangian itself [10,11] while the dynamical model is not explicitly needed in the analysis. In addition, it will be shown that the no-controlled dynamical model can be built from the control laws, so that the proposed methodology appears as an

NATO ASI Series, Vol. F 69
Real-Time Integration Methods for Mechanical System Simulation
Edited by E. J. Haug and R. C. Deyo

interesting technique for the design of efficient simulation codes devoted to controlled mechanisms.

More precisely, the first task of most codes is to allow the computer to carry out an automatic formulation of mechanisms through the use of Euler-Lagrange's equations, for example. It generally results in a set of algebraic differential equations which describes the dynamical model with constraint equations results. In addition, because most of mechanisms must be controlled, a specific controller is to be designed in such a way that the dynamics of the resulting system can be chosen arbitrarily. Introduced by Freund in the robotic area [4], the Nonlinear Decoupling Method is an efficient procedure to derive automatically the nonlinear feedback laws which lead to decoupled controls, exact linearization and pole assignment for any dynamical systems. However, it is to be noted that this technique requires the knowledge of motion equations of mechanisms to establish the nonlinear feedback laws which are to be written in a state space representation. This makes its application somewhat tedious for relatively complicated systems.

In an opposite design strategy, the feedback control laws to be implemented in a combined control and mechanical system will be directly derived from the Lagrangian itself [10]. So, the dynamical model of the system is not needed in the synthesis process while the required amount of calculations is reduced with respect to the usual method. This approach, called the Direct Nonlinear Decoupling Method (DNDM), takes advantage of the fact that Euler-Lagrange's equations and the common formulation of the Nonlinear Decoupling Method can be combined together. This leads to new formulaes or generating rules which give in an explicit and analytic form, the control algorithms in terms of the Lagrangian and of output equations only. In addition this formulation permits the derivation of dynamical equations of a mechanism from its control laws, so that a specific code involving these principles can be built to run on a small computer.

This paper presents the derivation of generating rules giving output decoupling and pole assignment for controlled mechanical systems. Principles involved in the derivation of control laws and dynamical equations of controlled mechanisms are introduced. Next, a phase-plane dynamical model of mechanisms and the phase-plane form of Euler-Lagrange's equations are given. The generating rules of feedback laws are established and the case of dissipative systems is investigated. The pole assignment problem is analysed and some illustrative examples are treated. The proposed methodology is next generalized to the case of dynamically driven mechanisms and the last part of the report investigates mechanical shock effects in terms of initial conditions.

I-DESIGN PHILOSOPHY OF THE GENERATING RULES

In this part the principles involved in the derivation of the generating rules [10-12] are outlined. Basically the proposed method works from the Lagrangian and output equations of the system. Next, use is made of a state space representation of Euler-Lagrange's formalism, i.e. a state-space generalized momentum equation or eventually a generalized phase-plane representation, from which the analytic form of nonlinear feedback laws are to be derived. After the application of the nonlinear decoupling method to find output decoupling and feedback linearization, a set of generating rules is obtained which involves the Lagrangian and output equations, i.e. the generalized coordinates vector to be controlled, as the Cartesian or the joint coordinates vector, for example. Many interesting features result from application of this new methodology. In particular, the generating rules can be successfully applied without even knowing the Nonlinear Decoupling Method and Euler-Lagrange's equations. The only mathematic tools required to derive control laws are essentially based on partial derivatives and matrix calculus while no derivative with respect to the time is needed in such a process. In addition, the methodology used to find the generating rules can be generalized to systems of any order such as mechanisms, dynamically driven mechanisms, compliant systems and dynamically driven compliant-systems, for example.

In the following, the control law synthesis of controlled mechanisms is investigated by means of a phase-plane approach for (i) a joint space model, (ii) a cartesian model and (iii) a phase-plane representation of Lagrange's equations.

II-PHASE-PLANE REPRESENTATION OF MECHANISMS

This part is concerned with mechanisms, i.e. stiff systems in which the dynamics of motors is not taken into account. Here, the joint and Cartesian space dynamical models, and Euler-Lagrange's formalism are written by means of a (nx1) generalized phase-plane representation. The usual joint-space model of a multi-body mechanism, such as a robot, is given by

$$A(q)\ddot{q} + B(q,\dot{q}) + g(q) = T \tag{1}$$

where **q** represents the joint coordinates of the mechanism, **A(q)** is the inertia matrix, $\mathbf{B}(\mathbf{q},\dot{\mathbf{q}})$ represents the Coriolis plus centripetal torque, **g(q)** is the gravity torque while **T** represents the generalized force applied to joints. On the other hand, the Cartesian dynamical of a robot model is

$$A(X)'\ddot{X} + B'(X,\dot{X}) + G(X) = F, \tag{2}$$

where **F** represents the cartesian driving force applied to the end-effector of the robot, i.e. for a stiff system $\mathbf{F} = \mathbf{J}^{-T}\mathbf{T}$, where **J(q)** is the Jacobian matrix of the system. Eqn(2) results, for example, from application of Euler-Lagrange's formalism to the Lagrangian L of a mechanical system. This formalism is defined by

$$\frac{d}{dt}\left(\frac{\partial L}{\partial \mathbf{p}}\right) - \frac{\partial L}{\partial \mathbf{q}} = T, \tag{3}$$

where $\mathbf{p} = d\mathbf{q}/dt$.

Now let us consider a generalized phase-plane form of both eqn(1,2) and Euler-Lagrange's formalism. A phase-plane representation of the joint space dynamical eqn(1) is

$$\dot{q} = p$$

$$\dot{p} = A^{-1}(q)[-B(q,p) - g(q) + T]. \tag{4}$$

When considering the cartesian coordinate speed of the end-link of the mechanism, the output-velocity coordinates are then described by the vector

$$\dot{Y} = J(q)\,p, \tag{5}$$

where **J(q)** represents the Jacobian matrix of the system. Naturally, when considering the joint variables **q** as the controller outputs, the output equation is to be written as

$$Y = q. \tag{6}$$

Alternatively, the phase-plane representation of the cartesian dynamical model of a mechanism can be easily derived from eqn(2) as

$$\dot{X} = \Phi$$
$$\dot{\Phi} = A'^{-1}[-B'(X,\Phi) - G(X) + F\,], \tag{7}$$

while the cartesian outputs of the system are defined by

$$Y = X. \tag{8}$$

Finally, a phase-plane representation of Euler-Lagrange's equations is

$$\dot{q} = p$$
$$\dot{p} = \left(\frac{\partial P}{\partial p}\right)^{-1} \left[\frac{\partial L}{\partial q} - \frac{\partial P}{\partial q} p + T \right] \tag{9}$$

where the generalized canonical-momentum vector **P**, which is derived from the Lagrangian, is defined by

$$P = \frac{\partial L}{\partial p}, \tag{10}$$

and its derivative with respect to t is

$$\dot{P} = \frac{\partial P}{\partial q} p + \frac{\partial P}{\partial p} \dot{p}. \tag{11}$$

The cartesian output **Y** is defined from its first derivative as

$$\dot{Y} = J(q)\, p. \tag{12}$$

All these three phase-plane representations can be written in a single canonical form defined by

$$\dot{Z} = F(Z) + H(Z)\, U(t). \tag{13}$$

For example, by writing in its canonical form the phase-plane representation of the joint dynamical model of a mechanism given by eqn(4), one gets

$$F(Z) = \begin{bmatrix} p \\ A^{-1}[-B(q,q)-g(q)] \end{bmatrix}, \quad H(Z) = \begin{bmatrix} 0 & 0 \\ 0 & A^{-1} \end{bmatrix}, \quad U(t) = \begin{bmatrix} 0 \\ T \end{bmatrix}. \tag{14}$$

Alternatively, when considering the cartesian model of a dynamical system, one gets

$$F(Z) = \begin{bmatrix} \dot{X} \\ A'^{-1}[-B'(X,\dot{X})-G(X)] \end{bmatrix}, \quad H(Z) = \begin{bmatrix} 0 & 0 \\ 0 & A'^{-1} \end{bmatrix}, \quad U(t) = \begin{bmatrix} 0 \\ F \end{bmatrix}. \tag{15}$$

Finally, the canonical phase-plane representation of Euler-Lagrange's eqns(9) can be derived from eqn(13) with

$$F(Z) = \begin{bmatrix} p \\ \left(\frac{\partial P}{\partial p}\right)^{-1} \left[\frac{\partial L}{\partial q} - \frac{\partial P}{\partial q} p \right] \end{bmatrix}, \quad H(Z) = \begin{bmatrix} 0 & 0 \\ 0 & \left(\frac{\partial P}{\partial p}\right)^{-1} \end{bmatrix}, \quad U(t) = \begin{bmatrix} 0 \\ T \end{bmatrix}. \tag{16}$$

Because all previous equations can be put into the same canonical form, the design of a controller can be analysed in a general manner from such a specific dynamical equation. Moreover, it could be shown that eqn(13) is a very efficient formulation to derive initial conditions resulting from the application of step or impulse commands on the system. In the following, the nonlinear decoupling method is directly applied to eqn(13).

III-EXPLICIT CONTROL LAWS SYNTHESIS FOR LAGRANGIAN SYSTEMS

In many applications, it is important to design dynamical decoupled systems in which one output obeys to one and only one input. In addition, the linearity of the input-output relationship is also required to permit, for example, a more easy off-line construction of trajectories. Though not easy to solve in the general case of multivariable nonlinear systems, these two problems can be simultaneously solved in using the Nonlinear Decoupling Method (NLDM). Essentially, this method allows to derive systematically the appropriate control laws giving simultaneously output decoupling and exact linearization by nonlinear feedback [12] of dyamical systems with constant parameters.

In fact, because mechanisms are modelled by second-order nonlinear and strongly coupled differential equations, the direct application of the nonlinear decoupling method represents a paramount task. In particular a state space representation of the dynamical model is required so that many computer calculations results. To simplify this synthesis problem, it is interesting to look at mechanisms only at the level of Euler-Lagrange's equations in using their canonical phase-plane representation. This leads to a set of analytic and explicit generating rules of the nonlinear control laws which are to be implemented in the controlled mechanical systems. The generating rules are derived as follows. Starting from a mechanical described by its Lagrangian, a particular methodology is used to avoid an explicit expansion of the dynamical model of the system in terms of differential equations. Namely, Euler-Lagrange's formalism is written in a particular form which allows the direct application on it of the NLDM. This is realized when eqn(3) is cast in the form of eqn(13), i.e.

$$\dot{\mathbf{Z}} = \mathbf{F}(\mathbf{Z}) + \mathbf{H}(\mathbf{Z})\ \mathbf{U}(t), \tag{17}$$

where

$$\mathbf{F}(\mathbf{Z}) = \mathrm{col}[\mathbf{p},\ \left(\frac{\partial \mathbf{P}}{\partial \mathbf{p}}\right)^{-1} \left(\frac{\partial \mathbf{L}}{\partial \mathbf{q}} - \frac{\partial \mathbf{P}}{\partial \mathbf{q}}\ \mathbf{p}\right)], \tag{18}$$

and with

$$\mathbf{Z} = \mathrm{col}(\mathbf{q},\dot{\mathbf{q}}),\quad \mathbf{H}(\mathbf{Z}) = \mathrm{diag}[0,\left(\frac{\partial \mathbf{P}}{\partial \mathbf{p}}\right)^{-1}],\quad \text{and}\quad \mathbf{U}(t) = \mathrm{col}(0,\mathbf{T}). \tag{19}$$

To design a controller, the outputs of interest which are to be decoupled are defined by

$$\mathbf{Y} = \mathbf{C}(\mathbf{Z}), \tag{20}$$

where **C(Z)** is a nonlinear vector depending upon **Z**. In usual cases, the outputs are such that **Y** = **C(q)**, and as expected, the decoupled controls can only be obtained when dim(**Y**) = dim(**T**), for example nx1. Theory shows that the feedback law solution, the implementation of which leads to output decoupling and linearization, has the following form:

$$\mathbf{U}(t) = \boldsymbol{\alpha}(\mathbf{Z}) + \boldsymbol{\beta}(\mathbf{Z})\ \mathbf{W}(t), \tag{21}$$

where **W**(t) represents the (nx1) input vector of the controlled mechanical system and

$$(2n\times 1)\qquad \boldsymbol{\alpha}(\mathbf{Z}) = \begin{bmatrix} \alpha_1 \\ \alpha_2 \end{bmatrix},\qquad \text{and}\qquad (n\times n)\qquad \boldsymbol{\beta}(\mathbf{Z}) = \begin{bmatrix} \beta_1 & 0 \\ 0 & \beta_2 \end{bmatrix}, \tag{22}$$

are to be computed. The synthesis of the control law is obtained by taking the successive derivatives of the ith output $\mathbf{Y}_i$ with respect to t. Because mechanisms are modelled by second-order differential equations, two derivatives are to be computed. One gets first:

$$\dot{Y}_i = \frac{\partial c_i}{\partial Z} F(Z), \qquad \text{because} \qquad \frac{\partial c_i}{\partial Z}(Z)\, H(Z) = 0. \tag{23}$$

To the next order, the output derivative is

$$\ddot{Y}_i = \frac{\partial}{\partial Z}\left[\frac{\partial c_i}{\partial Z}(Z)\, F(Z)\right] [F(Z) + H(Z)\, U(t)]. \tag{24}$$

Substituting for **U**(t) from eqn(21) into eqn(24), $\alpha(\mathbf{Z})$ and $\beta(\mathbf{Z})$ are obtained by exactly linearizing eqn(24) when

$$\frac{\partial}{\partial Z}\left[\frac{\partial c_i}{\partial Z} F(Z)\right] [F(Z) + H(Z)\, \alpha(Z)] = 0, \tag{25}$$

and

$$\frac{\partial}{\partial Z}\left[\frac{\partial c_i}{\partial Z} F(Z)\right] H(Z)\beta(Z) = 1. \tag{26}$$

Because decoupled outputs and exact linearization are simultaneously obtained when the input-output relationship is written as

$$\ddot{Y}_i = W_i, \tag{27}$$

the feedback laws solution of eqns(25,26) are given by the following generating rules

$$\alpha_2 = \left[\frac{\partial c}{\partial q} \frac{\partial p}{\partial P}\right]^{-1} \left[- \frac{\partial}{\partial q}\left(\frac{\partial c}{\partial q} p\right) p\right] - \frac{\partial L}{\partial q} + \frac{\partial P}{\partial q} p, \tag{28}$$

and

$$\beta_2 = \left[\frac{\partial c}{\partial q} \frac{\partial p}{\partial P}\right]^{-1}. \tag{29}$$

where

$$\alpha(Z) = \mathrm{col}[0, \alpha_2(Z)], \quad \beta(Z) = \mathrm{diag}[0, \beta_2(Z)]. \tag{30}$$

The first components α_1 and β_1 are not determined here, because the feedback law is not acting on the variable **p**, and they can be taken as zero. Note that the proposed explicit form of the control laws as given by eqns(28-30), only requires the knowledge of the Lagrangian and the output equations of the system so that the dynamical equations and Jacobian matrix are not explicitly needed in the present approach to derive the control laws. Moreover, the generating rules are valid for the construction of any controlled mechanism whatever in joint space, cartesian space or mixed space. It follows that the algorithms for computing control laws can be implemented in a code as written in eqns(28,29) when outputs are specified by eqn(20). Finally, many alternate forms of the generating rules can be derived by using eqns(6,8,12,14,15), because these equations involve the Jacobian, the joint and the cartesian dynamical model of a mechanism.

IV-DISSIPATIVE OR CONSTRAINED SYSTEMS

The generating rules are now designed for the case of dissipative and constrained systems. The dynamics of a dissipative mechanical system can be described by

$$\frac{d}{dt}\left(\frac{\partial L}{\partial p}\right) - \frac{\partial L}{\partial q} + \mathbf{D}\,\mathbf{p} = \mathbf{T}, \tag{31}$$

where $\mathbf{D} = \text{diag}(D_1, D_2, \ldots D_n)$ is the viscous friction while n represents the number of degree of freedom of the system. The canonical form of eqn(31) is easily derived as

$$\dot{\mathbf{q}} = \mathbf{p}$$

$$\dot{\mathbf{p}} = \left(\frac{\partial P}{\partial p}\right)^{-1}\left[\frac{\partial L}{\partial q} - \frac{\partial P}{\partial q}\,\mathbf{p} - \mathbf{D}\mathbf{p}\right] + \mathbf{T}. \tag{32}$$

By writing these equations in a canonical form as defined by eqn(17), one gets

$$F(Z) = \text{col}\left[\,\mathbf{p},\ \left(\frac{\partial P}{\partial p}\right)^{-1}\left(\frac{\partial L}{\partial q} - \frac{\partial P}{\partial q}\,\mathbf{p} - \mathbf{D}\,\mathbf{p}\right)\right], \tag{33}$$

and

$$Z = \text{col}(q,p), \quad H(Z) = \text{diag}\left[0, \left(\frac{\partial P}{\partial p}\right)^{-1}\right], \quad \text{and} \quad U(t) = \text{col}(0,T). \tag{34}$$

When the outputs to be controlled are specified by eqn(20), the control laws giving output decoupling and exact linearization of the dissipative system defined by eqn(32) are now given by

$$\alpha_2 = \left[\frac{\partial c}{\partial q}\frac{\partial p}{\partial P}\right]^{-1}\left[-\frac{\partial(}{\partial q}\frac{\partial c}{\partial q}p)\,p\right] - \frac{\partial L}{\partial q} + \frac{\partial P}{\partial q}p + Dp, \tag{35}$$

and

$$\beta_2 = \left[\frac{\partial c}{\partial q}\frac{\partial p}{\partial P}\right]^{-1}. \tag{36}$$

To investigate the case of systems with constraints, the Lagrange multiplier form of Euler-Lagrange's equations is to be used. In these equations an extra-term appears with the Lagrange's multipliers $\boldsymbol{\lambda}$, and it can be formally viewed as a generalized dissipative factor so that eqn(35) is always valid, if **Dp** is replaced by $Dp + \left(\frac{\partial \Phi}{\partial q}\right)^T \lambda$, where $\boldsymbol{\Phi}$ represents a vector of nonlinear constraint functions of the system coordinates **q**. So, the previously derived equations appear as generating rules from which the nonlinear control laws giving decoupled controls and output linearization can be derived in terms of the Lagrangian and outputs equations only. The main advantage of using the generating rules lies in the fact that these relations, as Euler-Lagrange's equations, are true no matter how the controlled output coordinates are chosen.

V-POLE ASSIGNMENT PROBLEM

In practice, it is important to design servo-mechanisms in which the closed loop dynamics can be specified whatever complex of the controlled system is. This leads to introduce two free (matrix) parameters in the synthesis process which permit the dynamical behavior adjustment of the resulting feedback system. To obtain output decoupling, exact linearization and pole assignment for controlled mechanisms, use is now made of the following general feedback law

$$U(t) = \alpha(Z) + \beta(Z)\left[K\overset{0}{Q}(Z) + \Gamma z\right], \tag{37}$$

where $\boldsymbol{\alpha}(\mathbf{Z}) = \mathrm{col}(0,\alpha_2)$, $\boldsymbol{\beta}(\mathbf{Z}) = \mathrm{diag}(0,\beta_2)$, $\mathbf{K} = \mathrm{diag}(\mathbf{K}_1,\mathbf{K}_2,.., \mathbf{K}_n)$, with $\mathbf{K}_i = (-k_i^o\ -k_i^1)$, $\Gamma = \mathrm{diag}(\sigma_1,\sigma_2,..\ \sigma_n)$ and $\mathbf{z} = \mathrm{col}(z_1,z_2,..z_n)$ is the new input of the controlled system. It can be shown that the implementation of this law leads the output to obey to the following differential equation

$$\ddot{Y} = - K^1 \dot{Y} - K^o Y + \Gamma z, \tag{38}$$

provided the control law is defined by a combined velocity-position feedback signal given by

$$KQ(Z) = - K^1 \dot{Y} - K^o Y. \tag{39}$$

Thus, the implementation of the new control law as defined by eqn(37) permits the pole location by choosing the appropriate parameters **K** and **Γz** such that

$$\Gamma z = -KQ(Z_d) + \ddot{Y}_d, \tag{40}$$

where $\mathbf{Z_d}$ corresponds to the desired state space input and $\ddot{\mathbf{Y}}_d$ is the desired value of the controller outputs acceleration. The motion of the controlled mechanical system is therefore described by

$$\ddot{Y} + K^1 \dot{Y} + K^o Y = K^o Y_d + K^1 \dot{Y}_d + \ddot{Y}_d. \tag{41}$$

In fact, eqn(41) is only valid when the desired input and its two first derivatives with respect to t are available; they appear as a generalized "input" of the controller when trajectories are specified from spline functions for example. On the other hand, the introduction of the generalized error term defined by $\mathbf{\Phi} = \mathbf{Y_d} - \mathbf{Y}$, leads the dynamics of the system to become

$$\ddot{\Phi} + K^1 \dot{\Phi} + K^o \Phi = 0, \tag{42}$$

an equation in which the parameters can be chosen arbitrarily by the designer. For example, a proper choice of parameters eqn(42) transforms into a Routh-Hurwitz's stable equation.

VI-A PRACTICAL EXAMPLE

In this part, the design of a controller for a five-link biped walking mechanism is built by means of the generating rules and the Mita's 2D biped mechanism [13-15] is used to provide common notations. The Lagrangian of a 5-link biped walking robot is given by

$$L = \tfrac{1}{2} \sum_{k=1}^{5} \left[\dot{\theta}^t K^t I_o K \dot{\theta} + \sum_{j=1}^{5} L_{kj} \dot{\theta}_j \dot{\theta}_k \cos(\theta_k - \theta_j) - 2 G_k \cos \theta_k \right], \tag{43}$$

where $I_{o,i}$ represents the inertia of the ith actuator and where the G_j coefficients (j=1,2...,5), can be found in ref [15]. For a 5-link system, the first matrix appearing in the Lagrangian defined by eqn(32) can be written as

$$K^t I_o K = \begin{bmatrix} I_{o1}+I_{o2} & -I_{o2} & 0 & 0 & 0 \\ -I_{o2} & I_{o1}+I_{o2} & -I_{o3} & 0 & 0 \\ 0 & -I_{o3} & I_{o3}+I_{o4} & -I_{o4} & 0 \\ 0 & 0 & -I_{o4} & I_{o4}+I_{o5} & -I_{o5} \\ 0 & 0 & 0 & -I_{o5} & I_{o5} \end{bmatrix}. \tag{44}$$

The motion equations for the biped mechanism are given by application of the Lagrange formalism in the form

$$\frac{d}{dt}\left(\frac{\partial L}{\partial \mathbf{p}}\right) - \frac{\partial L}{\partial \boldsymbol{\theta}} + \mathbf{K}^t \mathbf{D} \mathbf{K} \dot{\boldsymbol{\theta}} = \mathbf{T}, \tag{45}$$

where $\mathbf{p} = d\boldsymbol{\theta}/dt$ is the absolute angular speed vectors of links, $\mathbf{K}^T$ is the transposed of the matrix $\mathbf{K}$, $\mathbf{D} = \mathrm{diag}(D_1, D_2, \ldots D_n)$ is the viscous friction at joints and $\mathbf{T} = \mathrm{col}(T_1, T_2, \ldots T_n)$ is the absolute torque vector applied to joints. Finally, the last term of the left hand side of eqn(35) introduces a dissipative torque effect which is usually described by the Rayleigh function

$$F = \tfrac{1}{2} \dot{\mathbf{q}}^T \mathbf{D} \dot{\mathbf{q}} = \tfrac{1}{2} \dot{\boldsymbol{\theta}}^t \mathbf{K}^t \mathbf{D} \mathbf{K} \dot{\boldsymbol{\theta}}. \tag{46}$$

The control laws are now derived by using the DNDM [12]. If the outputs to be controlled are the absolute angles $\boldsymbol{\theta}$, the output eqn(8) becomes $\mathbf{Y} = \boldsymbol{\theta}$, and the generalized variables $\mathbf{q}$ are to be replaced by $\boldsymbol{\theta}$ in the control laws defined by eqns(17,24). From these equations and with the help of eqn(3), the generating term of the generalized momentum can be written as

$$p_k = (I_{o,k} + I_{o,k+1})\dot{\theta}_k - I_{o,k}\dot{\theta}_{k-1} - I_{o,k+1}\dot{\theta}_{k+1} + \sum_{j=1}^{5} L_{kj} \dot{\theta}_j \cos(\theta_k - \theta_j). \tag{47}$$

In matrix form, eqn(47) becomes

$$\mathbf{P} = \mathbf{A}(\boldsymbol{\theta})\ \mathbf{p}, \tag{48}$$

where $\mathbf{p} = \dot{\boldsymbol{\theta}}$, and $\mathbf{A}(\boldsymbol{\theta}) = [A_{kj}]$ with

$$A_{kj} = (I_{o,k}+I_{o,k+1})\delta_{kj} - I_{o,k}\delta_{k-1,j} - I_{o,k+1}\delta_{k+1,j} + L_{kj}\cos(\theta_k-\theta_j), \tag{49}$$

where $\delta_{k,j}$, $\delta_{k-1,j}$ and $\delta_{k+1,j}$ are the Kronecker's symbols, i.e. $\delta_{k,j} = 1$ when k=j and $\delta_{k,j} = 0$ elsewhere. Application of eqn(17) to the case of a 5-link biped walking system in which the link absolute-angle are controlled, leads to

$$\boldsymbol{\beta}_2 = \left[\frac{\partial \mathbf{P}}{\partial \mathbf{p}}\right] = \mathbf{A}, \quad \text{because} \quad \frac{\partial \mathbf{c}}{\partial \boldsymbol{\theta}} = 1. \tag{50}$$

To proceed, the vector $\frac{\partial L}{\partial \boldsymbol{\theta}}$ is then considered. Its general form is

$$\frac{\partial L}{\partial \theta_k} = \sum_{j=1}^{5} - L_{kj}\ \dot{\theta}_k\dot{\theta}_j\ \sin(\theta_k-\theta_j) + G_k\ \sin\theta_k. \tag{51}$$

On the other hand, the vector $\mathbf{K}^T\mathbf{D}\mathbf{K}\dot{\boldsymbol{\theta}}$ is defined by

$$\mathbf{K}^t\mathbf{D}\mathbf{K}\dot{\boldsymbol{\theta}} = \begin{bmatrix} D_1+D_2 & -D_2 & 0 & 0 & 0 \\ -D_2 & D_1+D_2 & -D_3 & 0 & 0 \\ 0 & -D_3 & D_3+D_4 & -D_4 & 0 \\ 0 & 0 & -D_4 & D_4+D_5 & -D_5 \\ 0 & 0 & 0 & -D_5 & D_5 \end{bmatrix} \dot{\boldsymbol{\theta}}. \tag{52}$$

where the generating term of the matrix is given by

$$\mathbf{K}^t\mathbf{D}\mathbf{K}\Big|_k = (D_{o,k} + D_{o,k+1})\ \delta_{k,j} - D_{o,k}\ \delta_{k-1,j} - D_{o,k+1}\ \delta_{k+1,j}. \tag{53}$$

Finally, the kth row of the control vector α_o is generated by

$$-\frac{\partial L}{\partial \boldsymbol{\theta}} + \frac{\partial \mathbf{P}}{\partial \boldsymbol{\theta}}\ \mathbf{p} + \mathbf{K}^t\mathbf{D}\mathbf{K}\dot{\boldsymbol{\theta}}\Big|_k = \sum_{j=1}^{5} L_{kj}\ \dot{\theta}_j^2\sin(\theta_k-\theta_j) - G_k\ \sin\theta_k + \mathbf{K}^t\mathbf{D}\mathbf{K}\dot{\boldsymbol{\theta}}\Big|_k \tag{54}$$

From eqn(43), it is now easy to compute the physical control algorithm leading to decoupled controls and linearization with respect to the link absolute-angles $\mathbf{u}^o{}_i = T_{ai}$, so that

$$u^o{}_i = \sum_{j=1}^{5} L_{ij}\dot{\theta}_j{}^2\sin(\theta_i-\theta_j) - G_i\sin\theta_i + K^tDK\dot{\theta}\Big]_i + Aw\Big]_i \qquad (55)$$

i.e.

$$u^o{}_i = \sum_{j=1}^{5} L_{ij}\dot{\theta}_j{}^2\sin(\theta_i-\theta_j) - G_i\sin\theta_i + (D_i+D_{o,i+1})\dot{\theta}_i - D_i\dot{\theta}_{i-1} +$$

$$-D_{i+1}\dot{\theta}_{i+1} +(I_{o,i}+I_{o,i+1})w_i -I_{o,i}w_{i-1} -I_{o,i+1}w_{i+1} +L_{ij}\cos(\theta_k-\theta_j)\ w_j, \qquad (56)$$

where $\mathbf{w}$(t) represents the input vector of the system. u_i represents the components of the vector $\mathbf{u}$(t) which is defined by $\mathbf{U}$(t) = col[0,$\mathbf{u}$(t)], and $\mathbf{u}^o$(t) represents its physical form, i.e. the torque control laws to be implemented in the system. For example, the first component of the control law $\mathbf{u}^o{}_1$(t) is given by

$$u^o{}_1 = L_{12}S12\dot{\theta}_2{}^2+ L_{13}S13\dot{\theta}_3{}^2+ L_{14}S14\dot{\theta}_4{}^2+ L_{15}S15\dot{\theta}_5{}^2-G_1S1+D_1\dot{\theta}_1+D_2(\dot{\theta}_1-\dot{\theta}_2)$$

$$+(I_{o1}+I_{o2}+L_{11})w_1 +(-I_{o2}+L_{12}C12)w_2 +L_{13}C13w_3 +L_{14}C14w_4 +L_{15}C15w_5. \qquad (57)$$

where symmetry relations between the coefficients have been accounted for. Note that these equations are directly derived from the nonlinear control laws which lead to linearization and decoupled controls of the 5-link biped skeleton. Because many terms computed in the synthesis of control laws are implied in the derivation of dynamical equations, the DNDM permits a reduction of the amount of computations.

VII-DERIVATION OF THE DYNAMICAL MODEL FROM THE CONTROL LAWS

This section shows how the dynamical equations of a mechanical system can be derived from the nonlinear feedback laws which lead to output decoupling and exact linearization. This useful feature of DNDM comes from the fact that the computation of both control laws and the dynamics of no-controlled mechanisms involves the same terms. In addition the generating rules to derive the dynamical model of no-controlled mechanisms can be established without needing any derivative with respect to the time. To see this point the canonical form of Lagrange's equations in variables **(q,p)** can be written from eqns(9,11) as

$$\dot{\mathbf{q}} = \mathbf{p}$$

$$\frac{\partial \mathbf{P}}{\partial \mathbf{p}} \dot{\mathbf{p}} = - \frac{\partial \mathbf{P}}{\partial \mathbf{q}} \mathbf{p} + \frac{\partial \mathrm{L}}{\partial \mathbf{q}} - \mathbf{D}\, \mathbf{p} + \mathrm{T}. \tag{58}$$

In term of control laws defined by eqns(35,36), the dynamical eqn(58) valid for no servo-controlled mechanisms becomes

$$\ddot{\mathbf{q}} = [\beta_2 \frac{\partial \mathbf{C}}{\partial \mathbf{q}}]^{-1} [-\alpha_2 - \beta_2 \frac{\partial (}{\partial \mathbf{q}} \frac{\partial \mathbf{C}}{\partial \mathbf{q}} \mathbf{p})\mathbf{p}) + \mathbf{T}], \tag{59}$$

which is the joint space dynamical model. When the outputs are the generalized coordinates **Y = q,** eqn(59) shows that the dynamical behavior of the decoupled system is defined by

$$\ddot{\mathbf{q}} = \mathbf{w}(t). \tag{60}$$

Thus, the dynamical equations of the generalized coordinates and the outputs variables obey the same diagonal differential equations. If the cartesian model is required, for example to consider the shock problem, eqn(59) is to be re-written in terms of cartesian outputs. Expanding the first derivative with respect to t of outputs defined by eqn(20) leads for a mechanism to

$$\dot{\mathbf{Y}} = \frac{\partial \mathbf{C}}{\partial \mathbf{q}} \mathbf{p}. \tag{61}$$

By combining the next derivative of eqn(61) with respect to t and eqns(18,28,29), the Cartesian dynamical model of a mechanism is then defined by

$$\mathbf{J}^{-t} (\beta_2 \ddot{\mathbf{Y}} + \alpha_2) = \mathbf{J}^{-t} \mathbf{T}. \tag{62}$$

Eqn(62) represents the dynamical cartesian model of the no-controlled mechanism, in terms of control laws which could be implemented to obtain an output-decoupled controlled-mechanism. It can be observed that all the terms required by eqn(62) are already computed in deriving the control laws. Just two extra matrix products are to be added to previous computations. In conclusion, the generating rules of control laws proposed in this paper yields both the feedback laws and the dynamical model of the investigated mechanism, and the above procedure can be applied to more complex systems such as a dynamically driven system or compliant system and sensored systems as well. In order to show how the previous derived expressions are to be used, the Slider-Crank problem investigated by Haug in ref [1] is now reconsidered. The Lagrangian of the system is

$$L = \tfrac{1}{2}[J_1+J_2 a r^2\cos^2\theta + m_2 r^2(1-l_1/l)^2\cos^2\theta + m_2(r+(l_1^2-r^2 l_1^2 l^{-2}\sin^2\theta)^{-\frac{1}{2}} r^2 l_1^2 l^{-2}\cos\theta]^2\sin^2\theta]\dot{\theta}^2 + m_2 g r(1-l_1 l^{-1})\cos\theta$$

or

$$L = \tfrac{1}{2}\dot{\theta}A\dot{\theta} - V, \tag{63}$$

where $a = (l^2-r^2\sin^2\theta)^{-1}$. When the output is chosen as $Y = \theta$, then the application of generating rules leads to compute the following terms

$$P = A\dot{\theta}, \quad \beta = A(\theta), \quad \frac{\partial P}{\partial\theta}\,p = \frac{\partial A}{\partial\theta}\,\dot{\theta}, \quad \text{and} \quad \frac{\partial L}{\partial\theta} = \tfrac{1}{2}\,\frac{\partial A}{\partial\theta}\,\dot{\theta}^2 - m_2 g r(1-l_1 l^{-1})\sin\theta,$$

when the applied torque to drive the coordinate θ is n. The control laws and the dynamical model can easily be written by means of eqns(28,29) and eqn(59) with $\partial c/\partial \mathbf{q} = 1$. In this last case, the motion equations of the system are

$$A\,\ddot{\theta} - \tfrac{1}{2}\,\frac{\partial A}{\partial\theta}\,\dot{\theta}^2 + \frac{\partial A}{\partial\theta}\,\dot{\theta} + m_2 g r(1-l_1 l^{-1})\sin\theta = n_1. \tag{64}$$

So, this calculation is probably shorter than those resulting from the direct application of Euler-Lagrange's equations, because it does not require any derivative with respect to t. As a second example, the biped system is again considered and the dynamical model is derived from eqn(56), i.e. from the nonlinear feedback control algorithms the implementation of which gives output decoupling and exact linearization. For the joint variables $\boldsymbol{\theta}$ eqn(59) becomes

$$\boldsymbol{\beta}_2\,\ddot{\boldsymbol{\theta}} = -\,\boldsymbol{\alpha}_2 + \mathbf{T}, \tag{65}$$

where the generalized coordinate vector $\mathbf{q}$ is replaced by $\boldsymbol{\theta}$, which represents the absolute-angle vector of links. So, owing to the initial conditions problem, the introduction of eqns(38,39) and eqn(43) into eqn(47) leads, for i=1,2..5, to the biped-motion equations

$$(I_{o,i}+I_{o,i+1})\ddot{\theta}_i - I_{o,i}\ddot{\theta}_{i-1} - I_{o,i+1}\ddot{\theta}_{i+1} + \sum_{j=1}^{5} L_{ij}\cos(\theta_k-\theta_j)\,\ddot{\theta}_j +$$

$$+ \sum_{j=1}^{5} L_{ij}\dot{\theta}_j{}^2\sin(\theta_i-\theta_j) - G_i\sin\theta_i + (D_i+D_{o,i+1})\dot{\theta}_i - D_i\dot{\theta}_{i-1} - D_{i+1}\dot{\theta}_{i+1} = T_i. \qquad (66)$$

In conclusion, it has been shown that the generating rules valid to establish the explicit form of feedback laws to be implemented in a mechanical system can be also used to derive the dynamical model of the mechanism, while no derivative with respect to t is needed in this approach. For simulation purpose, small codes based on the generating rules can be built since the dynamical model and the related control laws can be both derived by means of the same algorithm.

VIII-GENERAL FEATURES OF THE NEW DESIGN APPROACH

In this section a comparison between the usual Lagrangian approach and the present method is introduced, in terms of computational efficiency and flexibility. To do that, it is first recalled that the use of the Lagrange formulation leads to dynamic modelling of free mechanisms (i.e. no servo-controlled systems), by means of second-order differential equations. On the other hand, note that both the derivation of feedback laws and the dynamical equations of mechanisms are simultaneously realized in applying the generating rules. So this last approach performs two tasks while the control laws cannot be directly designed (in particular in Cartesian-space) by only applying Euler-Lagrange's equations to the Lagrangian of the system. Owing to the control theory which permits to establish the generating rules, a comparison of terms involved in the two approaches is now given. The Lagrange multiplier form of Euler-Lagrange's equations and the generating rules are defined by

$$\frac{d}{dt}\left(\frac{\partial L}{\partial \mathbf{p}}\right) - \frac{\partial L}{\partial \mathbf{q}} + \mathbf{D}\mathbf{p} + \left(\frac{\partial \mathbf{\Phi}}{\partial \mathbf{q}}\right)^T \boldsymbol{\lambda} = \mathbf{T}, \qquad (67)$$

and

$$\alpha_2 = [\frac{\partial c}{\partial q}\frac{\partial p}{\partial P}]^{-1} [-\frac{\partial(}{\partial q}\frac{\partial c}{\partial q} p) p] - \frac{\partial L}{\partial q} + \frac{\partial P}{\partial q} p + Dp + (\frac{\partial \Phi}{\partial q})^T \lambda, \tag{68}$$

with

$$\beta_2 = [\frac{\partial c}{\partial q}\frac{\partial p}{\partial P}]^{-1}. \tag{36}$$

where

$$Y = C(q), \quad P = \frac{\partial L}{\partial p}, \quad p = dq/dt. \tag{69}$$

Eqns(66-68) permit the design of the control law driving the joint generalized forces through the relation

$$T = u(t) = \alpha(q) + \beta(q)\, w(t), \tag{70}$$

where **w**(t) represents the input of the controlled system. Moreover, it has been shown that the control laws can be used to derive the joint dynamical model of the no-controlled mechanical system by means of eqn(59). So, when using Euler-Lagrange's equations, the dynamical model derivation of a mechanism involves the computation of the following terms

$$\frac{\partial L}{\partial q}, \qquad P = \frac{\partial L}{\partial p}, \qquad \text{and} \qquad \frac{dP}{dt} = \frac{d}{dt}(\frac{\partial L}{\partial p}),$$

while the generating rules require the computation of

$$\frac{\partial L}{\partial q}, \qquad P = \frac{\partial L}{\partial p}, \qquad \frac{\partial P}{\partial q} p \qquad \text{and} \qquad \frac{\partial P}{\partial p} \dot{p},$$

this because for a joint controller **C(q) = q**, so that

$$\frac{\partial c(q)}{\partial q} = 1 \text{ and } \frac{\partial[}{\partial q}\frac{\partial c}{\partial q}(q)p]\, p = 0.$$

In conclusion, the same expressions are involved whatever by applying Euler-Lagrange's equations or the generating rules because

$$\frac{dP}{dt} = \frac{\partial P}{\partial q} p + \frac{\partial P}{\partial p} \dot{p}.$$

It is to be noted that on the contrary of the classical method, the generating rules gives both the feedback laws and the dynamical model of the system (in joint or Cartesian spaces) while no derivative with respect to t is needed in the computations. So, in comparison with Euler-Lagrange's algorithm, the present method can work well on computers with small storage capabilities because the symbolic operations only involve partial derivatives. Now, the classical and the present approaches are compared at a more detailed level. For the Cartesian controller design, the joint model derived by means of Euler-Lagrange's equations requires to be transformed into its Cartesian counterpart. To do that, use is to be made in addition to eqns(70) of the following expressions:

$$\dot{\mathbf{X}} = \mathbf{J}(\mathbf{q})\,\dot{\mathbf{q}} \qquad \text{and} \qquad \ddot{\mathbf{X}} = \dot{\mathbf{J}}(\mathbf{q})\,\dot{\mathbf{q}} + \mathbf{J}(\mathbf{q})\,\ddot{\mathbf{q}},$$

where **J(q)** represents the Jacobian matrix. As expected, the application of the generating rules to design a Cartesian controller involves the same expressions though they are written in a slightly different form as

$$\frac{\partial \underline{c}(\mathbf{q})}{\partial \mathbf{q}}, \quad \text{and} \quad \frac{\partial}{\partial \mathbf{q}}\left(\frac{\partial \underline{c}(\mathbf{q})}{\partial \mathbf{q}}\,\mathbf{p}\right)\mathbf{p}.$$

But here again, these last developments are sufficient to derive in the same time (i) the dynamical model (ii) its related control laws and this from the Lagrangian (a scalar) and the output equation (i.e. a vector). In fact the generating rules can be viewed as the result of a direct implementation of control laws onto Euler-Lagrange's equations so that a new formalism is obtained. Consequently, as the Lagrange formalism is, these new rules are true no matter how the output coordinate are chosen. In particular when output are mixed joint and Cartesian coordinates, the generating rules can be applied as well. Moreover, the usual application of the nonlinear decoupling method requires a state space representation of the dynamical equations of mechanisms. This is usually achieved by means of a nonlinear transformation in connection with inverse matrice operations so that a large amount of calculation results. Here because the feedback laws are directly derived from the Lagrangian, there is therefore no need for such developments, the explicit form of the dynamical model of a mechanisms is never directly used to derive the control laws. This probably constitutes a great advantage of this new methodology over the other techniques as applied to the Lagrangian systems area.

IX-DYNAMICALLY DRIVEN MECHANISMS

This part introduces a generalization of the generating rules to the case of dynamically driven mechanisms. In many practical controlled mechanisms, the dynamics of driving motors are to be taken into account in the model equations. So, the simulation results are much closer to reality and more realistic and stable controllers can be built. In the following, the nonlinear feedback laws to be implemented in a dynamically driven mechanism modelled as a third-order system are synthetized by means of a phase-plane representation of the model equations. As previously, the resulting generating rules permit a direct derivation of nonlinear feedback control laws from the Lagrangian and output equation while the knowledge of the nonlinear decoupling method and Euler-Lagrange's equations are not needed. Moreover, no derivative with respect to t is required by applying these generating rules which are now established. Let us consider a mechanism driven by D.C. electric motors in which the armature inductance plays an important role. In a phase-plane representation **(q,p=q)**, the system equations is given by

$$\dot{\mathbf{q}} = \mathbf{p}$$

$$\dot{\mathbf{p}} = \left(\frac{\partial P}{\partial p}\right)^{-1}\left[\frac{\partial L}{\partial q} - \frac{\partial P}{\partial q}\,\mathbf{p} + K_m \mathbf{I}\right]$$

$$\dot{\mathbf{I}} = L_m^{-1}(-R_m \mathbf{I} - K_m \mathbf{p}) + L_m^{-1}\mathbf{V}. \tag{71}$$

where $\mathbf{V} = \mathrm{col}(V_1,V_2,..,V_n)$ represents the voltage vector applied to motor armatures, $\mathbf{L}_m = \mathrm{diag}(L_1,L_2..,L_n)$ is the matrix of the armature inductance, $\mathbf{K}_m = \mathrm{diag}(k_1,k_2..,k_n)$ is the torque constant matrix, $\mathbf{R}_m = \mathrm{diag}(R_1,R_2,..,R_n)$ is the armature resistance matrix and $\mathbf{I} = \mathrm{col}(I_1,I_2,..,I_n)$ is the armature current vector. The canonical expression of eqns(43) is

$$\dot{\mathbf{Z}} = F(\mathbf{Z}) + H(\mathbf{Z})\,U(t), \tag{72}$$

where

$$F(\mathbf{Z}) = \mathrm{col}\left[\mathbf{p},\ \left(\frac{\partial P}{\partial p}\right)^{-1}\left(\frac{\partial L}{\partial q} - \frac{\partial P}{\partial q}\,\mathbf{p}\right),\ \mathbf{I}\right], \tag{73}$$

with

$$\mathbf{Z} = \mathrm{col}(\mathbf{q},\mathbf{p},\mathbf{I}),\quad H(\mathbf{Z}) = \mathrm{diag}(0,0,L_m^{-1}),\quad \text{and}\quad U(t) = \mathrm{col}(0,0,\mathbf{V}). \tag{74}$$

When a cartesian robot controller is to be designed, the outputs to be controlled are to be written as

$$\mathbf{Y} = \mathbf{C}(\mathbf{Z}), \tag{75}$$

where in fact, **C(Z) = C(q)**. By using a control law defined by

$$\mathbf{U}(t) = \boldsymbol{\alpha}(\mathbf{Z}) + \boldsymbol{\beta}(\mathbf{Z})\mathbf{W}(t), \tag{76}$$

with

$$\boldsymbol{\alpha}(\mathbf{Z}) = \mathrm{col}[0,0,\alpha_3(\mathbf{Z})], \quad \boldsymbol{\beta}(\mathbf{Z}) = \mathrm{diag}[0,0,\beta_3(\mathbf{Z})], \tag{77}$$

by taking the third derivative of outputs defined by eqn(47) with respect to t, one gets

$$\begin{aligned}\dddot{\mathbf{Y}} &= \frac{\partial}{\partial \mathbf{q}}[\frac{\partial}{\partial \mathbf{q}}(\frac{\partial \mathbf{C}}{\partial \mathbf{q}}\mathbf{p})\mathbf{p}]\mathbf{p} + \frac{\partial}{\partial \mathbf{q}}[\frac{\partial \mathbf{C}}{\partial \mathbf{q}}(\frac{\partial \mathbf{P}}{\partial \mathbf{p}})^{-1}(\frac{\partial L}{\partial \mathbf{q}} - \frac{\partial \mathbf{P}}{\partial \mathbf{q}}\mathbf{p} + \mathbf{K}_m\mathbf{I})]\mathbf{p} \\ &+\left\{\frac{\partial}{\partial \mathbf{q}}(\frac{\partial \mathbf{C}}{\partial \mathbf{q}}\mathbf{p}) + \frac{\partial}{\partial \mathbf{p}}(\frac{\partial \mathbf{C}}{\partial \mathbf{q}}(\frac{\partial \mathbf{P}}{\partial \mathbf{p}})^{-1}(\frac{\partial L}{\partial \mathbf{q}} - \frac{\partial \mathbf{P}}{\partial \mathbf{q}}\mathbf{p}))\right\}.(\frac{\partial \mathbf{P}}{\partial \mathbf{p}})^{-1}(\frac{\partial L}{\partial \mathbf{q}} - \frac{\partial \mathbf{P}}{\partial \mathbf{q}}\mathbf{p} + \mathbf{K}_m\mathbf{I}) \\ &+ \frac{\partial \mathbf{C}}{\partial \mathbf{q}}(\frac{\partial \mathbf{P}}{\partial \mathbf{p}})^{-1}\mathbf{K}_m\mathbf{L}_m^{-1}(-\mathbf{R}_m\mathbf{I} - \mathbf{K}_m\mathbf{p} + \mathbf{V}).\end{aligned} \tag{78}$$

By introducing eqn(48) into eqn(50) and solving to obtain output decoupling and exact linearization by nonlinear feedback, one gets

$$\beta_3(\mathbf{Z}) = \mathbf{L}_m\mathbf{K}_m^{-1}\left(\frac{\partial \mathbf{P}}{\partial \mathbf{p}}\right)\left(\frac{\partial \mathbf{C}}{\partial \mathbf{q}}\right)^{-1}, \tag{79}$$

$$\begin{aligned}\alpha_3(\mathbf{Z}) &= \mathbf{R}_m\mathbf{I} + \mathbf{K}_m\mathbf{p} \\ &-\beta_3(\mathbf{Z})\left\{\frac{\partial}{\partial \mathbf{q}}[\frac{\partial}{\partial \mathbf{q}}(\frac{\partial \mathbf{C}}{\partial \mathbf{q}}\mathbf{p})\mathbf{p})]\mathbf{p} + \frac{\partial}{\partial \mathbf{q}}[\frac{\partial \mathbf{C}}{\partial \mathbf{q}}(\frac{\partial \mathbf{P}}{\partial \mathbf{p}})^{-1}(\frac{\partial L}{\partial \mathbf{q}} - \frac{\partial \mathbf{P}}{\partial \mathbf{q}}\mathbf{p} + \mathbf{K}_m\mathbf{I})]\mathbf{p}\right. \\ &\left.+\{\frac{\partial}{\partial \mathbf{q}}(\frac{\partial \mathbf{C}}{\partial \mathbf{q}}\mathbf{p}) + \frac{\partial}{\partial \mathbf{p}}(\frac{\partial \mathbf{C}}{\partial \mathbf{q}}(\frac{\partial \mathbf{P}}{\partial \mathbf{p}})^{-1}(\frac{\partial L}{\partial \mathbf{q}} - \frac{\partial \mathbf{P}}{\partial \mathbf{q}}\mathbf{p}))\}.(\frac{\partial \mathbf{P}}{\partial \mathbf{p}})^{-1}(\frac{\partial L}{\partial \mathbf{q}} - \frac{\partial \mathbf{P}}{\partial \mathbf{q}}\mathbf{p} + \mathbf{K}_m\mathbf{I})\right\}.\end{aligned} \tag{80}$$

With the aim of to compare two different approaches in deriving the control laws for the above third-order system, the phase-plane representation of dynamical equations in joint space is now used. The system equations becomes

$$\dot{q} = p$$
$$\dot{p} = A(q)^{-1}[-B(q,\dot{q}) - g(q) + K_m I]$$
$$\dot{I} = L_m^{-1}(-R_m I - K_m p) + L_m^{-1} V. \tag{81}$$

The canonical form of eqn(81) is given by eqn(44), but here

$$Z = \text{col}(q,p,I), \quad H(Z) = \text{diag}(0,0,L_m^{-1}), \quad U(t) = \text{col}(0,0,V), \tag{82}$$

and

$$F(Z) = \begin{bmatrix} p \\ A(q)^{-1}[-B(q,\dot{q}) - g(q) + K_m I] \\ L_m^{-1}(-R_m I - K_m p) \end{bmatrix}. \tag{83}$$

When the outputs are specified by eqn(48), the third-derivative with respect to t of the outputs **Y** is defined by

$$\dddot{Y} = \frac{d^2(Jp)}{dt^2} + \frac{\partial}{\partial q}[JA(q)^{-1}(-B(q,\dot{q})-g(q)+ K_m I)]\, p$$
$$+ \left[\frac{dJ}{dt} + \frac{\partial(Jp)}{\partial q} - J\right]A^{-1}(-B(q,\dot{q})-g(q)+ K_m I)$$
$$+ JA^{-1}K_m L_m^{-1}(-R_m I - K_m p + V). \tag{84}$$

This equation constitutes an alternate form of the output third-derivative with respect to t. In particular, eqn(71) can be used to find the meaning of each expression involved in eqns(69,70), in terms of joint space equations and Jacobian matrix. Owing to the arguments of vectors and matrices, this leads to

$$\frac{\partial[\partial(\partial c\; p)p)]}{\partial q \partial q \partial q}\, p = \frac{d^2(Jp)}{dt^2} \tag{85}$$

$$\frac{\partial}{\partial q}\left[\frac{\partial C}{\partial q}\left(\frac{\partial P}{\partial p}\right)^{-1}\left(\frac{\partial L}{\partial q} - \frac{\partial P}{\partial q}\,p + K_m I\right)\right] p = \frac{\partial}{\partial q}\left[JA(q)^{-1}(-B(q,\dot{q})-g(q)+K_m I)\right] p \tag{86}$$

$$\left[\frac{\partial}{\partial q}\left(\frac{\partial C}{\partial q}\right)p+\frac{\partial}{\partial q}\left(\frac{\partial C}{\partial q}\,p\right)-\frac{\partial C}{\partial q}\right]\left(\frac{\partial P}{\partial p}\right)^{-1}\left(\frac{\partial L}{\partial q}-\frac{\partial P}{\partial q}\,p+K_m I\right) = \left[\frac{dJ}{dt}+\frac{\partial}{\partial q}(Jp)-J\right]A^{-1}(-B(q,\dot{q})-g(q)+K_m I) \tag{87}$$

$$\frac{\partial C}{\partial q}\left(\frac{\partial P}{\partial p}\right)^{-1} K_m L_m^{-1}(-R_m I - K_m p) = JA^{-1}K_m L_m^{-1}(-R_m I - K_m p). \tag{88}$$

X-TOWARD THE SHOCK EFFECT INVESTIGATION

Some aspects of the shock effect problem encountered in mechanisms and controlled systems are investigated in this paragraph. Until now, this paper has shown that the canonical approach to derive control laws is a method which works at a probably more general level than other techniques. In particular the dynamical model of mechanisms is not required when using the phase plane approach to derive control laws and the case of dynamically driven system including or not the transducers time constant, the compliance etc.. can be easily included in the equations to be solved in the analytical procedure used in previous paragraphs and sometimes referred as the Direct Nonlinear Decoupling Method. In addition, the canonical form of the phase plane equations of mechanisms permits the derivation of the model of a mechanism in joint or in cartesian spaces from the the control laws themselves [12]. In fact, the cartesian model plays an important role in the analysis of the shock effects which appear in a mechanical system, and it is interesting to see how this investigation can be related to the canonical formulation. To do that, the cartesian equation of a simple mechanism is now considered. Its model is first derived from the phase-plane eqn(41) as follows. By introducing the derivative with respect to t of the Jacobian eqn(46) and writing hereafter the cartesian coordinates as **X**, the work space differential equation of the robot can be derived from eqn(44) as

$$\dot{X} = J(q)\,p$$

$$\dot{p} = \left(\frac{\partial P}{\partial p}\right)^{-1}\left[\frac{\partial L}{\partial q} - \frac{\partial P}{\partial q}\,p + T\right]. \tag{89}$$

By taking the time derivative of the first component of eqns(89) and using the second one, the work space model of the system can be written as

$$\ddot{X} - \dot{J}(q)\, p = J(q) \left(\frac{\partial P}{\partial p}\right)^{-1} \left[\frac{\partial L}{\partial q} - \frac{\partial P}{\partial q} p + T \right]. \tag{90}$$

By introducing the inverse transposed Jacobian matrix of the robot, the work space dynamical equation becomes

$$J(q)^{-T} \frac{\partial P}{\partial p} J(q)^{-1} [\ddot{X} - \dot{J}(q)\, p] = J(q)^{-T} \left[\frac{\partial L}{\partial q} - \frac{\partial P'}{\partial q} p \right] + F. \tag{91}$$

where **F** represents the cartesian view of the generalized torque which drives the mechanism from the joints. Now the shock effect problem is investigated from the cartesian mechanical model and a mechanical shock which appears in cartesian space will be viewed as resulting from a particular impulse driving force $\mathbf{F}_o$, which, for example, can stop instantaneously the mechanism. From the motion point of view, the corresponding jump of the cartesian speed is found by taking the integral of eqn(82) during a short interval of the time taken around the instant of the shock. Another way to find the initial conditions resulting from a transient command **F** consists to use a block-scheme representation of the work space dynamical equation in which some loops are to be opened just at the instant of the shock [17]. From these considerations, it results that the jump of the cartesian speed is given by

$$J(q)^{-T} \frac{\partial P}{\partial p} J(q)^{-1}\, \delta\dot{X} = F_o, \tag{92}$$

where $\delta\dot{\mathbf{X}} = \dot{\mathbf{X}}^+ - \dot{\mathbf{X}}^-$ is the speed jump, with $\dot{\mathbf{X}}^+$ is the speed after the shock and $\dot{\mathbf{X}}^-$ is the speed before the shock. In terms of generalized coordinates of the system, the corresponding jump of the joint speed is

$$\frac{\partial P}{\partial p}\, \delta\dot{q} = J(q)^T F_o. \tag{93}$$

To obtain a stop point, when the cartesian speed before the shock is $\dot{\mathbf{X}}^-$, the impulse cartesian force required to stop the mechanism motion is therefore derived from eqn(83) as

$$J(q)^{-T} \frac{\partial P}{\partial p} J(q)^{-1} (0 - \dot{X}^{-}) = F_0, \tag{94}$$

where **q** and **p** represent respectively the generalized coordinate and speed vectors at the instant of the shock. Alternatively, when the joint motors are used to establish such a force to stop instantaneously the system, the needed impulse torque and the corresponding jump of the joint speed vectors are then given by eqn(66). Moreover, note that the left hand side of eqn(85) represents the intensity of the impulse cartesian force leading the mechanism to a rest position, as a true shock can do. On the other hand and from the control point of view, eqn(85) shows that the shock effects could only be controlled by impulse laws, which is not a practical situation when considering the unavoidable saturating effects involved in the input/output hardware computer systems. Finally, it can be noted that the speed jump in eqns(80-85) which results of a mechanical shock sequence are expressed from the terms involved in the canonical dynamical equations of the system. It follows that the procedure used can be generalized to investigate electric and mechanical shocks and, in particular, applied to higher-order systems (as dynamically driven and sensored mechanisms), written in a canonical form.

CONCLUSION

This paper has introduced a new methodology to derive systematically from generating rules, the nonlinear control laws given exact linearization and decoupled controls of a mechanical system. Some interesting features of this method over the other available techniques have been shown depicted through the use of examples. In particular it has been shown that because the new method operates on the Lagrangian itself, it follows that a differential form or a state space form of dynamical equations of mechanisms are not required in this analysis. Moreover, it is not necessary to know the Nonlinear Decoupling Method as well as Euler-Lagrange's equations in applying the proposed generating rules. The control laws to implement in the system are directly obtained in an analytic and explicit form in which, on the contrary of other techniques, none derivative with respect to t is needed. Finally, the method is applied to the case of dynamically driven mechanisms to design cartesian, joint or any controllers leading to specific generating rules, i.e. a particular algorithm working from the

Lagrangian and an output equation. In addition, it has been shown that the dynamical model of no-controlled mechanisms can be directly derived from the control laws. Thus the computer manipulation of equations is reduced when combined control and mechanical systems are designed because the two problems are analysed together, in using the same algorithm. In conclusion, this report has introduced a new way to design small and fast codes devoted to the simulation of controlled mechanisms on small computers. To analyse theoretical results and design a general purpose code, a program based both on Euler-Lagrange's equations and on the generating rules which uses a fourth-order Runge-Kutta routine written in C-language to solve the differential equations is under development on XT. The resulting data will be then used to animate off-line, skeleton graphics on SIMULATIX, a 3D XT workstation.

REFERENCES

1. E. Haug. Computer Aided Analysis Design and Optimization of Mechanical Systems Dynamics. NATO ASI, Iowa Univ, Aug 1-12, 1983. Edited by E.J. Haug, Springer Verlag, NATO ASI Vol. 9, 1984
2. G. Andrews. A Brief Survey of Self-formulating Simulation Programs for Multi-body Dynamic Systems. IASTED, Int. Symp. on Simulation and Modelling, Orlando, Florida, Nov 9-11 1983
3. J. Wittenburg. Dynamics of Systems of Rigid Bodies. Teubner, Stuttgart 1977
4. E. Freund. A Nonlinear Control Concept for Computer-controlled Manipulators. Proc. of IFAC Symp. on Multivariable Techn. Systems, Fredericton, Canada 1977, N.Y. Pergamon Press, pp 395-403
5. E. Freund. Fast Nonlinear Control with Arbitrary Pole-placement for Industrial Robots and Manipulators, Robotic Research: 1,1 65-78, 1981
6. Y. Chen. Nonlinear Feedback and Computer Control of Robot Arms. Doctorat thesis, Washington University, Saint Louis MO, Dec 1983
7. T. Tarn, A. Bejczy, A. Isodori and Y. Chen. Nonlinear Feedback in Robot Arm Control. Proc. of the 23rd IEEE Conf. on Decision and Control, Las Vegas, Nevada 1984
8. A. Bejczy, T. Tarn and Y. Chen. Robot Arm Dynamic Control by Computer. 1985 IEEE Conf. on Robotics and Automation, Saint Louis MO, pp 960-970
9. C. Vibet. Design of Robot Controllers. Advanced Robotics, 1987 Vol 2, No 1, pp 9-20
10. M. Cotsaftis and C. Vibet. An Explicit Form of Control Algorithms. 2nd Int. Conf. on Robotics and Automotion. San Diego, July 1987, Edited by R. Radharamanan, Springer Verlag (1988) pp 461-466
11. M. Cotsaftis and C. Vibet. A New Method for the Robot Controller Design. Robotics and Autonomous Systems, Vol 4, No1 1988 pp 237-242
12. M. Cotsaftis and C. Vibet. Explicit Forms to Derive Control Laws of Mechanisms. To appear in Computer Methods in Applied Mechanisms, 1989
13. A. Cappozo and T. Leo. A General Computing Method for the Analysis of Human Locomotion. J. of Biom: 8, 307-320, 1975
14. S. Onyskho and D. Winter. A Mathematical Model for the Dynamics of Human Locomotion. J. Biom.: 13, 361-368, 1980
15. T. Mita, T. Yaamaguchi, T. Kashiwase and T. Kawase. Realization of High Speed Biped Using Modern Control Theory. Int. J. of Control 40: 107-109, 1984
16. M. Cotsaftis and C. Vibet. Control Low Decoupling for 2D Biped Walking System. IEEE Engin in Medicine and Biology, Vol 7 No 3, Aug 1988 pp 51-45
17. C. Vibet. General Method of Finding Initial Conditions. IEEE Trans. on Educ. Vol E-31, No 1 1988 pp 46-48 and see: The Initial Conditions Problem. IJEEE, Vol 25, No 2, 1988 pp 141-149

A Comparison of Numerical Integration Methods with a View to Fast Simulation of Mechanical Dynamical Systems

J. P. Meijaard
Delft University of Technology
Mekelweg 2
2628 CD Delft
The Netherlands

Abstract

Mechanical dynamical systems, as they occur for instance in machine dynamics and robotics, often give rise to systems of moderately stiff ordinary differential equations. In this paper it will be shown that one of the most widely used classes of integration methods, multistep methods with variable step size and order, is not always optimal, especially not for systems with small damping. The classical fourth–order Runge–Kutta method has a small advantage in this case and methods that exploit the second–order structure of the equations of motion again have an advantage over these.

Implicit integration methods, which allow of a larger step size than explicit methods, but require more work for each step, will be compared to the given explicit integration methods. The Runge–Kutta–Rosenbrock methods, a class of so–called semi–implicit methods, appear to be superior in efficiency to fully implicit methods such as the Gauss–Legendre methods or the Newmark method, notwithstanding the weaker stability properties.

1. Introduction

In this paper we will consider numerical integration methods for the equations of motion of mechanical systems,

$$M\ddot{q} = Q(t,q,\dot{q}), \tag{1.1}$$

or written as an explicit system of first–order equations,

NATO ASI Series, Vol. F 69
Real-Time Integration Methods for Mechanical System Simulation
Edited by E. J. Haug and R. C. Deyo

$$\dot{q} = v,$$
$$\dot{v} = M^{-1}Q(t,q,v). \tag{1.2}$$

The linearized equations can be written as

$$M\delta\ddot{q} + C\delta\dot{q} + K\delta q = 0, \tag{1.3}$$

where

$$C = -\partial Q/\partial\dot{q}, \qquad K = -\partial Q/\partial q + \partial(M\ddot{q})/\partial q. \tag{1.4}$$

Explicit integration methods, that are methods which do not require the solution of some in general nonlinear algebraic equations, are only conditionally stable: the step size to be chosen not only depends on the required accuracy, but also on stability considerations. If, in a given problem, the step size is limited by the numerical stability requirement, we call the problem stiff. Obviously, whether a given problem will be called stiff depends on the the required accuracy, the method used and the initial conditions. We will call a problem moderately stiff if the step size required for stability is not more than about an order of magnitude smaller than the step size that would be needed for the desired accuracy if the method were unconditionally stable. For this class of problems, the efficiency of implicit methods, which allow of a larger step size but require more work per step than explicit methods, should be compared to that of explicit methods.

We will mainly deal with single step methods. In the next section, explicit and implicit Runge-Kutta methods for systems of first-order and second-order differential equations and the so-called semi-implicit Runge-Kutta-Rosenbrock methods will be discussed. In section 3, these methods and a multistep method will be compared. We end with some concluding remarks.

2. Runge-Kutta methods

2.1. Methods for systems of first-order differential equations

An initial value problem for ordinary differential equations can be formulated as

Find the solution for the system of differential equations

$$\frac{dy}{dt} \equiv \dot{y} = f(t,y), \qquad y,f \in \mathbb{R}^n,$$

on the interval $[t_0,t_e]$ $(t_e > t_0)$ that satisfies (2.1)

$$y(t_0) = y_0,$$

where $y_0 \in \mathbb{R}^n$ is a given vector.

The vector-valued function f depends on t, a real-valued variable ("time"), and y, the state vector of the system. A dot denotes a derivative with respect to t.

In a numerical integration method, the solution in a number of discrete points t_0, $t_1,\ldots$, $t_m = t_e$, $t_{i-1} < t_i$ $(i=1,2,\ldots,m)$, will be approximated by y_0, $y_1,\ldots$, y_m. Methods can be classified on several grounds. If only the directly preceding approximation y_n is used for the determination of y_{n+1}, we speak of a single step method and if also other preceding approximations, for instance y_{n-1}, $y_{n-2},\ldots$, y_{n-k}, are used, we speak of a multistep method. A method is called explicit if no algebraic equations have to be solved for the calculation of y_{n+1} and implicit otherwise.

For the moment we will restrict ourselves to single step methods. For the problem (2.1), y_{n+1} is calculated as

$$y_{n+1} = y_n + \tau\Phi(\tau,f,t_n,y_n), \qquad \tau = t_{n+1} - t_n, \tag{2.2}$$

while we have for the exact solution

$$y(t_{n+1}) = y(t_n) + \tau\Delta(\tau,f,t_n,y(t_n)). \tag{2.3}$$

Here, Φ is the numerical increment function and Δ the exact increment function. The order of a numerical integration method is the greatest integral number p for which we have for all sufficiently smooth functions f and arguments t_n and y_n,

$$\|\Phi(\tau,f,t_n,y_n) - \Delta(\tau,f,t_n,y_n)\| = O(\tau^P) \text{ for } \tau \to 0. \tag{2.4}$$

Now we can define the function that determines the principal term in the local truncation error, the principal error function ϕ, as

$$\Phi(\tau,f,t_n,y_n) - \Delta(\tau,f,t_n,y_n) = \phi(f,t_n,y_n) + r, \tag{2.5}$$

where $\|r\|$ is $O(\tau^{p+1})$ as $\tau \rightarrow 0$. The function ϕ can be used to compare methods which have the same order.

A class of single step methods is formed by the Runge–Kutta family. The general form of Runge–Kutta methods is

$$\begin{aligned} y_{n+1} &= y_n+\tau\textstyle\sum_{i=1}^{s} b_i k_i, \\ k_i &= f(t_n+c_i\tau,\ y_n+\tau\textstyle\sum_{j=1}^{s} a_{ij}k_j). \qquad (i=1,\ldots,s) \end{aligned} \tag{2.6}$$

These methods are explicit if $a_{ij}=0$ for $j\geq i$, diagonally implicit if $a_{ij}=0$ for $j>i$ and not all a_{ii} equal to zero, and fully implicit otherwise. The coefficients c_i, b_i and a_{ij} can be put in an array (Butcher) as

$$\begin{array}{c|c} c & A \\ \hline & b^T \end{array} \quad = \quad \begin{array}{c|ccc} c_1 & a_{11} & \cdots & a_{1s} \\ \vdots & \vdots & & \vdots \\ c_s & a_{s1} & \cdots & a_{ss} \\ \hline & b_1 & \cdots & b_s \end{array}. \tag{2.7}$$

Only methods satisfying the convention

$$c_i = \textstyle\sum_{j=1}^{s} a_{ij} \tag{2.8}$$

will be considered, by which the explicit dependence of f on t can be lifted by adding an additional equation to the system, $f_{n+1}=1$, $y_{n+1}=t$. The application of the method to this extended system will give the same results.

The test equation is the complex scalar differential equation

$$\dot{y}(t) = \lambda y(t), \qquad y,\lambda \in \mathbb{C},\ t\geq 0,\ y(0)=y_0. \tag{2.9}$$

When we apply the method (2.6) to this equation, we get

$$y_{n+1} = R(z)y_n, \qquad (z = \tau\lambda) \tag{2.10}$$

where $R(z)$ is called the stability function of the method (2.6). The stability region for a method is the region in the complex z–plane in which $|R(z)|\leq 1$. A method will be called absolutely stable (or A–stable) if $|R(z)|\leq 1$ for $\mathrm{Re}\ z\leq 0$ and conditionally stable otherwise. In most cases the coefficients in (2.7) are chosen in such a way that the highest possible order is achieved for a given s, but sometimes also in a way to obtain an advantageous stability region.

As examples, consider explicit 3–stage $(s=3)$ third–order and 4–stage fourth–order methods. A third–order method is given by

$$\begin{array}{c|ccc} 0 & 0 & 0 & 0 \\ \frac{1}{2} & \frac{1}{2} & 0 & 0 \\ 1 & -1 & 2 & 0 \\ \hline & \frac{1}{6} & \frac{2}{3} & \frac{1}{6} \end{array} . \tag{2.11}$$

The stability function for 3–stage third–order methods is always

$$R(z) = 1 + z + \frac{1}{2}z^2 + \frac{1}{6}z^3 \tag{2.12}$$

and the stability region contains the real interval $-2.512... \le z \le 0$ and the part $|z| \le \sqrt{3}$ of the imaginary axis.

The classical fourth–order Runge–Kutta method is given by

$$\begin{array}{c|cccc} 0 & 0 & 0 & 0 & 0 \\ \frac{1}{2} & \frac{1}{2} & 0 & 0 & 0 \\ \frac{1}{2} & 0 & \frac{1}{2} & 0 & 0 \\ 1 & 0 & 0 & 1 & 0 \\ \hline & \frac{1}{6} & \frac{1}{3} & \frac{1}{3} & \frac{1}{6} \end{array} \tag{2.13}$$

and the stability function is

$$R(z) = 1 + z + \frac{1}{2}z^2 + \frac{1}{6}z^3 + \frac{1}{24}z^4. \tag{2.14}$$

The stability region contains the real interval $-2.785... \le z \le 0$ and the part $|z| \le 2\sqrt{2}$ of the imaginary axis.

2.2. Methods for second–order differential equations

Although it can be brought in the form (2.1), we will also consider the initial value problem for systems of second–order differential equations:

> Find the solution for the system of differential equations
> $$\ddot{y} = f(t,y,\dot{y}), \qquad y,f \in \mathbb{R}^n,$$
> on the interval $[t_0,t_e]$ $(t_0 < t_e)$ that satisfies (2.15)
> $$\dot{y}(t_0) = z_0, \qquad y(t_0) = y_0,$$
> where $z_0,y_0 \in \mathbb{R}^n$ are given vectors.

Single step methods for the numerical integration of (2.15) have the general form

$$y_{n+1} = y_n + \tau\Phi(\tau,f,t_n,y_n,z_n), \qquad \tau = t_{n+1} - t_n,$$
$$z_{n+1} = z_n + \tau\Psi(\tau,f,t_n,y_n,z_n). \tag{2.16}$$

Here, z_n is an approximation for $\dot{y}(t_n)$ and Φ and Ψ are numerical increment functions. With $z(t_n) \equiv \dot{y}(t_n)$, we can write for the exact solution

$$y(t_{n+1}) = y(t_n) + \tau\Delta_y(\tau,f,t_n,y(t_n),z(t_n)),$$
$$z(t_{n+1}) = z(t_n) + \tau\Delta_z(\tau,f,t_n,y(t_n),z(t_n)). \tag{2.17}$$

The order of the numerical method (2.16) is in this case the largest integral number p such that for all sufficiently smooth functions f and arguments t_n, y_n, z_n we have

$$\|\Phi(\tau,f,t_n,y_n,z_n) - \Delta_y(\tau,f,t_n,y_n,z_n)\| = O(\tau^p) \tag{2.18^a}$$

and

$$\|\Psi(\tau,f,t_n,y_n,z_n) - \Delta_z(\tau,f,t_n,y_n,z_n)\| = O(\tau^p) \tag{2.18^b}$$

as $\tau \longrightarrow 0$

The general form of Runge–Kutta methods for second–order differential equations is

$$y_{n+1} = y_n + \tau z_n + \tau^2\textstyle\sum_{i=1}^s b_i^y k_i,$$
$$z_{n+1} = z_n + \tau\textstyle\sum_{i=1}^s b_i^z k_i, \tag{2.19}$$
$$k_i = f(t_n + c_i\tau,\ y_n + \overset{*}{c}_i\tau z_n + \tau^2\textstyle\sum_{j=1}^s a_{ij}^y k_j,\ z_n + \tau\sum_{j=1}^s a_{ij}^z k_j). \quad (i=1,\dots,s)$$

This method is explicit if $a_{ij}^y = 0$ and $a_{ij}^z = 0$ for $j \geq i$. We will adopt the convention

$$c_i = \overset{*}{c}_i, \tag{2.20}$$

so the explicit dependence of f on t can again be lifted by adding the equation $\ddot{y}_{n+1} = f_{n+1} = 0$ with the initial conditions $y_{n+1}(t_0) = t_0$, $\dot{y}_{n+1}(t_0) = 1$. Again, the coefficients can be put in an array as

$$\begin{array}{c|c|c} c & A^y & A^z \\ \hline & b^{yT} & b^{zT} \end{array} \;=\; \begin{array}{c|ccc|ccc} c_1 & a_{11}^y & \cdots & a_{1s}^y & a_{11}^z & \cdots & a_{1s}^z \\ \vdots & \vdots & & \vdots & \vdots & & \vdots \\ c_s & a_{s1}^y & \cdots & a_{ss}^y & a_{s1}^z & \cdots & a_{ss}^z \\ \hline & b_1^y & \cdots & b_s^y & b_1^z & \cdots & b_s^z \end{array}. \tag{2.21}$$

A suitable test equation for methods for second–order differential equations is

$$\ddot{y} = ay + bz, \quad y,z,a,b \in \mathbb{R}, \quad t \geq 0, \quad y(0) = y_0, \quad z(0) \equiv \dot{y}(0) = z_0. \tag{2.22}$$

When we apply the method (2.19) to this test equation, we get

$$\begin{pmatrix} y_{n+1} \\ \tau z_{n+1} \end{pmatrix} = C(X,Y) \begin{pmatrix} y_n \\ \tau z_n \end{pmatrix} \qquad (X = a\tau^2,\ Y = b\tau), \tag{2.23}$$

where C is a 2 by 2 amplification matrix. The stability region is the region of the X–Y–plane in which the moduli of the eigenvalues of C do not exceed unity, or stated in terms of the determinant and trace of C,

$$\det(C) \le 1, \qquad \det(C) + \mathrm{tr}(C) + 1 \ge 0, \qquad \det(C) - \mathrm{tr}(C) + 1 \ge 0 \tag{2.24}$$

A 1–stage method having order 1, and order 2 if f depends only weakly on z, is given by

$$\begin{array}{c|c|c} \frac{1}{2} & 0 & 0 \\ \hline & \frac{1}{2} & 1 \end{array}. \tag{2.25}$$

Applying (2.25) to the test equation yields the amplification matrix

$$C = \begin{pmatrix} 1+\frac{1}{2}X & 1+\frac{1}{2}Y+\frac{1}{4}X \\ X & 1+\ Y+\frac{1}{2}X \end{pmatrix} \tag{2.26}$$

and the stability conditions become

$$Y \le 0, \qquad X \le 0, \qquad 4+2Y+X \ge 0. \tag{2.27}$$

We see that it is possible to integrate undamped systems ($b=0$, $Y=0$) in a numerically stable way.

A 2–stage method having order 2, and order 3 if f depends only weakly on z, is given by

$$\begin{array}{c|cc|cc} \frac{1}{2} - \frac{1}{6}\sqrt{3} & 0 & 0 & 0 & 0 \\ \frac{1}{2} + \frac{1}{6}\sqrt{3} & \frac{1}{3} & 0 & 1 & 0 \\ \hline & \frac{1}{4} + \frac{1}{12}\sqrt{3} & \frac{1}{4} - \frac{1}{12}\sqrt{3} & \frac{1}{2} & \frac{1}{2} \end{array}. \tag{2.28}$$

Applying (2.28) to the test equation yields the amplification matrix

$$C_{11} = 1 + \tfrac{1}{2}X + (\tfrac{1}{4}-\tfrac{1}{12}\sqrt{3})XY + (\tfrac{1}{12}-\tfrac{1}{36}\sqrt{3})X^2,$$

$$C_{12} = 1 + \tfrac{1}{2}Y + \tfrac{1}{6}X + (\tfrac{1}{4}-\tfrac{1}{12}\sqrt{3})Y^2 + (\tfrac{1}{4}-\tfrac{1}{9}\sqrt{3})XY + (\tfrac{1}{18}-\tfrac{1}{36}\sqrt{3})X^2,$$

$$C_{21} = X + \frac{1}{2}XY + \frac{1}{6}X^2,$$

$$C_{22} = 1 + Y + \frac{1}{2}X + \frac{1}{2}Y^2 + (\frac{5}{12} - \frac{1}{12}\sqrt{3})XY + (\frac{1}{12} - \frac{1}{36}\sqrt{3})X^2, \qquad (2.29)$$

and the determinant and trace are given by

$$\det(C) = 1 + Y + \frac{1}{2}Y^2 + (\frac{1}{6} - \frac{1}{6}\sqrt{3})XY + (\frac{1}{12} - \frac{1}{18}\sqrt{3})X^2,$$
$$\mathrm{tr}(C) = 2 + Y + X + \frac{1}{2}Y^2 + (\frac{2}{3} - \frac{1}{6}\sqrt{3})XY + (\frac{1}{6} - \frac{1}{18}\sqrt{3})X^2. \qquad (2.30)$$

The stability region contains the interval [-6.24303...,0] of the X-axis and the interval [-2,0] of the Y-axis.

2.3. Runge-Kutta-Rosenbrock methods

When an implicit method is used, the resulting algebraic equations have to be solved, for instance by a Newton-Raphson iteration process. Now the idea of semi-implicit methods is, to incorporate the solution procedure in the development of the integration method. A class of single step methods based on this concept was derived by Rosenbrock(1963). The general form of these methods is

$$y_{n+1} = y_n + \tau\textstyle\sum_{i=1}^{s} b_i k_i,$$
$$[I - \gamma\tau A]k_i = f(t_n + c_i\tau,\ y_n + \tau\textstyle\sum_{j=1}^{i-1} a_{ij}k_j) + \tau A\textstyle\sum_{j=1}^{i-1}\gamma_{ij}k_j, \qquad (2.31)$$

where I is the unit matrix and A is an approximation for the Jacobian matrix f_y. In principle, it is again possible to lift the explicit dependence of f on t, but we will not do this here, so we do not have to calculate the partial derivative of f with respect to t. This would lead to different methods, too. Furthermore, we will take $A = f_y(t_n, y_n)$, and we will adopt the convention (2.8).

For $s = 1$, we have the order condition

$$b_1 = 1, \qquad (2.32)$$

while γ is still free. The stability function of this method is

$$R(z) = \frac{1 + (1 - \gamma)z}{1 - \gamma z}, \tag{2.33}$$

from which we deduce that the method is absolutely stable if $\gamma \geq \frac{1}{2}$. The requirement $R(\infty) = 0$ (L–stability), which will cause the uninteresting fast components in the solution to decay almost in a single step, will fix γ to $\gamma = 1$.

For $s = 2$, the order conditions for a second–order method are

$$\begin{aligned} &b_1 + b_2 = 1, \\ &c_2 b_2 = \tfrac{1}{2}, \\ &\gamma(b_1 + b_2) + (a_{21} + \gamma_{21})b_2 = \tfrac{1}{2}. \end{aligned} \tag{2.34}$$

The general solution of (2.34) is $a_{21} = c_2 = 1/(2b_2)$, $\gamma_{21} = -\gamma/b_2$, $b_1 = 1 - b_2$, where b_2 and γ are still free. The stability function is

$$R(z) = \frac{1 + (1-2\gamma)z + (\frac{1}{2} - 2\gamma + \gamma^2)z^2}{(1-\gamma z)^2}, \tag{2.35}$$

which shows that the method is absolutely stable if $\gamma \geq \frac{1}{4}$. A convenient choice for the coefficients seems to be $\gamma = 1 - \frac{1}{2}\sqrt{2}$, for which value of γ we have $R(\infty) = 0$, $c_2 = a_{21} = 1$, $b_1 = b_2 = \frac{1}{2}$, $\gamma_{21} = -2 + \sqrt{2}$.

For a 3–stage, third order method we have the order conditions

$$\begin{aligned} &b_1 + b_2 + b_3 = 1, \\ &c_2 b_2 + c_3 b_3 = \tfrac{1}{2}, \\ &\gamma(b_1 + b_2 + b_3) + b_2 c_2 + b_3 c_3 + b_2 \gamma_{21} + b_3(\gamma_{31} + \gamma_{32}) = \tfrac{1}{2}, \\ &c_2^2 b_2 + c_3^2 b_3 = \frac{1}{3}, \\ &\gamma(c_2 b_2 + c_3 b_3) + c_2(a_{32} + \gamma_{32})b_3 = \frac{1}{6}, \\ &\gamma^2(b_1 + b_2 + b_3) + 2\gamma(c_2 b_2 + c_3 b_3 + \gamma_{21} b_2 + (\gamma_{31} + \gamma_{32})b_3) + \\ &+ (a_{32} + \gamma_{32})(c_2 + \gamma_{21})b_3 = \frac{1}{6}, \end{aligned} \tag{2.36}$$

and the stability function

$$R(z) = \frac{1 + (1-3\gamma)z + (\frac{1}{2} - 3\gamma + 3\gamma^2)z^2 + (\frac{1}{6} - \frac{3}{2}\gamma + 3\gamma^2 - \gamma^3)z^3}{(1-\gamma z)^3}. \tag{2.37}$$

We obtain an absolutely stable method for which $R(\infty) = 0$ if we choose $\gamma = 0.4358665$. Furthermore, we choose, a little arbitrarily, $c_1 = 0.0$, $c_2 = 0.5$,

$c_3 = 1.0$, $b_1 = 1/6$, $b_2 = 2/3$, $b_3 = 1/6$, $a_{32} = 3.0905211$, $a_{31} = -2.0905211$, $\gamma_{21} = 0.27263026$, $\gamma_{31} = 0$, $\gamma_{32} = -3.7057198$.

A 4-stage fourth-order method which is A-stable and L-stable is given by $\gamma = 0.57281606$, $c_1 = 0.0$, $c_2 = 0.33333333$, $c_3 = 0.66666667$, $c_4 = 1.0$, $b_1 = 0.125$, $b_2 = 0.375$, $b_3 = 0.375$, $b_4 = 0.125$, $a_{21} = 0.33333333$, $a_{31} = 3.81887292$, $a_{32} = -3.15220625$, $a_{41} = -4.87065444$, $a_{42} = 2.43689637$, $a_{43} = 3.43375807$, $\gamma_{21} = 1.00757865$, $\gamma_{31} = -2.31656710$, $\gamma_{32} = 3.00657413$, $\gamma_{41} = -3.80463110$, $\gamma_{42} = 0.0$, $\gamma_{43} = -5.87065444$.

3. Comparison of some methods

If we want to solve a system of differential equations in an efficient way, for instance when the solution has to be calculated in real time, we shall prefer methods with a fixed step size over methods with variable step size, because the time required to calculate the solution then has a predictable limit. Furthermore, only a moderate accuracy can be imposed, so the step size will be limited by the stability requirements in many cases. The eigenvalues of linearized mechanical dynamical systems with small damping will be close to the imaginary axis, so a good measure for the efficiency of explicit integration methods will be the maximal step size for which the method is stable, divided by the number of function evaluations per step, provided all eigenvalues are purely imaginary.

3.1. Explicit methods

A class of widely used methods for the integration of systems of first-order differential equations consists of multistep methods, possibly with variable step size and order. As a basis for reference, we will consider the method described by Shampine and Gordon (1975). In Table 1 this method and the explicit methods are compared as to the above mentioned efficiency measure.

Table 1. Efficiency of explicit methods for the integration of the equations of motion of mechanical systems.

method	$\lvert z\rvert_{max}$	nfe	eff.
Shampine, Gordon	1.20	2	0.60
RK1,3 (2.11)	1.732	3	0.577
RK1,4 (2.13)	2.828	4	0.707
RK2,1 (2.25)	2	1	2
RK2,2 (2.28)	2.498	2	1.249

nfe: number of function evaluations per step
eff.: efficiency measure = $\lvert z\rvert_{max}$ / nfe

We see that the classical fourth-order Runge-Kutta method performs better than the routine of Shampine and Gordon, and that the methods for second-order differential equations are the most efficient ones. If the method (2.25) gives a too poor accuracy, the method (2.28) can be used.

3.2. (Semi-)implicit methods

If we compare the semi-implicit Rosenbrock methods to fully implicit methods, we see that in the former only one linearization and matrix inversion is needed, whereas in the latter more linearizations and matrix inversions are needed if the full Newton-Raphson iteration method is used, or with the modified Newton-Raphson method, an undefined number of function evaluations and back substitutions are needed. Furthermore, a larger system has to be solved, unless the implicit method is diagonally implicit. Another advantage is the L-stability of the semi-implicit methods, while for the methods based on Gauss-Legendre quadrature, the Newmark-β method with $\gamma=\frac{1}{2}$ and also some diagonally implicit methods, we have $R(\infty)=1$ or $R(\infty)=-1$.

For mechanical systems like (1.2), the semi-implicit methods can be modified in order to prevent the inversion of the system mass matrix. If we define

$$\bar{M} = \begin{bmatrix} I & 0 \\ 0 & M \end{bmatrix}, \quad L = \begin{bmatrix} 0 & I \\ -K & -C \end{bmatrix}, \quad f = \begin{bmatrix} 0 \\ Q \end{bmatrix}, \tag{3.1}$$

the modified methods can be written as

$$\begin{aligned} y_{n+1} &= y_n + \tau\textstyle\sum_{i=1}^{s} b_i k_i, \\ [\bar{M} - \gamma\tau L]k_i &= f(t_n + c_i\tau,\ y_n + \tau\textstyle\sum_{j=1}^{i-1} a_{ij}k_j) + \tau L\textstyle\sum_{j=1}^{i-1}\gamma_{ij}k_j\ . \end{aligned} \tag{3.2}$$

Two principal methods for the calculation of the linearized equations are possible, a numerical one and an analytic one. The numerical differentiation requires at least n additional function evaluations, and the analytic differentiation requires only c times the time to calculate one function evaluation, where c is a constant number, typically $c \approx 10$. The analytical method is therefore not only more accurate, but also faster than the numerical method if the number of degrees of freedom is larger than about 5. The implicit method becomes more efficient than the explicit method (2.25) when the step size can be increased by about a factor 10 or more.

3.3 An example problem

As an example we will consider a plane slider–crank mechanism with a flexible connecting rod. This problem was used by Song and Haug (1980), Bakr and Shabana (1986), Jonker (1988,1989) and Koppens (1989) as a benchmark. The system consists of a rigid crank of length 0.15 m, a flexible connecting rod of 0.3 m and a plunger. The crank and the connecting rod have a uniform mass distribution of 0.2225 kgm^{-1}, the flexural rigidity of the connecting rod is $EI = 12.72345\ Nm^2$ and the mass of the plunger is 0.033375 kg. The crank is rotated at a constant rate of 150 $rad.s^{-1}$. The measured quantity is the dimensionless deflection of the centre point of the connecting rod. The connecting rod is modelled by two beam elements, of which only the two bending deformations are taken into count. The system has thus four degrees of freedom. For more details see Jonker(1988,1989). The highest natural circular frequency of the discretized model is 16871.6 $rad.s^{-1}$, if the system is in rest.

The system was integrated over 50 ms with an error tolerance of 1% with the methods of Table 1. The dimensionless deflection is given in Fig. 1. Regarding the highest natural frequency, the multistep method would need at least 1400 function evaluations (f.e.); in practice it turned out that about 1700 f.e. were needed. The number of function evaluations depended only weakly on the required accuracy, indicating that we deal with a stiff problem. With the classical fourth-order Runge-Kutta method, only 1200 f.e. were needed, whereas the third-order method needed 1500 f.e. With the method for second-order differential equations (2.25), only 450 f.e. were required, where the step sizes on the basis of accuracy and stability requirements were about the same.

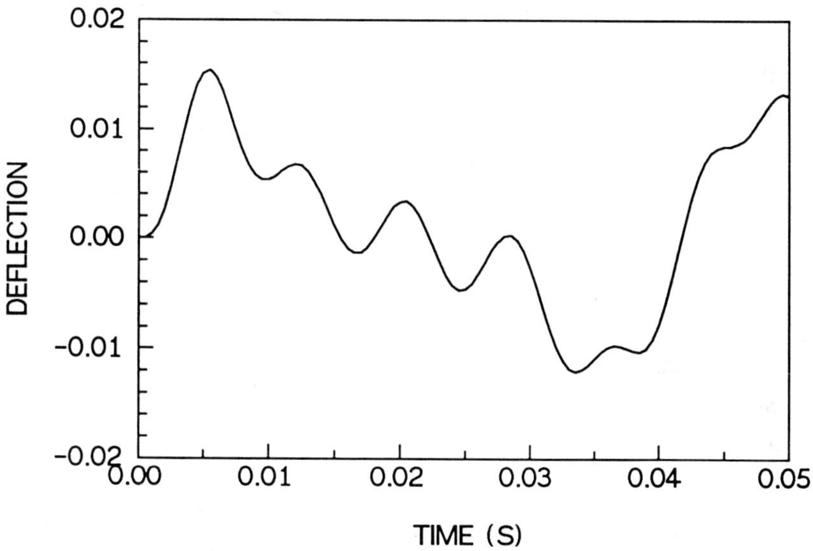

Fig. 1. Deflection of the centre point of the connecting rod

With the 3-stage semi-implicit method discussed in 2.3., about 120 steps were needed in order to obtain an accurate solution, each step requiring about the time for 9 f.e., so the amount of work was equivalent to about 1100 f.e. The 4-stage method needed about 90 steps, with an amount of work equivalent to about 900 f.e.

We can conclude that the theoretical considerations led to valid assumptions, and that the simplest method, (2.25), is the best for this problem. However, if we would increase the flexural rigidity of the connecting rod by a factor 10, keeping fixed other quantities, and diminish the required relative accuracy, as the deflections would be smaller, the explicit methods would need 3.16 times the number of f.e. given above, whereas with implicit methods, the step size could even be increased, so the last would be the most efficient one. If the system would be coupled to another system described by first–order differential equations, it would be more convenient to use an integration method for first–order equations, which would mean that the 4–stage semi–implicit method would be the most efficient one.

4. Concluding remarks

For many mechanical systems, method (2.25) is preferable over other explicit methods. If an increased accuracy is needed, (2.28) can be used. For stiff systems, semi–implicit methods work conveniently.

For real time integration, methods that have a well defined minimal speed should be used; this means in general that methods with a fixed step size should be used or semi–implicit methods when an implicit method has to be used.

From the point of view of dynamical systems theory, fixed order, fixed step size single step methods are much nicer than other methods. They turn a continuous time system in a well defined discrete time system with the same dimension of the state space.

The problem of choosing a method for the numerical integration of ordinary differential equations remains difficult, and it is in many cases impossible to determine the best method *a priori*.

Literature

Bakr, E.M., and Shabana, A.A. (1986), Geometrically nonlinear analysis of multibody systems. Computers & Structures **23**, pp.739–751.

Dekker, K., and Verwer, J.G. (1984), Stability of Runge–Kutta methods for stiff nonlinear differential equations. CWI Monograph 2, North–Holland, Amsterdam/New York/Oxford.

Henrici, P. (1962), Discrete variable methods in ordinary differential equations. John Wiley & Sons, Inc., New York/London.

Gear, C.W. (1971), Numerical initial value problems in ordinary differential equations. Prentice–Hall, Inc., Englewood Cliffs.

Jonker, J. B. (1988), A finite element dynamic analysis of flexible spatial mechanisms and manipulators. Dissertation, Delft University of Technology, Delft.

Jonker, J.B. (1989), A finite element dynamic analysis of spatial mechanisms with flexible links. To appear in Comp. Meths. Appl. Mech. Eng.

Koppens, W.P. (1989), The dynamics of systems of deformable bodies. Dissertation, Eindhoven University of Technology, Eindhoven.

Rosenbrock, H.H. (1963), Some general implicit processes for the numerical solution of differential equations. Computer J. **5**, pp.329–330.

Shampine, L.F., and Gordon, M.K. (1975), Computer solution of ordinary differential equations. The initial value problem. W.H. Freeman and company, San Francisco.

Song, J.O., and Haug, E.J. (1980), Dynamic analysis of planar flexible mechanisms. Comp. Meths. Appl. Mech. Eng. **24**, pp.359–381.

BDF Methods for DAEs in Multi-body Dynamics : Shortcomings and Improvements

Michael F. Steigerwald

Mechanical Dynamics, Inc.
3055 Plymouth Road
Ann Arbor, MI 48105-3203

Abstract

If backward differentiation formula (BDF) methods are used to solve sets of differential-algebraic equations (DAEs), problems may arise if the step size (h), becomes very small. The step size may decrease for a variety of reasons, but the most difficult problem to solve involves a sudden change, or (near) discontinuity in any of the system variables.

In general, BDF methods encounter stability problems if used in programs that allow for sudden changes in the system variables. To solve problems such as these, in the general case, the program will decrease the step size to integrate through the discontinuity. As the step size decreases, the Jacobian matrix, if used for Newton iterations, becomes ill-conditioned. As a result, round-off error makes it almost impossible to solve the equations of motion. Details of the problem and solutions are discussed.

Introduction

Many commercially available programs use BDF methods to solve DAEs that model multi-body systems. These simulations occasionally include sudden changes in the system. Examples include: impacts, digital or bang-bang controls, switches, and locking mechanisms. These discontinuous effects usually cause BDF methods to become unstable.

As the step size decreases during the change, the BDF formula may become inaccurate and the Jacobian matrix, if used, becomes ill-conditioned. Secondly, the discontinuity in the derivatives caused by the change makes BDF methods unreliable, because such a discontinuity is tantamount to restarting the integration with erroneous initial conditions.

There are several ways to avoid or offset these problems. Ideally, the system would be modeled in such a way that the small step size could be avoided. This is impractical for a general purpose program since it would require a great deal of artificial intelligence. Another potential solution is to switch away from the BDF method when the step size becomes small. This may be difficult to implement.

A simpler solution is to monitor (and scale) the ill-conditioned Jacobian, then restart the integration with a consistent set of initial conditions after the discontinuity. This is comparatively simple to implement, and usually achieves the desired results.

NATO ASI Series, Vol. F 69
Real-Time Integration Methods for Mechanical System Simulation
Edited by E. J. Haug and R. C. Deyo

General Purpose Multibody Dynamics Programs

General purpose multibody dynamics programs automatically formulate and solve the equations of motion for mechanical systems. Many formulations are designed to produce a sparse system of mixed differential and algebraic equations. For each body, a set of first order differential equations are used. For each constraint (joints, motions, etc.), an algebraic equation is added. Additionally, other algebraic variables are used to increase sparsity and reduce complexity.

Many studies require the simulation to account for sudden changes in the system. Impacts, for example, are often simple modeled as forces that jump from zero to nonzero values in (nearly) zero time. Imparted motions may switch from a smooth function to another value suddenly, as in a circuit breaker mechanism. Such discontinuities are discouraged, but must be accounted for in a general program.

As a simple example, consider the bouncing ball in figure 1. Until the body strikes the surface, gravity is the only force acting, and all equations are smooth. At impact, the force opposing gravity jumps from zero to to a large value.

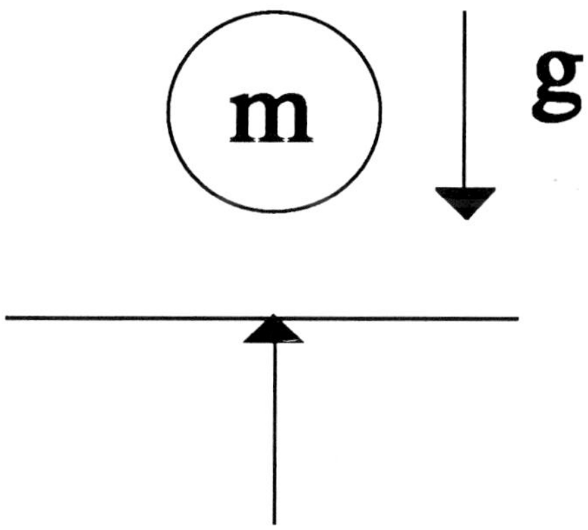

Figure 1 . Bouncing Ball

A more common phenomenon is that of a vehicle traveling over an irregular road surface (figure 2). Until the obstacle or hole is encountered, all transient effects have damped out and the forces are in a steady state. When the tire strikes the irregularity, most forces in the system experience a discontinuity.

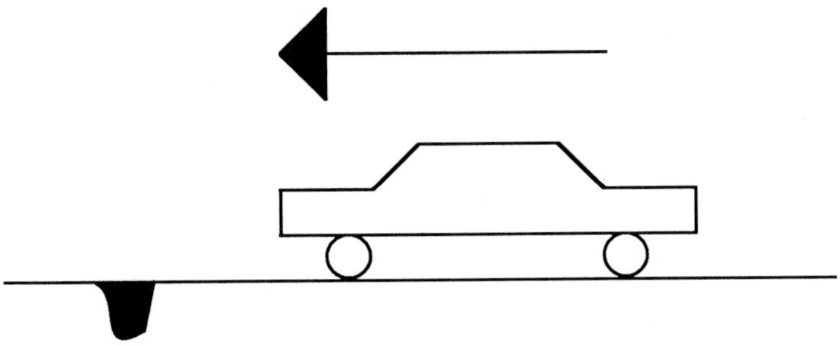

Figure 2 . Vehicle Over Irregular Surface

Problems with BDF Methods

Discontinuities in the system create considerable difficulties for BDF methods. As the integration step size decreases to account for the change, the system Jacobian matrix becomes poorly conditioned. The resulting discontinuity renders further solution from the BDF method unreliable, if the conditions after the discontinuity are inconsistent with the algebraic equations.

The BDF method extrapolates a polynomial through past solutions to predict the solution at the end of the integration step. To fit a polynomial through the discontinuity, the integration step size must be drastically reduced. As a result, the Jacobian matrix usually becomes ill-conditioned, as it is dominated by terms that are inversely proportional to h.

A general form of the BDF formula is given by:

$$\dot{q}_n = \frac{1}{h}\sum_{i=0}^{k} \alpha_i \, q_{n-i}$$

As a result, many terms of the Jacobian matrix are inversely proportional to the integration step size, h. As $h \rightarrow 0$, these entries $\rightarrow \infty$, and dominate the matrix.

While iterating for the solution, Gaussian elimination may introduce error by magnifying round-off errors with the dominant terms in the matrix. The Newton-Raphson iterates may be near a solution, but unable to converge.

Sudden changes in the system result in discontinuities, and error may be introduced. After the discontinuity, the integration is restarted with the resulting solution as initial conditions. If these initial conditions are erroneous or inconsistent with the constraints, further solutions using a BDF are suspect.

Integration error should only be controlled for displacement variables, because the Lagrangian formulation for the equations of motion is an index three formulation [2]. BDF methods for index three problems usually fail if higher order or algebraic variables are controlled.

The equation set using the Lagrangian formulation has an index of three:

$$M(q)\dot{q} - f(q,t) - \frac{\partial\phi}{\partial q}\lambda = 0$$

$$\phi(q,t) = 0$$

The index is three since the constraint equations would need to be differentiated three times to obtain a standard set of ordinary equations.

Solutions

To counter the problems introduced by Jacobian ill-conditioning, the program can automatically detect and avoid a poorly conditioned matrix. To remove the error caused by discontinuities, an additional solution can be performed to restart the integration with consistent initial conditions.

To detect an ill-condtioned Jacobian, an estimate of the matrix condition number is needed. The matrix condition number can be approximated by the ratio of the smallest to largest pivot elements from the matrix factorization [3]. This ratio is cheap to compute, and has proven to be not only an excellent approximation to the condition number, but also a good indicator of probable convergence difficulties using Newton-Raphson.

Once the condition number grows above a specified limit, the effects of ill-conditioning can be countered using the scaling algorithm prescribed in [2]. The second order (converted to first order) equations are scaled by h^2 and first order equations are scaled by h. For small steps, this has the effect of placing greater emphasis on the algebraic equations and damping out differential equations. This is ideal, since the constraint equations are most difficult to solve during sudden changes and the differential variables tend not to change substantially over such a small step. For impacts, this is physically equivalent to setting the step size and all non-impact forces to zero, while solving for the impact during a frozen snapshot in time.

To remove the error caused by discontinuities, an off-line solution can be performed to correct the initial conditions according to the constraints. The constraints are differentiated once to obtain equations for the velocities, once more for the accelerations. These calculations are performed separately from the integration, then substituted at the beginning of the next step. This is the same procedure that is used to compute consistent initial conditions at the beginning of the simulation.

Results

To illustrate the effectiveness of the solution, consider the bouncing ball example. Let the mass of the ball be 1kg, the radius of the ball r = 10mm, approximate gravity as $8000\mathrm{mm/s^2}$, and model the impact force as a stiffening spring:

$$f = k(z-r)^2, \; k = 1E12\frac{N}{mm^2}$$

The initial conditions of the ball are z = 1000mm, zero velocity. The ball strikes the surface at ~.5 seconds and the surface repels the ball with a force of 2E20 N. The step size reduces dramatically:

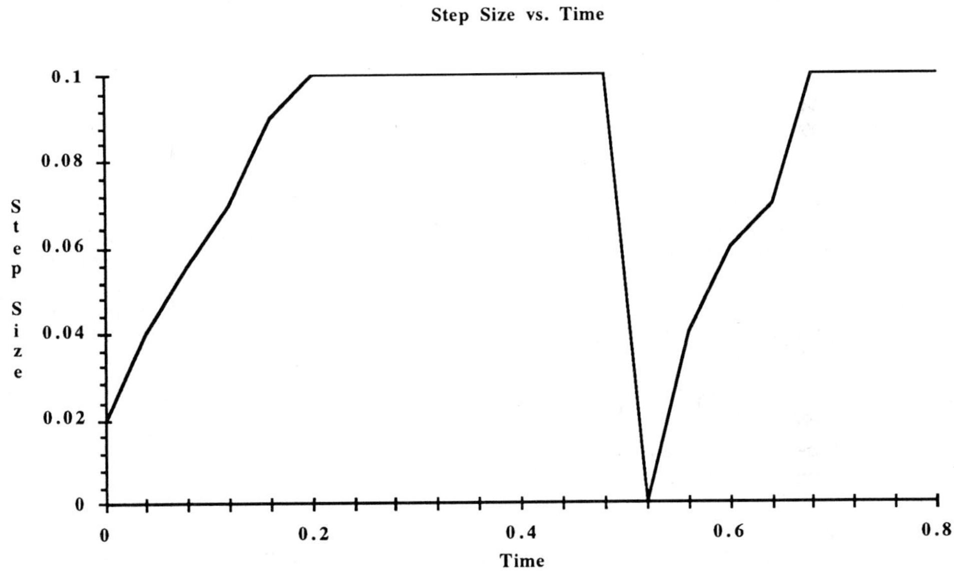

As the step size decreases, the condition number of the matrix goes from an average value of ~ 1000 to a high of 1E16:

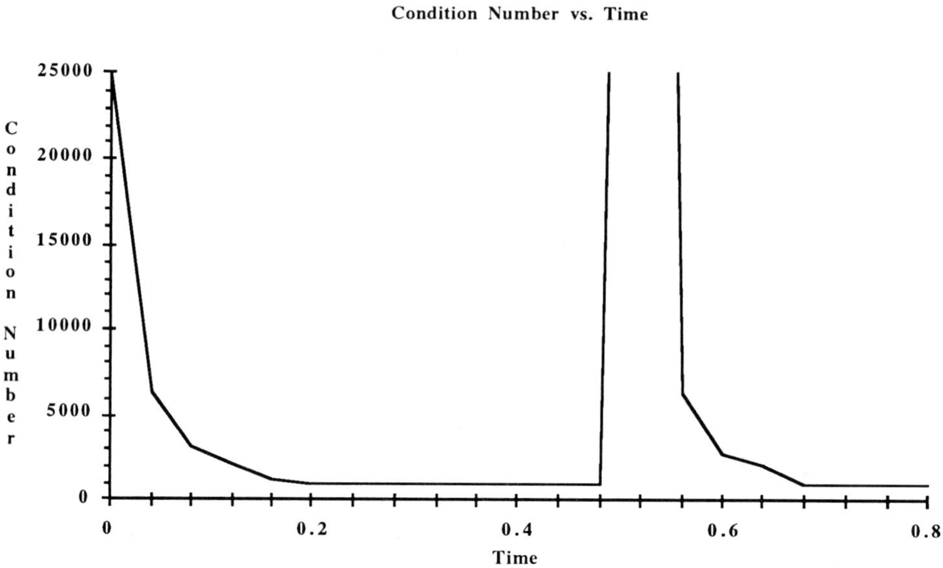

When constraints are added to the model, the matrix becomes even more ill-conditioned. If we constrain the ball to move only along the z-axis (which should be, of course, unnecessary), the condition number of the matrix increases by a factor that is, approximately, inversely proportional to the step size. The average value is 1E5, with a high of 1E22:

Condition Number (with constraints) vs. Time

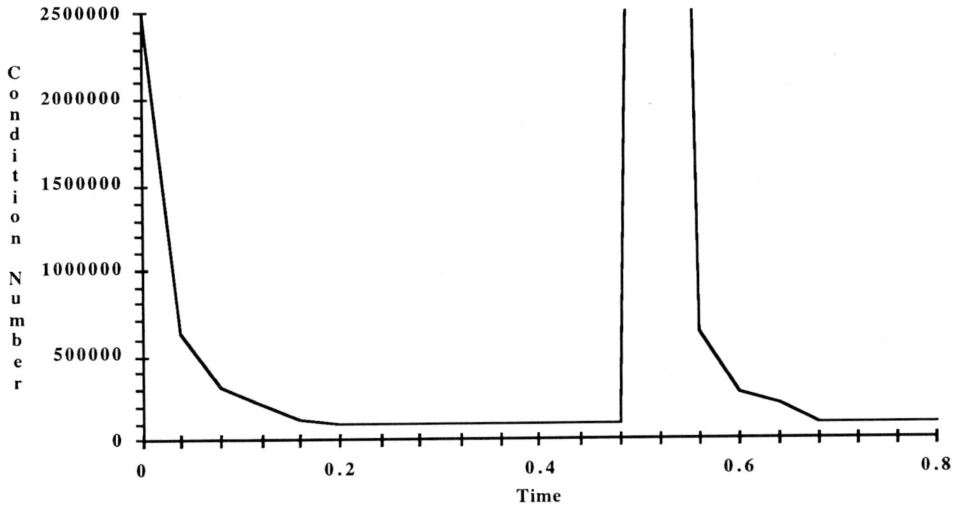

When the equations are scaled, the average condition number is reduced to ~ 1000, and the extreme value is reduced to 1E18 during impact.

We can also see that the impact introduces an error in the angular acceleration of the ball. Although the ball has been constrained to move only in the z-direction, after the impact, there is a jump discontinuity in the angular acceleration of the ball:

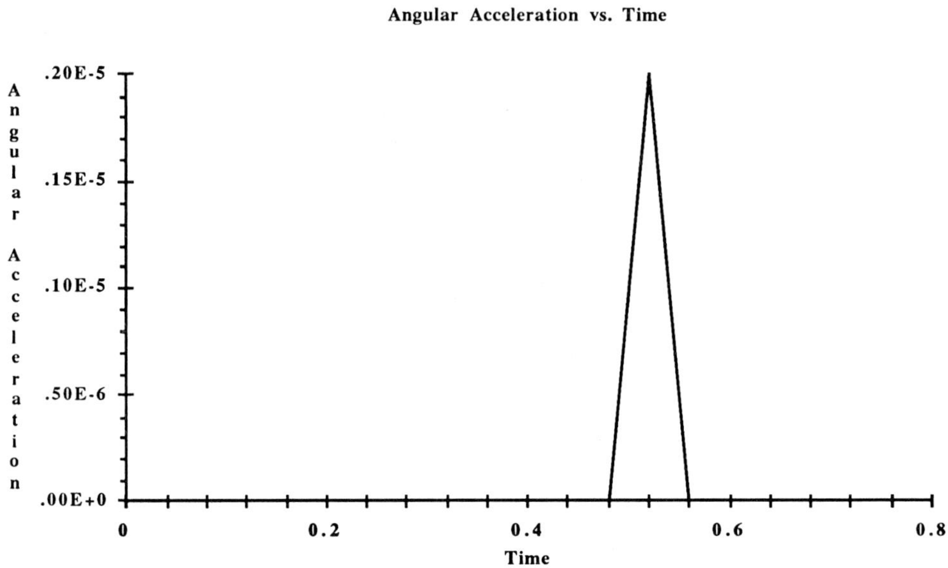

Needless to say, the angular acceleration should remain zero. This effect is corrected by the additional calculation that fits velocities and accelerations to the constraints.

Conclusion

In order to use BDF methods and DAEs to simulate mechanical systems that experience sudden changes, the method must account for the fact that this usually causes BDF methods to become unstable. As the step size decreases for the change, the ill-conditioned Jacobian matrix must be detected and scaled. Secondly, the initial conditions must be consistent with the constraints after the change.

The condition of the Jacobian is improved by scaling the equations by powers of the step size. The discontinuity is corrected by doing off-line corrections that ensure that the new initial conditions satisfy the constraints.

References

1. C. W. Gear, *The Automatic Integration of Ordinary Differential Equations,* Communications of the ACM, Volume 14, Number 3 (1971), pp. 176-190.

2. L. R. Petzold and P. Lötstedt, *Numerical Solution of Nonlinear Differential Equations with Algebraic Constraints II: Practical Implications,* SIAM J. Sci. Stat. Comput., Volume 7, Number 3 (1986), pp. 720-733.

3. T. Park and E. Haug, *Ill-conditioned Equations in Kinematics and Dynamics of Machines,* International Journal for Numerical Methods in Engineering, Volume 26 (1988), pp. 217-230.

NATO ASI Series F

Including Special Programmes on Sensory Systems for Robotic Control (ROB) and on Advanced Educational Technology (AET)

Vol. 1: Issues in Acoustic Signal – Image Processing and Recognition. Edited by C. H. Chen. VIII, 333 pages. 1983.

Vol. 2: Image Sequence Processing and Dynamic Scene Analysis. Edited by T. S. Huang. IX, 749 pages. 1983.

Vol. 3: Electronic Systems Effectiveness and Life Cycle Costing. Edited by J. K. Skwirzynski. XVII, 732 pages. 1983.

Vol. 4: Pictorial Data Analysis. Edited by R. M. Haralick. VIII, 468 pages. 1983.

Vol. 5: International Calibration Study of Traffic Conflict Techniques. Edited by E. Asmussen. VII, 229 pages. 1984.

Vol. 6: Information Technology and the Computer Network. Edited by K. G. Beauchamp. VIII, 271 pages. 1984.

Vol. 7: High-Speed Computation. Edited by J. S. Kowalik. IX, 441 pages. 1984.

Vol. 8: Program Transformation and Programming Environments. Report on a Workshop directed by F. L. Bauer and H. Remus. Edited by P. Pepper. XIV, 378 pages. 1984.

Vol. 9: Computer Aided Analysis and Optimization of Mechanical System Dynamics. Edited by E. J. Haug. XXII, 700 pages. 1984.

Vol. 10: Simulation and Model-Based Methodologies: An Integrative View. Edited by T. I. Ören, B. P. Zeigler, M. S. Elzas. XIII, 651 pages. 1984.

Vol. 11: Robotics and Artificial Intelligence. Edited by M. Brady, L. A. Gerhardt, H. F. Davidson. XVII, 693 pages. 1984.

Vol. 12: Combinatorial Algorithms on Words. Edited by A. Apostolico, Z. Galil. VIII, 361 pages. 1985.

Vol. 13: Logics and Models of Concurrent Systems. Edited by K. R. Apt. VIII, 498 pages. 1985.

Vol. 14: Control Flow and Data Flow: Concepts of Distributed Programming. Edited by M. Broy. VIII, 525 pages. 1985.

Vol. 15: Computational Mathematical Programming. Edited by K. Schittkowski. VIII, 451 pages. 1985.

Vol. 16: New Systems and Architectures for Automatic Speech Recognition and Synthesis. Edited by R. De Mori, C.Y. Suen. XIII, 630 pages. 1985.

Vol. 17: Fundamental Algorithms for Computer Graphics. Edited by R.A. Earnshaw. XVI, 1042 pages. 1985.

Vol. 18: Computer Architectures for Spatially Distributed Data. Edited by H. Freeman and G. G. Pieroni. VIII, 391 pages. 1985.

Vol. 19: Pictorial Information Systems in Medicine. Edited by K. H. Höhne. XII, 525 pages. 1986.

Vol. 20: Disordered Systems and Biological Organization. Edited by E. Bienenstock, F. Fogelman Soulié, G. Weisbuch. XXI, 405 pages.1986.

Vol. 21: Intelligent Decision Support in Process Environments. Edited by E. Hollnagel, G. Mancini, D.D. Woods. XV, 524 pages. 1986.

NATO ASI Series F

Vol. 22: Software System Design Methods. The Challenge of Advanced Computing Technology. Edited by J.K. Skwirzynski. XIII, 747 pages. 1986.

Vol. 23: Designing Computer-Based Learning Materials. Edited by H. Weinstock and A. Bork. IX, 285 pages. 1986.

Vol. 24: Database Machines. Modern Trends and Applications. Edited by A.K. Sood and A.H. Qureshi. VIII, 570 pages. 1986.

Vol. 25: Pyramidal Systems for Computer Vision. Edited by V. Cantoni and S. Levialdi. VIII, 392 pages. 1986. *(ROB)*

Vol. 26: Modelling and Analysis in Arms Control. Edited by R. Avenhaus, R.K. Huber and J.D. Kettelle. VIII, 488 pages. 1986.

Vol. 27: Computer Aided Optimal Design: Structural and Mechanical Systems. Edited by C.A. Mota Soares. XIII, 1029 pages. 1987.

Vol. 28: Distributed Operating Systems. Theory und Practice. Edited by Y. Paker, J.-P. Banatre and M. Bozyiğit. X, 379 pages. 1987.

Vol. 29: Languages for Sensor-Based Control in Robotics. Edited by U. Rembold and K. Hörmann. IX, 625 pages. 1987. *(ROB)*

Vol. 30: Pattern Recognition Theory and Applications. Edited by P.A. Devijver and J. Kittler. XI, 543 pages. 1987.

Vol. 31: Decision Support Systems: Theory and Application. Edited by C.W. Holsapple and A.B. Whinston. X, 500 pages. 1987.

Vol. 32: Information Systems: Failure Analysis. Edited by J.A. Wise and A. Debons. XV, 338 pages. 1987.

Vol. 33: Machine Intelligence and Knowledge Engineering for Robotic Applications. Edited by A.K.C. Wong and A. Pugh. XIV, 486 pages. 1987. *(ROB)*

Vol. 34: Modelling, Robustness and Sensitivity Reduction in Control Systems. Edited by R.F. Curtain. IX, 492 pages. 1987.

Vol. 35: Expert Judgment and Expert Systems. Edited by J.L. Mumpower, L.D. Phillips, O. Renn and V.R.R. Uppuluri. VIII, 361 pages. 1987.

Vol. 36: Logic of Programming and Calculi of Discrete Design. Edited by M. Broy. VII, 415 pages. 1987.

Vol. 37: Dynamics of Infinite Dimensional Systems. Edited by S.-N. Chow and J.K. Hale. IX, 514 pages. 1987.

Vol. 38: Flow Control of Congested Networks. Edited by A.R. Odoni, L. Bianco and G. Szegö. XII, 355 pages. 1987.

Vol. 39: Mathematics and Computer Science in Medical Imaging. Edited by M.A. Viergever and A. Todd-Pokropek. VIII, 546 pages. 1988.

Vol. 40: Theoretical Foundations of Computer Graphics and CAD. Edited by R.A. Earnshaw. XX, 1246 pages. 1988.

Vol. 41: Neural Computers. Edited by R. Eckmiller and Ch. v. d. Malsburg. XIII, 566 pages. 1988.

NATO ASI Series F

Vol. 42: Real-Time Object Measurement and Classification. Edited by A. K. Jain. VIII, 407 pages. 1988. *(ROB)*

Vol. 43: Sensors and Sensory Systems for Advanced Robots. Edited by P. Dario. XI, 597 pages. 1988. *(ROB)*

Vol. 44: Signal Processing and Pattern Recognition in Nondestructive Evaluation of Materials. Edited by C. H. Chen. VIII, 344 pages. 1988. *(ROB)*

Vol. 45: Syntactic and Structural Pattern Recognition. Edited by G. Ferraté, T. Pavlidis, A. Sanfeliu and H. Bunke. XVI, 467 pages. 1988. *(ROB)*

Vol. 46: Recent Advances in Speech Understanding and Dialog Systems. Edited by H. Niemann, M. Lang and G. Sagerer. X, 521 pages. 1988.

Vol. 47: Advanced Computing Concepts and Techniques in Control Engineering. Edited by M. J. Denham and A. J. Laub. XI, 518 pages. 1988.

Vol. 48: Mathematical Models for Decision Support. Edited by G. Mitra. IX, 762 pages. 1988.

Vol. 49: Computer Integrated Manufacturing. Edited by I. B. Turksen. VIII, 568 pages. 1988.

Vol. 50: CAD Based Programming for Sensory Robots. Edited by B. Ravani. IX, 565 pages. 1988. *(ROB)*

Vol. 51: Algorithms and Model Formulations in Mathematical Programming. Edited by S. W. Wallace. IX, 190 pages. 1989.

Vol. 52: Sensor Devices and Systems for Robotics. Edited by A. Casals. IX, 362 pages. 1989. *(ROB)*

Vol. 53: Advanced Information Technologies for Industrial Material Flow Systems. Edited by S. Y. Nof and C. L. Moodie. IX, 710 pages. 1989.

Vol. 54: A Reappraisal of the Efficiency of Financial Markets. Edited by R. M. C. Guimarães, B. G. Kingsman and S. J. Taylor. X, 804 pages. 1989.

Vol. 55: Constructive Methods in Computing Science. Edited by M. Broy. VII, 478 pages. 1989.

Vol. 56: Multiple Criteria Decision Making and Risk Analysis Using Microcomputers. Edited by B. Karpak and S. Zionts. VII, 399 pages. 1989.

Vol. 57: Kinematics and Dynamic Issues in Sensor Based Control. Edited by G. E. Taylor. XI, 456 pages. 1990. *(ROB)*

Vol. 58: Highly Redundant Sensing in Robotic Systems. Edited by J. T. Tou and J. G. Balchen. X, 322 pages. 1990. *(ROB)*

Vol. 59: Superconducting Electronics. Edited by H. Weinstock and M. Nisenoff. X, 441 pages. 1989.

Vol. 60: 3D Imaging in Medicine. Algorithms, Systems, Applications. Edited by K. H. Höhne, H. Fuchs and S. M. Pizer. IX, 460 pages. 1990.

Vol. 61: Knowledge, Data and Computer-Assisted Decisions. Edited by M. Schader and W. Gaul. VIII, 421 pages. 1990.

Vol. 62: Supercomputing. Edited by J. S. Kowalik. X, 425 pages. 1990.

Vol. 63: Traditional and Non-Traditional Robotic Sensors. Edited by T. C. Henderson. VIII, 468 pages. 1990. *(ROB)*

Vol. 64: Sensory Robotics for the Handling of Limp Materials. Edited by P. M. Taylor. IX, 343 pages. 1990. *(ROB)*

Vol. 65: Mapping and Spatial Modelling for Navigation. Edited by L. F. Pau. VIII, 357 pages. 1990. *(ROB)*

NATO ASI Series F

Vol. 66: Sensor-Based Robots: Algorithms and Architectures. Edited by C. S. G. Lee. 1990. *(ROB)*

Vol. 67: Designing Hypermedia for Learning. Edited by D. H. Jonassen and H. Mandl. XXV, 457 pages. 1990. *(AET)*

Vol. 68: Neuro-Computing. Algorithms, Architectures and Applications. Edited by F. Fogelman Soulié and J. Hérault. XI, 455 pages. 1990.

Vol. 69: Real-Time Integration Methods for Mechanical System Simulation. Edited by E. J. Haug and R. C. Deyo. VIII, 352 pages. 1991.